Jill + George Perry

Augusta Feb 2008

D1776058

DISCARD

*Ritualist on a Tricycle*

# Ritualist on a Tricycle

## FREDERICK GOLDSMITH

Church, Nationalism and Society in
Western Australia
1880–1920

### COLIN HOLDEN

The Charles and Joy Staples
South West Region Publications Fund

UNIVERSITY OF WESTERN AUSTRALIA PRESS

First published in 1997 by
University of Western Australia Press
Nedlands, Western Australia 6907
for the Charles and Joy Staples
South West Region Publications Fund

This book is copyright. Apart from any fair dealing for the purpose of private study, research, criticism or review, as permitted under the Copyright Act 1968, no part may be reproduced by any process without written permission. Enquiries should be made to the publisher.

Copyright © Colin Holden 1997

National Library of Australia
Cataloguing-in-Publication entry:

Holden, Colin.
Ritualist on a tricycle: Frederick Goldsmith, church, nationalism and society in Western Australia, 1880–1920.

ISBN 1 875560 98 X.

1. Goldsmith, Frederick William, 1853–1932. 2. Church of England – Western Australia – Bishops – Biography. 3. Church and state – Western Australia – Church of England. 4. Oxford movement – Western Australia. 5. Western Australia – Religion. I. Charles and Joy Staples South West Region Publications Fund. II. Title. (Series: Staples South West Region publication series).

283.941092

Produced by Benchmark Publications Management, Melbourne
Designed and typeset by Pauline McClenahan, Captured Concepts, Melbourne
Typeset in 9 pt Leawood Book
Printed by Brown Prior Anderson, Melbourne

For Ted, David and Christopher
*ambulavimus in domum Domini amici*

Also published by
University of Western Australia Press for
the Charles and Joy Staples
South West Region Publications Fund:

*A Tribute to the Group Settlers*
by P.E.M. Blond

*For Their Own Good*
by A. Haebich

*Dearest Isabella*
by P. Joske

*Portraits of the South West*
edited by B.K. de Garis

*A Guide to Sources for the History of South Western Australia*
compiled by Ronald Richards

*Jardee: The Mill that Cheated Time*
by Doreen Owens

*Blacklegs: The Scottish Colliery Strike of 1911*
by Bill Latter

*Barefoot in the Creek*
by L.C. Burton

*Western Australia as it is today, 1906*
by Leopoldo Zunini, edited and translated by Margot Melia
and Richard Bosworth

The Charles and Joy Staples South West Region Publications Fund was established in 1984 on the basis of a generous donation made to The University of Western Australia by Charles and Joy Staples.

The purpose of the fund was to make the results of research on the South West region of Western Australia widely available so as to assist the people of the region and those in government and private organizations concerned with South West projects to appreciate the needs and possibilities of the region in the widest possible historical perspective.

The fund is administered by a committee whose aims are to make possible the publication (either by full or part funding), by the University of Western Australia Press, of scholarly research in any discipline relevant to the South West region.

# Contents

| | | |
|---|---|---:|
| Acknowledgements | | xi |
| Introduction | | 1 |
| 1 | Figure in the Shadows: the Early Years | 19 |
| 2 | Throwing Down the Gauntlet | 41 |
| 3 | Reaction and Response | 61 |
| 4 | A Slowly Expanding Front | 77 |
| 5 | The Critics and their Position | 103 |
| 6 | From the Tolerant to the Favourable | 127 |
| 7 | Nationalism, Autonomy and Churchmanship: Perth Synod 1899 and General Synod 1900 | 153 |
| 8 | An Episcopal Mendicant: Goldsmith, Bunbury and the North-West: 1904–1910 | 179 |
| 9 | From 'A Nation in the Mill' to 'England's Green and Pleasant Land': 1910–1932 | 205 |
| 10 | Doctrine and Devotion: a Theory of Spiritual Independence Reinforces its Opposite? | 231 |
| 11 | Bunbury Diocese as an Anglo-Catholic Cause | 259 |
| 12 | Bringing Monasticism to the Bush: the Brotherhood of St Boniface | 285 |
| 13 | Resonances | 313 |
| Glossary | | 347 |
| Notes | | 351 |
| Bibliography | | 394 |
| Index | | 405 |

# Illustrations

| | |
|---|---|
| The Deanery, Perth, *c.* 1863<br>Author's collection | 46 |
| Interior of St George's Cathedral, *c.* 1904<br>St George's Cathedral collection, courtesy of the Dean of Perth | 54 |
| Alexander Forrest as Mayor of Perth<br>Battye Library | 63 |
| Sir Winthrop Hackett in Windsor Court dress<br>University of Western Australia Archives 2042P | 68 |
| St Nicholas' Australind: altar frontal, *c.* 1916<br>Battye Library mf 2426A/1 5794B/14 | 88 |
| The Venerable Frederick Barton-Parkes, *c.* 1898<br>Family collection, courtesy of Mrs E. W. Doncaster | 94 |
| Mr Justice Edward Stone, *c.* 1895<br>Battye Library 2243B | 104 |
| The Hon. Arthur Lovekin, 1929<br>Battye Library 3268B 2453P | 105 |
| The Most Reverend C. O. L. Riley<br>Battye Library | 132 |
| Bunbury and the South-West<br>Battye Library, *Bunbury Occasional Papers* 281.Bun | 181 |

# ILLUSTRATIONS

An aerial view of Bunbury, *c.* 1899   187
Battye Library 24925P

Aboriginal prisoners at Roebourne   190
La Trobe collection, State Library of Victoria

Bunbury Grammar School staff and children, 1911   208
Battye Library 5794B/5

A general view of Bunbury, *c.* 1920   209
Battye Library 369P

F. W. Goldsmith in cope and mitre   219
Battye Library mf 2426A/1 WN 5372

'Those damnatory clauses'   244
La Trobe collection, State Library of Victoria

'The Australian Synod sends home a grumble'   245
La Trobe collection, State Library of Victoria

A bullock driver's view of the Athanasian Creed   247
La Trobe collection, State Library of Victoria

F. W. Goldsmith and family group in the garden at 'Hillside', 1912   267
Courtesy of Mrs Marigold Crook

St George's Brede, 1928   279
Courtesy of Mrs Marigold Crook

Consecration of All Saints Collie, 1915   281
Battye Library mf 2426A/1 WN 5752

Exterior, All Saints Collie, 1923   282
*West Australian Church News*

The Chapel of the House of Grace, Williams   283
Battye Library mf 2426A/1 5794B/10

A page from *Constitution and Rule of the Brotherhood of St Boniface*   293
Battye Library mf 2426A/1 WN 5752

House of Grace, Williams, 1914   298
Battye Library mf 2426A/1 5794B/3

John Frewer on the roof of the House of Grace, Williams     325
Battye Library mf 2426A/1 5794B/20

The Right Reverend Edward Elsey     327
Courtesy of John Elsey

'A New Problem for the Bunbury Diocese'     333
Battye Library

The Bishop's Chapel, Kalgoorlie     339
Battye Library

Collapse of a church—Broome Hill     340
Battye Library

Interior, All Saints Collie     342
Battye Library

# Acknowledgements

Although this work centres on Bunbury's first bishop, the wide distribution of the circles in which Goldsmith worked and moved has meant that I have been helped during the course of my research by an equally diverse group of men and women.

I am particularly grateful to the Most Reverend Dr Peter Carnley for awarding me a grant from the Lockett Bequest, and to Dr Evan Burge and the Council of Trinity College for nominating me as the Sir George Turner Fellow in 1991; these two generous gifts made possible my research in England that year.

The publication of the results of my research in its present form would not have taken place without two other generous grants, one from the Western Australia History Foundation, and the other through The University of Western Australia from the South West Region Publication Fund (Clive and Joy Staples Bequest).

In England, Marigold and Peter Crook, then of Bishopsgarth, Brede, who hold an extensive collection of Goldsmith and Frewer papers, were unstintingly generous in offering hospitality as well as giving access to the relevant documents. I am grateful to the United Society for the Propagation of the Gospel for granting me permission to quote extensively from correspondence in its archives. Dr Harry Smythe, former representative of the Archbishop of Canterbury to the Vatican, and Librarian of Pusey House, Oxford, gave access to the collection of pamphlets and tracts from the nineteenth century relating to the Oxford Movement, which numbers almost half a million items, and gave valuable direction for research, as did Dr Geoffrey Rowell, then chaplain of Keble College. I am also grateful to the librarians and staff of St John's College and of Lambeth Palace Library for access to relevant materials, and for permission to quote from them. I also wish to thank the staff of the Battye Library, Perth, and of Trinity College, particularly Sandra Piggott at the former, and Gillian Forwood and Janet Bell at the latter.

Material for illustrations has been reproduced with the kind permission of the Public Records Office of Western Australia, the Picture Collection of the State Library of Victoria and the Archives of the University of Western Australia. I am likewise grateful to Mrs Marigold Crook, Mr John Elsey and Mrs E. W. Doncaster for making available photogaphs from family collections.

The late Dr John Foster was confident enough of the work that I was already envisaging in 1991 to undertake my supervision as a doctoral candidate and to arrange my entry into a department at Melbourne University with which I had no previous connection. At that time he was directing five candidates whose theses all involved a biographical treatment of an Australian ecclesiastical figure, and the exchange of ideas, and the sharing of mutual frustrations between members of that group were both rewarding and encouraging. When John's ill health made it difficult for him to continue the supervision, Mr Charles Zika took up his role and continued to offer encouragement and advice, but it was largely Dr Paul Nicholls who oversaw the shaping of my research in thesis form. Not only was he an invaluable source of advice, but conscientiously annotated and corrected the text in the manner of a first-class editor. Professor John Tonkin generously offered me access to materials he had assembled during his own extensive research into the history of St George's Cathedral, and more recently pointed out to me the location of the correspondence between Stone and Goldsmith over prayers for the departed, which I had been unable to identify. Lastly, throughout the transformation of my research from its original thesis form to its present shape, I have enjoyed the support of Dr Tom Stannage, beginning with occasional conversations, which eventually developed into a warm and personal interchange between us. It is such fruits that make the sometimes isolating and often painstaking nature of research doubly rewarding.

# Introduction

Up the steep incline, along a dusty track, a man who must have been approaching sixty, if he were not actually a little older, was pushing a cycle. The ruthlessly bright light on the warm summer's day could easily have persuaded a viewer that the setting was somewhere in southern Europe, but it was the south-west port town of Bunbury in 1912. There was a haze, but not rising from water, as in J. M. W. Turner's visions of the Venetian canals. Motes of dust danced in the heat, making the breathing of the man with the cycle more difficult: he was an asthmatic. His path led to a quite new single-storey building that could be hardly ten years old, surrounded on the north and west sides by an invitingly shady verandah. It was no usual cycle, but a large iron-frame tricycle, and the man propelling it was an equally unusual figure, the tails of his frock coat flapping in the wind to reveal well-developed calves enclosed in gaiters. Even if one only had the local nicknames to go by, the athletic form immediately distinguished its owner from the other Bunbury cleric to wear gaiters, the rotund archdeacon, 'Porky' Adams.

As the bishop laboriously ascended the steep slope, he recalled a very different hillside landscape, a village green with a tavern on one side, and a Gothic chuch surrounded by its graveyard on the other, with the land falling away sharply into the Brede River valley to the south. Over a decade ago he had asked in a public forum whether this new society was ever going to be regarded as having a history of its own. But European history, not to mention local history, had been written across the landscape that was in his mind, for what seemed a very long time. There had been Emma, the widow of Ethelred the Unready, bestowing the manor of Brede on the Benedictine abbey of Fecamp in Normandy even before the Norman conquest; in the church's chantry chapel a knight, recumbent in sculpture on his tomb, was related to the mythical and cannibal giant who was said to haunt the local 'groaning bridge'; and more recent local rumour had it that the regency rector of St George's, a Mr Maher, who had eventually gone insane, was a repentant buccaneer, who had finally been traced by a crew member he had marooned on a Caribbean island.

Here in this landscape all was so new, so clearly defined, so raw. Back there, there were gentler challenges to the mind and to the feelings. When his nephew John had arrived in Bunbury just a year ago, he complained bitterly about the absence of good actors for amateur theatricals. After all, Bunbury was larger: it should have some good actors. Even though Brede was small, it seemed to attract remarkable enough visitors, some long-term. There was the American journalist, Stephen Crane, living at Brede Place with the woman everyone had been told was his wife; close by, at Rye, there was Henry James, while H. G. Wells came down to Brede to act as one of this formidable trio: John Frewer had joined them. And Crane and James were both Americans: now *there* was a new society that could produce people of culture and refinement, that sought to imitate its parents, even though it stoutly proclaimed its autonomy.

Or there were his two sisters-in-law, Ellen and Alice, living in Hillside, the two-storey timber house near the edge of the green, beyond the east end of the church. Was Ellen still translating novels by Jules Verne for their relatives, the Low family, partners in the firm that had acquired the rights to publish the novelist's output in English? Here it was different. In the new house on the hillside his wife still played the piano like her sisters, but she was no missionary of civilization and higher culture to the rest of Bunbury. How often had he tried to persuade her that it did not matter that one of her eyes was blue and the other brown? But she still withdrew behind the net veil. She told people that her delicate skin would not tolerate the extremes of climate, but it was her eyes, not her skin, that made her withdraw. And there were no children . . .

Just then, as the absent and distant landscape seemed more real than the present, his reverie was interrupted by a small girl. His critics would have said that he began to talk to her because Jesuits in disguise like himself, the admirers of Edward Bouverie Pusey and John Henry Newman, sought every opportunity to beguile and manipulate the minds of children and women, incapable as they were of strong and independent thought. So they had suggested in Halling almost thirty years ago, when he initiated a liturgy for children. But the truth was that it was out of a desire for company, a desire heightened by his recollection of all that was seemingly absent, that made him welcome this interruption. His asthma tired him. And their childlessness still rankled.

The little girl lived across the dusty track from the new Bishopscourt. He did not see beyond her apparent innocence to the cruelty of children; he could not see in her a little girl who approved when her friends locked the inexperienced and incompetent teacher at the Grammar School he had established into the outdoor privy on a day as hot as this one. He had reassured an Australian audience that the purity of its family life was one of the jewels in the crown of British culture, and, here, it was children like her who were growing up in this new society to be the inheritors of a greater empire in the south. 'Can I help you push your bike?' came the improbable offer. The huge iron frame fascinated her, but it was even better to see it with its rider astride it, his coat-tails flapping in the wind like some giant insect on a merry-go-round. 'That's very kind of you, but we don't have far to go now. How is your father?' This turned out to be the wrong tack. 'My father says that I mustn't walk to school with my friend Joe. He goes to the other church.' 'You mean St Patrick's?' The bishop recalled another child going to school half a century before: he could not remember either any Roman Catholics in his part of Hampstead, or any nonconformists. Obviously the girl's father was making sure that until an Anglican identity was firmly fixed in the child's mind, she would not be exposed to the possibility of any alternative. 'Father said that it was because his father was a carpenter. But I said that if Jesus was a carpenter, what was wrong with talking to Joe?' Fortunately, their next steps brought them abreast of the path to Bishopscourt, and offered a way of avoiding comment on this awkward insight. What could he, who cautiously encouraged Bunbury's Anglicans to recover their awareness of their Catholic identity, say that would neither challenge the father's role, nor seem to contradict some part of his gospel? Father was certainly as worried about his daughter mixing with the children of the lower classes as any possibility of doctrinal deviation. The seemingly new and raw society was not as different from the old, despite the heat, the dust, the lack of dignified buildings for reverent and Catholic worship, the weight of history and culture. Perhaps there was solid ground even here for his vision to be established.

In some ways, the genesis of this study lies in my time as an undergraduate at Melbourne University when I was a resident of Trinity College. Here several Western Australian candidates for ordination were studying for their theology degrees. In the inevitable discussions of the many differences between West and East, they assured me that Western Australian Anglicanism did not have, and never had experienced, the strong divisions between different streams of churchmanship that they encountered from time to time in Melbourne. The nearest equivalent in Perth to Sydney's Christ Church St Laurence and St James' King Street, or Melbourne's St Peter's Eastern Hill, or Adelaide's St George's Goodwood, they assured me, was its cathedral. They also suggested that at the other end of the spectrum of Anglican churchmanship, with the exception of one or two centres such as St Alban's Highgate, there were few churches with a strongly evangelical identity. They could be excused for being unaware that, at the beginning of the century, St Alban's had a pronounced Anglo-Catholic tinge, and had maintained a quite Catholic profile in the face of a congregational decline after World War II. When I invited them to offer some definition of the churchmanship of the diocese as a whole, the answers ranged from moderately high to neither high nor low. The common denominator in all of these descriptions and definitions was an avoidance of extremes. At the same time, I was told that Anglo-Catholicism had a stronger hold in Western Australia's rural south-west in the diocese of Bunbury, and that it had been an influence in the formerly autonomous diocese of Kalgoorlie, which had been reabsorbed into Perth in 1973.

I subsequently spent eight years working in the diocese of Bunbury, and the comments of the friends of my undergraduate days about the Anglo-Catholic influence in rural Western Australia were confirmed in various ways. On the afternoon of my arrival in Bunbury, a very warm 17 October in 1978, I viewed the first mitre worn in Western Australia, a small cloth of gold medieval style specimen that had belonged to Frederick Goldsmith, Bunbury's first bishop, displayed like a relic in a glass showcase in the cathedral of St Boniface, a pale brick building designed by Louis Williams and situated across the road from Bishopscourt. I walked under the west gallery, and looking up, saw the wooden statue of St Boniface, the patron of the only Western Australian bush brotherhood, a relic from their house at Williams, raising a hand in blessing above me. In the chapel the burnished bronze panels of St Paul and St Boniface almost shone in its subdued light. These finely crafted fittings, showing the influence of the arts and crafts school, witnessed to the way in which the Oxford Movement harnessed the arts; they were part of the output of Gordon Holdsworth, whose first works were created when Goldsmith was bishop. Not long after, I was asked to act as master of ceremonies for a rural deanery liturgy at Harvey, over which Cecil Muschamp, sometime Bishop of Kalgoorlie, presided. I noticed that he wore something that had been out of fashion since the second Vatican Council—a lace alb, but mistakenly thought that this might just be a superficial manifestation, an attraction to 'bells and smells'. I soon realized why I had been asked to act as his master of ceremonies, because as I stood beside him at the beginning of the liturgy, I heard the preparation prayers from the Tridentine Latin rite being said in Latin in a low but audible voice, and he continued to use Tridentine formulae for many prayers that were not heard beyond the sanctuary. Later I heard anecdotes of the members of the Brotherhood of St Boniface, of Father John Foley-Whaling of St David's South Bunbury, and of Bishop Frewer in the North-West.

But it was not until I left Bunbury for Perth that I began to realize how influential Frederick Goldsmith had been in bringing many values of the Oxford Movement to influence the Anglican community of Western Australia, though he was far from the first Anglican influenced by it to come to the state. In Bunbury I had celebrated the eucharist week by week in the church of St Mark built by John Wollaston, the colony's first Anglican archdeacon. He noted in his journal the combination of curiosity, ignorance and suspicion concerning the Tractarian movement that was emerging in England at the time, a response that was partly conditioned in the Western Australian setting by the tyranny of distance.[1] He also noted that the layout of church interiors in Western Australia was such as to minimize any focus on the altar—quite the reverse of the emphasis of the Oxford Movement.[2] There were hostile comments in the *Perth Gazette*, one of which took the form of a verse satire reproduced from *Punch*.[3] Before coming to Western Australia, George Pownall, Perth's first dean, had been a member of the Cambridge Camden Society, an organization that was significant in promoting the revival of Gothic as the most appropriate style for church architecture, but there was little in his ministry in Perth to suggest that he had been strongly influenced by its more Catholic members, such as John Mason Neale.[4] But the tendencies of a curate at the cathedral in 1874 who seems to have been strongly influenced by the Oxford Movement provoked a definitely negative response from some quarters; and at Albany, complaints by the parishioners of William Wardell Johnson led to an investigation by Bishop Hale to see whether his eucharistic theology was compatible with Anglican standards.[5]

The picture of Western Australian churchmanship was becoming a much more complex one than the outline drawn by my friends of undergraduate days. A careful examination of the Perth press of the 1890s in particular revealed something very different from their picture of an absence of infighting and an avoidance of extremes. Instead, here was the editor of the *West Australian*, the Irish Winthrop Hackett, preventing any possibility of Goldsmith's election as bishop of Perth following the death of Henry Hutton Parry, attacking the dean and his churchmanship, sometimes subtly, sometimes quite directly. Instead of toleration and openness, there were impassioned letters in the press, alternately denouncing and defending a wide range of practices, many of which are now dispersed among Anglicans over a range of churchmanship, but then perceived as signs of Anglo-Catholicism. The correspondence in the Perth press was as extended and fiery as exchanges in the press in Melbourne and Sydney over centres such as St Peter's Eastern Hill or St James' King Street. Far from being exempt from the infighting that took place in other states, despite its isolation and its smaller dimensions, Perth's Anglican community was deeply embroiled.

However, my college friends were right in presenting a claim to moderation and an avoidance of extremes as a Perth tradition. But now it appeared in a new light: not as an unbroken inheritance that distinguished Perth's Anglican history from that of some other Anglican communities elsewhere in Australia, but as a tradition, manufactured in order to create, as much as possible, an unawareness of any such dissension. On the one hand, it became clear that C. O. L. Riley, Perth's first archbishop, had felt himself unable to handle such dissension, despite his public image as a no-nonsense, bluff and direct figure. He sought to deflect attention from the existence of polarities, and perhaps the most successful method was to encourage a middle way—to urge, despite his own distaste for ceremonial of any kind, that all the clergy should use the less controversial and obvious ceremonial usages, in order that, outwardly at least, variations between those of different churchmanship should be kept to a minimum. His private diaries reveal a very different picture from the one of consensus that he painted for public consumption. Later, I was to hear echoes of this story of harmony and moderation in the church in a different context, as I read Tom Stannage's *The People of Perth*, and its account of the Western Australian gentry's stress on harmony and consensus as a way of both rewriting the history of the colony, and imposing particular controls: it was a way of telling the story of a community that wrote out others who dissented in any way, those who did not conform to the values of those in power. Consciously or unconsciously, the myth of consensus that Riley had tried to create, and which my friends repeated in their own way, was of a piece with the mythology of a dominant group in society in general.

And I understood the surprise of my Western Australian friends at the strength of the parishes that had developed an overtly Anglo-Catholic tradition in other cities all the more when I discovered that it was not until Archbishop Le Fanu's time in 1933 that St Paul's Carr Street became the first church within Perth's inner-city area to develop a definite Anglo-Catholic profile. That this partly came about as a result of support both from Le Fanu himself, and from a group that were largely born and educated in England, in turn raised questions in my mind about the extent to which the Oxford Movement, in its most overt expressions, had taken root in Perth. It gave further confirmation that it might not have done so to the same extent as in some other large Australian cities. But while there were those on the edges who were bound to be dissatisfied, like those involved with the establishment of St Paul's as an overtly Anglo-Catholic centre, the devotional needs of many other Anglicans were being adequately met through the expressions of a more modest form of churchmanship, widely distributed throughout city and country. Riley's promotion of something like a middle line had borne fruit.

Ceremonial restraint and the strong contribution of those born and educated in England were not the only characteristics that seemed to distinguish Western Australia from Melbourne and Sydney in its experience of the Oxford Movement in the period under consideration—though Queensland also shared some common ground with Western Australia at this time in the high proportion of British clergy. There was also the issue of the interrelationship between Anglo-Catholicism, social work and Christian socialism, which had been a fruitful one in many cases in England, and which had a variety of expressions, particularly in Melbourne and Sydney. In Western Australia the seeds for some developments of this kind were not lacking. In Edward Mallan Collick, the remarkable goldfields priest who became rector of Fremantle, the Anglican community had a priest who had not only worked in that field which was to become a source of mythology for Anglo-Catholics, an east-end London slum parish, but one who transferred the ideals and approaches of the Anglo-Catholic slum mission priest to the goldfields, and especially to their aboriginal populations.[6] And at the cathedral, following their arrival in Perth in 1901, the Sisters of the Church provided a ministry to those who came to them off its streets, the homeless, the addicted, the marginalized.[7] It may well have been the results of the Great Depression that dashed the hopes of Robert Henry Moore, the dean during the Great Depression, that the cathedral parish might be able to perform effective social work and reach into the community of working families who lived just north of the railway line in the inner city. Le Fanu had been influenced in his earlier years by the Christian Social Union and by other expressions of Christian Socialism, however mild they might have been: later in Perth, when he was branded by some as a communist for signing a pacifist petition, a contemporary described him as 'inclined to a pale pink opinion'.[8]

Yet despite such figures as Collick, the early work of the sisters, and the awareness of others such as Moore and Le Fanu, there seemed to be a consistent absence of a cutting edge for either socialism or social work among Western Australian Anglo-Catholics, compared with the political radicalism of F. E. Maynard in Melbourne, or the engagement with social issues undertaken by the Brotherhood of St Laurence. An absence of radicalism seemed to be another characteristic of the Catholic tradition within Western Australian Anglicanism. As archbishop of Perth during the 1970s, Geoffrey Sambell, admittedly not an English priest, but one born and educated in Melbourne, and strongly influenced by the Brotherhood of St Laurence, more recently gave considerable dynamism to this aspect of the Anglican church's life in Perth. Meanwhile, was I going too far in tracing some of the slow growth in this area of the Perth Anglican consciousness to Goldsmith's conservative values? A critic who thought that I was going too far, and trying to use Goldsmith as an explanation for things far beyond the scope of his influence, might well point out that in the 1890s Perth had nothing that resembled the congested east end of London or similar areas in other large European cities. It lacked the kind of surrounds whose existence jarred the consciences of Christian Socialists elsewhere, so the seed would not germinate. I must finally leave the reader to decide the answer to this.

If my Western Australian friends in my undergraduate years introduced me, however broadly, to some of the questions that I have sought to answer, I have also been both stimulated and frustrated by the current state of writing on this area. While the impact of Tractarianism, the first stage of the Oxford Movement, has received some attention in studies based on regions, and in the biographies of one or two individuals, there is still much room for charting the development of the Anglo-Catholic movement. In her recent study, *Little Grey Sparrows*, Merle Bignell has provided a detailed study of a particular expression of Anglo-Catholicism in Western Australia, the community of the sisters of St Elizabeth of Hungary. But the impact of the Oxford Movement in Western Australia has generally been treated inadequately, or ignored, in accounts of Anglicanism in Western Australia. Alfred Burton, the state's pioneer church historian and the first candidate whom Riley ordained after his own arrival, made only passing reference to the issue of churchmanship in his *Church Beginnings in the West*.[9] The absence of any real discussion of this subject seems all the more strange, given that Burton himself regarded a debate over churchmanship as one of the most important factors that led to the resignation of Bishop Mathew Hale. By the time he published his work, it was no longer possible to question, as his parents' generation might well have done, whether the Oxford Movement was more than a temporary phenomenon, without significant or lasting impact. It is true that Burton gave no more consideration to the piety of the Evangelical revival. In this respect, he conforms to Riley's consensus myth. Much more recently, in the last decade, despite the title of Janet Scarfe's contribution to Colonial Tractarians—'The Diocese of Adelaide (and the West)'—her essay is exclusively the story of Tractarian influence in South Australia.[10] Even more peculiar are the omissions in a recent popular work by A. E. Williams, *West Anglican Way*, which surveys Anglicanism within the state from 1829 to 1929. Not a single reference is made to the Oxford Movement as such. This seems peculiar, given that by 1914, with the creation of Kalgoorlie, the last of the three rural dioceses in the province, the rural bishops in the state were all imbued with its influences. Nor is there any reference in what amounts to the best part of a chapter given over to Frederick Goldsmith and his circle.[11]

An exception to this is C. L. M. Hawtrey's *The Availing Struggle*, dated though it is in many other ways. There were other areas in which Hawtrey showed herself to be perceptive, but here it is almost certainly her own Anglo-Catholicism that drove her: she was a regular worshipper at St Paul's Carr Street, and contributed from time to time to the *Australian Church Quarterly*. She was the first historian of the state's Anglicanism to note the more distinct regional trends in churchmanship. She commented on the presence by the turn of the century of a core of priests in Perth diocese who 'would have liked to have accepted the ceremonial corollaries of the Catholic Revival', and noted that, despite them, and despite Goldsmith's long tenure as dean of Perth, restrained usages such as altar lights did not appear in the cathedral until 1925, eight years after his return to England, and three deans further on in time.[12]

She attributed some of this restraint to C. O. L. Riley. She stated elsewhere that it was due to his thirty-four-year episcopate that churchmanship in the diocese was neither distinctly high nor low, and that it was as a result of Le Fanu's initiatives that St Paul's Carr Street developed a definite Anglo-Catholic profile.[13] She devoted a chapter to Goldsmith's time as bishop of Bunbury, and, in introducing her subject, commented on his role as a careful teacher of the doctrinal emphases of the Oxford Movement during his Perth years. And while she devoted most of this chapter to an account of the organization of diocesan life, she also illustrated the churchmanship of the people of the new diocese with an anecdote that suggested to her that Goldsmith began his episcopate by facing even more resistance to his distinctive position in Bunbury than he did in Perth.

In 1957 Peter Boyce used the private diaries of C. O. L. Riley to create a perceptive re-evaluation of that prelate—perceptive enough to make members of the Riley family press for the destruction of these documents that showed the underside of the consensus he had created. The diaries referred to the clashes between dean and bishop, clashes that centred on the dual issues of the dean's authority in the cathedral, which Riley sought to curtail, and the dean's churchmanship. Boyce suggested that Riley's own attempt to avoid public identification with a particular party resulted in the 'avoidance and elimination of party friction' within the diocese. Although he noted Riley's attempt to change the cathedral statute while Goldsmith was in England, Boyce concluded that 'Goldsmith soon overlooked the offence', an interpretation that is called into question by subsequent entries in the diaries that record a continuing undercurrent of tension.[14]

In an entry in the *Australian Dictionary of Biography* Wilfrid Henn, a priest and son of another prominent Perth cleric and contemporary of Goldsmith, paid tribute to Goldsmith's definite churchmanship, but presented an equally benign account of his relationship with Riley.[15] Henn described Goldsmith's churchmanship as Tractarian, and made no reference to his introduction of the more controversial ritual usages in both Perth and Bunbury. He did not distinguish between Tractarianism and the ritualism or Anglo-Catholicism that followed it: he described the ongoing tradition of the diocese of Bunbury as Tractarian, whereas under Cecil Wilson, Goldsmith's successor, the majority of the clergy openly described themselves as Anglo-Catholic.

Boyce's study of Riley appeared in a collection of essays devoted to the first four bishops of Perth, and was the only essay to make any comment on how the currents of churchmanship were reflected in the lives of the individual bishops, or surfaced in the broader life of the diocese. In this regard, the treatments of Hale and Parry in *Four Bishops and Their See* were disappointing, as was the treatment of the diocese of Bunbury. This made no reference to the churchmanship with which the first bishop was so clearly identified, nor did it refer to the Anglo-Catholic colouring that it assumed under Wilson, when it was the home for more experiments with community life than any other rural diocese in Australia, despite its small overall population. The writer who dealt with the history of the south-west before its establishment as a separate diocese was oblivious to the churchmanship tensions that erupted in Bunbury in the last decade of the century. And it seems an even greater pity that almost forty years after the publication of Boyce's perceptive treatment of Riley, Williams could take up Boyce's charitable summing up of his subject as 'a godly but very human bishop' and turn it into an effusive compliment of a kind never intended by its coiner: the humanity that Boyce revealed in his study was one characterized by fallibility and limitation, not by personal insight, warmth or breadth.[16]

To sum up, historians of Western Australian Anglicanism, whether in biographical or broader studies, have generally provided an account of the influence of the Oxford Movement in its various aspects only in so far as these writers have touched on isolated individuals. There has been little examination of the broader social context. Boyce made passing reference to the press in the *West Australian*'s veiled criticism of Goldsmith in 1895, which was appropriate in the scope of his study. However, none of the writers already mentioned was aware of the acrimonious debates over churchmanship in the press in the 1890s. And while Boyce referred to Riley's distaste for ritualism and Hawtrey commented on the restrained nature of Perth cathedral worship under Goldsmith, no attempt was made to compare the emergence of Anglo-Catholicism in England with its appearance in Western Australia in such a way as to account for either similarities or differences.

These writers described Western Australian Anglicanism at the turn of the century as a religion of a substantially united community that was occasionally ruffled by minor personality clashes. As this study shows, it was a forum for acrimonious debates, revealing the divisions within the community. Were their accounts shaped by concepts of the unity and harmony of the Western Australian church and society—even if the influence of such concepts may have been one of which they were not conscious?

A consideration of history that does not in some way illuminate the present is of very limited application, and is little more than antiquarianism. For me, at the end of this treatment of a movement that engendered considerable controversy, the period under question came to pose its own questions of Anglicanism of the present both in Western Australia and elsewhere. Like all revival movements in Christian churches, the Oxford Movement provoked emotional responses among Anglicans, ranging from deep loyalty to outright rejection. There were points in the debate when to those involved there appeared to be the choice of only one of two points of view—for or against. Those who consider this part of Anglican history may well ask themselves: how do we now respond, and how have we responded, to a variety of movements within contemporary Anglicanism?

But, perhaps most importantly, there is a lesson to be gleaned from the way in which the story of this period was rewritten, or written out, of much of the public and official memory of the church in Perth. The same attractions beckon to those who want to tell the story of recent controversies in Perth, perhaps particularly over the ordination of women, an issue in which there are some parallels that can be drawn with the debate over Anglo-Catholicism last century, especially in the tensions between dean and (arch)bishop. Those who opposed such action risk the danger of describing their involvement as that of a small but heroic group (or sometimes even a silent majority), alone able to identify the essential teachings of the church and alone in preserving them. Some members of this group have been quick to criticize their opponents as being driven by the values and pressures of the wider society, while they have claimed to remain impervious to all such influences, resolutely turning their backs on them. If my analysis of the debate over what was perceived as Anglo-Catholicism in Perth at the end of the nineteenth century is any indication, the participants on both sides of a debate such as this one are responding to elements in their wider cultural setting, though they may be responding in different ways, and to different elements. On the other hand, those who supported the ordination of women need to recall the danger of succumbing to a retelling of the story that smoothes out the differences, reduces or denies the incidence of genuine pain on both sides, denies that high-profile figures taking different positions provoked one another, or pretends that those who differed from them were principally motivated by their human limitations, while those who supported were mainly driven by a deeply idealistic commitment.

However, history does not repeat itself identically in any two situations. If in the 1890s those perceived as Anglo-Catholics were regarded as radical or subversive, in the debate over the ordination of women their role had now changed to a conservative one. Again, while the nineteenth century churchmanship debate appears to have tested the comprehensiveness of Anglicanism to its limits at the time, it ended in accommodation, whereas the more recent debate has ended in the existence of bodies that are out of communion with one another, particularly in North America, but to a much lesser extent in Australia. In both the earlier and later controversies, there is no way of assessing how many Western Australian Anglicans responded by ceasing to worship;[17] and while the churchmanship debate contains references to a number of Anglicans who changed their denominational allegiance, there are a small number of more recent examples of the same response—but towards Orthodoxy or Roman Catholicism, as distinct from the Methodism or Congregationalism that provided options in the earlier debate. Such figures, both as individuals, and as statistics, generally remain hidden in the shadows, beyond the historian's reach.

A significant matter, and one essential for a proper reading of the text, is that of terminology. The term high church, which had emerged by the end of the seventeenth century, was first used to denote those Anglicans in the seventeenth and eighteenth centuries who combined a conservative political position with a stress on sacramental theology and liturgical scholarship. But since the 1830s it has also enjoyed a much wider use in describing a variety of liturgical, devotional and theological positions that show some influence of the Oxford Movement. The Oxford Movement, in turn, is a term that has been used in an umbrella fashion to describe a revival movement in Anglicanism which had some roots in this earlier high churchmanship, but which is generally identified as commencing with John Keble's Assize Sermon of 1833.[18] It had its beginnings in academic circles in Oxford, and its influence broadened beyond the realms of academe through the publication of substantial texts, somewhat ineptly described as tracts—hence the term Tractarian for the first phase of this revival, which focused on doctrine, though it was not necessarily uninterested in liturgy.[19]

Since the 1830s the range of those Anglican clergy embraced by the term high church has included those who have been restrained in their presentation, priests who neither wore vestments nor insisted on elaborate eucharistic ceremonial, but who taught the desirability of confession or the real presence in the eucharist; but it has been equally used of those who celebrated the eucharist as a high mass, using vestments and incense, and those who have taught an advanced eucharistic and Marian doctrine and devotions.

In Victorian England, responses to both of these levels of manifestation, the restrained and the overt, have included violence. In the 1840s it was one of the most restrained manifestations—the wearing of a surplice—that provoked the so-called surplice riots at St Sidwell's Exeter in 1845. The emergence of the more overt expressions was marked by bitter conflict. The riots at St Barnabas' Pimlico in 1850 and at St Peter's London Docks in 1859–60 were part of the first period of controversy, which culminated in the attempt to use parliamentary legislation to control 'ritualism' through the Public Regulation Act of 1874, under which six clergy were gaoled.[20] The failure of the Act to suppress manifestations of Catholic doctrine, ceremonial and devotion led to another wave of unease in the 1890s when John Kensit, a London bookseller, played a prominent role as an agitator, and pressure was once more brought to bear by opponents in an attempt to find a legal solution.[21]

The term Anglo-Catholic was used in the nineteenth century of the whole range of clergy described above, but came to be restricted to those who belonged in the second group. By the period of the Anglo-Catholic congresses of the 1920s and 1930s it had been firmly taken over by those whose liturgical practices included what the English Church Union had described in the nineteenth century as 'the six points' and eventually came to be called 'full Catholic privileges'.[22] In doctrine, they were committed at least to affirming seven sacraments, the real presence and a sacrificial doctrine of the eucharist, and a proclamation of the religious life. Marian doctrine and devotion was an area that engendered some debate; so did the desirability of eucharistic devotions; and, in the area of ecumenism and authority, a minority, who believed that Anglicanism was largely in error in not being in communion with Rome, were happy to be described as 'Anglo-Papalists'. In the second half of the nineteenth century the use of the term had been more inclusive, reflecting the uncertain legal position of the time. While it was used of those who followed the Church Union's 'six points', it was also used of those who were more restrained in their liturgical practices, but who taught the doctrinal and devotional positions that have already been mentioned. Fear of legal repercussions or of acrimonious public controversy made some cautious in revealing their true position; and some of these in turn would take comfort in the doctrine of 'reserve' over issues of faith that might be misunderstood. Priests of that ilk might have refused to accept the gift of a set of candlesticks, until the Lincoln Judgement ruled them to be lawful ornaments, but would still declare the desirability of confession, the beauty of the religious life, and modestly stand at the altar in a surplice and stole facing east, while believing that they were offering a sacrifice. Many such individuals described themselves, and were described, as Anglo-Catholics. Significantly, the critics of those who staunchly upheld 'full Catholic privileges', often termed ritualists in derision, used the same derogatory term to describe those who preached Catholic doctrine while using the Prayer Book text in the most restrained liturgical setting. To them, Goldsmith in Perth, using stoles but no other eucharistic vestments in the cathedral, in the absence of altar lights, but teaching the real presence, the desirability of confession, and the possibility of the religious life for those who had such a vocation, was a ritualist or an Anglo-Catholic.

Attempts to create a revival among the heirs of the Oxford Movement in the 1970s and 1980s saw many eschew the 'Anglo-' prefix and opt for

Catholic; the former was identified with the doctrinal, devotional and liturgical positions of the Anglo-Catholic congresses of the 1930s and the pre-Vatican II era. If the term Anglo-Catholic had up to this point denoted a fairly clear doctrinal package, with some argument about the borders, the emergence of those who identified themselves as liberal Catholics and became supporters of the ordination of women, and the growth of the charismatic movement, all contributed to a degree of fragmentation. While before World War II and the Second Vatican Council the terms Anglo-Catholic, broad and low church were useful labels for describing groupings within Anglicanism, they can now only be used in guarded and qualified ways.[23]

Throughout this text I would have preferred to avoid the term high church except when referring to those seventeenth- and eighteenth-century Anglicans for whom the term was first used, although I have obviously retained it without comment in those sources cited that use it. However, I have occasionally used it of later generations of Anglicans. I use the term Tractarian only to describe the first phase of the Oxford Movement, but use Anglo-Catholic before World War I of those who subscribed to Catholic doctrine, irrespective of their liturgical practices, while using it subsequently of those committed not only to particular doctrines, but to a liturgical platform. At the same time, I recognize that the Oxford Movement extended its influence beyond this well-defined group.

Colin Holden<br>1997

— ONE —

# Figure in the Shadows: the Early Years

As the *Albany* discharged her passengers at Fremantle on Friday 27 April 1888, a small but excited group gathered, waiting to welcome the new dean of Perth, Frederick Goldsmith, along with his wife, Edith Emma.[1] The welcoming party comprised members of Perth's religious and civic establishment. As well as the mayor of Fremantle, several members of the cathedral, and some nameless 'gentlemen', there were others who would be powerful supporters or strong opponents of the dean in the future. Among the former were Henry Hutton Parry, Bishop of Perth, the son of a bishop of Barbados, whose ancestors included two archbishops of York and an archbishop of Canterbury. Among the future opponents and most prominent among the laymen was one of the two churchwardens of the cathedral, John Winthrop Hackett, later to become the first vice-chancellor of the University of Western Australia. From 1887 until 1916 he was also a part owner and editor of Perth's most prominent newspaper, the *West Australian*. His brother became archdeacon of Dublin, and their father was also a priest in the Church of Ireland, which emphasized its Reformation inheritance and was suspicious of Tractarianism and its successors.[2]

The Goldsmiths were rapidly whisked away to the home of another of Perth's establishment figures, Anthony O'Grady Lefroy, where they remained until all was ready at their new home, the cathedral's deanery. Situated on the corner of St George's Terrace and Pier Street, the charming Gothic cottage *ornée* designed by R. R. Jewell, was then only one of many residences along this major thoroughfare, but now, the oldest house in the city centre still occupying its original site, it is dwarfed and isolated by high-rise buildings.[3] Goldsmith and the Lefroy family began to form a friendship as well as a personal relationship which enraged and puzzled C. O. L. Riley, Parry's successor, when he found out that it was the dean, and not he, who was called to the dying man's bedside nearly a decade later.[4]

While a journalist described Goldsmith, in preaching his first sermon in the cathedral on Sunday 29 April, as 'making a very distinct impression', the same writer suggested a definite presence in his appearance at a public reception in Perth Town Hall on Wednesday 2 May: 'The Dean ... is still a young man, being 35 years of age. He is tall, with sharply cut, pleasant intelligent features, and he gives the idea of being an active man, with a good capacity for work'.[5] The impression conveyed by the journalist is confirmed by a photograph of Goldsmith which he sent back to his former parish of St John's Halling, and which survives in its archives: it shows Goldsmith seated in a revival Jacobean armchair wearing a cassock, gown and hood, and in the prime of life, with vivacious eyes, a firm jaw and broad forehead, his whole pose conveying determination and assurance. Even if the Perth journalists made the wrong connections when they wrote of his past patrons, he had conveyed this sense of assurance to them: they incorrectly described his patron at Charlton as 'that well-known Australian colonist, Sir Samuel Wilson', confusing the Maryon-Wilson family, who were patrons of the living of Charlton, with the family of Sir Samuel Wilson, who after a distinguished career in the eastern part of Australia retired to England to unsuccessfully contest the seat of Buckinghamshire.[6]

Nostalgia for the home country and a sense of the strangeness of the new underlay Hackett's speech at his civic reception. He expressed 'peculiar satisfaction' that Goldsmith's predecessor, Joseph Gegg, had been replaced by an Englishman, because this would reinforce 'the ties which bind the church and people of the older country to us who live

> *By the long wash of Australasian seas,*
> *Far off, and raise our heads to other stars,*
> *And breathe in converse seasons'.*[7]

Hackett's satisfaction must have echoed the sentiments of much of Perth's Anglican population, even if others did not express their feeling in unmemorable blank verse: the high proportion of the population born in England, compared with that of other state capitals, and the consequent impression of a greater degree of Englishness, was commented upon by new arrivals.8 But the new dean was warned not to allow such appearances to deceive him: 'he would find things very different from what they were in England . . .'9 His response acknowledged this, as well as evidencing some of his characteristic determination to embrace the task in hand:

> In England when anyone became a dean, it was supposed to mean his retirement, with a nice house to live in, and little to do. Some of his friends, when they heard that he was appointed dean of Perth, thought he was going into retirement . . . He had come out here to work and he hoped God would give him the strength, wisdom and discretion, that he might do His work as it ought to be done, and as they had a right to expect that it should be done . . .10

But at the same time he showed how unaware he really was of the different dynamics of his new setting. Though the account of his reception does not indicate precisely how, he eventually revealed that he was unaware that there were members of other denominations present, and he was quickly enlightened by Mr Justice Stone, who had married into a leading Perth Methodist family, the Shentons.11 His assumption that the function was an exclusively Anglican affair may have been simply a momentary oversight; equally, it may have reflected the prevailing atmosphere of his childhood, particular assumptions about the relationship between the Anglican church and society which were reinforced in the patterns of life which were at hand in the part of London in which he grew up.

Frederick William Goldsmith was born on 3 August 1853, and was given the same names as his father, a writing master of Merchant Taylors' School, one of two such positions created in 1828 by William Bellamy.12 Father and son were both long-lived: the father died at the age of ninety-one in 1914, shortly after the outbreak of World War I. The son's tendency to respiratory complaints may also have been inherited. The immediate cause of his father's death is given as 'bronchitis and cardiac failure, increasing for some weeks',13 and on the bishop's own death, the writer of an obituary questioned whether it had been wise for him to return to the 'sharp' air of Hampstead after his time in Australia, when he suffered from a respiratory weakness.[14] His father was certainly the source of the interest in education which he showed in his later years in establishing church day schools as dean of Perth, and later, a small grammar school in Bunbury.[15]

His baptismal certificate shows that he was baptized at St Clement Danes, and gives his parents' address as 13 Arundel Street, only a stone's throw from the unattractive and overcrowded area which was cleared in the following decade to form a site for the new Law Courts facing on to the Strand, towards the east of the church. The church was one of several where almost daily burials during the 1849 cholera epidemic had led to complaints.[16] And perhaps it was the birth of their first child and the desire to find a more attractive and healthy environment for his future that encouraged Frederick's parents to move to Hampstead, where their address is given as West View House, Hampstead Road.[17]

The architectural historian, Nicholas Pevsner, described this north London borough as one which preserved much of the character that it had taken on during the eighteenth century.[18] While Hampstead had become a select residential town and a summer home for the wealthy by the second half of the eighteenth century, it relied for much of its character on the growth of a professional population, having virtually no resident nobility,[19] and census figures for the second half of the nineteenth century show that the professional stratum, of which Goldsmith's father was a part, was still increasing.[20]

The population of the whole borough increased twentyfold in the century. The Hampstead into which Goldsmith moved was described by one writer in 1851 as a 'picturesque and pretty village' with a 'beautiful aspect', where 'on either side elegant villas, cottages and mansions meet the eye' . . . 'a favourite abode with invalids and persons of rank and fortune'.[21] But significant population growth occurred in Goldsmith's formative years, and eleven years later George Rose Emerson could write that it was 'now nearly joined to London by rows of villas and white terraces . . .'[22]

To the mind of a growing child, the suburb's orderly proportions might well have confirmed the rightness of the claims made by members of the

Victorian middle classes that, as the bulwark of wider social stability, they deserved to prosper, and that their prosperity was a proof that they were fulfilling that role responsibly. In later years, on a number of occasions, Goldsmith was to articulate a view of a renewed society based on social harmony rather than structural reorganization. Above all, clearly articulated responsibilities were a significant part of his own understanding of his office as dean and bishop, whose exercise he saw as vital for the establishment and maintenance of a stable, cohesive fabric.

Its witness to stable social order was not the only way in which the life of the borough may have impressed itself on him. The census of 1851, the only census to attempt to assess religious attendance in England, found that across the nation Anglicans were only a bare majority of those who attended church. But Hampstead did better than the national average. On the census Sunday of 1851 nearly half the total population of Hampstead attended a church, even when allowance was made for the double attendance of some; it was assumed that only 58 per cent of the total population was free to worship, invalids, children and servants being included in the category of those assumed to be absent. To a child becoming conscious of the fabric of life in such a setting, institutionalized Christianity can only have seemed normal, indeed typical; and it is hardly surprising that coming from such a background, he should in later life envisage institutionalized Christianity as a social as well as a religious force. The religious complexion of the Hampstead of Goldsmith's childhood was overwhelmingly Anglican. In the census year of 1851, Anglicans formed 80 per cent of the total worshipping population of the borough. Within the borough two significant landholders, the Dean and Chapter of Westminster, and Eton College, deliberately excluded non-Anglicans from the eight estates which they controlled; it was only in 1883 that the first of these landowners allowed the building of a Congregationalist church, which with the Fleet Road Methodist Chapel, constituted the only nonconformist churches on the Chalcot and Belsize estates.[23]

In later life Goldsmith was to make statements which assumed the existence of a natural Anglican hegemony. In the case of his initial welcome in Perth Town Hall he could be excused for thinking that he was addressing an exclusively Anglican gathering. However, in other

Australian contexts, such as the six years during which he exercised missionary jurisdiction over the north-west of Western Australia, with a skeleton staff of clergy and lay-readers, such an assumption could only seem faintly ludicrous.[24]

Another formative influence was that of his school, Merchant Taylors'. The school had been founded by Sir Thomas White and Richard Hilles in 1561,[25] but by the first half of the nineteenth century the unattractive conditions which existed were those of a school living on its past. It was predominantly a day school, with up to one hundred boarders.[26] In 1864, Goldsmith's first year at Merchant Taylors', the school was visited by parliamentary commissioners who recommended the removal to the country of the larger schools, such as Westminster and Charterhouse, on whose surroundings the city had begun to encroach. However, it was not until 1875, three years after Goldsmith had left, that Merchant Taylors' was relocated at the old Charterhouse.[27] The narrow curriculum of Merchant Taylors' and other public schools had also been an object of the commissioners' criticisms. At the beginning of the nineteenth century its focus was on a purely classical course of Greek, Latin and Hebrew. Bellamy's introduction of mathematics was unusual, and the commissioners regarded the time given to its study as disproportionate. James August Hessey, the principal when Goldsmith entered the school, had introduced French, modern history and drawing but, as yet, little time was devoted to them, and this vein of conservatism continued to predominate until the century ended. The school's sporting enthusiasms were likewise conservative, concentrating on running and cricket.[28] The emphasis on high standards in classical languages remained with Goldsmith in later life. As dean of Perth, he was an examiner in Latin, as well as French and English for Perth High School, and on at least one occasion his standards were regarded by that school as being too rigorous.[29]

The school's religious practice was equally conservative. Under Hessey, monitors continued to lead in the recitation of Latin prayers; Baker, his successor, opted for prayers in English.[30] The fates of some of its earlier heads, supporters of the Stuarts and the non-juring tradition—the latter comprising those bishops, priests and the smaller body of laymen who scrupled to take the oath of allegiance to William and Mary after 1688 on the ground that this would break their previous oath to James II and his successors—indicated that it had leaned in the past in the direction of an earlier high churchmanship, of which a component was a conservative, even reactionary, political position.[31] If in the 1860s there was certainly nothing outwardly Anglo-Catholic, there was not likely to have been anything evangelical either. And if in the first half of the nineteenth century a school head such as Arnold at Rugby could espouse an anti-Tractarian position, it was only from the middle of the century onwards in a school such as Eton that the distaste for any form of religion involving experiential conviction or conversion slowly dissipated; and it was probably as true of Merchant Taylors' as of larger public schools that 'the boys themselves felt militant objection to suspect zeal'.[32]

On leaving Merchant Taylors', Goldsmith entered St John's College, Oxford, in 1872 as Sir Thomas White scholar, and was awarded the degree of Bachelor of Arts with third class honours in modern history in 1876.[33] This somewhat undistinguished record may well be due to the prevailing atmosphere, which was hardly favourable to any serious study. A near contemporary at St John's, C. Y. Fell, one of the few undergraduates who did not come from a public school, wrote the following account:

> Of the men, say twenty or twenty-five were 'Scholars', all I think from Merchant Taylors', the great London School, who had all gone through the mill, and many were in for classical honours. They mostly had some well-known coach outside. The rest of us were either hopeless idlers, intent only on pleasure, or like myself, willing enough to work if they only knew how. It was not at all a reading college like Balliol or New and our reading men were sorely at a disadvantage ... In those days temperance was unheard of and the wine and beer that was daily put away seems now idiotic and worse. It was the day when 'Wines' were almost the only recognized form of entertainment, the 'Wine' being a dessert supplied by the grocer, with unlimited Port and Sherry and Tobacco, songs were sung with rattling choruses, and sometimes things went on till all hours and half the men were more or less drunk.[34]

As dean of Perth, Goldsmith, along with C. O. L. Riley, was to be a strong supporter of the temperance movement, particularly as a means of influencing the leisure patterns of working people; but by his own admission, he never embraced total abstinence himself. Was this because he felt confident of his own individual propensity for self-control; or because as a class, 'gentlemen' such as those whom Fell described, stood in less danger of falling permanent victims to the effects of the 'demon drink' than their weaker working brethren?

Other aspects of life within the college can only have reinforced the lessons in conservatism that he had already learnt. From its foundation in 1555, in which Sir Thomas White, founder of Merchant Taylors', also played a part, it was a close corporation. By the time Goldsmith went there, most of its fellowships were still held by scholars from Merchant Taylors', and when the Liberal government began its enquiry into the colleges, St John's showed itself to be amongst the most conservative by refusing to supply them with even a copy of its statutes.[35] Despite some concessions to their recommendations, a strongly Tory atmosphere was maintained. Mark Pattison, then rector of Lincoln College, described St John's as 'entirely eaten up with the canker of Toryism and ecclesiasticism'.[36] Prys Morgan identifies Toryism as the political position embraced by James Bellamy, its president from 1871 until 1909, a position which he is said to have shared with most undergraduates and fellows.[37] With a few notable exceptions, high Tory politics had indeed characterized the college in the seventeenth and eighteenth centuries and Bellamy's predecessor as president, Philip Wynter (1827–71), had been a leader of the University's conservative party.[38] As Goldsmith entered the college only a year after Wynter's retirement, he can hardly have avoided imbibing an atmosphere already saturated with his political convictions. Bellamy continued in a similar role, allowing members of the party to meet in the college lodgings at election time. Despite the imposition of new statutes shortly after Goldsmith left, the ultra-conservative character of the college was to endure.[39] The social and political conservatism of his school and university college account for his own conservative social position in contrast to the more radical social and political stance taken by some other contemporary Anglo-Catholics.

Ecclesiastical, as much as political and social, conservatism pervaded the air of St John's. While Biblical higher criticism was raising questions in the minds of people elsewhere about how Scripture could be read with integrity in the light of new insights provided by a variety of disciplines, in St John's, theology and scriptural interpretation still seem to have been treated as an assured body of knowledge, the transmission of which could be taken for granted, as though independent of personal conviction or the need for a revision in the means of approach. Instead, Bellamy offered the only tuition in this area in the dining room of the president's lodge: the students gathered around the table while he sat astride a mahogany wine-cooler from under the sideboard, on which he resembled the cartoons of him riding a charger, which were sold in the Broad Street shops.[40] Goldsmith and other divinity candidates were taught theology more adequately elsewhere, as is shown by the certificate issued by C. A. Heurtley, the Lady Margaret Professor, as evidence of Goldsmith's attendance at divinity lectures.[41]

The advanced positions in theology and liturgics that Goldsmith later openly espoused were the opposite of those favoured by the college's previous president, Wynter, who had just retired. Known as *malleus haereticorum* when vice-chancellor of the University on account of his denunciations of Pusey, when the latter was a leading voice of the infant Tractarian movement,[42] he was reputed to have given the Laudian vestments of his college, which had survived since the seventeenth century, to his children as fancy dress for charades.[43] Even if this anecdote is apocryphal, it suggests an attitude of relaxation towards the accessories of worship diametrically opposed to the deliberate reverence consistently expressed by Goldsmith in later years. Bellamy, Wynter's successor, may have sympathized with Pusey, and according to Benjamin Jowett, advised him on how to vote in debates,[44] but worship in the college chapel remained restrained. The college was even described by the evangelical journal, *The Flail*, as late as 1897 as 'that well-known seat of evangelical interest', and it was not until a later period that a more consciously high-church image was to emerge.[45] In Goldsmith's day its liturgy, like that of other university college chapels, was that of the *Book of Common Prayer* without addition or deviation.[46] If the Anglo-Catholic emphases of his later years had their genesis in his Oxford days, their birthplace was certainly not the college chapel. Indeed, it is possible to say in general, that the wellsprings of undergraduate religion in both Oxford and Cambridge lay not in the college chapels at this time, or even in other official forms of college life, but in unofficial bodies or external institutions.[47]

There remains one other way in which St John's College may have influenced Goldsmith in his ultimate adoption of a position combining political and social conservatism with religious commitment. Just as Merchant Taylors' enjoyed a strong non-juring tradition, so St John's also displayed prominent signs of its past loyalty to the Stuart line: it still houses many relics of Archbishop Laud, one of its patrons, and prominent life-size statues of Charles the First and Henrietta Maria by Le Soeur dominate the Canterbury quadrangle. The non-jurors were the Anglican tradition's self-deniers; and by the inclusion in the Prayer Book of 1662 of a liturgical commemoration of the death of Charles the First as 'King and Martyr', for high churchmen, the Stuarts became its martyrs. Despite the removal of this celebration from the Prayer Book in 1859, the Caroline and non-juring elements of the Anglican tradition were often to be invoked by Victorian high churchmen of varying shades. The status of the non-jurors as a persecuted minority was seen not as a weakness but as a virtue: they could be upheld as examples of how truth might be preserved by a persecuted remnant in spite of pressure from the state. Such models harmonized with the claim of the Oxford Movement that the church was an institution of divine foundation which stood in no need of any external authentication.

Goldsmith was one of twenty-four candidates ordained to the priesthood on 20 December 1877, the eve of the feast of St Thomas.[48] From then until his appointment as dean of Perth in 1888 he remained within the diocese of Rochester. No documents have survived from this early period of his life that throw any light on his motivation. However, a strong sense of vocation characterizes several statements made later in his career, such as the one he made at his reception in Perth, and this is consistent with the professional ethos of which his father, as a public schoolmaster, was a part. And the family into which he married had a strong sense of the professional, both as schoolmasters and members of the clergy.

It is just possible that his association with Rochester was a result of an early connection with the Maryon-Wilson family, who were major landholders in Hampstead and Blackheath, and who were patrons of the livings of St John's Hampstead and of the parish of Charlton, to which Goldsmith was appointed for his first curacy.[49] Goldsmith's public school background and his father's professional status would be consistent with the possibility of an early date for such an association. While Goldsmith, later in life, was definitely friendly with the Maryon-Wilsons (hence his appointment to St John's Hampstead in 1917 by the younger Sir Spencer Maryon-Wilson, whom he had tutored), there is no proof of any connection before 1876, and one indication that points in the other direction. When worshipping in Hampstead, the Maryon-Wilsons attended St John's, but Goldsmith's *Si Quis*, a legal document which had to be read in the parish church of any candidate for ordination, is signed by E. H. Bickersteth, vicar of Christ Church Hampstead, which suggests that Goldsmith's family did not worship at St John's.[50]

Churchmanship may equally have played a part in his introduction to Rochester. His deaconing on 8 October 1876 took place at the hands of Thomas Legh Claughton, who was regarded as being sympathetic to a high church rather than an evangelical position. He numbered among his close friends Samuel Wilberforce, Bishop of Oxford and subsequently of Winchester, a conservative high churchman of an older school, suspicious of Anglo-Catholicism.[51] While Claughton's distaste for ritualism was as well known as Wilberforce's, Goldsmith may well have reposed some confidence concerning his own future in the bishop's known sympathy towards Tractarians.

But things turned out differently. The most notable incident of Claughton's episcopate was to demonstrate his hostility to Anglo-Catholicism—the case of Father Tooth of St James' Hatcham, the first priest to be gaoled under the provisions of the Public Worship Regulation Act. The Act of 1874 sought to control ritualism by means of a court established to discipline clergy after it had investigated complaints by aggrieved parishioners concerning alleged breaches of ritual. It had not been the intention of its framers that penal sanctions should be used, but it was an Act administered by a civil court, and the assumption that all clergy would accept the jurisdiction of such a court was to be the Act's weakest point.[52]

Formal proceedings against Tooth began in June 1876, the year of Goldsmith's deaconing. Tooth refused to appear before the court, and in the face of his persistence in ignoring the initial monition of Lord Penzance, the court declared in December that year that he was suspended for three months from performing priestly functions. Tooth refused to acknowledge the court's monition and suspension, continuing to use the disputed—and controversial—ritual. A body of Tooth's supporters frustrated Claughton's opening attempts to appoint other clergy during the period of suspension by controlling access to the church. Claughton himself eventually appealed to the police to intervene and Tooth was committed to the debtors' ward of Horsemonger Gaol on 22 January 1877. Nor was Tooth's release from prison the end of the Hatcham saga, which involved an appeal against Tooth. After a lengthy dialectic with Archbishop Tait, a legal technicality allowed the Queen's Bench to quash it on 19 November 1877.

How might this case and its successors have appeared to Goldsmith as a young curate in a nearby parish? The impact of this particular case on the diocesan clergy is not easy to assess. Some journals reported it as a *cause célèbre*, but the two major Kent papers available in Charlton in Goldsmith's time, the *Kentish Mercury* and the *Kentish Independent,* paid it little attention, though both were hostile to advanced churchmanship.[53] The significance of the Tooth case, as the first of a series that would eventually bring discredit to the Public Worship Regulation Act, was only to become apparent in the following years. The frequent reports in their columns of meetings of local branches of the Church Association, and occasional correspondence, suggest that, in the year leading up to Goldsmith's deaconing, the ongoing life of such pressure groups, rather than reaction to a single specific case such as Tooth's, led to the maintenance of a strongly Protestant profile among Anglicans in the archdeaconry of Greenwich. Moreover, prominent Rochester clergy were numbered among the opponents of Anglo-Catholicism: these included John Cale Miller, archdeacon of Rochester and vicar of Greenwich, the author of uncompromising pamphlets. He was regarded as the leading clerical spokesman for the anti-ritualists in the Canterbury Convocation.[54]

But while the general atmosphere accounts for the caution in matters of ritual that Goldsmith displayed as a curate and then as a young incumbent, the whole sequence of gaolings under the Act that began with the Tooth case and ended in 1887 may still have had a cumulative effect on him. The last case, that of James Bell Cox in Liverpool, gaoled for a year and a half, was certainly a cause of concern and an object of discussion in Goldsmith's family circle: the first page in the journals of George

Ernest Frewer, Goldsmith's clerical brother-in-law, features a printed card, asking for prayers for Cox.[55] A clerical life lived through these years of tension over Anglo-Catholicism explains some of the caution that marked Goldsmith's actions over ceremonial as Bishop of Bunbury, though this caution in later years was also a response to a variety of subsequent factors.

Meanwhile, later in 1876, Claughton left Rochester to become the first Bishop of St Albans, a new diocese formed from Hertford, Essex and North Woolwich. Any prospect of future preferment that Goldsmith might have hoped for at Claughton's hands was cast under a deep shadow with the appointment of Anthony Wilson Thorold, who was consecrated on 25 July 1877.[56]

Thorold was impressed by the sermons of Canon Carter of Clewer, the founder of one of the earliest religious communities for women in the Anglican church, and had been a regular worshipper during the Holy Week of 1863 at All Saints Margaret Street, already regarded as a leading centre of Tractarian, and then Anglo-Catholic, influence. Yet his close friends were all of the evangelical school, and 'every year he had become more definitely associated with the leaders of the Evangelical party, on Committees, on Trusts, as a Revivalist . . .'[57]

One of his early official acts as Bishop of Rochester was a visit to St James' Hatcham, on 19 August 1877, which he described as 'an anxious day'. Despite his admiration for individual churchmen at the heart of the Tractarian movement such as Carter, he made his position clear as far as the diocesan clergy were concerned in 1878 in a policy statement that he described as his Pastoral. He said this about Anglo-Catholicism:

> A Church with a foreign body in it, such as the Ritual polity declares itself to be, must very soon either absorb, modify, or expel it. It comes to this, that what in the army would be called mutiny, and in the State outlawry, in the Church is schism. My own course is clear . . .

He 'isolated' such churches, refusing to perform any function in them as bishop, until they had conformed to what was deemed lawful in accordance with the Public Worship Regulation Act.

Apart from St James' Hatcham, there were other churches whose ritualism he sought to contain. One at which Goldsmith preached regularly on his return visits to England as a bishop was St Stephen's Lewisham, where the teaching on confession by the vicar, R. R. Bristow, brought rapid responses within the first month of Thorold's appointment.[58]

As deacon, and then as a junior priest, Goldsmith worked as assistant curate in the parish of Charlton, across the heath from Greenwich and close enough to one of the centres that distressed Thorold, St John's Walworth. Here, in 1872, George Nugee entered into a private agreement with the vicar that a male community which he had founded, the Order of St Augustine, should live and work in the parish. The splendid revival baroque decoration of the refurbished oratory of the community and the colourful and dramatic outdoor processions associated with the liturgy, especially in Holy Week, were visible evidence to the public of a degree and kind of ceremonial that was not based on the rubrics of the Prayer Book. Exotic worship, causing scandal and sensation, was something that Nugee could support from his extensive private income, while ignoring the bishop's strictures.[59] It was one of those expressions of an Anglo-Catholicism that enjoyed thumbing its nose at the establishment, and attracted people by its suggestion of rebellion, a *frisson* of naughtiness.

Charlton, on the other hand, was a parish in which social structures and historical associations would have made it far less tempting for a rector and his curate to adopt any such startling innovations. Charlton's rector, Charles Swainson, appointed in 1874, distinguished himself not by advanced ceremonial practices, but by the much safer publication of *A Handbook of Weather Folklore*, and later, in 1890, with *Historical Memoirs of the Maryon-Wilson Family*, a respectable, uncommentable kind of activity.[60]

There is nothing to suggest that as the patrons of the living, the Maryon-Wilsons ever encouraged ritual deviancy. Their centre was Charlton House, near Greenwich, one of the two remaining Jacobean mansions 'of the first order in the precincts of London'.[61] Charlton House, with its chapel dedicated to St James, still complete in Goldsmith's time with its original Caroline oak altar and frontals, had been built by Sir Adam Newton, tutor to Henry, Prince of Wales, in the first decade of the seventeenth century.[62] The chapel was a setting designed for the performance of the Prayer Book rite without any of the ceremonial beloved of Anglo-Catholics, whose ideals were far better realized in revival Gothic or rococo buildings. Equally redolent of the Prayer Book era was the parish church of St Luke's, built just before the outbreak of the English

Civil War in the classical Italian style, then unusual for English churches, but subsequently adopted by Christopher Wren, a style which gave visible expression to the principles espoused by the Caroline high church party.[63] The setting as Goldsmith knew it was sympathetic to any priest seeking to instil a Tractarian emphasis, but nothing more. Nor is it possible to learn anything from the liturgical patterns of the parish, as the only registers that survive from this period are those for baptisms, weddings and funerals.[64]

Charlton's roots were in the same soil of an older high churchmanship, combined with social conservatism, that Goldsmith already knew from Merchant Taylors' and St John's College. Swainson was no ritualist, but was among the growing number of clergy who used the less controversial of the Church Union's 'six points': in 1871, he was one of almost 4,700 clergy who signed a petition appealing to the archbishop and bishops 'to preserve the ancient liberty of the Church of England' against the Purchas judgement, in which the Judicial Committee of the Privy Council declared the use of the eastward position to be illegal.[65] Nor were the Maryon-Wilsons averse to high churchmen, as distinct from ritualists: in July 1875 the Reverend George Maryon-Wilson, Sir John Maryon-Wilson's youngest son, married a daughter of the Tractarian Bishop of Adelaide, Augustus Short.[66]

Goldsmith's period at Charlton was notable for another reason: on 22 April 1880 he married Edith Emma Frewer, one of three daughters of George Frewer, a former mathematics master and housemaster of Eton College, who became rector of Hitcham in Buckinghamshire on his retirement from the school.[67] This alliance was also significant because Edith had two brothers who were priests.

Both George Ernest and George Herbert Frewer were distinctly Anglo-Catholic, and Goldsmith's marriage to Edith Frewer is the first definite evidence of his exposure to Anglo-Catholic influences. If it was indeed his introduction to that world, there was already sympathetic ground to build on in his previous associations with institutions such as Merchant Taylors' and St John's College that had their roots in the older 'high and dry' school, and Charlton itself. But if a family tradition is correct, which identified the friendship between Goldsmith and G. E. Frewer as dating back to their days together as Oxford undergraduates, he may well have first encountered Anglo-Catholicism in Oxford itself. There were several significant centres outside the colleges and their chapels. These included the Cowley Fathers' church, then more notable as a centre of teaching than for its liturgy,[68] and the church of St Thomas the Martyr, where eucharistic vestments, hastily made up from an academic hood, had been worn for the first time in Oxford.[69] That church, and St Barnabas Jericho, another Anglo-Catholic centre, were frequented by the members of women's religious communities.[70] And Edmund King, who then held the seat of Pastoral Theology, conducted informal, mission style services and lectured in his home to a wide circle of Oxford men.[71]

Goldsmith moved in 1881 from Charlton to Cheam, a village lying on the east side of the Little Park of Nonsuch. Its vicar, Charles Hobbes Rice, had come to Cheam in 1867 from a fellowship at St John's College, which held the patronage of this parish,[72] and it is presumably through their common collegiate background that Goldsmith was appointed assistant curate. Cheam was also the site for two churches that sprang up in the Victorian enthusiasm for church building: St Dunstan's, 1862–64, and St Philips, Cheam Common Road, commenced in 1874 and opened in 1876; on Goldsmith's arrival it was relatively new but was not an independent parish centre of its own. Probably wanting to hasten this process, Rice gave Goldsmith particular responsibility for St Philip's; the *West Australian* later described him as having been in charge of the independent district of Worcester Park for five years.[73] The Cheam *Parish Chronicle* of 1882 mentioned that if sufficient financial support were forthcoming, St Philips could become an independent parish. By 1883 Rice commented that the increase in giving that had already taken place amply justified his previous statement, and added that it was 'one among many proofs that the work of the Revd. F. Goldsmith has been successful'.[74]

Like Swainson, Rice had signed the protest against the Purchas judgement, suggesting that he was Tractarian in sympathy.[75] The service registers of the time provide no evidence of anything ritualistic in the worship of the parish;[76] a weekly celebration of the eucharist had been customary since 1878 but Matins retained its traditional pride of place, and Tractarians as much as Anglo-Catholics would have disapproved of its offering of a eucharist on Ash Wednesday in the evening.

At Cheam, Goldsmith exhibited a characteristic of the first years of his Perth ministry, the energetic organization of pastoral work. Also,

Goldsmith's time at Cheam shows the developing links with the Frewer family: the baptismal register shows G. E. Frewer administering baptisms in June 1884, presumably to allow his brother-in-law some time for holidays.

In 1885 the parish of Halling, then in the gift of the chapter of Rochester cathedral and its scholarly dean, the Greek lexicographer R. Scott, became vacant and was accepted by Goldsmith. Of the medieval palace of the bishops of Rochester that was located at Halling only a small length of wall still remains in St John's churchyard, a witness to an earlier period when the town had some significance. But in the fifteen years before 1888 the population of the town, most of whom were involved in the production of cement, had grown from eight hundred to just over two thousand—much of this increase occurred in a single decade.[77]

Compared with the previous incumbent, Joshua Nalson, who assumed office in 1852, Goldsmith's tenure was to be short.[78] His first signed entry in the preacher's book is for 31 October 1885, and the completeness of this register allows the drawing of a somewhat fuller picture than for his previous appointments. Though there are still no signs of the controversial liturgical usages, there are clearer indications of a particular churchmanship than in the past.

The parish register records the daily recitation of the offices and the offering of the eucharist on Sunday after matins at 11.00 a.m., and also on the red-letter days of the Prayer Book calendar. This is consistent with standards proclaimed by the Tractarians and their successors, as were the more frequent celebrations of the eucharist in Advent in 1886.

If the record at Cheam of baptisms of those 'able to answer for themselves' suggests that Goldsmith had already developed a pattern of teaching aimed at adults, clearer evidence is provided in Halling. On 27 May 1886, almost eight months after his induction, he presented fifty-four candidates for confirmation. Another twenty-two were presented at Aylesford on 3 February 1887. Opportunity for teaching, as well as worship, was also provided by the introduction in 1887 of 'children's vespers'. That the children's service took the form of an office and not a eucharist, was certainly a concession to the known propensities of Bishop Thorold: eucharists for children were still seen over a decade later as evidence of advanced churchmanship. And for adults who were already members of the church he provided additional teaching: in Advent of 1886 he ran a special series of addresses for men.

As the population grew, extensions and alterations to the fabric of St John's were made, and these offered a tactical point for Goldsmith to make obvious changes. At the reopening of the church on 10 February 1888 he introduced a surpliced choir, by then a common enough feature elsewhere, but still suggestive of a particular kind of churchmanship. On the same day his brother-in-law preached at a festal evensong at which the choir was accompanied by an orchestra. On the following Tuesday, Shrove Tuesday, one of the services was marked by a festal *Te Deum* and a procession.[79] The resources available can hardly have allowed the celebration to be anything other than simple—but this is consistent with the later record in Perth, where Goldsmith's emphasis was initially on dignity and restraint rather than elaborate ceremonial as such, even where resources richer than those at Halling were available.

Goldsmith's churchmanship was indicated by his organizational interests as well as his liturgical patterns. In 1887 he established a branch of the Church of England Working Men's Association in Halling: this organization had grown out of the need to provide 'minders' for a number of controversial Anglo-Catholic churches.[80] The means by which the Halling branch was established was equally suggestive: Goldsmith invited his brother-in-law to join him in holding a mission, for which preparations took place in December 1886. The mission itself occurred in Lent 1887, with a series of addresses given by G. E. Frewer; the branch of the Working Men's Association was inaugurated on 15 February, in the week before Ash Wednesday.[81] In 1887 Goldsmith had also joined the English Church Union, the largest and most powerful of several associations of laity and clergy then in existence to promote Anglo-Catholicism.[82] The increasing strength of the English Church Union may have been attraction enough for Goldsmith to join, but the Frewer family certainly offered encouragement—both George Ernest and George Herbert Frewer were already members of the Church Union and of the Confraternity of the Blessed Sacrament, another Anglo-Catholic organization, whose aims were concentrated on the promotion of particular eucharistic doctrines, devotional attitudes and liturgical practices.

At Halling the closest that Goldsmith came to anything controversial in terms of Anglo-Catholicism was when he invited his brother-in-law as parish missioner. G. E. Frewer already had such strong views on confession that he felt unable to take part in a mission unless he were free to preach on this contentious topic.[83] Despite the lack of controversial ceremonial, it was clear to others that Goldsmith already held a particular position: 'young as he may be, and decided in his views, there is nothing bumptious in his way of expressing them' was the rather guarded way he was described in 1888 by C. H. Rice, his vicar at Cheam, while another referee felt it necessary to add that Goldsmith could have 'liberal sympathies with those who might not in all respects agree with him'.[84] Whatever liberality of sympathy he may really have possessed, it was for the strength of his views in areas of churchmanship that he was noted in Perth.

G. E. Frewer's journal contains a handbill advertising another mission which was to have taken place in 1888, beginning at the end of January, and obviously designed to lead up to the reopening of the extended church. But that mission did not take place: Goldsmith had already accepted the offer of the deanery of Perth. Although his last Sunday was not until 4 March, the parish register lists G. P. Howes as vicar-designate by 15 January.

What motivated Goldsmith's resignation and moved him to leave for such a distant shore? Despite the apparent increasing dignity of worship and some sense of achievement at the reopening of the extended building, the small number of communicants at St John's shows that the impact of Anglicanism, and particularly Goldsmith's eucharistically centred expression of it, was limited. The *Church Times* referred to the numbers as 'fair' and 'good'; but the building extensions which were designed to allow an increase in seating from 137 to 450, with room for another 150 in a chapel, were for a church whose average number of Sunday communicants, according to its registers, varied from ten to twenty.[85] And despite the large number of confirmees in May 1886, the same low average number of communicants on Sunday prevailed afterwards. Workers living in small terrace houses constituted most of the town's population. The reopening of the church in February 1888 saw a choral eucharist at 4.30 a.m., 'to meet the convenience of the working people in the parish' and the Shrove Tuesday anniversary of the founding of the branch of the Working Men's Association likewise saw a eucharist at 4.30 a.m., presumably for the same reason. Its attendance was praised by the *Church Times* 'notwithstanding the deep snow'.[86] But Frewer's journals also record that the communicants—fewer than thirty—on Ash Wednesday morning the previous year, included most of the members of the newly formed branch, which points to its small number in the total village population. Winnington-Ingram's dictum that the Victorian Church of England had never lost the working classes because she never had them to begin with must have seemed sadly evident. And in contrast to his brother-in-law, whose wife had sufficient private means at her disposal to enable her to assist her husband generously in refurbishing the parish church of Brede along more pronouncedly Catholic lines, Goldsmith had no such support in Halling through any local gentry family.

Furthermore, little could be expected in the way of preferment in the future from Bishop Thorold. True, in common with a number of other bishops whose diocese included large, ugly and overcrowded inner-urban developments, pragmatism allied with a genuine sense of responsibility and a concern for the urban poor brought him to forge alliances with those of a quite different churchmanship, who nevertheless shared a similar concern and appeared to have some success in these areas. He brought an end to his policy of 'isolation', claiming as a justification that the church at large had 'condoned' ritualism. But despite the visits he now made to some of the previously isolated churches, in his appointments Thorold still exercised preferences based on churchmanship as well as on 'good connections', and even his hagiographical biographer was critical of them.[87] In contrast to his current setting and future prospects, the appeal of an executive position, offering scope for initiative and the exercise of influence over a large number and wider range of people, must in itself have seemed highly attractive to Goldsmith.

The task of selecting a new dean for Perth to fill the vacancy created by the resignation of Joseph Gegg fell to the members of the Perth English Committee, an organization that Bishop Parry had founded in 1886 on a visit to England to raise finances for the completion of the new cathedral. Although many of these were clergy, one of its most powerful figures was a layman, Herbert Laurence. Parry's diary refers to a letter from Laurence that named Goldsmith as the successful candidate.[88] Two of Laurence's brothers had worked in Western Australia, Henry as a priest, and Hayes as a magistrate, and a Western Australian colonial secretary, H. P. Barlee, was his cousin.[89] Later, Canon Tucker, the Organizing Secretary of the Society for the Propagation of the Gospel, one of the Anglican church's largest missionary organizations, expressed considerable frustration that Laurence spoke of himself as 'selecting and appointing' clergy for Perth.[90] In 1876 Laurence had sufficient influence to be invited by Archbishop Tait to suggest a suitable candidate for the see of Perth, then vacant after the translation of Mathew Hale to Brisbane. Significantly, he nominated George P. Viner, a curate of Christ Church Lee, who subsequently distinguished himself as a high churchman as the first vicar of Mottingham.

Herbert Laurence clearly favoured high churchmen. And while Tait did not accept Laurence's advice, the man whom he nominated to Perth as Hale's successor, Henry Hutton Parry, was also more receptive to Goldsmith's churchmanship than was Thorold in Rochester. Parry's father, the Bishop of Barbados, had consecrated him as his coadjutor, but failed when he tried to arrange for his son to succeed him.[91] It was in 1871 when he was in England awaiting the result of his father's machinations that he had his first experience of ritualism: he attended St Alban's Holborn, then a centre of legal controversy, and wrote disapprovingly of what he saw. A year later he noted that one of his sisters, Beatrice, known in the family as 'Bee', was 'smitten with modern notions in religion'.[92] One of his sisters soon joined the nursing community of St John the Divine as Sister Aimee, when the community was still operating under the rule established by its original founder, Sister Caroline.[93]

How the various members of the Parry family responded to such an entry into community life can only be conjectured, but by 1886, when H. H. Parry visited England, his attitude towards Anglo-Catholicism was markedly different. On the ship on the way home he engaged in conversation with a Wantage sister, Rose Emily, who had been working at the Cowley Fathers' mission at Poonah.[94] On arrival in London, the first evening was spent at a festival of Gregorian chant at St Paul's cathedral, featuring a massed choir of nearly one thousand. Presumably unused in

Perth to Gregorian chant of any quality, even poor, he concluded that it was 'glorious'. Not satisfied, and like a child sampling a range of sweets, the next morning he attended an early morning service at All Saints Margaret Street. Later in the month he was in correspondence with the mother superior of the convent of St John the Baptist at Clewer, and was prepared to invite this community to work in Perth. And at his own sister's community in Lewisham the chaplain was Rhodes Bristow, whose forthright teaching of confession had drawn a prompt response from Bishop Thorold that has already been noted. Parry found this 'enemy in disguise' as a neighbour at the dinner table and near Christmas he attended solemn evensong at St Stephen's Lewisham, exposing himself to all the dangers of a coped officiant and the use of incense at the *Magnificat*. On this occasion his diary does not record any of the disapproval he voiced of such ceremonial at Holborn a decade and a half previously. He also visited other churches with equally definite profiles.[95]

Unlike Hale, whose advisers showed no signs of being influenced by the Oxford Movement, Parry trusted individuals such as Laurence and gave places to a number of clergy of the same ilk. In 1878 he appointed as his chaplain James Allen, a priest who favoured the use of confession and the restoration of eucharistic vestments.[96] Others included Charles Groser, three of whose sons became Anglo-Catholic priests,[97] R. H. Purnell, who concealed a crucifix in his Prayer Book and equally concealed his churchmanship from the people of Bunbury,[98] Thomas Louch, who later became archdeacon of Bunbury under Goldsmith,[99] and F. C. Gillett, a former member of the Church of England Working Men's Association and a member of the English Church Union.[100] But this did not mean that Parry himself encouraged full-blown ritualism for his own diocese. In his synod addresses he acknowledged that the face of Anglicanism had changed over the previous half-century, but remained guarded and cautious about any ceremonial that might cause controversy in the small and isolated community.[101] He was not party to criticism of the churchmanship that embodied its principles, but would make no dramatic alterations himself. It was Goldsmith who was to take the more pronounced initiatives. As he does so, his figure moves out of the shadows, to be defined sharply in the bright, sometimes harsh, West Australian light.

— TWO —

# Throwing Down the Gauntlet

The Perth in which Goldsmith arrived in 1888 was a very different centre from the city shaped by the gold rushes of the following decade. It was still a market town with no suburbs. Its total adult male population was little more than three thousand, of whom six out of ten were born in the colony, while the rest came chiefly from England and Ireland.[1] Nor was the transition to an independent legislature in 1890, and the departure of the autocratic Governor Broome (whose figure had been burnt in effigy during the 'Onslow affair'), the prelude to the emergence of a less conservative body. Until the departure of Sir John Forrest into federal politics, the Perth political arena would remain small enough for a significant part in his hegemony to be played by his wide circle of family connections and the social circle centred on his wife and home.[2]

Across St George's Terrace, and just west of the imposing Government House that Governor Hampton had built, stood the almost completed new cathedral church of St George, designed in an early English Gothic style by the Sydney architect Edmund Blacket. It was to replace the neo-classical building that had served since 1845. The urge for a new building was spurred by the commencement of a Gothic Roman Catholic cathedral in 1865 and the equally Gothic Wesley church soon after, but it was in the old building that Goldsmith was installed as dean. The progress of the new building had already been fitful, and the combination of a depression in 1888 with a perennial lack of funds (despite Parry's fund-raising trip to England in 1886) meant that even when the old cathedral was used for the last time on 5 August 1888, the interior of the new one was still unfinished.[3]

However, Goldsmith moved into a magnificent shell whose overall design was already sympathetic to his churchmanship in a way the old cathedral could never be. As its dean in the years 1888–1904, he moulded its fittings even more to this end and expressed the emphases of the Oxford Movement in doctrinal statements, liturgy and devotional attitudes.

We have already met him on the dock, being greeted by prominent laity and clergy, and attended the reception following his installation. How might the new dean have appeared to Perth citizens in general, and Perth Anglicans in particular, in the opening years of his appointment? How might his contemporaries have read the signs that delineated the man?

If, as we shall see, he frustrated those who were conservatives as far as their Anglican profile was concerned, he must have appeared as an intriguing, perhaps even enigmatic, mixture; for while the kind of Anglicanism with which he became increasingly identified was seen as radical, even subversive, the view from a different perspective, the perspective that took in his pronouncements on social issues, ranging from sport to gambling and temperance, was of a conservative, a man who believed that if the existing structures were made to function efficiently, much, if not all, would be well.

The photograph that Goldsmith sent back to Halling shortly after his appointment to Perth showed him with an expression of controlled determination. He was also driven by a determination to control.

Within a year of arrival, Goldsmith had already established the cathedral as a centre for a variety of organizations catering for different kinds of needs, at a time when only a handful of Western Australia's Anglican churches offered any activities beyond their Sunday services.[4] In so doing, he established a legacy which was to become permanent. For while these organizations began by catering for the needs of local residents, and in this sense functioned as 'parish' organizations, they included organizations which would have a continuing and diocesan impact, such as the Girls' Friendly Society (GFS), and were the forerunners of many other occasional organizations which successive deans would introduce at the cathedral.

There were the predictable Sunday schools, run by teachers who met weekly. Goldsmith began with a morning Sunday school at the cathedral, and an afternoon children's service, but by 1890, he claimed that six hundred children attended three Sunday schools, two of them in the daughter parishes of St Alban's and St John's.[5]

Polite society might well have noticed that the St Georges Young Men's Society had been re-established, and had rooms at the cathedral; its patrons were an impressive, though predictable, list of VIPS. It offered a pattern of correct social activities for young gentlemen—evenings of music and recitations; a patronal festival picnic expedition by steam launch to Peppermint Grove, followed by sports and prizegiving; classes in painting and drawing by a Mr Gibbs.[6] Its young men were certainly rather idealistic—after a debate on the virtues of moderation as opposed to total abstinence, they voted unanimously in favour of the latter. This is more an indication of the Victorian middle-class conviction of the importance of self-improvement than of any likelihood that the young men concerned were indulging in some kind of double standard. Were reported fluctuations in membership due to too much enthusiasm for total abstinence? Or was it because the dean, like some other clergy, assumed a greater knowledge of historical theology on the part of the laity than was reasonable, when he delivered an address on marriage and divorce to its members? Its many references from classical and early Christian writers would have made it no easy listening for a theology undergraduate, let alone a Perth cathedral gentleman, more interested in impressing suitable young ladies with his skill in painting, or his physical prowess.[7]

Care was also taken to provide suitable activities for the class whose lives would be spent in waiting on such young men, and their distinguished patrons. Girls 'in service' could attend a scripture class or bible study on a weekday afternoon.[8] In order to foster the virtues of 'purity, thrift and faithfulness', a branch of the GFS, then a new organization in the Anglican church, was also opened, which Goldsmith noted was likewise for 'working girls'.[9] Its rooms would be open for two hours every evening for recreation, under the guidance of one of twenty-six associates. Elsewhere, Goldsmith expressed anxiety that the lives of such 'working girls' were not more rigidly supervised through government controls from the moment of their arrival in Perth. Hand in hand with a concern for 'purity' (no doubt heightened by the ratio of males to females in Perth's population in the last years of the century), went the possibility of moulding faithful servants who would accept orders unquestioningly, and whose 'thrift' would make them content with their wages.[10]

When Goldsmith arrived in Perth, it was far from obvious to late Victorians that the state would assume the comprehensive role that it now holds in what are considered to be social service areas, although the role of the government in such areas was gradually being defined, and expectations were increasing, as at least one editorial in the *West Australian* suggests.[11] This period saw the churches involved in a growing questioning of their relationship to the wider society around them. At the same time, governments came to redefine many of their own areas of responsibility. But meanwhile, before the peak of the gold rush, Perth was still small enough for some areas of social work to be dealt with on the scale of a cottage industry: during the 1893 smallpox epidemic the deanery was transformed into a centre for receiving and distributing gifts of linen by Edith Emma, Goldsmith's wife.[12] Goldsmith's concern over the lack of supervision of the living conditions of young female servants on their first arrival in the colony has already been mentioned. He went on to suggest that a need existed for a 'House of Mercy,' a home for prostitutes, which he saw as a part of the 'parochial machinery' of the cathedral.[13] The proposal of such programmes indicates the extent to which Goldsmith, and those who supported him, were still convinced of the ultimate workability of the existing social order, and conceived their answers to problems in terms of moulding individuals to better fit the structure.

A common enough conviction that the working classes needed to be protected from themselves motivated Goldsmith's involvement in temperance movements, and his convictions as to the nature of married life were interwoven with his temperance concerns. During his very first Advent in Perth a series of addresses which he gave to 'men only' were on three subjects which he saw as interrelated—marriage, gambling, and temperance.[14] It might have behoved Winthrop Hackett not to bewail the supposedly reactionary and impractical visionary quality of the

Tractarian movement, but to question the accuracy of the dean's conviction that the purity of family life formed the jewel in the crown of Anglo-Saxon civilization.[15] For while he never publicly acknowledged any awareness of the existence of domestic violence among the middle classes of Perth, the stress placed by alcohol on working-class marriages moved him to be a vigorous supporter of the establishment of a branch of the Church of England Temperance Society in Perth. In this, he received—for a change—Hackett's praise. In 1889, while synod was in session, he called a meeting at the Town Hall, attended by five hundred, at which membership cards for the Temperance Society were handed out by members of the Cathedral Young Men's Society; but a low attendance marked the first meeting in the cathedral school room, which was attributed to the rain, rather than any dying down of enthusiasm by members caught up in a first flush.[16]

The muscles of the temperance movement flexed at the beginning of 1893. When proposals for Sunday trading were made, 'exciting scenes' was the title used to head the description of another meeting at which the dean, among others, addressed the general public urging that public houses remain closed on Sundays. The deanery was made into a centre for a petition. But the press chided Goldsmith for describing those in favour of Sunday trading as the 'local vagabonds' association', just as it had earlier criticized total abstinence as an extreme response to the issue.[17]

Goldsmith's advocacy of temperance was hardly unusual among Anglican clergy at the time; the temperance movement found another strong supporter in Bishop Riley, and total abstinence was becoming a requirement for membership of a number of Anglican associations, including the Church Army. However, sectarian rivalry may also have acted as a goad to action in this area, particularly as Anglicans looked across the denominational fence at their Methodist neighbours. Methodism had generally taken a high profile over the temperance issue in Western Australia, as it had also done in England, and had acquired a middle-class respectability, from which it was beginning to recognize a need to reach out to the working classes who had been noticeable in its earlier membership.[18]

The violent instincts of the working classes also needed curbing. Although a boxing academy had been established in Perth for its middle-class men, boxing received more of its support from the city's workers. Again, the dean became involved in large meetings, and deputations to both the Mayor and the Premier to urge that the sport be declared illegal. In this, he was unsuccessful. And while his involvement with this issue took place early in 1894, just within the perimeters in time to which this chapter is otherwise limited, his attitudes here are consistent with the forays into social issues that have already been recorded. And in this area too, his attitude—that sporting controls should reflect social order and ranking—was one that persisted for some time among members of Perth's middle classes.[19]

By the beginning of the twentieth century it was admitted, with much regret in some quarters, that gambling was almost a national characteristic. Perhaps it was the apparently relaxed attitude to gambling in Perth which also led Goldsmith to attack it on his arrival. Both his attitude, and the views expressed by a number of the clergy in synod at a later date, were criticized in editorials in the press as being unbalanced.[20]

The Deanery, Perth, c. 1863, photograph by Alfred Hawes Stone
The home of the Goldsmiths for sixteen years

In all of these different areas of social outreach, Goldsmith applied models of institutionalization, control and conformity to men and women alike. It was as much a part of his vision for dealing with men, and he could petition politicians equally concerning restricted trading or sport, as over the 'inexcusable laxity under which female immigrants are brought to this colony'.21

Had Goldsmith simply maintained the kind of conservative attitudes in his ecclesiastical activities that he displayed in the range of social involvements that have already been outlined, his profile might have remained an otherwise fairly unremarkable one. In one sense, the position for which he became Perth's leading spokesman was also a conservative one, in that Anglo-Catholicism understood itself to be a return to an earlier and authentic tradition. But in the eyes of critics, this position was neither a maintenance, nor a restoration, of any kind of status quo, but a revolutionary and subversive one. It is necessary to examine his churchmanship, expressed in doctrinal statements and liturgical and devotional life, and placed in the context of the Anglo-Catholic movement among clergy in Australia. Not that this is a matter that is exclusively or narrowly ecclesiastical, for there were distinctive features in the colony's political situation, particularly the maintenance of state aid to religious bodies, that gave a wider focus to the churchmanship issues in Western Australia. And finally, because Goldsmith was the only local candidate—albeit an unsuccessful one—for the vacant see of Perth after the death of Bishop Parry in November 1893, a careful examination of the division over churchmanship in Perth's Anglican community prepares the way for new light to be cast on the election of C. O. L. Riley, Parry's successor.

By 1893, in a correspondence provoked by an editorial over Welsh disestablishment, Winthrop Hackett, the editor of the *West Australian*, referred to Goldsmith's churchmanship as though it were a widely known and verifiable fact.22 As early as 1888 he had made his position clear enough in a sermon to synod. It is enough to say here that his statement that Anglicanism regarded episcopally conferred orders alone as valid and regular, and the emphasis placed on the doctrine of Apostolic Succession, marked his approach to authority unmistakably as that of an advocate of the Oxford Movement.²³ His picture of the faithful 'safe in the unity of the Catholic Church . . . free from every subtle heresy that has arisen to vex Christendom . . .'²⁴ represented an approach as old as Cyprian of Carthage's *De Unitate Ecclesiae,* but which his predecessors and Bishop Parry (let alone the evangelical Bishop Hale) never used: his hearers would have associated it with Roman Catholic homiletics. He put the sacraments higher than the Word. Defining prayer, he asserted that the individual and individual judgement should submit to the worshipping and believing community. He hinted at the unreliability of private judgement when he spoke of 'the selfishness which destroys all true religion'. All this was likely, if not calculated, to enrage evangelical Anglicans. Such sermons give credence to Hackett's claim in 1895 that one party in particular felt that its position was being repudiated angrily from the cathedral pulpit.²⁵

As well as using the pulpit, Goldsmith created additional opportunities for teaching by establishing a guild for communicants very soon after his arrival. He began by enrolling between fifty and sixty members who met for monthly instruction on 'ecclesiastical topics'.²⁶ The subject of its inaugural meeting, 'The Growth and Development of the Early Church and Its Warnings to Ourselves', adopted the Oxford Movement's rejection of the Reformation as the normative period of church history and its replacement by the patristic era. The titles of other addresses equally point to the emphases of the Oxford Movement.²⁷

In addition to the communicants' guild, a guild for the newly confirmed was established in 1889. It grew at the end of 1888 from what Parry claimed was the largest group of candidates he had ever confirmed, and the purpose of the guild, as explained by Goldsmith, was unashamedly devotional and didactic: 'the promotion of regular Communion, and careful preparation'.²⁸

Beginning in 1889, regular entries in the cathedral register on Good Friday, recording services of Preparation for Holy Communion, are consistent with the guild's second aim. The description of the aims of the guild and the register entries are too guarded to form clear proof that Goldsmith was already encouraging the revival of confession, but if this were the case, they would have avoided drawing unwelcome attention to a controversial and misunderstood practice. Even if they simply show that Goldsmith encouraged regular self-examination by communicants, he was already moving steadily in a direction that was to become more pronounced after 1894.[29] The guilds were thus a forum for teaching both doctrine and devotional attitudes.

If the Tractarians had first been concerned with the reassertion of doctrine rather than a liturgical revival, the model of action discernible in Goldsmith's term of office was one of doctrinal teaching accompanied by liturgical usages that were restrained by English standards. But like his doctrinal emphases, these liturgical usages were consistent with a particular churchmanship and were recognized as such.

Matins remained the central Sunday morning service at the cathedral, despite Goldsmith's obvious conviction about the centrality of the eucharist. In 1894, in the interregnum between bishops Parry and Riley, Goldsmith tried to shift the fortnightly sung eucharist into a place of greater prominence by placing it at 9.45 before matins. The attempt was shortlived.[30] Such a pattern was still unusual in England, apart from a few parishes where all of the 'six points' were established. Even a ritualist such as Goldsmith's brother-in-law, G. E. Frewer, faced pressure to maintain the priority of matins, pressure that was too strong to resist, notwithstanding his success in introducing other elements of ritual far in advance of Goldsmith or other clergy in Australia.[31]

To the existing pattern of cathedral services Goldsmith added celebrations of the eucharist wherever possible. One such addition was the offering of an early morning eucharist on saints' days and holy days at 7.30 a.m; an address at evensong on holy days gave the opportunity for further teaching. An additional, weekday, eucharist was also offered in Lent beginning in 1890.[32] On Sundays the eucharist was celebrated weekly at 8.00, and fortnightly, there was a choral celebration after the 11.00 matins. The major festivals were marked by an increase in the number of eucharists offered: by 1890 Goldsmith had established another pattern for Christmas and Easter involving four or five celebrations, a number which was expanded before the end of the century to six; the actual hours of most of these services are still part of the cathedral's regular liturgical programme for these seasons.[33]

But Goldsmith did not feel free to move beyond this increased emphasis on eucharistic offering on the days of the Prayer Book calendar to a celebration of other feasts. In this he differed from his brother-in-law, who revived the feast of Corpus Christi in his parish in 1889, and of many other English ritualists who had already gone much further in supplementing the Prayer Book calendar.³⁴ At St George's, Goldsmith later introduced only one additional observance, that of All Souls' day.

What happened at the eucharist in these first years was understated enough. During Goldsmith's incumbency only the most uncontroversial of the English Church Union's six points were used at the cathedral—the eastward position and the mixed chalice.³⁵ Although the use of altar lights also increased significantly in England,³⁶ the cathedral possessed only a pair of standards at each corner of the altar, each carrying nine lights, which were for purely practical purposes. The Lincoln judgement which ended the trial of Bishop King over ceremonial usages had declared altar lights to be lawful, and it may well have been this decision, and the good relations that he enjoyed with Parry, that encouraged Goldsmith to approach the bishop on Maundy Thursday of 1892 and ask for permission for altar lights for the cathedral. Whether the request was a matter of courtesy or a legal necessity is not clear, since no copy of the original cathedral statute under which Goldsmith worked has survived. It may have been as a result of his poor health that Parry noted the request in a more than usually cramped hand in a diagonal across the corner of a page in his diary.³⁷ He became housebound the following day, and Goldsmith celebrated the eucharist privately with the Parrys on Easter Day. Five days before the request was noted in his diary, the bishop had been reading a learned tome on liturgical history from the Tractarian period, Scudamore's *Notitia Eucharistica*. If, as this suggests, discussion over matters liturgical had been going on for some time between the two men, the reading of Scudamore did not convice the bishop. It seems that concession to local conservatism rather than hesitancy over the status of the Lincoln judgement made the bishop cautious: when the judgement was upheld against appeals in England on 2 August, no lights appeared in the cathedral either then or afterwards.

While symbols were few and even gestures seem to have been kept to a minimum, there were other aspects of the performance of the eucharist that were indicative of Goldsmith's theology. The singing of the celebration that followed the Sunday matins twice every month marked one advance, and sung eucharists also became the norm for major festivals, even those occurring on weekdays, such as the anniversary of the cathedral's opening.[38] It certainly reflected influences beyond the narrower questions of churchmanship: the second half of the nineteenth century saw a general revival of choral music in English churches. However, even in England in the 1880s, the introduction of a sung eucharist, as distinct from the singing of the offices, was still regarded as a sign, not so much of out-and-out Anglo-Catholicism, but at least of a respectably high churchmanship: so, in his journal, George Frewer noted the first *missa cantata* offered in Brede parish church in June 1888 as a special event, as another landmark in establishing standards.[39] At Perth's cathedral the singing did not mean a unison setting in which the congregation joined: instead the choir alone sang the liturgical ordinary, creating a sympathetic atmosphere in which the congregation might be made aware of the transcendant mystery, which Tractarians and their heirs stressed to be at the core of worship. In Australia in 1857 the objection to musical settings by Melbourne's Bishop Perry had some English parallels. But by 1878 the singing of the offices had become sufficiently widespread in city churches for even a Perth Anglican of conservative tastes to regard his own dislike of this practice as old-fashioned.[40]

As well as the Creed, *Sanctus* and *Benedictus* and *Gloria in Excelsis*, the texts of which were part of the 1662 Prayer Book, the Perth cathedral rite included two other standard elements of the Latin rite not appearing in the 1662 Prayer Book. One was the *Kyries*. These were sung at Christmas in Goldsmith's first year as dean to a setting by Mendelssohn.[41] The other was the *Agnus Dei*. It might have been easy to justify the *Kyries* on account of the composer—he was Queen Victoria's favourite. The use of the *Agnus Dei* could not be defended with such expedient arguments. Moreover, it was a clear indication of churchmanship: it was one of the usages against which the plaintiffs protested at Bishop King's trial. Opponents of its restoration claimed that it expressed a doctrine of the real presence that was incompatible with the standards of the Prayer Book or the 39 Articles.[42]

But the most remarkable feature of the sung eucharist was the singing of the Latin hymn of St Thomas Aquinas, *O Salutaris Hostia*, as a treble solo immediately following the consecration prayer.[43] This text, originally the two final verses of a longer hymn, was familiar to Roman Catholics as the opening hymn of the rite of Benediction in which the consecrated Host is exposed for adoration by the faithful. The actual rite itself was then only used in a tiny handful of the most advanced Anglican parishes and religious communities, and provoked irate responses from Anglican bishops in Australia well into the twentieth century.[44] The use of such a text instead of some kind of ceremonial was a less controversial way for Goldsmith to express a very definite theology of the eucharist. While there was no visible adoration of the sacrament following its consecration, the presence of such a text nevertheless would have suggested to a worshipper sufficiently aware of its origin, that the consecration prayer had as its end Christ's presence in the elements, and that, through the adoration of that presence, worship was offered to God the Father.

The style of the new cathedral was certainly conducive to Goldsmith's approach to liturgy and spirituality. And it was not just Goldsmith who viewed the building in this way. A writer who had witnessed Parry's installation in the old cathedral commented that the new building made for the successful performance of solemn and grand ceremonial, something that was impossible in the old.[45] And even when the erection of the new cathedral was only being contemplated, another writer linked the Victorian revival of Gothic architecture with the revival of 'medieval ritual and doctrine'—the Tractarian and Anglo-Catholic movements.[46]

The grand shell into which Goldsmith moved already had basic inner structural features common in English high churches in the second half of the century: its graduated levels between nave and chancel, and between chancel and sanctuary, creating a focus on the sanctuary and high altar.[47]

More characteristic of churches built along the architectural principles of the revival was the chancel, proportionately long in relation to the rest of the building, filled with choir and clergy stalls and separated from the nave by a screen. This effectively divided the clergy and those immediately involved in the rite from the congregation. Though at first particularly characteristic of early Tractarian churches, by the 1870s such an arrangement had ceased to be limited to high churches.[48] A wooden screen of this kind separated the chancel from the nave in Perth cathedral from Goldsmith's early years until it was replaced by a wrought iron screen in 1906. While the screen was not embellished within anything that might offend evangelical sensibilities, this clear architectural demarcation line could only reinforce the well-developed sense of the uniqueness of the priestly role which Goldsmith expressed in sermons in later years, such as one in which he defended the lawfulness of confession.[49]

The cathedral's first high altar was an uncontroversial one of wood; already, elaborate stone altars which would have been unthinkable in the first decade of the Tractarian movement were being installed in some English churches by the 1870s. The use of timber instead of stone is more likely to reflect the limits of local craftsmen and the need for economy, as the cathedral opened with a debt of £5,000.[50]

Goldsmith may have preferred to see himself as representing the van of progress rather than medievalism, but he certainly took advantage of the opportunities to harness the inherent possibilities of the building in order to reinforce his point of view. The altar, already thrown into focus by the three levels of nave, chancel and sanctuary floor, was made even more central by dressing it with seasonal frontals and superfrontals, sometimes highly embellished with embroidery. And this apparently simple visual device did not go unnoticed in the media. In its description of the opening service in the cathedral in August 1888 the press commented generally on the decoration of the altar. The *Western Mail* remarked on the beauty of the white frontal at Christmas in 1892. At the other extreme of the liturgical year, the dossal, curtains and frontal were all of black for Good Friday. In 1892 two unnamed female donors gave the materials for a new frontal, which was 'exquisitely embroidered' in England.[51]

Another of Goldsmith's innovations was one that was still uncommon in England except in a few ritualist churches: the creation of a side chapel. When his brother-in-law's church at Brede was reopened after restoration, the *Church Times* commented that all six points except incense were in use and that it had two altars.[52] As early as 1892 Goldsmith asked the vestry's permission to set up an area in the north transept for the use of small groups that had occasional services.[53] Against the east wall he placed an altar, surrounded by curtains hanging

Gertrude Ford, St George's Cathedral, interior, c. 1904, oils on board
Note the Chapel of the Good Shepherd in the north transept, its altar flanked by riddel posts and curtains

on riddel posts in what was believed to be a pattern characteristic of medieval English churches—actually, it was largely a cleverly marketed creation of Sir Ninian Comper.[54] The chapel eventually became known as the Chapel of the Good Shepherd. Somewhat later, in Melbourne in 1906, opponents of ritualism complained, *à propos* of the Handfield chapel at St Peter's Eastern Hill, that the presence of more than one 'communion table' in a church contravened ecclesiastical law.[55] If the sanctuaries of the early Western Australian settlers had 'exalted' the Word above the Sacraments in Wollaston's eyes, the circle was definitely turning.

Another part of the shell of the new building that could be developed to reinforce a particular emphasis was the window space, which was filled with clear glass to begin with. When the new cathedral was opened, the governor, Frederick Napier Broome, himself the son of an Anglican cleric, offered to provide windows for the east end. The press report refers to the offer being made to the dean, and if the choice of subject was not entirely Goldsmith's, he still played some part.[56] The subject of the windows, the events of Christ's life from Palm Sunday to the Ascension, was consistent with the Tractarian and Anglo-Catholic stress on the observance of the ecclesiastical seasons, and in this case provided a visual commentary on Holy Week and Eastertide. The central crucifixion panel may also have been intended to provide a substitute for an altar crucifix.

That Goldsmith intended the windows of the cathedral to underpin his theology and spirituality is clearer in a series that were originally suspended within the building with the clear glass lancets of the north transept behind them. Their subjects were the four major prophets and the four evangelists. When these first arrived, the press commented that four more windows were to come, and presumed that their subjects were to be the saints after whom Goldsmith and Parry had already named the canons' stalls.[57] Goldsmith was obviously concerned to use various fittings in order to remind worshippers of the communion of saints, another doctrine on which Tractarians and ritualists placed a much more positive stress than evangelicals and low churchmen. Two windows depicting St Michael and St George were referred to in the same article as being already *in situ* 'close to the north transept door'.[58] These windows were eventually removed.

In 1892 the Lefroy family, with whom the Goldsmiths first stayed on arriving in Perth, also gave a window depicting St Michael as a warrior angel.[59] It was placed in the north transept. The warrior figure was a suitable one with which to commemorate Lefroy's father-in-law, a former Indian army officer who also occupied significant military roles in Western Australia. But the Lefroy's early association with the dean, and the installation of the window near the time he established the chapel in the north transept, make it likely that it was another bearer of the dean's message. It might have reminded kneeling worshippers in the chapel as the priest introduced the *Sanctus* ('therefore with angels and archangels . . .') of their union in prayer with the heavenly armines, rather than with the former acting governor, Colonel Bruce.

The cathedral fabric, the building itself, silent, was yet made to speak eloquently—not to an audience of largely illiterate men and women, as had the original Gothic buildings on which it was modelled, but to an audience for whom it was a powerful way of harnessing visual symbolism, and one to which this late nineteenth-century audience responded, with appreciation—or alarm.

And in its worshipping life, a variety of miscellaneous usages, all of which had been current for some time in England, were more in the nature of gentle hints than controversial affirmations. Goldsmith himself maintained that a decade and a half before his arrival, a surpliced choir that had been introduced in 1872.[60] A common badge of Tractarianism in the first two decades of the movement, by the 1880s the surpliced choir was used in over half of London's churches, making it commoner than the eastward position, the most widely used of the six points.[61] But it is certainly indicative of Australian perceptions that when George Parker commented on the 'advanced ritual' of St George's cathedral, he was referring to its surpliced choir.[62] And in 1882, not long before Goldsmith's arrival, the Western Australian diarist Alfred Hillman had referred contemptuously to the cathedral's surplices as 'nightshirts'.[63] What were no longer signs of advanced churchmanship in England still had much more distinct connotations in a colonial setting. Goldsmith also veiled his female confirmation candidates, another practice against which Bishop Perry had earlier protested in Melbourne and which also provoked a comment from Hillman in the west in 1882.[64]

He was beginning to grope his way beyond the minimal provisions of the Prayer Book for Holy Week, but unlike his brother-in-law, who introduced a procession with palms in 1888 only two years after arriving in Brede, no additional ceremonies marked Holy Week at the cathedral. G. E. Frewer's Palm Sunday processions had the added attraction—or justification—that the palms came from Israel.[65] Palm Sunday acts of communion recorded in the cathedral registers after 1883 show no sign that worshippers regarded it as the beginning of a significant week in the ecclesiastical year.[66] The absence of the slightest hint of Anglo-Catholicism in the celebration of Holy Week is also shown by the confirmation of forty candidates on Maundy Thursday in 1895, an occasion that would have been unthinkable in any advanced church in England at the time, such as Christ Church St Leonard's-on-Sea, which Goldsmith visited in 1891. It already had Holy Week ceremonies based on the

Roman rite. Goldsmith did introduce one new service in his first year which henceforth formed a regular part of Holy Week in the cathedral: the Three Hours' Devotion on Good Friday. This series of addresses was delivered at the time assigned by tradition between Christ's crucifixion and death. His brother-in-law likewise introduced it and maintained it in Brede, beginning in 1886, his first year.[67] The devotion began among Anglicans in 1868 under the distinguished Anglo-Catholic and slum mission priest, A. H. Mackonochie, at St Alban's Holborn, the London church whose Anglo-Catholicism had disturbed Parry.[68] It did not involve any controversial symbol or ritual. Any distinct emphasis was communicated through words—in content and technique, it was not substantially different from an evangelical mission.

This cautious approach, combining teaching and some textual additions to the liturgy, such as the *Kyries* and the *Agnus Dei*, which could be justified as scriptural quotations, and using fixtures and furnishings—the altar and its fittings, and windows—over which there could be little or no legal challenge, placed the cathedral abreast of other high church centres in Australia at the time. Only a tiny number were committed to usages that were still controversial in England. St Peter's Eastern Hill, then under the ageing Canon Handfield, had neither eucharistic vestments nor a daily eucharist until 1900. Closer to Perth, St George's Goodwood, which later became a significant point on the Anglo-Catholic map in Australia, had neither a surpliced choir nor a choral eucharist until after 1900. South Australian parishes in which eucharistic vestments and incense were beginning to appear between 1888 and 1893 formed part of the vanguard, and eucharistic vestments were also used at Christ Church Saint Laurence in Sydney in the 1880s.[69]

Later, in 1895, Bishop Riley claimed that Goldsmith sought to control the appointment of clerical staff in Perth by making all new centres in the metropolitan area into outcentres of the cathedral so as to be able to maintain a uniform churchmanship, which he described as 'high'.[70] The unusual situation of control in which Goldsmith found himself on arrival made it at least a possibility. In 1888, except for the cathedral, the area that now comprises Perth's suburbs was devoid of Anglican churches.

Beyond the city there was only St Matthew's at Guildford and St John's at Fremantle. Each was separated from Perth by largely unsettled land. Beyond Guildford lay the two churches of the Swan valley, All Saints and St Mary's, serving what were then isolated rural hamlets. Before Goldsmith's arrival it was expected that the cathedral would minister to Anglicans scattered over the present metropolitan area.[71]

Though Riley's comment undoubtedly reflected his own dissatisfactions, there is some evidence to substantiate it. The strongest comes from St Alban's Highgate, the cathedral's first daughter church, which Goldsmith himself founded. Highgate Hill, an area to the north of the city, housed working class people as well as middle-class families.[72] Goldsmith began holding outdoor services in the area at the end of 1888 and by June the following year he was able to open a brick chapel which was later extended. In addition to Goldsmith, the leading figure in this operation was Annie Hare, wife of Augustus Cockburn Hare, former Albany magistrate, and mother of Louisa Burt, the wife of Septimus Burt, prominent lawyer and conservative politician.[73]

Its altar was highlighted in the same way as the cathedral's. When a parishioner of St Alban's presented the church with a frontal from England which was first used on Christmas Day in 1892, a journalist stumbled over the term used for the narrow vertical panels of material contrasting with the base material of the frontal—orphreys—and his report suggests that the frontal included live birds in its decorations: 'delicate light blue ospreys [sic] are beautifully embroidered with white lilies, and in the centre is a highly raised design of exquisite workmanship'. Further gifts of frontals were made early in 1894.[74] Terminology used to describe the services here occasionally suggested a particular churchmanship, though whether of the journalists, or Goldsmith himself, is not quite clear: the main Christmas Day liturgy in 1893 was described as the 'High Celebration', a term used in contemporary editions of the *Church Times* to describe the main eucharistic celebration in Anglo-Catholic churches.[75]

Perhaps because it was a daughter church, Goldsmith felt less restricted in making any departure from the Prayer Book. On Good Friday 1892, the evening service consisted of a sermon preceded by a 'litany of the Passion', which, like the penitential psalms used at the cathedral that year, was the kind of devotion that was provided in Anglo-Catholic manuals.[76]

For the use of Anglicans in East Perth, predominantly a working-class area,[77] Goldsmith harnessed an existing building, the cemetery chapel. He provided additional furnishings by using some from the old cathedral, and began weekly services in August 1888. The chapel became known as St Bartholomew's. The area was partly worked by Goldsmith and partly by the senior cathedral curate.[78] Although there were fewer references to St Bartholomew's than St Alban's in surviving sources (perhaps because East Perth had a clearer working-class identity than Highgate), one celebration there is significant: the first Christmas midnight mass to be celebrated in the colony by Anglicans, which took place in 1892. Goldsmith claimed the precedent so dear to the Tractarians—antiquity ('according to ancient Church custom, at the hour when old tradition says our Blessed Lord was born').[79] The report of a small number of communicants ('several') was characteristic of communion figures at Christmas at St Bartholomew's for the rest of the century: the sheer novelty of the exercise explains why only a small number attended. But there is no record of any further celebration of midnight mass at Christmas at any of the cathedral's centres. The celebration at St Bartholomew's may have been carefully calculated. East Perth was not a centre in which prominent 'ancient colonists' of the middle class lived, that is, those who showed the greatest resistance to Goldsmith's churchmanship.[80]

St Alban's and St Bartholomew's thus followed in the footsteps of the cathedral. The exception was St John's West Perth. This church developed when a chancel was added to the former West Perth Mission Room. It was consecrated as the mission church of St John the Baptist at the end of June 1888.[81] The area of West Perth that it bordered, south of the railway line, was predominantly a comfortable middle-class area, and its clientele was one that might be predicted to resist Goldsmith's churchmanship to some extent.[82] James Allen, who had already worked in this area, was licensed as curate of the cathedral but conducted most services at St John's as well as continuing to visit Freshwater Bay.

Even here at St John's the dean's conservative innovations were moderately influential. Under his predecessor, it only had an evening service on Sundays, but a weekly morning eucharist was added to this pattern and a sung eucharist marked its patronal festival.[83] But when it was closed in 1927, it was recalled that some worshippers who regarded the singing of the psalms at the cathedral as high church had preferred to worship at St John's, and the issue of the singing of the psalms, for which the dean expressed a predictable preference, was briefly raised at the cathedral's annual general meeting in 1893. Though divergence from the dean's churchmanship is unlikely to have been the sole cause, St John's definitely enjoyed some popularity, as by Easter of 1894 the church was so full on some occasions that intending worshippers had to be turned away.[84] Later, in 1897, a speaker at a parish meeting referred to the desirability of the continuing existence of a 'moderate' church such as St John's for those who might not 'like a cathedral service',[85] which was another way of saying that if St John's were an exception to the dean's churchmanship, it was the exception that proved the rule that a uniform pattern was generally maintained through the cathedral's outcentres.

Another episode is highly suggestive. In 1893 St Bartholomew's unsuccessfully sought independent parish status.[86] Although the issue of churchmanship is not mentioned in the existing records concerning St Bartholomew's, Parry's diary contains an entry that is significant in the light of later disputes: under the heading of correspondence in connection with the division of the cathedral parish two letters are listed: the first to the rector and churchwarden of the cathedral parish, and the second to Messrs Simpson and Rowley.[87] The latter was to be a significant figure in Perth synod in 1899 in attempts to attack Anglo-Catholic practices. Given that the dean had already established a generally uniform pattern of churchmanship in the daughter churches, Rowley's request for some kind of division may well have been based on early misgivings over churchmanship. Sources relating to other centres in which services were conducted regularly or intermittently do not provide further material that illuminates this particular question. If these episodes make it clear that Goldsmith was understood to be throwing down some kind of gauntlet, it remains now to chart a response, which accelerated sharply, to reach a climax following the death of Bishop Parry.

— THREE —

# Reaction and Response

While negative responses to Goldsmith's churchmanship reached a peak following Bishop Parry's death, and expressed themselves most powerfully in the process that led to Riley's election, the build-up to this point was a gradual one, that encompassed a number of interwoven strands. The maintenance of state aid to religious bodies gave a wider focus to the churchmanship issues in Western Australia, and it was in the debate over educational policies that responses to Goldsmith's churchmanship were also strongly articulated. But as well as these more obvious areas, there were others in which the distant mutterings of the rising storm can be detected: mutterings over teaching through sermon as well as symbol. If the position he enunciated was presented by way of symbols and signs that were restrained when compared with the contemporary English scene, the response indicates that for all the apparent restraint, there was still an identifiable profile.

The diary of Alfred Hillman, a public servant who regularly worshipped at Perth's first cathedral, contains many entries in which sermons delivered in the old cathedral are evaluated. The standards used to assess these sermons show that the old cathedral congregation regarded the sermon less as a forum for doctrinal instruction than for a practical (which could mean ethical) discourse, delivered in a style that charmed by its artlessness. In the period of Goldsmith's tenure, when some correspondents complained about cathedral sermons, it was not always the dean to whom they were objecting, but even here, there were still signs. During his absence in England (1891–92) it was the 'portentious [sic] dimensions' of the curate's sermons that caused offence.[1] The situation was repeated in 1893. Following the return to England of E. P. Hood and J. E. Harston that year, Goldsmith appointed F. J. Price as cathedral curate.[2] He had served in three Melbourne parishes where there were clear Oxford Movement influences.[3] His preaching prompted a correspondent to recall Sydney Smith's definition of torture as being preached to death by wild curates, and to complain of 'unpalatable dogmas' delivered 'with all the self-sufficiency of infallibility' on 'an unwilling and disbelieving but helpless congregation'.[4]

But other statements which at first appear unconnected with the dean and his teaching appear on closer examination to be smaller pieces in a more complex pattern. In 1893 'C. T. B.', a correspondent in the *West Australian*, claimed that Anglicans were attending nonconformist churches because they preferred a particular style of sermon delivery—impromptu.[5] In the previous decade the son of an Anglican cleric in Adelaide had commented that Australian churchgoers generally showed a preference for this style of preaching, which he regarded as deplorable, and Alfred Hillman had commented on what he thought of as the poor standard of preaching in the old cathedral, which tempted him to go to a nonconformist church.[6] To that extent, 'C. T. B.'s' comment reads as part of a general attitude. Another correspondent in the Perth press had made general criticism of the style and delivery of the Anglican clergy in 1889, the year after Goldsmith's arrival.[7] However, it was also a response to the dean, whose tendency to read from notes was commented on at his reception in the Perth Town Hall in 1888.[8]

That same year Alexander Forrest complained in a similar vein to 'C. T. B.' in state parliament during the annual debate on the Ecclesiastical Grant. In a speech in which he argued that the continuation of the grant was weakening the 'vitality' of the churches that received it—among which the Church of England was the greatest benefactor—he alleged that 'the one great reason why people did not attend and support the Churches' in Western Australia was that 'the clergymen sent out here' were not 'first-class preachers'. By contrast, in the other colonies, where state aid had long been abolished, 'great and eloquent preachers' to whom one could listen with pleasure 'for an hour or two'(!), attracted capacity congregations.⁹ Given that the Forrests were city-dwelling Anglicans, it is difficult to avoid concluding that these comments formed an attack on the dean.

It was in October 1894 that an editorial in the *West Australian* linked growing hostility to the Ecclesiastical Grant with Anglican churchmanship and the content of sermons:

> It is greatly to be feared that in the Church which has enjoyed the largest share of the subsidy that feeling has been awakened by the unwise teaching and proceedings on the part of some of its clergy. To the needless controversial vigour with which doctrines of an exceedingly unpalatable character to so many have been urged in season and out of season, especially the latter, by some men who were young and some who were not so young, and the strangely unintelligent discourses too often heard must be attributed a good part of the indifference which has brought about what in the present state of the colony is little short of a calamity.¹⁰

Alexander Forrest as Mayor of Perth 1892–1894
The chairman of the directors of the *Morning Herald* in his mayoral robes: Forrest was critical of the cathedral's preaching tradition under Goldsmith.

Read in the light of an editorial of 1895 that identified the cathedral as a centre of 'extreme' churchmanship, at which the position of other Anglicans was being 'repudiated' from the pulpit,¹¹ these strictures are obviously directed against what were seen to have been the unpalatable and offensive doctrines of the Oxford Movement. The most articulate and consistent criticism of Goldsmith's churchmanship had a political edge. It occurred in the debate over state aid for religious bodies. Given that Western Australia was the only Australian colony that still had state aid, largely because it was the last colony to achieve responsible government (1890), Western Australia's particular social and political structures thus gave Goldsmith's churchmanship a focus that it would have lacked elsewhere in the country. At the same time, the issue of Anglican churchmanship added an extra dimension of unpleasantness to an already tense debate, and some of the bitterness with which that issue was discussed also spilled over on to what, for Anglicans, might otherwise have been more of an internal matter.

State aid took two forms. The Imperial Grant provided by the British Colonial Office was already being withdrawn. The bones of contention were the Ecclesiastical Grant and the Assisted Schools Grant provided by the Western Australian government. The Ecclesiastical Grant was apportioned on the basis of the number of adherents of the major denominations in the colony: Roman Catholic, Anglican, Wesleyan and Presbyterian—on principle, the Congregationalists refused to accept it.[12] Although the grant was unconditional, most churches appear to have used it as a means of supplementing stipends, particularly in country areas.[13] Under the provisions of the Elementary Education Act of 1871, the Assisted Schools Grant was intended to assist in the funding of general staff and facilities, not the teaching of any doctrine: catechetics were to be taught outside school hours.[14]

Goldsmith wittingly or unwittingly made his own entry into this contentious area in his first year in Perth. On his arrival, he found that there were no Anglican assisted schools in the colony and thus no system of Anglican parish schools like those in England. Given the educational interests of his father and his father-in-law, his subsequent action was hardly surprising. Along with at least one layman, he helped to fund an Anglican school in the cathedral parish,[15] and by Easter of 1890 he reported that there were two day schools belonging to the church, one of which, St John's, in Duke Street (the one he helped to fund), had 'about 60 pupils' and was receiving assistance from the Education Department.[16] By 1892 the school had been shifted to Newcastle Street, and had over 100 pupils, a day school attached to St Alban's had been opened at Highgate and another school was projected for South Perth.[17] The latter did not materialize and, by 1894, St John's remained the only Anglican assisted school in operation.[18]

Goldsmith described the recognition of St John's school by the Central Board of Education as 'tardy'; a year earlier he complained that the Board had refused an application for a grant 'similar to that which assisted schools have obtained in all parts of the colony'.[19] His action was similar to that of Anglican clergy in England almost half a century earlier, but the passive resistance that he encountered suggests that there was political opposition to any desire to expand activities in an area over which there was an increasingly heated debate. The assisted schools system was seen as a concession to the Roman Catholic community, not the embodiment of a principle on which Anglicans also should work.

Winthrop Hackett, a complex mixture of cultural, political and religious motives, was diametrically opposed to Goldsmith. While Goldsmith obviously had an interest in the Assisted Schools Act, Hackett's opposition was so determined that, in 1893, he proposed inserting a clause into the Amended Education Act forbidding the building of any additional assisted schools.[20] He was prepared to attack Goldsmith, and the churchmanship he represented, from every possible angle, even if the consistency with which he used it as a whipping-post brought him close to contradiction from another point of view. Thus in his campaign against the divisive dogmatism that he claimed was the poisoned fruit of the Assisted Schools Grant and the dual system, Hackett attacked the dean, stating that his motive in supporting the dual system was his desire to preserve the right to teach his own particular dogmas.[21] But Hackett had also claimed that if it were not for unease over a particular brand of Anglican churchmanship (which he just stopped short of identifying), what he described as 'sudden' hostility to the grant would not have developed[22]—'extreme' churchmanship could thus be attacked even when it was supposedly hastening the end of the system of state aid and bringing about a result that Hackett himself wanted.

His Church of Ireland background explains only a part of his attitude. He was certainly a child of the Protestant ascendancy in Ireland. His generally controlled prose could not quite cover a vein of Irish sectarian bitterness that occasionally came to the surface, especially when he contemplated the disestablishment of the Church of Ireland.[23] The Catholic community was at the heart of his objection to the dual system. Their 'consciences, liberties and pockets' alone would benefit by the maintenance of 'this most mischievous system'.[24] Anglican support for its continuance might frustrate his aim and thus had to be defeated. To that extent the education debate triggered Hackett's most consistent attacks on Goldsmith and his churchmanship. Significantly, he made no editorial comment on the 1888 synod sermon by Goldsmith, even though it was an obvious Oxford Movement manifesto; but when fellow Anglo-Catholic Charles Groser preached a synod sermon on education in 1890, Hackett was quick to attack.[25]

But it was as much on liberal intellectual grounds as on sectarian and conservative ecclesiastical ones that he criticized the Oxford Movement and its advocates. In 1890, on Newman's death, he had identified Tractarianism as an idealistic and romantic but reactionary system that had based its blueprint for a renovated society on a return to a past that had never existed outside its own reconstructive mind. He regarded it as being at odds with the practicality of the 'coldly critical world of today'. His analysis was, in its own way, quite perceptive—as far as it went.[26]

He was not beyond distorting to some extent the support that existed for the maintenance of assisted schools. In 1894 he described the dean as the leader of a 'misguided but happily scant band of Anglicans' who supported the dual system. This may have been a reasonably accurate description of lay support both in and outside parliament; the laity neither struggled to resist the abolition of the act nor sought to actively support the creation of any Anglican school system of their own. But as a synod member, he must have been aware of the widespread support that the clergy were prepared to offer to schemes of education to which laymen might often be apathetic. In 1892 Hackett himself played a leading part in introducing a motion that sought the synod's support for amendments to the Education Act to allow for separate denominational religious instruction in state schools. Significantly, some clerical speakers, such as Canons Groser and Louch, used the occasion to express their own approval of the concept of Anglican parish schools and thus (at least by implication) of the dual system. Their statements in this area went unchallenged by other clergy. Not everyone saw an amended Education Act and the dual system as mutually exclusive. Hackett, who supported an amended Act as an alternative to the dual system, later took the dean to task for wanting to have his cake and eat it by supporting an amended Act *and* the dual system. The Amended Education Act was passed in 1893, allowing the clergy or accredited lay teachers to give religious instruction in the government schools to children of their own persuasion. This replaced what were regarded as undenominational lessons that were based on Bible readings and given by school staff. The amendment was modelled on clause 17 of the New South Wales Public Instruction Act.[27]

In attacking Goldsmith, Hackett was joined by nonconformists. They had their own particular concerns. Though, like other Australian colonies, Western Australia had never given Anglicanism fully established status, dissenters retained a residual fear lest Anglicans should act as a quasi-establishment, and complained against anything they regarded as evidence of such an attitude.[28] Nonconformists later identified pressure, exerted on the government following the synod of 1892, as one of the forces that brought about the passing of the Amended Act of 1893, and voiced their fears of a virtual Anglican monopolization of government schools, especially in the country.[29]

But in 1892 and 1893, even before the amendment, two Congregationalist clergy in the colony had already written to the press, voicing their fears over the proposed amendment to the Education Act. B. C. Matthews wished to rid 'our State schools . . . from the domination of parson and priest of any sect whatever', but specifically attacked what he called 'the proud assumption of the Anglican church'. E. T. Dunstan, Perth's leading Congregationalist and minister of the Trinity Church, just a short distance along St George's Terrace from Goldsmith's cathedral, objected that because the Church of England was the only religious body with clergy in many country areas, the only instruction available would be from Anglicans, who in practice would be the only teachers of religious instruction in half of the colony's schools. Further, nonconformist parents might be unwilling to remove their children from classes lest they be stigmatized.[30]

Matthews also asked why Congregationalists should not accept any funding themselves when, through state aid, they and others helped to support the teaching of doctrines with which they did not agree; he continued by claiming that the Assisted Schools were economically unjustifiable, but reached his climax with a denunciation of high churchmen: 'We should like to ask the Dean, who, among the multitude of teachers, all of whom claim the right to interpret the Bible, the Government are to

Sir Winthrop Hackett in Windsor Court dress
Goldsmith's most powerful public critic, the Vicar of Bray's brother, decked with the trappings of imperial loyalty

authorize? Are they to be adherents of the high, low, broad or Evangelical school . . .' He concluded in a vitriolic and anti-clerical outburst that behind the proposed amendment to the Education Act lay 'the specious sophism of crafty ecclesiastics whose zeal is to make converts more to their own peculiar and narrow views than to truth and principle . . .'[31] That ritualist error would no longer be funded was thus another reason to abolish state aid. Dunstan likewise rejected Goldsmith and his churchmanship. He drew his readers' attention to a quotation from a sermon by Goldsmith in the same issue of the paper, a passage in which Goldsmith advocated daily communion. Dunstan urged them to be vigilant: 'let every Protestant read this sample of the "definite religious instruction" which the State is to provide a means for inculcating'.[32]

Nonconformists in England had also attacked Anglo-Catholicism in connection with education. As early as 1876 it was feared that proposed educational legislation would oblige children to attend Anglican church schools in areas where there was no available alternative, particularly in country areas.[33] Nonconformists also feared that Anglo-Catholic clergy would use their position as teachers to disseminate their own doctrines: this fear persisted to the end of the century.[34] The growth of Anglo-Catholicism fuelled their support for disestablishment as well as their criticism of the government funding of denominational schools, lest the state encourage 'the enemy in disguise'.[35] Though there were elements in the English educational situation that were different from the Western Australian one, nonconformist ciricism of ritualism, real or perceived, was bound to be similar as long as some form of state aid was involved.

Both Hackett and the Congregationalist clergy already quoted provided oversimplified analyses of Anglican support for the Amended Education Act or the Assisted Schools Act, treating it as a creature of a group of extreme churchmen. The strong support in the 1892 synod for the Amended Act by a cleric such as Archdeacon Brown, a staunch evangelical, qualifies any such conclusions. But as long as these issues were supported by men such as Canons Groser and Louch and D. J. Garland, all of whom spoke strongly in favour of the Amended Education Act in the 1892 synod, such a conclusion could sound convincing enough. Goldsmith, who proposed the motion, had been aided by D. J. Garland in researching the New South Wales Act on which the amendments were based. He had come to Western Australia from New South Wales earlier in the year.[36]

Goldsmith's nonconformist critics generally differed from Hackett in the way they viewed the proposal for religious instruction in state schools. Hackett supported it as an alternative to the dual system, viewing the one as rendering the other unnecessary, but Goldsmith and his Congregationalist critics were agreed, even if they stood in opposite corners of the ring, that support for one could mean the survival of the other and that the teaching of doctrine through one system was linked to the possibility of teaching doctrine through the other. In expressing his fear lest the Amended Act allow the teaching of Anglo-Catholic doctrine in state schools, B. C. Matthews also attacked the dean for proposing the establishment of Anglican assisted schools.[37] In the continuing public debate leading up to the amendment, a meeting representing the Wesleyan, Congregationalist and Presbyterian churches in Perth protested to the Premier that the proposed amendment would 'indefinitely prolong the present dual system'.[38] After the amendment had been passed, nonconformists continued to identify it as a reinforcement to the dual system.[39]

The passing of the Amended Act in 1893 was in one sense a victory for Goldsmith: the right for all mainstream churches to teach their particular doctrines had been ensured. This included the right of clergy influenced by the Oxford Movement to propagate their particular doctrinal emphases. But it was a victory fraught with danger. The Act's very provision of denominational instruction which protected Goldsmith's right to teach Anglican dogma represented the most satisfactory answer to the question of religious instruction as far as most Anglicans were concerned. At a time when no Anglicans who desired the abolition of state aid actually favoured an exclusively secular and 'godless' education—Hackett's position in supporting the amendment in the press and as a member of synod was in this way highly representative—it ensured the teaching of doctrine without necessitating the building and maintenance of a denominational school system. To Anglicans who claimed to have lacked the means but in reality were more lacking in inclination to do this, all they could want had now been provided—by the dean's pressure group.

Churchmanship was also a weapon, if a less obvious one, in the debate over the other form of state aid, the Ecclesiastical Grant. For Alexander Forrest, whose opposition to the Ecclesiastical Grant remained consistent until its abolition, it was precisely that—a weapon—and nothing more. Churchmanship issues did not colour any of his other political pronouncements, but his seemingly general comment concerning the attendances in Perth churches and the quality of the preachers is difficult to dissociate from Goldsmith, given other comments in the press that linked low attendances with a particular preacher or topics of preaching.[40] His continuing burden of complaint was that no account of expenditure of the grant was available—although on this he was contradicted by his brother.[41] Elsewhere, he stated that if Fremantle and Perth were excluded from receiving the grant and its application were limited to country districts, he 'would not object very strongly'.[42]

Had Alexander Forrest's suggestions been carried out, the area from which aid would have been withdrawn was the city, all of whose churches were identified by Riley on his arrival as 'high'. The weapon being used by Alexander Forrest was also picked up by Hackett: an editorial in the *West Australian* in 1891 contrasted the need of country parishes for the grant in order to maintain a basic ministry, with the city parishes, whose 'services . . . are more elaborate and the buildings more costly'. The grant was more likely to continue if it were seen to be meeting essential needs, rather than 'what might be termed purposes of spectacular display'.[43] Readers could easily have linked the tone of this editorial with other criticisms of ritualism such as Bishop Hale's, deploring its misplaced emphasis on material things and cultivation of the grand and theatrical.

The suggestions of an attack on high churchmanship latent in these comments were made explicit in the *West Australian*'s identification of the preaching of 'unpalatable' doctrines as a factor in continuing support for the withdrawal of the grant. That the earlier suggestions of an unbalanced expenditure on 'extravagant display' to the detriment of the genuine needs of the country were all part of a well-directed polemic is also indicated by the persistence of counterbalancing statements: W. T. Loton's statement that Perth and Fremantle were not provided for at the expense of the country; Sir John Forrest's correction of his brother's claim that no account of expenditure was provided; Septimus Burt's insistence that the Anglican portion of the grant was spent on country rather than city needs.[44] Most of all, there was a belated statement in 1894 in the *West Australian*'s editorial to the same effect[45]—belated and carefully calculated in its delayed presentation because, as a member of synod and of the cathedral vestry, Winthrop Hackett had access to the relevant financial figures in annual diocesan reports that would have shown the inaccuracy of the earlier assertions made about the distribution of the grant—had he been interested in correcting the misinformation in the first place. By 1894 the misinformation concerning the balance between city and country in the Anglican application of the grant had created sufficient impact to need addressing in synod, where a detailed statement was presented, in which it was pointed out that the cathedral gave over half of its portion of the grant to country parishes.[46]

For Goldsmith the Amended Education Act of 1893 meant winning the battle but losing the war; his apparent success in this area singled him out as a threat to the opponents of state aid if he were to become an even more prominent figure. In 1892 George Randell, a Congregationalist politician and firm supporter of the abolition of state aid, stated that any attempt to change the existing system of education would create 'a severe struggle'.[47] The end of the dual system was not then taken for granted. The rallying point outside the Catholic community formed by the dean made his churchmanship a political as well as a religious threat.

The debate over education had shown that it was in the interest of particular political positions as well as religious ones that Goldsmith should be isolated. The opportunity arose at the end of 1893. He had enjoyed a degree of personal friendship with Bishop Parry as well as receiving professional support. Parry, whose cast of mind was academic—he read in Greek every day—enjoyed Goldsmith's company in an otherwise theologically arid environment and frequently attended meetings of the Communicants' Guild at the cathedral. Unlike Hackett, he had come to look favourably on the Oxford Movement.[48]

In Bunbury on 15 November 1893, the anniversary of his own consecration as a bishop as well as that of the new cathedral, Parry died after a short illness. In St Paul's Bunbury, the rector celebrated a choral requiem (described as such in the Bunbury and Perth press) before the bishop's body was taken by train to Perth. There, after it had lain in state in the cathedral, Goldsmith celebrated three eucharists in the morning prior to the funeral—the beginning of his attempt to create a revival of prayer for the departed among Perth Anglicans. On the following Sunday special services commemorating Parry were held, not only at the cathedral, but also in nonconformist churches. Eulogizing Parry's somewhat retiring and seemingly uncomplicated personality, Goldsmith found the most appropriate estimate in lines written of Nathaniel, 'the Israelite in which there is no guile', by the Tractarian priest-poet, John Keble, already regarded as a saint-cum-hero of the Oxford Movement.[49]

The election of a successor was the responsibility of the diocesan synod, which could itself elect a candidate whose name would then be submitted to the Anglican Primate of Australia for confirmation. Alternately, it could delegate its electoral role to others. The synod was summoned to meet on the evening of Wednesday 13 December; but before it met, opposite forces were at work in an attempt to influence the election. From one direction Winthrop Hackett produced an editorial that summed up the qualifications of a modern bishop. He extolled the episcopal role in the Anglican church. It had been shorn of its political connections and had reverted to its original spiritual and pastoral function—a description that accorded more with Victorian piety than with reality. But he went on to warn synodsmen that they would be discharging their duty responsibly only if they chose a man who was 'in touch with the spirit of the times' and did not represent any 'party spirit'. In elaborating on what this meant, he ruled out men given to 'shrinking back into the mists and cloudy symbols of medievalism', who substituted 'ineffective for effective modes of calling the attention of the people to their own shortcomings, and the need for improvement'. To this thinly veiled attack on the dean's churchmanship he added a further claim he was to repeat on Riley's arrival—the claim that Anglicanism was 'comparatively losing ground among us, and has been doing so for some time past'. He made it clear that Anglican losses were in response to churchmanship as he concluded that this trend would only continue 'if the choice now to be made prove an unfortunate one'.[50] That Hackett should have intervened in this way provides more evidence of something that has already been clear in the debate over state aid—the extent to which the press had become an influential agent in forming the public's perceptions of religious issues.

While Hackett lobbied from his powerful editorial seat, others did so on Goldsmith's behalf. K. E. Courthope, a lay member of synod, referred to pressure on behalf of a particular candidate having been exerted among clergy from the country who had gathered in Perth before synod began, and Edward Stone referred to preliminary lobbying having been carried out, both for and against the dean. Their own distaste for Goldsmith showed in the caucus terminology they used to describe this. Courthope viewed caucuses as an American institution that undermined 'independence, honesty and conviction' (thus being thoroughly un-British) and the conservative Stone cast a slur on the wisdom of caucuses and elections because they were the machinery of democracy, 'the form of Government now in existence in this country, and which they hesitated a long time before adopting'.[51]

The opposition to proceeding by means of a local election was commenced by the archdeacon of Fremantle, D. G. Watkins, who argued that no one local candidate would be acceptable to the majority. Canon Sweeting supported him: it was unlikely that a man of 'broad sympathies, no partisan', was locally available.[52] Goldsmith's own position was invidious. As diocesan administrator he had to chair the election, but was himself nervous of any open discussion of churchmanship. When D. J. Garland began to relate the question of churchmanship to the recent election of the Bishop of Grafton and Armidale, Arthur Vincent Green, Goldsmith directed him to desist. Despite his attempts to steer the ecclesiastical ship from the reefs of contentiousness, the opposition scored a *coup de grâce* in a singularly tactless speech by the dean's own curate, F. J. Price. Price stated that opposition to a local election was grounded on the identification of the dean as a 'party man', and accused the dean's opponents of being the real party men. Price was denounced somewhat inconsistently by a lay representative, H. G. Anstey. He complained that Price had erred by bringing a clearly identifiable personality into the discussion—and at the same time attacked him on the grounds of obscurity, claiming that he did not know to whom Price was referring![53]

Opposition to the dean proceeded from a variety of motives but when the vote was finally taken, the nature of support for him was clear enough: the press not only reported the names of voters but indicated the direction in which they cast their votes.[54] Even if they varied in their degree of altitude, the clergy who voted in favour of a local election were all high churchmen, such as W. F. Marshall, Price, James Allen, Charles Groser and F. C. Gillett. The laity were principally cathedral stalwarts, such as Octavius Burt, J. T. Hobbs, J. F. Law, J. J. Harwood, T. Sherwood, E. W. Haynes, A. Burt, and W. C. Bowra, whose family was strongly associated with St Alban's Highgate; there is evidence that another lay supporter, A. E. Woodruffe, sympathized with the dean's churchmanship.[55]

The 'no' voters were more diverse. They included members of the cathedral congregation such as J. B. Roe, W. T. Loton, and, most notably, Septimus Burt. His family's gifts to the cathedral in the coming years were hardly characteristic of an evangelical cast of mind. Canon Louch and D. J. Garland, the latter to be identified with Goldsmith before the century ended as a leading Perth Anglo-Catholic, also cast 'no' votes; jealousy of the dean that was later more directly expressed may already have influenced Garland's vote. Hackett (presumably sufficiently confident of the effect of his editorial to refrain from making any speech at synod) voted in the negative along with Charles Harper, joint owner of the *West Australian*, conservative politician and pastoralist. Other 'no' voters were involved in the debate over ritualism later in the decade—the Stone brothers and W. D. Moore.[56] Lastly, there were clergy such as Archdeacon James Brown and C. J. Nicolay who came to the diocese under Hale. The overall vote—38 noes against 18 ayes—also demonstrated other trends. It showed the conservatism of the laity: twice as many laity voted against as voted for (27/13), compared with the clergy (11/7). That a higher proportion of clergy than laity was prepared to vote for a man who embodied Oxford Movement influences was not a sign of deep commitment to Anglo-Catholicism as such. The way it articulated the professional status of the clergy was attractive in the brave new world of colonial society, as Tractarianism had been to an earlier generation of colonial bishops.

While Goldsmith was effectively prevented from being raised to the episcopate—at least for the time being—the election of C. O. L. Riley by the synod's nominees did not end the dispute over Anglo-Catholicism. Instead, it introduced a new figure who would play a significant role in determining the way in which differences in churchmanship were accommodated in Western Australia.

— FOUR —

# A Slowly Expanding Front

Instead of being deterred by the Perth electoral synod of 1893, Goldsmith continued to promote Catholic teaching and liturgical practices even more openly in the period between December 1893 and February 1895 when he was administrator of the diocese before Riley's arrival. Although the abolition of state aid to religious bodies meant the end to high churchmanship as a political issue, a new and stormier controversy erupted, reaching a peak between 1898 and 1901, as sympathetic clergy became more self-confident and gave visible expression to their convictions.

## The Interregnum: Goldsmith Undeterred 1894–1895

The Wesleyan preacher in Perth who greeted Newman's death with a series of reflections, culminating in the assertion that Tractarianism and ritualism were eventually bound to founder in the wake of the growing swell of an ascendant Protestantism, presented one version of a triumphalist conviction that varied according to the position of the preacher.[1] We do not know whether Goldsmith himself used such language from the cathedral pulpit to describe the future of the Oxford Movement in the colony, though his brother-in-law was certainly using it over a decade later.[2] However, something of the same sense of possession of the future characterized Goldsmith's activities in 1894.

He seems to have introduced eucharistic vestments to the colony at this time, carefully using an isolated country centre. The duties of administration may have functioned as an excuse for a change in the time of the cathedral's sung eucharist that year which gave it priority over the Sunday morning matins. The titles of his addresses in this period reflect Anglo-Catholic emphases—a series on the Blessed Virgin at St Alban's during Lent, and an address at evensong on Good Friday on 'The Condition of the Departed in Paradise'. That same Good Friday, at the Mechanics' Institute Hall, his curate F. J. Price (whose high church sermons had led to complaints in the press in the previous year), was showing a series of lantern slides of pictures in Antwerp Cathedral under the title of the Way of the Cross—a thinly disguised version of Stations of the Cross.[3] The dean celebrated the anniversary of Bishop Parry's death with a requiem.

Bishop Riley marked his arrival with expressions of gratitude for the dean's helpful advice, and there was nothing in the events of his opening weeks to suggest the rift that would eventually become apparent. Goldsmith might have been excused for thinking that, from his point of view, it would be 'business as usual'. Well before Riley's arrival, the Western Australian press reported that his parish, St Paul's Preston, had an active communicant life.[4] At his enthronement his vesture was an odd combination—episcopal choir habit (rochet and chimere) over which he wore a stole. Choir habit on its own would have been more usual, but at least the peculiar addition hardly indicated a strict evangelical, instead suggesting a tolerance or acceptance of the Oxford Movement. At Riley's public welcome, Goldsmith made a veiled reference in passing to the earlier tensions in the diocese, without identifying churchmanship as their source. Given the subsequent heated clashes between Goldsmith and Riley, it was ironic that it was Goldsmith who should regard churchmanship debates to be at an end, because the presence of a bishop provided a centre of unity more effective than any other. He confidently claimed that the bishop's authority would be acknowledged by all.[5]

## The End of State Aid

If synod had not been prepared to endorse Goldsmith as an episcopal candidate, neither was the wider electorate prepared to support the kind of educational structures for which he was Anglicanism's strongest spokesman. The dual system and the Ecclesiastical Grant were abolished at the end of 1895, after the 1894 election, the first under responsible government in the colony's history. The education system and state aid had been its most important single issue. In some country seats, electors returned representatives who were still pledged to the maintenance of the dual system, but in urban seats, candidates were returned on the basis of their opposition to the system.[6] Although the dual system, and not the Ecclesiastical Grant, had been the election's key religious issue, the pressure for the end of the one sounded the death knell for the other. A significant factor (though not necessarily the determining one) in this election was the vote of 't'othersiders' who were arriving in the colony in increasing numbers because of the gold rush.[7]

The campaign opened in February 1894, and a pressure group, the Education Defence League, was founded to counter the claims of another body, the National Defence League, which opposed state aid. Goldsmith explained to a meeting of the Education Defence League in the Town Hall that he continued to support the dual system, despite the provisions of the Amended Education Act. He preferred to see the teaching of a doctrine with which he did not agree, rather than the 'wishy-washy stuff known as non-sectarianism'. This statement showed that he still sought the maintenance of a dual system which would eventually include Anglican schools, in which Anglican doctrine and his own churchmanship could be taught. Hackett's editorial statement, that the dean's position was due to 'his fervid attachment to dogma' was thus not unfounded.[8] And another incident suggests that he still hoped to establish a number of Anglican schools under the dual system. He was openly attacked in 1894 by nonconformists, who claimed that he had persuaded a number of them to support the Amended Education Act in the previous year, on the understanding that Anglicans would withdraw their support for the dual system—an alleged promise which his subsequent support for the Education Defence League negated.[9]

Hackett's attacks on the dual system, and on the dean as its leading Anglican supporter, continued.[10] Hackett still named only the Roman Catholic portion of the population as its beneficiaries, as did many parliamentary discussions.[11] But anxieties about Anglicanism continued: in his editorials Hackett remained concerned as an Anglican lest extreme churchmanship prejudice the already narrow social and financial base on which the church in Western Australia stood; and the nonconformists were also determined that (whatever its churchmanship might be) Anglicanism should be prevented from being anything more than one among equals. In speaking on the Ecclesiastical Grant, Randell even raised the old spectre of arrogant privilege by claiming that Anglicanism had originally enjoyed the same established status in Western Australia that it possessed in England.[12]

Hackett stirred nonconformist sensitivities by claiming that Roman Catholic and Anglican clergy viewed with 'perfect complacency' the disregard of the 'rights of this minority'.[13] Thus he tacitly acknowledged the support for the dual system offered by Anglican clergy, a support that could only confirm the nonconformist fear that, in country areas, state aid of any kind would reinforce Anglicanism as much as Roman Catholicism.[14] Two statements illustrate this ongoing fear. E. T. Dunstan said that the dual system could work, as far as nonconformists were concerned, only in built up areas, and that in the country, 'it must be a Government system or no system at all'.[15] And the Congregationalist leader of the opposition, George Randell, reminded parliament that the Anglican denominational school system that operated in England created difficulty for the parents of nonconformist children who lived in rural areas—precisely the areas over which concern had already been expressed about the churchmanship of the Anglican clergy.[16] In parliament in September, just before synod met, two members suggested that the Ecclesiastical Grant should be retained as long as it was exclusively used for churches in country areas. This conformed with Hackett's suggestions three years earlier, but was hardly likely to calm previous dissenting fears of an Anglican dominance in the country and the possibility that Anglo-Catholic doctrine might be taught in schools.[17] The small but influential cross-section of Anglicans who publicly supported the Education Defence League may well have fuelled nonconformist fears of an Anglican attempt to retain social dominance through educational means. They were more than a high church clique, and included Mr Justice Stone and the principal of Perth High School, two future critics of Goldsmith's churchmanship.[18]

Presiding at the Perth synod in 1894 as diocesan administrator, Goldsmith acknowledged both the nonconformist unease and Hackett's editorial criticism. At the beginning of the month in which synod met, Hackett referred to 'dissatisfaction at the preaching of certain doctrines' as the cause of increased opposition to the Ecclesiastical Grant—a claim he did not substantiate with any hard evidence.[19] Goldsmith emphatically denied that the promotion of any particular churchmanship had any such effect.[20] He also criticized the Congregationalists, without naming them, stating that those who had churches only in the built up areas because they either did not recognize or respond to the needs of country areas 'can well afford to maintain themselves'.[21] However, he must have sensed that the diocesan synod would not unanimously support the dual system as it had supported the Amended Education Act, because he focused on the Eccesiastical Grant and urged synodsmen to bring pressure to bear on country members to support the grant's continuation.[22]

Those who led the attack on the dual system in the new parliament were George Randell, F. T. Illingworth (a Church of Christ lay-preacher), W. H. James (an Anglican, later a member of the cathedral chapter) and the member for Geraldton, G. T. Simpson. The part played by the last two confirms the impression that, as far as the Anglican laity was concerned, Hackett's analysis of the situation was substantially correct. In introducing the bill which finally abolished the Ecclesiastical Grant in 1895, Sir John Forrest explained that this would bring Western Australian practice into line with that of the other colonies (an argument that had been advanced by other speakers against the grant in earlier parliaments), and that this was a natural result of self-government. In addition, as though to confirm that their opposition had been a significant factor, he also reminded the house that each year, a member had spoken against the grant on behalf of the Congregationalists.[23] As if to reinforce the message that it was not the Roman Catholic community alone to which the nonconformists objected, Simpson reiterated assertions that he had made in speeches in previous years. Those churches 'whose vitality is promoted without any assistance from the state' performed the most active and useful work. Here his prime object of attack was Anglicanism, and his statement implied that it had survived in the past in England only because of its established status. The 'vitality' of the smaller Protestant bodies would ensure that they would come out in front in any race in a society that refused to give preferential treatment to a particular body.[24]

J. M. Medley has argued persuasively that the 't'othersiders', to whom state aid was unknown, were a significant new component in the 1894 election and were important participants in the state aid debate.[25] In most of the Australian colonies, an impatience with the manoeuvering of ecclesiastical pressure groups, and not a dismissal of religion as such, was a factor in the abolition of state aid. In a religiously divided society, it was concluded, often with reluctance, that the state could not fund overtly religious teaching. But as D. Grundy also suggested, the secularist lobby contained a strong anti-clerical element, and was not just motivated by a benignly neutral liberal philosophy.[26] Something of the manouvering of pressure groups in Western Australia, in which Goldsmith played a part, has been obvious throughout this episode. To the 't'othersiders', the slightly earlier nonconformist perception of Goldsmith as a large high church fish in the small pond of pre-gold-rush Perth was largely irrelevant. Nevertheless, the support for the abolition of state aid in Western Australia combined impatience at sectarian dispute with its all too healthy survival in the abolitionists. The key factor remained the funding of Roman Catholic schools. While nonconformists could resent Anglicanism in any of its manifestations and feared a resurgence of Anglican hegemony, uneasiness over a perceived rise of Anglo-Catholicism played at least a part in intensifying their determination to end any kind of state aid.

Goldsmith's first decade in office as dean of Perth was thus marked by two defeats, one in the more narrowly ecclesiastical area, the other in a somewhat wider political sphere. But far from being the signal for some kind of withdrawal on the part of the dean, these two episodes were followed by a decade in which the churchmanship of Goldsmith and those in his immediate circle generated ongoing controversy. This controversy was conducted not only, or even primarily, within ecclesiastical settings, but in the eyes of the widest possible audience, through the correspondence columns of the daily press. The very forum in which much of the discussion of Anglo-Catholicism was conducted, as well as the grounds on which exception was taken to many Anglo-Catholic practices, and the way in which they were in turn defended, shows that what might at first glance appear to be matters of doctrine, devotion or liturgy, were perceived to have wide-ranging social implications.

And while heated controversy ensued, in which strongly worded statements were produced on both sides, there were clear indications that some of the standards promoted by Goldsmith and others as a result of the Oxford Movement were acceptable to an increasing number of Perth Anglicans, even if the key to this increasing acceptability did not lie in areas of doctrine alone, but embraced wider social and cultural attitudes. If the standards Goldsmith was promoting were regarded by their critics as subversive, there were Anglicans who were not beyond being subverted. What were the signs of subversion?

'Above all, the practice of auricular confession, show(s) a wanton boldness and determination to trample underfoot the known lines of church worship before the Oxford party had their traitrous existence.'[27] So wrote 'Apocalypse' in a letter to the Perth *Morning Herald* in 1901; the writer's poor grammar is perhaps a result of the vehemence of the feelings generated by the subject on hand.

The Tractarians were active in encouraging the revival of confession. The translation into English of Roman Catholic manuals providing pastoral direction for priest-confessors, and the private publication in 1877 of *The Priest in Absolution*, a manual for Anglican confessors, provoked debates in the British parliament that year. By the last two decades of the century the opponents of Anglo-Catholicism regarded it as one of the distinguishing marks of an advanced priest.[28] Confession continued to occupy a significant place in the controversy as the century drew to an end, for reasons examined in more detail in the next chapter.

The very limited documentary evidence that remains because of the intrinsic nature of the practice, presents problems of interpretation, and limits the scope of the conclusions that can be reached. Two factors have encouraged a silence difficult for the historian to penetrate—the obligation of confidentiality, binding in Anglican canon law, and the desire of a number of the clergy to avoid undue attention from both unsympathetic ecclesiastical authorities and influential and hostile laity. Only one prominent Anglo-Catholic priest in Australia, Percy Wise of St George's Goodwood, kept a systematic record of the number of confessions heard; this document is exceptional; some of the Queensland diaries of F. E. Maynard also indicate the number of penitents he was hearing.[29]

It is possible that Goldsmith himself was discreetly encouraging its use for a number of years before hostile allegations were made. The register entries listing services of 'Preparation for Communion', which begin in 1889, continue regularly throughout the years 1894–1904, principally at Easter, and less frequently at Christmas in most of the following years, as well as on a few other occasions.[30] The times at which such services were regularly provided corresponded with the two seasons of the church calendar at which Roman Catholic discipline encouraged the laity to communicate and obliged them to prepare for this by making their confession. Anglican priests seeking to encourage the restoration of confession as a spiritual discipline had no canon law that made confession obligatory, but they often encouraged the observation of a similar seasonal discipline.

Forms for such services of preparation were provided in a number of devotional manuals by Anglo-Catholic clergy, and generally consisted of appropriate psalms, scriptural readings, an address and prayers; a priest remaining after the conclusion of the service could give advice in informal interviews or formally hear confessions; laity who attended the advertised service could easily disperse at its conclusion without being aware of its sequel. Notice of such services formed a means of advertising the availability of a priest for such a purpose, without drawing unwelcome attention. Bishop Riley's 'special service and sermon', noted in the register before preparation on Good Friday in 1896, need not have disturbed such a pattern. The relatively late hour at which they took place—8.45 or 9.00 p.m. in Goldsmith's later years at the cathedral—shows that they were for a small number of committed worshippers—the kind of cross-section of Anglicans from which regular penitents might be expected to come.

Goldsmith's brother-in-law had been discreetly advertising in Lenten handbills since 1895 that he would be available at specified times in his parish church to hear confessions, and by 1897 Goldsmith had followed suit in Perth cathedral. A notice published in the cathedral pewsheet in

Lent in 1897 stated that one of the clergy would be present in the cathedral for an hour before evensong on every weekday except Thursday, in order to provide 'comfort, counsel or ghostly advice'.[31] This last phrase—little more than a paraphrase of the words from the exhortation in the 1662 Prayer Book communion rite in which the priest states his availability as a confessor—would have been familiar to those who had been taught to make their confessions, the exhortation itself being a standard element in justifications of the 'lawfulness' of the custom. By 1898 F. J. Price, Goldsmith's former cathedral curate, then rector of St Alban's Highgate, advertised in the parish Lenten leaflet: 'if you need advice and direction in any difficulty, as God's minister I offer you all the help which he has placed in my power to give you'. Price advertised that he would be present in the church at set hours each day.[32]

By 1898 Riley felt that the subject was in need of comment and preached a sermon on the subject at Christ Church Claremont. In his diary he regretted that there was no press reporter to record his view for the benefit of the general public. From this it is reasonable to infer that he was responding to a current objection, though its precise nature is not stated.[33]

In a lengthy debate concerning the revival of Catholic practices in the Anglican church in the *West Australian* between August and September 1898, confession was referred to in general terms, but no specific allegations were made that throw any light on its practice in Perth at the time. However, anxiety about the revival of confession, and especially the instruction of children, was a significant factor behind the questions about the circulation of particular devotional manuals and the educational material used in Sunday schools put to the Perth diocesan synod in 1899 and 1900.[34]

In December 1900 the *Morning Herald* began the last major public debate over ritualism when it published a series of allegations made by an unnamed but 'prominent churchman'. They were headed 'Illegal Practices in Anglican Churches'.[35] The article claimed that the superintendent of the Protestant Orphanage had an argument with Goldsmith, who was the Orphanage's manager, in which she criticized him for compelling the girls to make their confessions. She subsequently resigned. Goldmith denied that the girls were coerced. Riley backed Goldsmith's denial in a public response, and ruled that, in certain circumstances, confession was enjoined by the Prayer Book, and that a priest in such circumstances was 'bound to exercise his office', but went on to reassure Goldsmith's accuser that the dean had promised not to hear any further confessions from the orphanage girls. In this incident Goldsmith never denied that he had been hearing confessions.[36]

'Prominent Churchman' also claimed that auricular confession had been revived in several Anglican churches, but only specifically identified St Alban's Highgate. Another correspondent who joined in the debate, 'Apocalypse', claimed that it was undeniable 'that the Dean hears, and has heard, the auricular confessions of persons outside the orphanages'. He went on to make the remarkable claim that Riley was aware that, in Kalgoorlie, confessions were heard in 'confession boxes' as in Roman Catholic churches.[37] This claim was an expression of the common anti-ritualist conviction that the bishops sided with the ritualists, or at least did nothing to restrain them; 'Prominent Churchman' repeated the claim. It showed little awareness of Riley's own position—he would have stood on secure legal grounds in ordering their removal, and would not have hesitated to do so. Confessionals were completely unknown in Anglican churches in Australia, and despite anti-ritualist propaganda, though they were not entirely unknown, they were still extremely uncommon in English churches. At most, this particular complaint reflected a perception, accurate enough in itself, that the churchmanship of most of the goldfields clergy was generally high.

Goldsmith responded from the cathedral pulpit by defending the legality of confession according to the Prayer Book rubrics, arguing on pastoral grounds—it was the most appropriate way of dealing with the needs of those with troubled consciences. His defence made no comment on the actual frequency with which he heard confessions. While Riley had stated that confession was permitted and advised in certain circumstances, habitual and compulsory confession was 'not according to the mind of the Church of England',[38] the dean's silence on this point does not make it clear whether he heard the confessions of regular penitents—and thus differed from Riley's more limited approach. His own plea based on pastoral need was discreetly ambiguous.[39] It is clear that the dean, F. J. Price and Canon Garland heard confessions; the frequency with which they heard, whom they heard, and whether other clergy also encouraged the practice without attracting hostile responses, is not possible to determine.

Although confession was often identified as the most distinctive practice of Anglo-Catholics by their opponents, the central thread that tied all else together was the eucharist. For the penitent, confession could be a devotional practice that grew primarily from a particular kind of attitude towards the eucharist, as much as from convictions about the authority of the priesthood. And that the eucharist, as a reverence-provoking mystery, could only be approached in surroundings and in gestures that would encourage and reflect such a response, is the rationale behind a variety of signs that provoked comment, both positive and negative.

'Apocalypse' complained that

> Every Anglican church has a throne and altar which, after Edward VI's first prayer book, were ordered by the Bishops to be cut down, and were never revived until the Newman Oxford party came into existence. I challenge Dr Riley to say there is a communion table, as prescribed by the Prayer Book, in any Anglican church in Perth . . . [40]

While it might well be argued that it was not since the early seventeenth century that the 'holy tables' in Anglican churches had been arranged precisely as Cranmer intended, the many photographs in early issues of the *West Australian Church News* of sanctuaries in newly opened or recently restored churches in Western Australia, show that, by 1900, the greater proportion had an altar dressed with a seasonal frontal, generally on a step or steps, and often furnished with lights. At the cathedral and its daughter churches Goldsmith continued to highlight the altar, and gifts of frontals were mentioned from time to time by the press, which took due note of the beautification of the sanctuary at Christmas and Easter. In 1896 Lady Barlee offered the gift of an alabaster altar to the cathedral, which became the first Anglican cathedral in an Australian capital city to have a stone altar. To worshippers such as 'Apocalypse', a wooden table, however it might be dressed, could notionally be regarded as a 'communion table', but a stone structure was unmistakeably an altar. It implied that the cathedral authorities, particularly the dean,

St Nicholas' Australind: altar frontal, c. 1916
The emphasis on the altar created by the use of embroidered frontals extended beyond large urban centres to small and isolated churches such as St Nicholas', formerly a workman's cottage. The frontal was probably the work of the Frewer sisters, since the transformation of the cottage into a church took place under the direction of John Frewer.

promoted a sacrificial doctrine of the eucharist, a doctrine that anti-ritualists believed had been repudiated by the Prayer Book reformers, and which they regarded as distinctively Roman Catholic.

Elsewhere, at Claremont, by 1896, the altar was raised on a step, incorrectly described by the press as a footpiece. Presumably the term Goldsmith used in his annual report from which the press created its 'howler' was footpace. Its only real alternative was the Italian *predella*—had the latter been used, the worst fears of 'Apocalypse' would have been confirmed.[41] In 1900, even in as distant a centre as Mount Magnet, the altar stood on three steps and had a double gradine. Its rector, B. G. Richardson, had not the necessary personnel to use the three steps for the ceremonial of high mass, in which a separate step was assigned to each of the three sacred ministers, but the hope that such ceremonial would one day come to this remote centre would have been consistent with his churchmanship.[42]

Though the increased focus on the altar was a legacy of the Oxford Movement that was already influencing a wide range of Anglican churches, the presence of more than one functioning altar in a church was still characteristic of only a few ritualist centres in England. Goldsmith's creation of the Chapel of the Good Shepherd had already been noted, and the presence of such a subsidiary altar and the devotional pattern of more frequent weekday communions which it fostered was another sign of the general direction of the dean's churchmanship. In 1898 an anonymous donor presented a set of frontals and a dossal for this chapel altar.[43] The only other Anglican church in the colony to have two altars in the last decade of the century was the church of the Ascension Helena Vale (now Midland), whose rector, C. E. C. Lefroy, supported Goldsmith.[44]

By 1899, as celebrant at the eucharist in the cathedral, Goldsmith had adopted liturgical gestures and devotional attitudes that provoked Judge Stone to complain to Riley that the dean elevated the chalice, bowed during the consecration prayer, and 'mumbled'.[45] The elevation of the consecrated elements following the words of institution was a ceremony common in late medieval devotion, made mandatory in the rubrics of the Tridentine missal of 1570, and specifically forbidden by a rubric in the first Anglican rite of 1549. In view of 'Apocalypse's' comment on the cathedral clergy, that 'the priests in charge, as they style themselves, are not only educated in theology but in genuflexion',[46] it seems most likely that Goldsmith was performing the extended but not so deep inclination during parts of the consecration prayer that was prescribed for the celebrant in the Roman rite and which was also recommended in a number of Anglican manuals on ritual by Anglo-Catholic writers. The 'mumbling' that distressed Stone was probably Goldsmith's attempt to approximate to the phenomenon known in the west as 'the silent canon', a custom common in both orthodox east and Latin west, by which most of the consecration prayer was recited at a level only clearly audible to those immediately around the altar. It was ordered by a rubric in the Roman rite.

These usages were identified by their critics as signs of a general Romeward movement. But it was also more than just a general trend: it was seen as part of a plan to reduce the Anglican liturgy systematically to conform as closely as possible to the pattern of the Roman rite: 'to make the Communion service fit into the lines of the Mass', as 'Apocalypse' put it.[47] He claimed that the Anglo-Catholics were achieving this by taking the liturgy of the First Prayer Book of Edward VI (1549), which was 'little varied from the Mass', as their model. Two of the most controversial practices in England at this time did not appear in Western Australia until considerably later—the use of incense, and the reservation of the consecrated elements. Incense was introduced at the House of Grace in 1916; reservation was introduced in Western Australian churches at a later date again.[48]

The Lincoln Judgement had declared the use of altar lights to be legal, as long as they were not lit ceremonially, that is, as a specific action during the liturgy, rather than 'outside' the liturgy—before its commencement. This somewhat specious avoidance of their symbolic significance was criticized in the *Morning Herald* by 'Apocalypse', who responded when Riley quoted the Lincoln Judgement: 'Why are there lights at all on the Perth church altars, if not ceremonially?'[49] Despite Goldsmith's attempt to introduce them under Parry, the cathedral remained devoid of altar lights. Something of the hesitancy that possessed Parry also characterized the vestry of St Matthew's Guildford in 1899, which declined a gift of altar lights but accepted an altar cross.[50] Lights did begin to appear in Perth churches whose clergy were identified with advanced churchmanship. 'Prominent Churchman' complained of their use at St Alban's Highgate, and they were part of the fittings at Victoria Park when the church was opened, and at South Perth.[51] The papers read at a clerical conference held at Dongarra in 1897 imply that lights were then standard fittings in the churches at Geraldton, Dongarra, Gingin and Carnarvon.[52] At Roebourne, when Riley confirmed there in 1901, the altar was furnished with both a pair of lights, and something much more unusual which would have rejoiced the heart of the most advanced Anglo-Catholic: an additional set of six, a number traditionally associated with the Roman rite. This parish had two decidedly Catholic priests in succession, E. Saunders and H. Pitts, but the numbers of worshippers reported on this and other occasions does not suggest that the accoutrements of the church caused any pronounced offence.[53]

An evangelical cleric visiting the West in 1901 commented upon their extensive use, compared with Victoria.[54] Significantly, despite the hesitancy of Parry and the Guildford vestry, there was at least one centre where their presence suggests that they were not always identified as signs of 'extreme' churchmanship. In the south-west, when Harry Darling was inducted as rector of Bunbury in 1898, the *West Australian Church News* commented that the altar was furnished with lighted candles and other legal ornaments, 'which had for many years been in use in this church'.[55] Yet altar lights were not mentioned in the bitter accusations of ritualism levelled at his predecessor, W. F. Marshall. But while it was not just his ritual that caused offence, the subsequent disuse of lights by his successor might indicate some degree of anti-ritualist aversion to them in Bunbury.[56] Elsewhere in Australia, responses to altar lights varied: they were certainly used by men who did not regard themselves as Anglo-Catholics, while they were regarded by others as definite signs of Anglo-Catholicism.[57]

Within Western Australia, Sydney Hawthorn, rector of Busselton in 1892, nearly became the first Anglican priest in the state to wear eucharistic vestments. He advertised in the *Church Times* for a set of vestments for Busselton, but left Western Australia that same year when he accepted the parish of Naseby in the diocese of Dunedin.[58] Eucharistic vestments were not introduced to St George's cathedral until the time of R. H. Moore. The allegations by 'Prominent Churchman' published in 1900 in the *Morning Herald* that 'at the services at the cathedral the Dean is in the habit of donning robes associated with Roman Catholicism'[59] refer to the use of embroidered stoles, not chasubles. As 'Apocalypse' pointed out, it was the embroidered sign of the cross on the stoles that caused offence, and distinguished them from the stoles (his term for the preaching scarf) worn by Evangelicals.[60]

An entry in the diary of the Brotherhood of St Boniface links the first appearance of eucharistic vestments in Western Australia with Goldsmith, who, on retiring from Bunbury, made a number of gifts to the House of Grace, including a green silk chasuble, 'the first chasuble worn in W. A.—by the bishop, then dean of Perth'.[61] This may have been part of the set of eucharistic vestments Riley was dismayed to find when he went to open the Perth Orphanage chapel on the Sunday evening of 26 February 1899:

> Home for dinner.
> Opened Girl's Orphanage.
> Good congregation.
> Very sorry to see they have set of Coloured Vestments—never told me anything about it—I do not see how, without causing trouble—I can stem the ritualism of the Dean and Garland.[62]

However, a passage in the *Perth Quarterly Magazine* lists various gifts for St George's Carnarvon, distinguishing between stoles and eucharistic vestments. The material for other eucharistic ornaments (veils and burses) was specified—silk.[63] The silk chasuble referred to in the earlier quotation is more likely to have been among the vestments made for Carnarvon. It was Goldsmith who, as diocesan administrator, opened St George's Carnarvon in May 1894.[64] The position he then held as diocesan administrator offered him freedom from restraint by higher authority in considering furnishing and fittings for new buildings in the diocese.

But for such an innovation as the introduction of vestments, the choice of Carnarvon was in some ways unusual. Its isolation from Perth might seem an advantage: the experiment could go on quietly with little risk of interference from outside. But objection from within, by a majority in a small community, was still a real risk, and in England the opponents of Anglo-Catholicism had criticized clergy who introduced practices in country centres whose isolation made it impossible for offended worshippers to find an alternative Anglican church. However, the experiment continued. The parish remained vacant during the remainder of the year, and D. J. Garland, who went there to celebrate from time to time, would certainly have been sympathetic to continuing such a use.[65] Although argument from a negative is not satisfactory on its own, it is also significant that W. Sharp, rector of Carnarvon from 1896 until 1922, never referred to any need to introduce vestments, a point he is likely to have made, had there been any opportunity to do so in the first place. He wrote frequently to the SPG in a painfully self-conscious way of his maintenance of Catholic standards in the face of indifference, and his concern for ceremonial irritated Riley. He eventually left a set of Spanish fiddle-back chasubles of his own at St George's, and the use of vestments cut in a style identified with the continental Counter-Reformation, rather than with medieval England, may explain the comment in Riley's diary on first worshipping in Carnarvon: 'very Romish'.[66]

But one amusing anecdote calls into question at once the anxiety of Riley, the suspicions of the anti-ritualists, and the cautiousness of some, though not all, the clergy who introduced them. In later life Moore recalled an Irish priest on the goldfields who had been persuaded to wear a chasuble for evensong, because his parishioners liked the visual effect: this occurred even in Riley's presence.[67] The peculiar scene that this conjures up—the priest happily wearing a vestment worn exclusively when celebrating the eucharist, outside its proper context, suggests that anti-ritualists were jumping to conclusions far too rapidly when they saw the use of such vestments as proof that particular doctrines had been systematically taught. Rather, for this cleric's parishioners, they really were the 'man-millinery' of the contemptuous anti-ritualist phrase, devoid of their traditional associations.

English publications that catalogued clergy and churches according to their churchmanship were often prone to inaccuracy and exaggeration. No evidence can be found to substantiate the claim made in the Church Association's *Ritualistic Clergy List* that J. Ellis was using vestments at St Paul's Palmerston Street in Perth by 1903, even though such usage would have been consistent with his churchmanship and his training by the Cowley Fathers.[68] But the entry for Carnarvon in the 1898 *English Church Union Tourists' Guide,* which states that vestments were used there, is consistent with what we know from local sources.[69] The *Guide* also lists Dongarra and Coolgardie as centres where vestments were in use. Photographs taken before the end of the century showing the rector of Coolgardie, F. J. Barton-Parkes, wearing a fiddle-back chasuble, have survived.[70] R. H. Moore, who was elected as dean of Perth in 1929, later recalled his introduction in the winter of 1898 to the goldfields, where

The Venerable Frederick Barton-Parkes, Archdeacon of Coolgardie, c. 1898
A rare photograph of a Western Australian goldfields priest in eucharistic vestments.
Photographer unknown

Barton-Parkes told him that the minimum liturgical standard throughout his archdeaconry included vestments, altar lights and the eastward position.[71] And while there is no evidence in Perth to substantiate the *Guide*'s claim that vestments were also worn at Highgate and Victoria Park (though this would equally be consistent with the churchmanship of F. J. Price and D. J. Garland), an article in an Anglo-Catholic publication almost a quarter of a century later also stated that vestments were worn at St Alban's for a short time.[72]

Hawthorn's advertisement, the reference to vestments made for St George's Carnarvon, and the evidence from the goldfields all point to a particular regional pattern in the introduction of vestments in Western Australia, one that differs from most other parts of Australia at the time—their appearance in the more remote country centres, rather than in urban ones. Their introduction in South Australia by F. T. Whitington in 1889 at Kapunda, a country centre, offers some parallel to Carnarvon—though near enough to Adelaide, it was not a fashionable middle-class suburban church, where large-scale protest might occur; they subsequently appeared in four urban parishes in Adelaide—Walkerville, Woodville, Parkside and Glenelg—in the 1890s.[73] The clergy who introduced them were generally, though not always, born and trained outside Australia. Sharp, though an American, came to Carnarvon through the English SPG.[74] And even men such as Brodribb and E. S. Hughes, who were among Melbourne's innovators in this area, though Australian born, were strongly influenced by English models.

Despite Goldsmith's introduction of vestments at the orphanage chapel, the cathedral did not have them. Riley's distaste for ritual signs is not the sole or main factor here. The bishops of Queensland before 1900, though sympathetic to the Oxford Movement, had not introduced vestments to their cathedral churches. J. B. Kyte, Hobart's dean, a Church Union member like Goldsmith, and a well-known advocate of confession, did not introduce them to St David's. Their introduction in Adelaide and some Queensland cathedrals occurred in the first decade of the present century. Adelaide Cathedral was the first capital city cathedral to receive a gift of vestments, but they do not appear to have been used until 1905, almost a decade after they had been given.[75] This nation-wide caution indicates a general conservatism in response to popular attitudes, including (presumably) those of lay members of chapters.

Since the seventeenth century Anglicans have argued as to whether the intention of Anglican formularies had been to forbid all forms of prayer for the departed, or only particular kinds of prayer. Objection to the reintroduction of some form of prayer for the departed was the basis of a debate in the *West Australian* between the 'ancient colonist' Judge Edward Stone and Goldsmith. Stone, who objected to a reference to the departed in a sermon by 'one of the clergy', wrote to the *West Australian* under the pseudonym 'Parishioner' but subsequently revealed his identity. The press eventually reprinted the whole correspondence in a separate supplement.[76] Stone complained to Riley in 1899 that he thought he had heard Goldsmith ask for prayer for a departed person in a cathedral eucharist just before the Prayer for the Church Militant.[77]

If a particular doctrine lay behind such a devotion, its precise nature is often impossible to discern from either anti-ritualist statements or more sympathetic sources. The Congregationalist cleric W. T. Kench attacked F. J. Price as 'an advocate for the Ritualistic party' in 1898, and listed 'the doctrine of Purgatory' among the doctrines that he claimed were being restored by ritualists. Unfortunately, Kench's statement was too general to indicate anything more definite than that Price had advocated some kind of prayer for the departed. Equally vague is the allegation of Langham Burdett in 1900 that he had recently encountered an Anglican priest 'who inculcated the obligation of prayers for the dead' not from the Bible, but from other books. The use of the term requiem in

1893 to describe the eucharist in Bunbury before Bishop Parry's body was taken to Perth, likewise may mean no more than an intention to pray for the departed and need not be understood to indicate a belief in any particular theory concerning the state of the departed or any alteration of that state as a result of the offering of the eucharist. The title of an address at evensong on Good Friday in 1894—'The Condition of the Departed in Paradise'—shows that Goldsmith himself was propagating some kind of teaching concerning the state of the departed, without indicating its content.[78]

For 15 November 1894, the first anniversary of Parry's death, the entry in the cathedral register reads 'Holy Communion and Memorial of the late Bishop, "Year's Mind" '. This last term was used by Anglo-Catholics to denote the offering of prayer for departed persons at a eucharist on the anniversary of their death, and recurs in the entry for 1896.[79] Goldsmith used the anniversary of Bishop Parry as an opportunity for a liturgical celebration in connection with the departed, and he may well have hoped that by offering an annual requiem for an apparently well-loved man, some kind of prayer for the departed would be accepted by Perth Anglicans.

Anglo-Catholics also revived the observance of 2 November as All Souls' day. At the Reformation it had been excised from the Anglican calendar because of its popular association with the doctrine of purgatory. It continued in the Roman calendar and was observed with the offering of requiems. Goldsmith entered 2 November as All Souls' day in the cathedral service register for the first time in 1896 and continued its observance until 1900: no observation was recorded for that, or subsequent, years. It is unclear whether this deletion was a result of some pressure from Bishop Riley following the controversies in the press between 1898 and 1900, or whether the decrease in the small numbers which originally attended led Goldsmith to discontinue the celebration.[80]

Some clergy in country centres also sought to encourage a revival of devotion involving the departed. The dedication of the newly-opened church at Mount Magnet, under the title of All Souls, was claimed to have been 'unanimously resolved' at a full meeting of the vestry, but the title is more likely to have reflected the teaching of its new rector,

B. G. Richardson.[81] At least one priest in an isolated centre, H. Pitts of Roebourne, used the death of Queen Victoria as an excuse for celebrating what he described in his correspondence as 'a Requiem Eucharist with Collect, Epistle and Gospel from the First Prayerbook of Edward VI— as authorized by the Bishop'. His chapter and verse citation of his sources demonstrates that very sympathy for the 1549 Prayer Book that opponents of Anglo-Catholicism saw as an ominous sign. His congregation of fifteen at ten in the morning in a black-draped church was heavily outnumbered by the ninety—'the largest congregation ever collected in Roebourne'—who gathered for an evening service. Rather than understanding the smaller morning congregation as evidence of a rejection by Anglicans of any kind of prayer for the departed, the much higher evening congregation reflects the continuing great popularity of non-eucharistic evening services at this time.[82]

An occasion such as the Queen's death, or the death of servicemen in the Boer War, could provoke a wave of feeling that would accept a muted form of prayer for the departed and interpret it as an expression of patriotic sentiment rather than as a part of a doctrine. A good example of this is an additional verse for the National Anthem published in the *West Australian Church News*:

> *Shield when the fight is high*
> *Those who in battle die.*
> *Grant, Lord, thy peace.*[83]

Anglo-Catholic manuals such as *Before the Altar,* which was attacked in Perth synod, often contained prayers for the departed either of a quite explicit, or else a more oblique, kind.

Thus there is evidence that clergy in a wide range of centres in the state encouraged some kind of prayer for the departed and sought to use occasions when popular sentiment might be receptive to such a devotion. However, despite the claims of anti-ritualists, there is nothing to prove that such a devotion implied a belief in the doctrines concerning the state of the departed expressed in official Roman Catholic formularies, and the hostile nature of most of the sources means that the conclusions that can be reached over this issue are limited.

Canon Louch's address at the end of 1897 on the legality of lights and cross as ornaments of the altar showed that in the minds of the more Catholic clergy the two belonged together, and were presumably in use at the centres whose clergy joined him that day—Carnarvon, Gingin and Dongarra, as well as his own parish of Geraldton.[84] Altar crosses were common enough ornaments in other churches in the colony, even those that were hesitant to introduce altar lights.[85] Perth cathedral had a plain cross on its high altar. Those desiring at least a visual image of the crucifixion close by would have found satisfaction in the cathedral's great east window with its central crucifixion panel.

But certain forms of the cross, as a ritualist symbol, were still offensive to some. It is unclear whether 'Prominent Churchman' was denouncing some kind of mission service, or simply the choir procession before a normal Sunday service, when he stated that 'at Highgate Hill there is frequently a procession into the streets, when crosses and other ritualistic signs are employed'.[86] 'Prominent Churchman' further objected to the dean for wearing a stole, which he defined as 'a garment with a cross worked on it . . . (a robe) associated with Roman Catholicism', and when Riley responded that stoles were worn by clergy of all schools of churchmanship, including evangelicals, 'Apocalypse' responded that the evangelical clergy wore undecorated stoles.[87]

One controversial practice was what the Lincoln Judgement, in the King case, described as 'making of the sign of the cross in the air' by the celebrant at the absolution and the blessing. Bishop King was forbidden from continuing it. W. H. Timperley specifically mentioned it when he denounced W. F. Marshall's ceremonial practices in Bunbury:

> The ritualistic practices which he followed were an abomination to the people. (Hear, hear, and applause.) He would say that if there was another place of worship of the Church of England where the clergyman was not promenading about and making the sign of the cross and other practices he would never put his foot in the church again. (Great applause.) These practices were repugnant to the people and he would like to know how much longer Mr Marshall desired to continue them. (Applause.) At this stage of the proceedings several ladies left the room.[88]

Joseph Withers, the previous incumbent, followed Timperley in condemning Marshall. Withers described his predecessor, R. H. Purnell, as a tactful high churchman—the proof of his tactfulness being his concealment of 'a crucifix in his prayerbook' where it was well hidden from view. But Withers revealed that he had given direction on how to run the parish to Marshall shortly after the latter's arrival in Bunbury, and this suggests that the churchmanship issue was interwoven with a personal power struggle between Marshall and his predecessor, who was not above manipulating public opinion.[89]

It is surprising that anti-ritualists did not denounce two devotions associated with the cross that Goldsmith adapted for Good Friday. Price's lantern slides of the Way of the Cross in the Mechanics' Institute Hall on Good Friday in 1894 had a sequel. In the St Alban's service register from 1897 onwards there are entries for the same service. In 1899 it was advertised as the Way of the Cross, but the register unambiguously lists it as Stations of the Cross, showing that it was based on the popular Roman Catholic devotion. It was attended that year by four hundred worshippers. On Good Friday, starting in 1897, the St Alban's registers also list the singing of the Reproaches after the Prayer Book liturgy of Morning Prayer and Ante-Communion.[90] At this same time the Reproaches also made their appearance in the cathedral on Good Friday.[91] The Reproaches, a dramatic dialogue, probably of eastern origin, were sung in the Latin rite on Good Friday during the veneration of the cross. Goldsmith made no attempt to introduce the liturgical action of the veneration, which had already appeared in the small number of advanced English churches that had replaced the Prayer Book Holy Week rites with the Roman rite services. The introduction of the veneration, commonly known as 'creeping to the cross', formed another focus for anti-ritualist unrest in England and was one of the practices to which attention was drawn in the Report of the Commission on liturgy in 1906.

Goldsmith's liturgical innovations were therefore modest. The reasons were his own caution and the conservatism of the laity, and many of the clergy, in this isolated community. However, the use of a text of the Reproaches both at St Albans and at the cathedral, is another example of his readiness to supplement the Prayer Book discreetly from the Roman rite—as was his interpolation of the *O Salutaris Hostia* after the consecration prayer in the sung eucharist. The absence of crucifixes from Western Australian churches at this time was consistent with standards elsewhere in Australia. Lord Kintore's gift of a carved crucifix and brass processional cross to Adelaide's St Peter's cathedral was still unusual for the time.[92] And in Sydney St Andrew's cathedral had found it necessary to modify the central panel in a reredos which was to have shown the crucifixion, lest it be treated as a crucifix by some worshippers; the figure with outstretched arms became an inoffensive Jesus on the Mount of Transfiguration.[93] In Tasmania Bishop Montgomery commented to Randall Davidson, then Bishop of Winchester, that the only 'extreme' in his diocese was represented by a group surrounding H. C. Wisdom of St George's Battery Point, who refused to enter any church in which there was so much as a plain cross.[94]

*T*he story of earlier responses to Goldsmith, not only to his churchmanship but to his engagement in the political arena through promoting state aid, is one of the power of the media, especially through the skilful manipulation of Winthrop Hackett. But colonial Anglo-Catholics were equally prepared to enter into the media arena on their own terms. And just as journals with a high church tinge appeared in Sydney and Melbourne in the last decade of the nineteenth century, so the *West Australian Church News* appeared in Perth.

The monthly journal, the *West Australian Church News,* is also another important sign of the emergence of Anglo-Catholicism in the colony, though its own assessment of the contemporary ecclesiastical scene cannot always be taken at face value. Unlike the *Perth Quarterly Magazine*, which was designed for English readers, the *West Australian Church News* circulated locally and its tone was unmistakeable. Portrait photographs of Anglo-Catholic heroes such as Father Charles Lowder of the notorious slum parish of St-George's-in-the-East, or current party symbols like the Church Union leader Viscount Halifax, sometimes took up most of its front page.[95] Between its inception in 1897 and the turn of the century, it carried substantial articles and editorial comments from an Anglo-Catholic standpoint on liturgical and ceremonial issues such as the Lincoln Judgement, the judgement of the two archbishops on the use of incense and processional lights, and the battle to win freedom for the 'six points' outlined by the English Church Union. It emphasized the theology and devotion of Anglo-Catholicism with articles on the eucharistic sacrifice and the real presence. It was all the more alarming to those who believed that they were being subjected to an overpowering Anglo-Catholic wave, because it appeared in the absence of an official diocesan organ, but bore the name of the diocesan secretary. Critics feared that this indicated diocesan support for its attitudes. Copies carried the legend 'printed for David John Garland': Garland had in fact financed its foundation.

Its contents and its promotion under the name of a priest regarded as a leading ritualist made it a predictable object of attack. Trying to attack Garland, some asked questions, in the 1899 Perth synod, about the paper. Riley quashed the attempt, but the assault continued elsewhere. 'Onlooker', a pseudonymous correspondent in the *West Australian*, described it as divisive, and the inappropriately named 'Charity' called it 'rude, one-sided, violent, a real discredit to a Christian clergyman', and 'shocking' to a 'great majority of church people', because Garland belonged to 'an extreme party in the church'.[96] Along with the attack on the *West Australian Church News* in the 1899 synod there were questions over the sale of devotional books, and one publication in particular, *Before the Altar*. Though the book was available at more than one outlet, only sales from the Church Book Depot, which was financed by Garland, were questioned. James Cowan also moved that only those books whose titles appeared on a list bearing the bishop's imprimatur should be circulated to the laity by the clergy. Laughter greeted this motion and Garland commented, 'The Archdeacon of Perth says it is a little Papacy. Mr Cowan: Perhaps you will find these books show a little Papacy'.[97] Because the motions concerning the *West Australian Church News* and the Church Book Depot were only masks for attacks on Garland, they show that, by this time, Garland as well as Goldsmith had become identified as leading promoters of advanced churchmanship, an identification which is confirmed by Riley's diary entry of 26 February 1899.

— FIVE —

# The Critics and their Position

So far, we have seen ample evidence of a suspicious or hostile reaction to what was perceived as Anglo-Catholic innovations. Of Western Australia's population at this time, which group or groups regarded Anglo-Catholicism as an alien and subversive movement? And what was the foundation for their hostility? The answers to the first of these questions brings us back to one of the main participants in the election of a successor to H. H. Parry: the Western Australian press, and those who directed and financed it. It also demands a consideration of the devotional patterns of different generations, and the possibility that at this point, for some people, there was a kind of religious generation gap. Answers to the second question involve a careful unravelling of texts that present concerns about race, culture and empire, using religious imagery.

The most significant press organ in Western Australia was the *West Australian,* whose weekly subsidiary, the *Western Mail,* reproduced editorials and correspondence about churchmanship from its parent paper. In addition, there was the *Morning Herald*. There were two reasons for the virulent tone of statements about Anglo-Catholicism in the Western Australian press. One was the personal stance of editors and owners, many of whom had already criticized the dean and his churchmanship. The other was the limited forum for anti-ritualist discontent: the press could both act as an outlet for discontent and nourish it.

Sir Edward Stone, whose distress at Goldsmith's liturgical and devotional practices has already been cited, was strongly associated with the

Mr Justice Edward Stone, c. 1895
A courteous legal critic of Goldsmith

*West Australian*: he had been a part-owner.[1] Its current joint owner with Hackett was Charles Harper, a conservative Anglican politician and pastoralist. Although Harper did not enter directly into the churchmanship fray, his pastoral interests may not have been unconnected with the editorial attitude to churchmanship issues. As well as opposing Goldmith's churchmanship, Hackett and Stone both made common cause in the interests of the rural community. Hackett complained that it would be disadvantaged through the cessation of the Ecclesiastical Grant. Yet simultaneously he provoked some of the hostility over churchmanship, hostility that he claimed was accelerating the demand for the abolition of state aid. Stone had urged Perth synod to pressure the government to continue the Ecclesiastical Grant on the ground that it was essential for the maintenance of clergy and churches in rural areas.[2] And because one of the identifiable anti-ritualist correspondents, and probably the longest standing, E. Parker, was a large rural landowner,[3] Stone and Hackett's personal distaste for Anglo-Catholicism seems to have coincided with the interests and views of a larger conservative rural bloc, in which Harper was a significant figure.

Certainly the differences between Goldsmith and Hackett were wider than merely issues of churchmanship. The liberal in Hackett clashed with Goldsmith not only over education, but over Goldsmith's stances on issues such as temperance and gambling, just as it had identified the Tractarian movement as reactionary, and made him sympathetic to a broad churchmanship. He certainly believed that the future primacy of Anglicanism in the colony depended on the ascendancy of such a churchmanship.[4] His most direct attacks on Goldsmith's churchmanship were in the context of the state aid debate, but there was still a hostility in later years, even if the style of attack was less direct. As we have already noted, an element of Irish sectarian bitterness underlay his attitudes in the campaign against state aid and may also have played a part in the undercurrent. In England, especially in Liverpool, Irish sectarianism heightened the intensity of the debate at this time.[5]

Significant 'ancient colonists' were also directors, part owners or prominent shareholders in the *Morning Herald*, and when he retired from his position as editor late in 1900, Arthur Lovekin specifically referred to the support that the paper gave to the interests of 'ancient colonists'. Its chairman of directors was Alexander Forrest. While the political interests of the Forrest family were the paper's first priority,[6] its initiation of the last large-scale anti-ritualist press controversy was quite consistent with the attitudes of the Forrest family to Goldsmith and his churchmanship. Alexander Forrest had made passing and veiled hostile references in the debate on state aid; Sir John equally expressed his distaste for Goldsmith in a letter to Riley at a later date and his absence from Goldsmith's enthronement as bishop of Bunbury, Forrest's home town, was duly noted, though not explained, by local papers.[7]

In this period the hostility of the *West Australian* was masked by an appearance of impartiality. Hackett was even prepared to reproduce a substantial passage from the *West Australian Church News*, which had clear Anglo-

The Hon. Arthur Lovekin, 1929
Lovekin's *Morning Herald* joined Hackett's *West Australian* in criticizing Anglo-Catholicism.

Catholic sympathies.[8] But the most protracted of the newspaper debates actually began when F. J. Price, Goldsmith's former cathedral curate, who had only recently been appointed as rector of St Alban's Highgate, complained in the correspondence columns of the *West Australian* that the press was creating a bias against Anglo-Catholicism in 'the uninstructed colonist'. His assertion that the press created and manipulated a hostile public opinion in the colonies was not the main topic of the ensuing correspondence: it became a battle between the attackers and defenders of Anglo-Catholicism. The debate, which involved over twenty letters and summaries of sermons and addresses, was small in volume compared with some other debates over similar issues in the columns of newspapers in other Australian cities. But it dragged on over almost five months; the first outburst ran from the end of August for over a month, and the debate was refuelled when a Wesleyan cleric delivered an address entitled 'Ritualistic Bats and Moles'.[9]

Price had reasonable enough grounds for his complaint. The *West Australian* used the heading 'lawlessness in the church' under which it reproduced cablegrams reporting unease over Anglo-Catholicism in England, and this title headed much of the subsequent correspondence in the press, presumably to Price's chagrin. Although the editor of the *West Australian* replied to Price that 'no thought was taken as to ritualistic or anti-ritualistic feeling',[10] the title 'Lawlessness in the Church' came from one of the most hostile of English sources, a series of nineteen letters by Sir William Harcourt, a leading figure in the renewed pressure in England for parliamentary legislation to control Anglo-Catholicism. His letters were published in both *The Times* and the *Guardian*, and then collectively under the title, 'Lawlessness in the National Church'.[11] The sheer quantity of cablegrams in the *West Australian*, reporting unease about or hostility to ritualism, was in itself remarkable by comparison with the coverage given at the same time in prominent newspapers in other colonial capitals.[12] The *West Australian Church News* had identified the stance taken by the sources that Hackett used: in 1899 it referred to 'cablegrams in the Australian press (though emanating as is notorious from an unfriendly source)'.[13]

The *West Australian* also claimed that its policy was to refuse to publish anonymous correspondence and statements—a way of distinguishing it from other papers such as the *Morning Herald*, which had no hesitation in initiating its outburst with a statement by an individual, 'Prominent Churchman', who remained cloaked in anonymity to the end. But again, the *West Australian*'s claim to be a more sophisticated and impartial organ was honoured in the breach as much as in the observance. In 1898 an Anglo-Catholic layman, E. H. Myerson, criticized the anonymity of most of the anti-ritualist correspondents. And during the outburst which the *Morning Herald* initiated in 1900, the *West Australian* excused itself from what it claimed was its normal policy of disallowing anonymous correspondence and published a letter signed by 'Churchman', stating that the writer was 'so well known and respected a member of the Church of England' as to justify the exception.[14]

The hostility shown by the press to advanced churchmanship was partly an 'ancient colonist' antagonism, a hostility from those who were among the colony's earliest, as well as wealthiest, settlers. The arrival of their families at an early point in the colony's history meant that Tractarianism and its offshoots had not influenced many of the parishes in England they had left behind. Other sources, especially the diary of the public servant, Alfred Hillman, confirm that among the colony's earlier settlers the norm in patterns of piety were of a different kind from those encouraged by the Oxford Movement. There is some direct evidence of the persistence of such patterns into the last decade of the century (and beyond) and they surface in mutual misunderstandings and tensions in the debate over Anglo-Catholicism. Though such patterns were often dismissed as 'evangelical' by Anglo-Catholics, their distribution across the Anglican spectrum is too comprehensive to make this an accurate description.

Perhaps the most conspicuous element of the earlier Anglican piety was the acceptance of frequent attendance at non-eucharistic worship as the norm, along with infrequent acts of communion. This was not necessarily because communicating was regarded as insignificant in itself: it could also reflect a belief in a particular degree or kind of preparation. Thus, when Alfred Hillman recorded his attendance at church on almost every Sunday between 1877 and 1884, he referred only once in 1878 to staying for Communion and commented, 'I always feel that I ought to attend it more, but it is such a serious and solemn duty that one cannot help hesitating'.¹⁵ On another occasion he had gone to church, but did not remain to communicate because he felt that he was not in a recollected state of mind 'suitable to such a solemn service'. On other occasions he remained to communicate.¹⁶ Hillman was following a pattern allowed by the Prayer Book rubrics, and which had been customary in England since the Reformation. He attended morning prayer and litany and remained until the end of the Prayer for the Church Militant, when those not intending to communicate would leave. A description in the *West Australian Church News* of the congregation at St Alban's Marradong in 1897 refers to the piety of the Oxford Movement encouraged by the rector, F. C. Gillett, in a way that shows that the other pattern was still prevalent. It commented favourably on how the whole congregation remained to communicate, without any departure of a body of non-communicants 'as is done in so many places'. Clergy influenced by the Oxford Movement disapproved strongly, but still had more headway to make.¹⁷ Meanwhile, they were quick to imply that such a pattern was a sign of lack of commitment or of due reverence, rather than a product of a particular attitude towards preparation and recollection of the kind shown by Hillman.

This pattern of infrequent communion also surfaces in disputes over churchmanship. Thus in the dispute surrounding W. F. Marshall, the rector of Bunbury 1892–97, one of Bunbury's early settlers, T. Hayward, repudiated the rule that church office-holders should be frequent communicants. He appealed to local feeling against Perth (represented by its bishop) and stressed the local social hierarchy by lauding the wisdom of the local patriarchs, but he also stated that it was a matter of conscience whether a man communicated three or thirteen times in a year.¹⁸ From the opposite point of view, in the debate at the end of 1900, the *West Australian Church News* asked whether the 'Prominent Churchman', whose allegations initiated the episode, were a 'regular communicant', and framed its question to imply that this indicated an absence of genuine devotion—he was a troublemaker with only a peripheral involvement in the church's life. The earlier comment concerning St Alban's Marradong shows that the writer was unwilling to acknowledge that infrequent communicating attendance might have been an ingredient in a genuine though quite different devotional tradition.¹⁹

Though there is evidence of some regional variation in the frequency with which Anglicans communicated at the end of the eighteenth and beginning of the nineteenth centuries in England, the kind of frequency encouraged by the Oxford Movement would have been exceptional or unknown to the generations that produced Western Australia's first settlers. Local conditions only strengthened an inherited pattern of infrequent communion: the colony's population remained small, and there were several small communities in which distance reinforced isolation. Communicant statistics, available from the last quarter of the century, which become much more complete and detailed with the passing of time, also support this interpretation. By 1889 only six churches in the diocese had a weekly eucharist, while twelve still only had a quarterly celebration. The ground between was occupied by seven churches with monthly celebrations, and six with celebrations twice a month. Bishop Parry then estimated the number of communicants throughout the diocese as 1500, representing about one twelfth of the total number of Anglicans, or almost one fifth of those over fourteen years of age.[20] Two other figures are instructive: in 1882 the cathedral had a communicant roll of four hundred, of whom an average of forty communicated each Sunday; at Bunbury in 1889, out of a roll of 150 communicants, between ten and thirteen would communicate at celebrations.[21]

Hillman's worshipping pattern shows other notable features which contrast with the attitude of the Oxford Movement. He does not appear to have observed the calendar of feasts and fasts centred around the life of Christ: he did not mark Lent and Holy Week with any distinctive observance and only once worshipped in church on a Christmas day, and that only when it fell on a Sunday.[22] The new cathedral's service registers suggest that this pattern also remained largely unaltered: its figures for attendances on saints' days and on major days in Lent and Holy Week throughout this period are all undeserving of comment. Hillman also disliked the singing of the offices, though he realized that this marked him as old-fashioned. He described surplices contemptuously as 'nightshirts'. Elsewhere he condemned 'high church fooleries'. The context in which he expressed this was significant—it was as he praised the simplicity of the service in an English village church which reminded him of the style of worship with which he was familiar in Perth. He described the village of Shaftesbury as 'sequestered'. As he likened the liturgy of the church there with worship in Perth, it was as though the isolation of the remote colony had kept its Anglicanism from corruption by the forces at work 'at home' in the more populous centres.[23]

Though Hillman was born in the colony, this consciousness of a relationship to an earlier pattern which had survived in the colonial wilderness was also apparent in the background of E. H. Parker of Dangin, near Beverley. In 1896 he denounced Riley for 'eulogizing' the Lincoln Judgement. Parker damned it for upholding the most modest ceremonial usages—the eastward position, altar lights and the mixed chalice. He praised all of Hale's clergy, whom he claimed to have known personally as a member of synod—according to Parker, they had all been evangelicals. He considered sympathy for the Oxford Movement to be a characteristic of young, English-trained clergymen: this tendency represented a threat to the purity of the colony's original tradition.[24] Parker had in fact come to the colony in 1830 when he was only ten, having known an England untouched by Tractarianism and its successors.

'V. M.', a correspondent who supported the dean's attempts to make services 'more lively' in 1893, described opposition as coming from 'the Protestants, I mean the members of the dear old Church of England', and asserted that it was time that they were 'roused up a bit, and brought out of their humdrum style of churchgoing'. In the same sequence of correspondence, 'Justice' wrote of the dean's attempts to improve the music of the cathedral that 'no sooner does the Dean do his utmost to make the worship of God a pleasure than these old fogies raise the hue and cry that "We are all going over to Rome"'.[25] This letter was sarcastic, yet it referred to a recognized local establishment, part of which was an older generation.

In the dispute over W. F. Marshall in Bunbury, T. Hayward's comment in the *Southern Times* that not a 'single old resident' was connected with 'the working of our Church', and claims by Joseph Withers that 'several heads of families . . . had never been to communion' in Marshall's time of office, suggest that most of the earlier generation of settlers in Bunbury stood behind the dividing line that marked out the opponents of Anglo-Catholicism from their antagonists. To them, the causes of offence were the singing of morning and evening prayer ('miserable droning monotoning ... loud voiced entoning [sic]', acknowledging the altar and the sign of the cross—a restrained level of ceremonial, akin to that disliked by the 'old-fashioned' Alfred Hillman.[26]

Thus anti-ritualism in the press manifested the polarization between the Anglicanism of the 'ancient colonists', or the early English settlers, and the theology of the younger, recently arrived clergy. The private reflections of Alfred Hillman provide further insight into the motives behind the hostility—a desire to preserve a pattern already consciously upheld as that of an England of a slightly earlier period—the period at which the earlier settlers came to the colony. And although Hillman did not explicitly identify the isolation of the colony as something which reinforced a sense of loyalty to the ways of the parent culture as the colonists remembered it, his identification of 'coming home' in the Shaftesbury church has precisely such a resonance.

At the beginning of 1895 an editorial by Hackett suggested that distress—at the particular churchmanship promoted from the cathedral pulpit—was leading worshippers 'gently down the incline of disbelief', or sending them 'to other places of worship'.[27] Later in the same year, in the midst of the acrimonious dispute between W. F. Marshall and his Bunbury vestry, a dispute that surfaced periodically in the Bunbury press from 1895 until 1898, 'A Former Friend' alleged that it was because of Marshall's ritualism that the Wesleyan church was 'crowded with Churchmen',[28] and the correspondence that closed the debate over 'illegal practices in Perth churches' was signed 'Ex-Anglican'.[29] In Adelaide, Perth's closest neighbour as a state capital, it was likewise claimed that 'churchmen' were attending nonconformist churches as a result of the preaching of high church doctrines.[30] In 1898 'Tocsin' made specific claims about the number of Anglicans who had left particular parishes over issues of churchmanship, but did not identify their new worshipping home.[31]

Concrete evidence of such a pattern is not easy to obtain. In Riley's diary, among the expressions of concern about the churchmanship of Goldsmith and others, there is only one such reference. It had been claimed that Perth's greatest philanthropist, Walter Padbury, had left the cathedral because of the choral eucharist, and that the principal of Perth High School had gone to the Congregationalist church.[32] Riley's main concern may have been the implications for the future finance of the diocese, rather than numbers and churchmanship. Riley's diary does not indicate when Padbury returned from his exodus, but it was certainly not permanent. On his death in 1907 Padbury was to become one of the most generous benefactors of both cathedral and diocese, and during his lifetime contributed liberally towards the establishment of Bunbury diocese.

In 1893, two years before Hackett's accusing editorial, 'Justice' commented on Anglicans who attended nonconformist churches. He explained this as a response not to churchmanship, nor the content of sermons, but rather to the style of delivery—the extemporaneous style cultivated by most nonconformist clergy was preferred.[33] Thirteen years before that, Alfred Hillman had commented on what he considered to be the generally poor standard of preaching at the cathedral, and felt that it would be appropriate to attend a nonconformist church simply for the sake of a good sermon. Thus before Goldsmith's arrival in Perth, there were factors other than churchmanship that could explain fluctuating attendances. One was the popularity of individual preachers, and antagonism to some preachers given to particular subjects such as total abstinence—the cathedral congregation could follow a particular preacher elsewhere or threaten not to attend if an unpopular preacher were to return; in an earlier generation, even the Governor had been known to display his displeasure by joining the nonconformists for a few Sundays, when Hampton was dissatisfied at the music of the cathedral and its performance.

In Bunbury a correspondent who signed himself 'Looking On' contested the claim that Marshall's churchmanship alone led to poor attendances at St Paul's. He pointed out that the churchmanship of his predecessor, Joseph Withers, had not guaranteed him a thriving congregation—he had attracted only a handful of the town's Anglicans to worship. As in Perth, the supposed revulsion generated by high churchmen and their doctrines was not matched by a corresponding attraction towards those of other schools.[34] Anglican attendance at nonconformist churches for varying periods of time was far from being a new phenomenon. 'High church doctrines' were simply another reason for following an accepted pattern. That nonconformist churches were generally chosen was indicative of one thing in particular—the degree to which Anglicans identified themselves as Protestant.

In England, hostile responses to Anglo-Catholicism inherited the popular identification of Tractarianism with Roman Catholicism, one which had been made in the first decade of that movement's life and which became firmly established in many minds following the conversion of a number of its prominent early members.[35] Further, several recent studies refer to a complex of ideas of race, nation and empire in hostile English responses to Anglo-Catholicism.[36]

Many opponents of Anglo-Catholicism in England combined their fear of Roman Catholicism with a belief that Britain's national character and her international primacy at the head of a powerful empire were built on her Protestant Reformation inheritance. Change in the character of the church would therefore be a prelude to a change in the nation at large. If tolerated, Tractarianism, then Anglo-Catholicism, would herald the disappearance of all that distinguished England from continental Roman Catholic countries. The 'Romanizing' of the church was regarded as part of a social and economic reconstruction: Tractarians and Anglo-Catholics were either dupes, or willing accomplices, in a Roman Catholic plot. The same arguments were repeated in Western Australia, in spite of its different social and political context—distance from Britain and the absence of an establishment did not lessen this concern.

As early as 1874 E. H. Parker of Beverley wrote in the *Perth Gazette* and *West Australian Times* that ritualism and Roman Catholicism alike should be denounced in all Protestant countries, and saw England's supremacy as a direct result of her Protestantism. At the opposite end of the scale stood the toal laziness of members of Roman Catholic religious orders—Parker would have agreed with other Anglicans who assumed that allegedly poor levels of education and the high incidence of crime and poverty in Southern European countries were direct outcomes of their Roman Catholicism.[37] Parker, who continued to write against Anglo-Catholicism into the 1890s, was convinced that the apocalyptic vindication of Protestantism was close at hand. The recent Franco-Prussian War of 1865 fulfilled the prophecy of 1260 days in Daniel, and was a sign that the suppression of the papacy was imminent. A similar apocalyptic vein characterized a letter of Langham Burdett in 1900, who wrote that as a result of the 'Romanizing of the Church of England' in these 'serious times', society was on the eve of 'terrible changes'. He regarded the freedom and liberties of Australia as being due to the Reformation—presumably because he understood Australia to be British, and identified Britishness with Protestantism. Those whom he held responsible for the changes that were looming were certainly part of something neither Protestant nor British—a plot.[38]

Variants that reflect the same assumptions in a simpler form are presented by other writers in the debate over Anglo-Catholicism. When 'Prominent Churchman' denounced the ritualism of Perth's cathedral and other churches, he stated that 'so long as we have an English church, the services should be conducted according to the Prayer Book'.[39] He clearly equated English and Protestant with what he considered to be the correct way of conducting Prayer Book services—the Anglo-Catholics were not only lawbreakers, and not truly Protestant, but were un-English. Two years previously, another writer, 'Tocsin', had referred to the ritualist clergy as agents of 'your old enemy, Rome. No surrender!'[40] If the image of the 'enemy' here may have been of a religious rather than a national kind, he went on to place Catholicism in the nationalist framework: its emotional appeal marked it as un-English. 'Watchman', who corresponded in the same series of letters as 'Tocsin', equally identified English, Anglican and Protestant, when he claimed that calling an Englishman a Catholic was tantamount to calling a (white) Australian 'a blackfellow'.[41]

The nationalist complex was acknowledged and turned on itself by those who were under attack. Anglo-Catholics saw themselves not as the subverters, but as being truer than any other stream of churchmanship to the national and cultural heritage of Anglicanism. Goldsmith, Garland and others referred to Anglicanism as the English church.[42] They equated Catholicism not with Rome, but with Anglicanism, presenting Anglicanism as the means by which pure and primitive Catholic doctrine and practice had been preserved. The opposite of English was not Catholic, but Roman, and Goldsmith and his friends were not supporters of a foreign system, nor were they 'the enemy in disguise', but the truest Englishmen of all. Thus Goldsmith himself could refer condescendingly to Roman Catholicism as 'a religion which is entirely alien in many of its principles and practices to the minds of English people, naturally conservative of the primitive ideal, and standard'.[43] He identifed the Catholic and Tractarian ideal of primitiveness and antiquity as an English one. Thus, instead of being a sign of something un-British and dishonest or disloyal, the term Catholic was truly English: 'every true English churchman uses it when he is loyal to his creed and the services of the Church', wrote 'One of the Laity' in reply to 'Tocsin'. Edward Myerson responded in a similar vein.[44]

Langham Burdett explicitly connected the cultural progress of Britain and her empire with its Protestantism, and saw any weakening in the one as fatal to the supremacy of the other. Anglo-Catholicism and the Oxford Movement were going to 'put back our civilization four hundred years'.[45] While he expressed his position in a more sophisticated way, Winthrop Hackett's editorials were perfectly consistent with the more overt nationalism of writers such as Burdett and Parker. The Tractarian movement sought to return to the 'mists and cloudy symbols of medievalism'; the 'ineffective' methods which its supporters sought to revive were not those used by any genuine 'spiritual regenerator'.[46] Its spirit was essentially reactionary, its romanticism the antithesis of the practical spirit of the present.[47] Inasmuch as Anglicanism in Western Australia was seen to be influenced by such standards, it was seen to be losing its former position of pre-eminence in the colony as the 'most powerful and successful' of the churches, while 'other bodies' were distinctly 'improving their position'.[48] Hackett's antitheses were no different from those of Burdett and Parker: Catholic ideals belonged to the past; Protestantism was allied with progress.

A more openly nationalist framework characterized his editorial on the enthronement of Bishop Riley. He attacked the cathedral as a centre which was unrepresentative of Anglicanism as a whole. 'Religion', which in this context meant Christianity, was one of the 'essential forces of civilization, of progress, of morality, of true greatness'. Anglicanism in particular in Western Australia inherited a warrant from its mother church ('representing the great Anglican Church of England, Ireland, and the colonies') for inspiring citizens to seek 'purer aims, higher desires, and the larger and grander hope which all wish to believe lies before the nation and the individual in the future'. The standards upheld at the cathedral impeded this aim. Hackett invited his reader to draw conclusions from what he claimed was the gradual decline of the Anglican pre-eminence in the colony. The God who gave spiritual inspiration and progress to the British empire would only fully bless the new society and its Anglicanism if he were offered the sacrifices of a contritely un-Tractarian heart. God was a liberal Protestant.

A definite element in the nationalist framework in which Anglo-Catholicism and Roman Catholicism were viewed was the identification of Protestantism as logical and restrained on the one hand, and Roman Catholicism as emotional and illogical on the other. Nineteenth-century Anglicanism had inherited a tradition which identified sober restraint and the avoidance of excessive emotional display as characteristic of its spirituality and its liturgical forms. A sober thoughtfulness was contrasted with the theatrical display of Roman Catholicism which used rich and sophisticated resources to work on the senses and the emotions; this likewise protected Anglicanism from the false simplicity of dissenting bodies. Such an identification dovetailed with nineteenth-century perceptions that reasonableness, logic and emotional restraint were British characteristics. These were held to distinguish the Briton from the southern European, whose tendency towards uncontrolled emotion was in keeping with his religion; and both were part of the latter's place among the less developed European nations.

A classic early description of a prominent Anglo-Catholic church, Lord Shaftesbury's account of St Alban's Holborn in 1866, coupled accusations of theatricality and emotional display with the suggestion that it was so exotic as to be not only foreign but heathen: 'in outward form and ritual, it is the worship of Jupiter and Juno . . . The Communicants went up to the tune of soft music, as though it had been a melodrama, and one was astonished at the close, that there was no fall of the curtain . . .'[49] In the lengthy correspondence on Anglo-Catholicism in the *West Australian* in 1898 'Tocsin' described Roman Catholicism as a religion of feeling, not of intelligence, which had been repudiated for this very reason by the English. In a later letter in the same sequence he repeated his initial claim, contrasting 'our birthright as Anglo Saxons' and 'our intellectual religion' with the 'lawlessness, sensuality and idolatry of ritualism'.[50]

Although the nationalist framework was not always so explicit in the responses of other Western Australian critics of ritualism, individual elements which 'Tocsin' linked together—the accusations of emotional excess, intellectual emptiness, theatricality and appeal to the senses—were all used to suggest that Anglo-Catholicism was something exotic or foreign. As early as 1875 the *West Australian Times* quoted a Melbourne Presbyterian who identified the 'logical outcome of Anglo-Catholic worship as 'the emotional response in the witnesses', and condemned it as 'theatrical'.[51] Western Australian opponents quoted English sources with the same emphasis. A description by Lady Wimborne of the 'extravagant behaviour' of the servers at an Anglo-Catholic liturgy produced a grotesque *faux pas* in the *West Australian*: 'the acolytes remained for long spaces with their heads on the floor, then swinging censors [sic] and going through elaborate changes of position, along with the priest, who was clad in gorgeous vestments'.[52] Given the absence of a single Anglican church in the colony where incense was used or where high mass was performed according to the ceremonial of either Sarum or Roman rites, a Western Australian reader was obliged by default to conjure up a vision of an exotic and foreign practice. Two years later 'Apocalypse' claimed that Bishop Riley was familiar with 'gorgeous ceremonial in his churches', again suggesting the promotion of an exotic appeal to the senses.[53]

The opponents of Anglo-Catholicism in England sometimes claimed that because it appealed to the emotions, it could only attract women and children. Here again it represented the antithesis of the simple and forthright masculine reasonableness of the Protestant John Bull. The Bunbury priest who became the centre of impassioned denunciations of ritualism, W. F. Marshall, was accused in his earlier Adelaide days of delivering sermons whose intellectual emptiness would appeal only to women and children.[54] Though many complaints had been made concerning the poor standard of preaching at the cathedral, only an editorial in October 1894 by Winthrop Hackett linked the supposedly poor quality with churchmanship. Restiveness was caused by the preaching of 'doctrines of an exceedingly unpalatable character' in the 'strangely unintelligent discourses too often heard, and which were apparently considered fit meat for the educational and intellectual acquirements of their hearers . . .'⁵⁵ The pre-eminence of Anglicanism in Western Australia and the progress of society as a whole would not be furthered by the intellectual emptiness that was reminiscent of the pseudo-medieval mists of Tractarian reactionariness.

Another ground of complaint has no obvious nationalist element, yet was still connected with this underlying theme. Accusations of 'lawlessness' against Anglo-Catholic clergy were sometimes coupled with suggestions of dishonesty—such clergy were consciously denying doctrinal positions which they had promised at their ordinations to uphold. Thus, in one letter, 'Watchman' provided instances of two kinds of dishonesty practised by Anglo-Catholic clergy, while in another letter, in which F. J. Price was the particular object of attack, he referred to them as 'false clerical guides who have perjured themselves by their wicked sayings and doings'.⁵⁶ At the height of the controversy over confession in 1900 Goldsmith considered that 'Prominent Churchman' had imputed some degree of dishonesty to him.⁵⁷ Although Western Australian correspondents did not criticize this alleged dishonesty in explicitly nationalist terms, behind it lay the assumption that truthfulness and directness were English characteristics. In other debates over Anglo-Catholicism in Australia and in England, this equation was clearly made: thus a Victorian correspondent, objecting to Anglo-Catholicism in 1901, complained that 'Englishmen, reared in the light of truth and honour', were now teaching 'heretical, idolatrous and damnable' doctrines.⁵⁸ Similarly, the claim made most conspicuously by Walter Walsh in *The Secret History of the Oxford Movement*, that Tractarianism and Anglo-Catholicism were part of a conspiracy, partly made its appeal on the assumption that indirectness, deviousness and plotting were characteristics of other nations, as much as of other religious groups, and that a simple truthfulness was not only a peculiarly Protestant, but a British, characteristic. Such a presentation of Anglo-Catholicism and Roman Catholicism had also been a stock-in-trade of Victorian religious novelists.⁵⁹ When 'Tocsin' described Anglo-Catholic clergy as 'disguised Jesuits', he drew on the same complex of associations.

The academic origins of Tractarianism were partly responsible for giving the whole Oxford Movement a strongly clerical identity in England. In colonial societies where there was no establishment to lend added support to the status of the clergy, the Tractarian movement could prove attractive because it posited a basis for their authority that was independent of the state. While some Tractarians, such as Tyrrell in Newcastle, promoted the movement's concepts of authority and hierarchy in a way that gained the endorsement of the laity, the potential for a lay–clerical divide remained.

Varying levels of sophistication marked the treatment of the relationship between clergy and laity by the opponents of Anglo-Catholicism. Before launching into an apocalyptic vein, 'Watchman' provided a short list of significant historical works, including Hallam's *Constitutional History*, Macaulay's *History of England*, Ranke's History of the Popes and E. Creasy's *History of the Constitution*, as a justification for his own position. These works all stressed the place of the laity rather than the clergy as the promoters of the Reformation and the preservers of its values.[60]

A much cruder anti-clericalism marked a number of anti-ritualist letters. 'Tocsin' claimed that the church and its property had been 'seized' by Anglo-Catholic clergy, and urged the 'sleeping laity' of Western Australia to reclaim it, by refusing to contribute to its upkeep until the clergy performed the Prayer Book services free from any Anglo-Catholic innovations. This provoked E. Myerson to counter by asking where the title deeds of property were, if the churches had really been seized.[61] In 'Tocsin's' view, an acceptable model for the response of the laity was provided in England by John Kensit, the secretary of the Protestant Truth Society, who organized a series of increasingly rowdy protests in which he and his supporters disrupted services at a number of Anglo-Catholic churches. The fanatical tone of his activity was typified by his attempt to sue the vicar of St Cuthbert's Philbeach Gardens for assault after he had been sprinkled with holy water during the *Asperges* before a high mass. His death in 1902 occurred shortly after violent clashes between his supporters and Irish opponents in Birkenhead, near Liverpool.[62] 'Prominent Churchman' equally appealed to the laity to 'combine and fight this (ritualist) movement', lest the Anglican churches of Australia should be 'Romanized' by the clergy. In the same passage he referred to the conduct of services according to the 'whims and fancies of our clergymen'. He joined 'Tocsin' in his interpretation of events in England, and in seeing the English situation as no different from that in Australia. In England it was the clergy who had tried to 'Romanize' the churches, but 'popular indignation intervened'.[63] 'Watchman' had equally branded ritualism as a clerical movement when he denounced the ritualist clergy, alleging dishonesty on their part, and referred to the movement's 'silly and idolatrous sacerdotalism'.[64] And the frequent charge, discussed below, that Anglo-Catholicism was 'lawlessness', was directed specifically at the clergy in view of their subscription to the 39 Articles and the oath of obedience.

The anti-clerical statements of 'Prominent Churchman' and 'Tocsin' assumed that the English and Australian experiences were identical—as well as assuming that the course of the movement in England was merely a matter of priestly deception encountering popular lay opposition. The same equation was less obviously made by 'M. C.', in quoting the critical description by Lady Wimborne of an Anglo-Catholic liturgy. But while Anglo-Catholic leaders in Western Australia were members of the clergy—Goldsmith, Garland and Price—the kind of liturgy that Lady Wimborne described as typical of an Anglo-Catholic church in England was not to be found in a single church in Perth, a fact that was not lost on Western Australian Anglo-Catholic sympathizers. Further, the absence of any popular agitation of the kind carried out by the Protestant Truth Society or the Wyclifites in England, shows that such critics depended heavily on English sources for the framework of their arguments. The failure of any Kensit-like figure to appear indicates that the activities of Anglo-Catholics in Perth caused less unease there than in contemporary England. It also shows that those who sought deliverance through such a figure had misread the signs of their own society. Their agitation in the correspondence column was a sufficient outlet for existing dissatisfaction.

Ever since the first decade of Tractarianism, the revival of sacramental confession had provoked consistent responses in which it was interpreted as a threat to family structures and thus to society at large. Even Samuel Wilberforce of Oxford, whose high churchmanship made him receptive to other aspects of the Oxford Movement, described it as 'a sort of spiritual dram-drinking'. It was more than the possibility that it might couple religion with excitement, that ingredient of foreign, but not English, religious practice. According to Wilberforce, it led the priest into casuistry, but more importantly it placed the relationship of exclusive and total knowledge (and therefore control) of husband and wife under threat. It was a moral threat to the nation, because it particularly involved dealing with the 'sins of uncleanness', in which even the most well-intentioned question of a penitent by a priest might result in the former becoming aware of hitherto unknown variations of sin—which they then ran the risk of being tempted to commit.[65]

By comparison with the number of complaints about the possible corruption of the minds of the young through confession, little concern was expressed concerning the threat posed by the confessor to the husband's role. A single quotation by 'Prominent Churchman', from a speech by the Marquis of Salisbury in the House of Lords, refers to this aspect, which provided anti-Tractarian and anti-ritualist novelists with a staple source of situations in which the wife's loyalty to her husband, or attachment to erroneous doctrine, was tested. But when a Perth nonconformist cleric referred to *The Priest in Absolution* as 'that unclean book', he was evidently showing a very Victorian concern that, in confession, a priest might cross-examine the penitent concerning sexual minutiae.[66] A vague sexual unease also underlay 'Prominent Churchman's' allegations concerning compulsory confession at the orphanage, allegations that he coupled with claims that Goldsmith kept the orphanage girls up at night to force them to go to chapel, and that access to the chapel itself was denied to the general public. The elements of his allegations—hints of cruelty, a group of young women whose activities were not entirely accessible to the public, and a sinisterly controlling cleric—were common enough themes in Gothic novels.

Until the end of the nineteenth century, criticism of revival of confession continued to centre on the threat it was believed to pose to family authority structures and to sexual morality. Thus Frederick Temple, Archbishop of Canterbury, stressed it as a threat to the role of the male in marriage as husband and father.[67] The attack in parliament in 1877 on a privately printed and distributed manual of guidance for confessors, *The Priest in Absolution*, provoked *The Times* to denounce Anglo-Catholicism as a 'conspiracy against public morals'.[68] In England the influence of the priest over children in their formative years provoked not only some of the anxiety felt by nonconformists over the position of

Anglican clergy in denominational schools, but stirred Anglicans hostile to the revival of confession. Many elements in this concern over the possibility of an undue influence over the young was focused in the Cavalier case, in which the teenage son of an Evangelical cleric of unblemished reputation secretly began to attend St Cuthbert's Philbeach Gardens. He disappeared from his home after his parents' attempts to discipline him had failed. He reappeared, after a police search, in the rectory of an Anglo-Catholic priest in Ilkestone (Yorkshire). The English press ruminated on the issue, and produced images of Anglo-Catholics as sinister manufacturers of forcible adolescent conversions, a position reinforced by a long tradition of forced conversions on the part of Roman Catholics. The case had some impact in Australia, as the father, a missionary speaker, postponed a tour as a result of his son's activities.[69]

Between 1898 and 1901 the same anxieties were expressed in Perth, and while English sources were also quoted by those who opposed it, specific local situations stimulated their concern. A major fear was that the clergy would use Sunday schools to disseminate teaching on confession. At the 1899 Perth synod, one motion addressed this possibility. O. L. Haines asked for the removal from the Sunday school syllabus of the *St Paul's Manuals on the Catechism*. A correspondent claimed that they were used in nine (Sunday) schools.[70] A month after synod had sat, 'Onlooker' attacked Garland for supporting the use of the manuals, and identified the cause of offence in them—they contradicted the 39 Articles by encouraging confession and belief in the real presence of Christ in the eucharist.[71] At a meeting shortly after synod, the diocesan Education Committee, which compiled the Sunday school syllabus, withdrew the *St Paul's Manuals* from the syllabus. Its clerical members in 1899 were all of a uniform churchmanship—Goldsmith, Garland, Price and Lefroy—which perhaps explains the appearance of the *Manuals* on the syllabus in the first place.[72] Despite the deletion of the *Manuals* from the education board's syllabus, James Cowan, an influential public servant, wrote to the press at the beginning of 1901, and commented concerning their use:

> It is not so much the minds of adult persons which some of our priests, by their preaching or teaching, hope to divert from the true doctrines of the Bible, but they know that they have great opportunities with the minds of the young, who are so trustfully placed in their hands at Sunday Schools, Bible classes, and preparation for confirmation and Sacrament.[73]

As examples of what caused him offence, he quoted only a single passage from the *St Paul's Manuals* (it dealt with the real presence), but went on to claim that the Anglo-Catholic devotional manual currently available in Perth, *Before the Altar*, offended on several grounds, and from it he reproduced a form of confession. That same book had stirred him at the 1899 synod to urge the creation of some kind of censorship of ecclesiastical literature. In that stratagem he is said to have had the support of at least one influential member of the Education Committee, who promised Cowan that the circulation of the book would be suppressed throughout the diocese.[74]

Equally, 'Prominent Churchman's' claim that compulsory confessions were being heard by Goldsmith at the orphanage, even if totally erroneous, is another example of anxiety about the role of the priest in his ministry with children. He had withdrawn a child of his own from a school at which Goldsmith taught, although the example of what he found offensive in the dean's teaching consisted in encouraging children to observe Friday as a day of self-denial. Another correspondent at the same time, Langham Burdett, generally condemned the teachings which he associated with the Oxford Movement, but referred specifically to the impression of truth and authority mistakenly received by the young from 'cultivated, amiable and courteous' clergy, whose image would impart an air of authority to the doctrines they taught.[75]

In justifying confession, Goldsmith did not refer to the aspect that appeared to make it a potential threat to the Victorian married man—the possibility that the confessor might become privy to facts which revealed the gap between the theory of the husband's role and its practice. His naïve view of the British family suggests that he was probably sheltered from any real awareness of marital violence in Perth: 'the greatest social glory of the Anglo-Saxon race [is] the beauty and purity of its home life'.[76] More importantly, the claim that confession threatened the family's authority structure was recognized by another dean of the time, Joseph Bertram Kyte of Hobart, whose churchmanship was similar to Goldsmith's. He regarded it as an issue that was too sensitive to challenge directly: instead, he protected himself by refusing to hear the confession of young female penitents, except when they had parental permission.[77] Goldsmith publicly sidestepped the whole question of penance and the young. At the height of the controversy which the

*Morning Herald* initiated, he justified the lawfulness of confession from the cathedral pulpit by referring to the adult pastoral needs to which it ministered.[78]

Earlier in the decade nonconformist attacks on Goldsmith's Anglo-Catholicism were aroused by fears that high church clergy would use their position as teachers of religious instruction to disseminate Anglo-Catholic doctrine. Though this concern ceased with the abolition of state aid, Western Australian nonconformists discovered a new ground for attack in the conspiracy theories about Anglo-Catholicism. Conspiracy theories had already been in circulation for some time in England: lists of 'unsound' clergy (members of Anglo-Catholic societies such as the Church Union, Confraternity of the Blessed Sacrament and the Order of the Holy Cross) reprinted from an ultra-Protestant paper, *The Rock*, were circulated in the 1870s under the title *The Ritualistic Conspiracy*. The Church Association, the Protestant answer to the Church Union, regularly published a *Ritualistic Clergy List* whose early editions included Goldsmith and his brothers-in-law. This work carried a subtitle which likewise identified members of Catholic societies as part of an organized 'Romeward' movement. Conspiracy theories gained a new popularity in England following the failure of the Public Worship Regulation Act to achieve the purpose for which it was created, the most significant single example being Walter Walsh's *Secret History of the Oxford Movement* (1897).

A short episode of correspondence in the *West Australian* was generated at the end of 1898 by an address by a Wesleyan cleric, a Mr Wheatley, entitled 'Ritualistic Bats and Moles: A Review of *The Secret History of the Oxford Movement*'. This crude popularization of an already sensationalist work described the Church Union as a secret society with thirty thousand members whose aim was corporate reunion, a society prepared to 'take the Church of England over to Rome'. Wheatley clearly drew on Walsh's text when it came to naming Australian conspirators: the one Australian whom he did name, Bishop Dawes of Rockhampton, was mentioned by Walsh. Had a copy of the Church Association's *Ritualistic Clergy List* been available to him, Wheatley would have found more Australians listed, including Goldsmith. However, at this point he could not be more specific than to report of the secret societies, that were supposed to be at the heart of Anglo-Catholicism, that 'some of them had branches in the colonies, and that they had members in every diocese'. Wheatley likewise relied heavily on Walsh when he denounced *The Priest in Absolution*. He was joined in the correspondence columns by W. T. Kench, a Congregationalist, who had already taken part in the dispute surrounding W. F. Marshall in Bunbury, and G. E. Rowe, the city's leading Wesleyan cleric, both of whom attacked F. J. Price of Highgate.[79]

Belief in a conspiracy theory in Perth was not confined to the nonconformists, though they were its most outspoken advocates. Langham Burdett referred to Anglican clergy in Western Australia as the dupes of 'Jesuitical wire-pullers'.[80] 'Apocalypse' quite incorrectly described Viscount Halifax, the president of the English Church Union, as a 'convert to Rome, following in the wake of Newman', and went on to describe Western Australian Anglicanism as being 'in the hands of the party led in England by Viscount Halifax'. George Kidson, the manager of the Church Book Depot, had already written in response to an earlier letter, pointing to 'Apocalypse's' dependence on Walsh, and commenting on the general dependence of anti-ritualist writers in Australia on British sources for their impression of ceremonial of a kind that was not then practised anywhere in the country.[81]

The critics of ritualism drew on a wide range of issues, articulated in such a way as to elicit powerful responses from those who had learnt to associate British imperial greatness with Protestantism, and who believed that social and economic structures were related to the maintenance of a markedly Protestant profile. Given that such convictions were both widely held, and powerful, why was it that the detractors of Anglo-Catholicism did not score a resounding victory in the war of criticism?

— SIX —

# From the Tolerant to the Favourable

If the critics of Anglo-Catholicism in Western Australia were able to articulate their criticism in a way that brought together issues of race, culture and empire, as well as religious identity and doctrine, the appeal of their position was modified as a result of an equally complex range of factors. Though on the surface the strongly evangelical background of C. O. L. Riley should have weighted the situation in favour of Anglo-Catholicism's critics, the considerable reservations that Riley himself felt about ritualists was balanced by his concept of the bishop's role—to ensure that, within the limits allowed by ecclesiastical discipline, the needs of Anglicans of different kinds of churchmanship were catered for. The growth of Perth and of other centres in the wake of the gold rush brought other factors into play. It brought a new population, some of whom were already formed by the influences of the Oxford Movement; and with the possibility of a more sophisticated lifestyle came an openness to a liturgical and devotional style that was less restrained, and that drew on a rich aesthetic and cultural resource in music and visual arts.

In accounting for responses to Anglo-Catholicism in Western Australia in general as well as to Goldsmith in particular, it is important to assess the place of Parry's successor, C. O. L. Riley. His diary records his own irritation and that of others over the dean's churchmanship. An oral tradition still persists among some senior Anglican clergy that portrays Riley as at least intolerant of Anglo-Catholicism, if not as a persecutor of Anglo-Catholics.

In a series of unpublished reminiscences A. A. Robertson, a layman who was employed as a diocesan official in Riley's last years, supports this view with a series of anecdotes. One tells of a letter by Riley headed 'washing day' in reply to another letter from an Anglo-Catholic priest who had piously dated his own correspondence according to the days of the church calendar. Another tells of a conspicuous Bunbury Anglo-Catholic, Father John Foley-Whaling (nicknamed 'holy failing' and 'slowly fading'), best known as rector of St David's South Bunbury, before the Great Depression. He knelt to kiss Riley's ring and was greeted with 'That's enough of this tomfoolery'. He nevertheless persisted in leaving Riley's presence by walking backwards at the end of the interview. To further illustrate Riley's apparently deliberate avoidance of symbols dear to Anglo-Catholics, Robertson repeated the comment of the bishop's son-in-law, R. H. Moore, that he had a mitre in the diocesan arms and on letterhead, but never where it most properly belonged. He was obviously ignorant of the incident in which he wore a mitre at Collie, described elsewhere in this text.[1]

That Riley came from an evangelical hothouse is clear: St Paul's, Preston, his last appointment in England before he came to Perth, was a parish that produced three evangelical bishops from among its vicars. His wife, Elizabeth, was a niece of Bishop Merriman of Grahamstown, who brought an unsuccessful suit against his dean in a dispute that boiled down to issues of churchmanship. But he was regarded as being a higher churchman than his immediate predecessor at Preston, Chavasse.[2] And even at Preston he cultivated a wider circle of acquaintance—when he attended the 1908 Lambeth Conference a home, run by the Sisters of the Church, welcomed him back as a frequent visitor in his earlier days.[3] R. H. Moore claimed that in Manchester, Riley had visited and communicated one of the priests gaoled under the Public Worship Regulation Act—presumably this was James Bell Cox.[4] (He was far from isolated in this kind of response to the controversy over Anglo-Catholicism: Field Flowers Goe, who became Bishop of Melbourne in 1887, had been one of many evangelical clergy who signed a petition protesting against the aggressive tactics of John Kensit and his followers.) In his first decade in Perth, Riley appointed two leading high church clergy to positions of trust in which they were to work closely with him—

D. J. Garland as the diocesan registrar and secretary, and F. J. Price as his chaplain. To the latter he gave considerable support during a protracted case of allegations of sexual misconduct in which he was defended by Septimus Burt, and which ended in a judgement against the *Sunday Times*.[5]

While he was anxious to contain the Anglo-Catholicism of Garland and the dean, in public Riley was careful to avoid courses of action that might be interpreted as examples of discrimination in favour of either party. In 1898, in his synod address, at a time of renewed agitation in England over the alleged 'lawlessness' of Anglo-Catholics and others more broadly influenced by the Oxford Movement, he stated that he believed the majority of his own clergy, including most of those accused of 'lawlessness', were law-abiding. He expressed a desire that the needs of all kinds of Anglicans might be catered for in large centres, but urged the avoidance of extremes of any form that might make some Anglicans feel alienated in country centres that had only one church—an exhortation that was not only natural enough in a diocese in which most of the centres were in rural areas, but was also a response to some of the country clergy whose advanced practices have already been detailed.[6] At the 1899 synod he quickly ruled out of order the questions which veiled the attack on Garland. In 1899 and 1900 he reiterated his emphasis on the breadth of the Anglican church, but regretted that an undue concentration on ritual matters created a spirit of disunity and led to the neglect of more important issues.[7] Most of all, on Goldsmith's election to Bunbury, Riley did not seek to replace him with a priest of different churchmanship, in spite of encouragement to do so from Sir John Forrest.[8] Instead, he put forward the name of another distinctly high churchman, Joseph Bertram Kyte, who had been the subject of a series of attacks which centred on his advocacy of confession.[9]

Riley's real aim was not to prevent the existence of a high church centre or centres within the metropolitan area, but to provide for the range of different schools of thought within Anglicanism. He not only stated this in public, but privately in the same vein at the end of 1895 to his English commissary, W. W. Firth.[10] At the time he wrote, this aim brought him into conflict with Goldsmith's use of his existing powers as dean, and in the future it would also fail to satisfy those who saw his role as one that obliged him to put down Anglo-Catholicism.

Riley's statement in this correspondence concerning the dean's desire to maintain a single churchmanship in Perth's churches contrasts with Goldsmith's public expressions of disinterest as to whether new centres in Perth were to come under the cathedral's control or exist as independent parishes.[11] As early as 1889 he had presented a paper at the Sydney Church Congress in which he discussed the disadvantages of applying English parochial structures to the church in Australia. He suggested that in an urban setting it was desirable to avoid the creation of a large number of small independent parishes, each under the direction of an individual priest, and replicating the services and functions of its neighbour; instead, a large central church should staff a number of smaller mission churches operated by a team of assistant priests and deacons, with whom a team of lay workers would also co-operate.[12] Such a scheme was presented as one that offered substantial monetary savings, and it was such a scheme that he was running in Perth when Riley arrived. As long as this *modus operandi* was maintained, the dean would hold the right of appointing clergy in the urban district served through the cathedral, and Riley's hopes for a diversity in churchmanship would be frustrated. Even more fundamental than this, the only way in which Riley would be free to appoint clergy in new areas would be by creating new parishes outside the cathedral's control. Otherwise the diocese would have a mere token bishop.

The subject of his prerogatives, in relation to the cathedral in particular, and parishes in general, became a dominant issue in his correspondence.[13] Goldsmith's executive position was made even stronger by the cathedral's administration. It had only a vestry possessing the limited powers of a parish organization, and not a chapter with wider powers, even though an act had been passed by synod in 1897 enabling a chapter to be formed, a point of which Peter Boyce was unaware when he wrote his account of their conflict, where he describes the body backing the dean as a chapter.[14] Riley used Goldsmith's absence on leave at the end of 1895 to attempt to curtail the dean's power. But despite being backed by the Diocesan Council, there was no change in the status quo. In the wake of the failure of this attempt to bridle the dean, Riley called on the jealousy of one of Goldsmith's own kind: in 1897 he persuaded Garland to remain as registrar on condition that he would support Riley in curbing the dean's power.[15]

Control over appointments, rather than churchmanship, continued to be a basic source of friction between the two men.[16] Goldsmith equally frustrated the bishop on issues of authority rather than churchmanship. In 1896 Riley urged Perth synod to vote in favour of a General Synod proposal to give the title of archbishop to the metropolitan provincial bishops; Goldsmith led the opposition. The motion was affirmed by only four votes in its favour but, other matters intervening, Riley's ambition of becoming the first archbishop was forced to wait another eighteen years.[17]

The key to the tense and worsening relations between the two men was not churchmanship. It was the fact that both men were determined and forceful characters. At the end of his first year as bishop, Riley wrote an assessment of all the diocesan clergy, in which he concluded that, apart from Goldsmith, there was only one strong figure in the diocese, Archdeacon Watkins.[18] In as small and isolated a society as Perth, such a limited range of strong figures among its clergy did not augur well for the future. The fact that Goldsmith had been the only likely candidate for election may have caused some unconscious tension. The two men were born within a year of one another, and it made it all the easier for them to consider each other as rivals.

However, Goldsmith's churchmanship was an unconscious irritant to a basic element of Riley's personality. The bishop was generally regarded as a muscular Christian: his bluff and uncompromising manner earned him respect in circles outside the church, but intimidated his clergy so much that close friends such as Sir Winthrop Hackett and Bishop Harmer of Adelaide cautioned him to soften his approach.[19] But the rugged exterior was to some extent a mask that hid a deep-seated self-questioning and insecurity. He gave vent to this in a series of entries in his diary in 1897, shortly before his return to England for the first time after his election. These extracts are unparalleled in the private writing of an Australian church leader of the period and have few equivalents in the writings of secular politicians. He was so overcome by stress when he wrote the first of these entries as to be unable to write legibly:

The Most Reverend C. O. L. Riley
The bluff northern English exterior that masked deep insecurity

21 March: (Esperance)
I have completely lost powers of speaking—The words come but I do not feel any virtue go out of me and so none can reach others. Somehow I do not <u>draw</u> people.

I am out of joint physically. perfectly lazy.
                morally. —perfectly fleshly
                mentally. perfectly feeble
                unable to think deeply.

Spiritually—dead—hold on Faith. I seem terribly weak and despondent . . . I seem a failure all round and even fear and dread going home—that too after all my looking forward should be a failure too.

I must try to pull myself together. I am becoming very ignorant—never read anything but a light novel now and again—(illegible) so sad. Everything turns out wrong.

10 May: Did not feel well enough to do anything—refused to have anything to do with transports and am becoming very selfish and grumpy in old age but now I have nothing to do have quite collapsed. Only fit to read and eat.

12 May: Had a better night. Rheumatism. Better a little. Must try to do a little work. It is hopeless wasting others[?] time chatting about nothing. I wish I had the faculty of drawing out men to tell me about their work etc. Some people seem afraid of me—most do in fact until they know me—is my character becoming impressed on my face?

26 May Birthday 43 *vide* Byron at 33
It wd. hardly do for me to put down where I am in fact I cdnt. Ones beliefs change so. Things wh. used to be difficult are now easy. Things wh. did not trouble me—now are difficulties.[20]

Unfortunately, this otherwise intimate sequence does not tell us precisely what it was that provoked Riley into this frenzy of self-revelation. However, his view of himself as an old, ignorant, bearish man, who either lacked faith or was exchanging once firmly held tenets of belief for others, is in stark contrast to at least two aspects of Goldsmith as others perceived him. Riley himself later described Goldsmith as the only theologically educated priest in the colony.[21] Most of all, the possibility here privately admitted by Riley that belief and action were centred on a hierarchy of truths whose content and order could change with time, was quite different from Goldsmith's confident public presentation of the Catholic faith as a clearly defined body of unchanging truths.

Doubt, and a desire to establish an authority for belief in the face of increasing questioning, were issues central to nineteenth-century Anglicanism, as were questions of authority for European society in general. The new orders being evolved in infant colonies threw them into heightened relief there as well. That a Catholic position could be used to answer or silence such self-doubts and agonizing as Riley expressed was one of its attractions, at least as many understood it. That he could not embrace such a position may have done more than simply make expressions of Anglo-Catholicism frustrating to Riley. The confidence they seemed to represent may well have stirred the sense of inadequacy he expressed in 1897 in his diary; they threatened something that was supposed to be hidden beneath the mask of muscular confidence.

In his correspondence and diary Riley certainly expressed a personal distaste for ceremonial, suggesting to Harry Darling, who had recently arrived from Ireland and was incumbent of St Paul's Bunbury, that the significance of certain ceremonies as party signs might be neutralized, not by their prohibition, but by their use by all the clergy.[22] So anti-ritualists did not see Riley as an unequivocal ally. Their complaints about his apparent lack of action, and his own responses in public and private, form another example of the way in which Western Australian Anglicanism reflected contemporary developments in its English parent and also throws into relief some of the elements in the Australian situation that differentiated it sharply from the English one.

By the 1890s English opponents of Anglo-Catholicism regarded the Public Worship Regulation Act as ineffective. They believed that, if anything, the bishops had contributed by using their right under the Act to veto prosecutions. Criticism of the bishops accompanied moves to introduce new and more effective legislation: hostile speakers said that the laity had lost their faith in the bishops.[23] For their own part, the bishops' exercise of the veto grew out of their desire to solve ecclesiastical matters without recourse to civil courts. The trial of Bishop King was a significant point in this process.[24] Machin suggests that a slowing in the growth of Anglo-Catholicism at the turn of the century was due not to a resurgence of Protestant feeling, but to the success with which the bishops were conducting out-of-court dialogue with Anglo-Catholic clergy.[25]

In Perth, 'Prominent Churchman' criticized Riley in the belief that, on legal grounds, he was able, and obliged, to discipline Anglo-Catholics. He wrote of confession: 'I strongly denounced the practice, and said that it ought to be put a stop to'. He stopped short of accusing Riley of condoning the actions of the ritualists, instead suggesting that he 'appears to be too weak to put a stop to them'.[26] After Riley made his public response, 'Apocalypse' reiterated 'Prominent Churchman's' claims of weakness. According to him, the bishop, far from maintaining reformation standards, actually condoned the undermining of them by Anglo-Catholics: he was aware of the confessional in the Kalgoorlie church; he tolerated altars in Perth's churches; and despite his claim that occasional confession was acceptable, he knew that the hearing of confessions in any circumstance contravened the 39 Articles. Thus Riley himself was a lawbreaker.[27] While these two writers accused the bishop of weakness or complicity, James Cowan wrote in a more temperate vein, but still expressed dissatisfaction at the bishop's responses to his questions at synod in 1899 and 1900 concerning the distribution of Anglo-Catholic devotional and doctrinal material.[28]

'Prominent Churchman's' interpretation of the legal situation was the most interesting. He wrote that the dean's recent motions proposing a change in the name of the church in Australia were part of 'an effort to take the church out of the jurisdiction of York and Canterbury, so that the priest might be free to carry on their ritualistic practices without interference from the church authorities in England'.[29] 'Prominent Churchman' seems to have believed that legal restraints applicable in England were also effective in Australia—or would be, but for the failure to apply them. And he assumed that it was English ecclesiastical law, rather than English civil law, that could be used to contain Anglo-Catholicism in Western Australia. 'Apocalypse' was equally under the impression that, at the last resort, some kind of legislation—he did not specify its exact nature—could be, and needed to be, used in Australia to deal with Anglo-Catholicism.[30]

The sheer complexity of the legal scene in England was of some advantage to Anglo-Catholics. The increasing number of conflicting judgements issued by different authorities offered them the possibility of invoking those portions of judgements which were in their favour as a defence, while ignoring others.[31] In Australia the legal situation could work in their favour, but for different reasons. The Australian bench of bishops was uncertain of the status of English canon law in Australia. A variety of motions in General Synod between 1880 and 1910 reveals the degree of confusion; some assumed that English canon law automatically extended to Australia, some suggested that it did not, while some were uncertain and sought clarity through a committee report.[32] In a letter to the Primate, Saumarez Smith, Riley confessed that he preferred not to invoke canon law himself, since ritualists used it to defend practices to which their bishops objected.[33] Uncertainty over the interpretation or status of canon law may have been behind his hesitancy to act over Goldsmith's introduction of vestments at the orphanage chapel. The legality of vestments depended on the interpretation of the Ornaments Rubric which at this time was both complex and unclear.[34] Hence his diary comment, after first seeing the offending vestments, that he anticipated that it would be difficult to restrain the Anglo-Catholicism of Goldsmith and Garland.

Like his English counterparts, Riley preferred to deal with alleged Anglo-Catholicism by discreet 'backrooming'. In defending Goldsmith over the allegations of enforced confession at the orphanage, he stated that, in order to remove any possibility of suspicion in the future, the dean had undertaken not to hear confessions at the orphanage, even if they were voluntary ones. Riley may well have made this undertaking by Goldsmith as a condition of the public defence: still, however the agreement was reached, to a certain extent it contained the issue within the church. Ultimately Riley did not see the putting down of ritualism as part of his function. As well as his privately expressed view that a city the size of Perth should cater for Anglicans of different churchmanship, he publicly articulated an understanding of the bishop as a moderator, not an inhibitor. In 1898, a year in which the Perth press carried a long sequence of correspondence on Anglo-Catholicism, and where there was renewed unrest in England, he said: 'With regard to ritual, I desire to permit the greatest liberty of thought and expression of devotion, having due regard to the lawful limits which must not be exceeded by one side or another . . .' He made a similar statement in 1900 in response to the allegations of illegal practices.[35]

This point of view was unlikely to endear him to Anglo-Catholics wishing their position to be endorsed as the model for the rest of the church. Certainly, it did not fit in with the triumphalism of priests such as Goldsmith's brother-in-law. To opponents seeking repression, it appeared either as a betrayal of reformation principles or a sign of weakness. But it was consistent with the approach of more and more English bishops. The course of events in England showed that even in a society where the church was established, recourse to civil law to solve ecclesiastical disputes was increasingly unproductive. And in Australia, where the church was not established, the bishop had an even greater burden of responsibility as a mediator, because those dissatisfied with episcopal decisions would rarely find any further authority to which to appeal— only by writing to the press could they express not merely their sense of grievance but their frustration that more could not be done.[36] The bishop was likely to bear the brunt of the complaints of those who continued to be aggrieved by his decision, and lay people were more likely than clergy to register discontent over episcopal decisions—their salaries did not come direct from a diocesan office, as did those of the diocesan clergy. It is perhaps fortunate that, in this apparently invidious position, Riley gauged the needs and mood of Perth Anglicans more accurately than did the opponents of Anglo-Catholicism. Despite their complaints, there were no further pronounced attacks on the followers of the Oxford Movement in the Western Australian press after the episode at the end of 1900.

The figures for attendances at the cathedral, and at other Perth centres in the years 1888–1904, are not complete in all respects, those of St Alban's Highgate being the most complete and consistently preserved. These figures reveal something of the context not only of the press hostility to ritualism, but of the conservative suspicions held by the older settlers, suspicions that partly motivated that hostility. In the light of the dispute over Marshall's supposed Anglo-Catholicism in Bunbury, it is unfortunate that no communicant registers survive from his time there.

Communicant figures reveal that the least impact was in the observance of the Lenten cycle and of saints' days. Celebrations of saints' days at the cathedral, although consistently held, attracted very small numbers of communicants. Ash Wednesday fared marginally better, but the communicant figures for Palm Sunday hardly suggest that Holy Week was marked by cathedral Anglicans as a significant feast in their calendar. At St John's, red-letter saints' days were only inconsistently observed. At St Alban's, in 1898, F. J. Price succeeded in establishing a daily eucharist in Lent, but the average number of communicants was small—five. It was probably this pattern of non-observance of holy days in general that doomed Goldsmith's attempt to secure a place for All Souls' day in the cathedral calendar, as much as any resistance to prayer for the departed.

At St John's Melbourne Road, the average figure for Sunday communicants each year remained low and the Sunday communicants were a small number compared with the total number of communicants on the parish roll, for those years when the latter figure is known. This may well reflect something of the 'ancient colonists' and their rearing in a pattern of infrequent communion—the area served by West Perth was surrounded by the homes of the well-to-do. It is unfortunate that there is no record of the numbers at non-eucharistic services, which one would expect to have been particularly well attended, given the occasional hints that St John's appealed to those who regarded the cathedral as being too 'high'.

Of all the centres that became independent parishes as a result of the subdivision of the cathedral parish, the one that shows the most remarkable service record is St Alban's, something that is all the more significant because its first rector, F. J. Price, was regarded as being as much an Anglo-Catholic as Goldsmith. Its figures present a record of a steady rise each year until 1900, in acts of communion, in averages for Sunday communicants and in Christmas and Easter communions. These generally steady increases do not in themselves constitute proof of a deep commitment to Anglo-Catholic doctrine. At the time English analysts who sought to explain the success of some Anglo-Catholic clergy were inclined to see attendances, especially by working-class worshippers, as a sign of personal respect for individual clergy. The support that Riley and Forrest gave Price during his lawsuit against the *Sunday Times* certainly indicates that Price commanded respect. Highgate's attendances may be a tribute to his own popularity, as well as reflecting the growth of the area north of the city. However the rising attendances there are to be explained, they contradict anti-ritualist claims of a falling-off among worshippers.

The cathedral's figures also offer a similar qualification to anti-ritualist claims. According to Goldsmith at Easter 1893, the total number of acts of communion in the previous year had risen by 44 per cent compared with the 1891–92 figures. At Easter 1896 he compared the Easter communion figures with those of the previous year, noted an increase of 20 per cent, and a further increase of 66 per cent on the figure for Easter four years previously. Such rises certainly suggest that, to the cross-section of Anglicans for whom their Easter communion remained a badge of affiliation, the cathedral's churchmanship did not act as a significant deterrent. But to balance such figures, the cathedral's average of Sunday communicants each year remained a comparatively low proportion of the total number of communicants on its roll (for the years for which this is known), and to that extent indicates the slow progress of the Oxford Movement in changing people's general pattern of communicating.

During a period of almost three years after Goldsmith's arrival there was a decline in the average of Sunday communicants. This may reflect the native-born Western Australian's suspicion of Goldsmith's churchmanship. The general rise in communicant figures after 1894 was marked by a sudden drop in the period 1898–99, but between 1900 and 1904, the figures began to rise again. The sharpest falls were between Christmas 1898 (384) and 1899 (298), and Easter 1899 (419) and 1900 (306). Disputes about churchmanship do not entirely explain this variation. Instead, it spans the period when St John's Melbourne Road, and the two centres closest to the cathedral on its west, St Mary's and St Paul's, became independent parishes. The number on the communicant roll for these last two parishes, provided in the *Statistical Register of the Colony of Western Australia*, sufficiently accounts for the fall in communicants at the cathedral, since these three parishes encompassed a significant section of the fashionable end of Perth, whose comfortable middle-class inhabitants would earlier have naturally looked to the cathedral.

Nor did the decline, in the Christmas and Easter attendances at the cathedral, coincide with outbursts in the press over churchmanship: the highest figure for communicants at Christmas came at the end of 1898, the year that saw the longest correspondence over Anglo-Catholicism in the *West Australian*, and after the predictable fall after the creation of three independent parishes in one year, the figures began to rise again, notwithstanding the outburst over confession which the *Morning Herald* fuelled in 1900–01.

In spite of the suggestion of Hillman and others that a sung liturgy was a sign of an undesirable churchmanship, the attendance figures for the sung eucharists at St Alban's and at the cathedral hardly indicate a progressive falling away. The Christmas sung eucharist of 1898 was a particular highlight, and its high attendance figure was probably as much a response to the unusual musical setting used on that occasion— Gounod's *Messe Solennelle*. It is perhaps these figures which, more than any other, provide a clue in understanding why the attitudes of a conservative native-born Anglicanism finally did not prevail. The figures for attendance at sung eucharists at St Alban's generally show an increase until the beginning of the present century. The cathedral pattern is interesting in that it shows a marked change in attitudes to the sung eucharist in the middle of the decade. Before 1895 the highest numbers of communicants at Christmas were found at said, not sung, celebrations; at Easter there was less noticeable difference between the said celebration with the highest number of communicants and the communicant numbers for the sung eucharist, but the said celebrations still had marginally higher figures, with the exception of 1894, when the contrast was dramatic—188 at a said celebration, compared with 47 at the sung eucharist. But from 1897 the sung celebration became the one that always had the highest number of communicants.

The communicant records for Sundays display the same pattern, only the change took place slightly more slowly. Until 1895, on a Sunday with a sung celebration, the number of communicants at the sung eucharist was almost half the number at a said celebration that day for a significant number of occasions each year (between a third and half of the Sundays when there was a sung celebration). Between 1895 and 1901 the discrepancy between communicant numbers at sung celebrations and at said celebrations became negligible, except in 1899, when there was a reversion to the pre-1895 pattern. In 1902 the sung celebration became the one which consistently maintained the highest number of communicants on the Sundays when it was held.

When Sir John Forrest commented to Riley that it would be desirable to replace Goldsmith with a different kind of churchman, he was acting as an unofficial spokesman of many native-born Western Australians who had entrenched suspicions of Goldsmith's churchmanship. Yet, despite these suspicions, the sung eucharist became increasingly accepted, especially as Perth's population grew because of gold rush immigration.[37] The newcomers—whether from England or from other parts of Australia—were more willing than local Anglicans to adapt to changes in styles of worship. However, the late nineteenth-century revival of choral music, sacred and secular, meant that liturgical singing could no longer be considered as an issue of churchmanship alone.[38] The preference of Perth's newer population of Anglican communicants reflects this, rather than a sudden injection of men and women with a commitment to Anglo-Catholic theology and ritual—though these came as well. One such was Edward Myerson, who came to Perth from New South Wales. He corresponded in defence of Anglo-Catholicism in 1898, but elsewhere expressed a preference for Gregorian chant as the basic staple for the cathedral's music, a preference which was then distinctly advanced. When the Sisters of the Church came to Perth, he became a regular supporter of their work.[39]

The attacks on what Perth critics perceived as Anglo-Catholicism did not go unanswered, and these sympathetic responses invite the further consideration of the reasons for, and extent of, the influence it wielded, in spite of the fierce criticism it encountered.

Apologists, as much as critics, backed their arguments with illustrations from the English experience which did not always have precise current parallels within Australia. The most obvious appeal of this kind was to the mystique that already surrounded Anglo-Catholic slum priests such as Charles Lowder of St George's-in-the-East, A. H. Stanton and A. H. Mackonochie of St Alban's Holborn, and Robert Dolling of Portsmouth. A small body of clergy inspired by them was only beginning to emerge in Australia in this decade. Conspicuous among them were E. M. Collick on the Western Australian goldfields and E. S. Hughes of

Melbourne, who sought to establish a mission in the Melbourne suburb of Fitzroy modelled in part on the 'settlement' run by the Oxford Mission in the parish of St Matthew's Bethnall Green. As curate at St Peter's Eastern Hill, he was also involved in a Melbourne branch of the modestly socialist organization, the Christian Social Union.[40]

Although at this time Perth did not have Anglican clergy of its own in this mould, some of its Anglicans were aware of their existence, and of the way in which the Anglo-Catholic movement was giving them an almost canonized status. The front page of the *West Australian Church News* sometimes carried a portrait of an English ritualist slum priest.[41] Its editor, D. J. Garland, was also in touch with other clergy who were inspired by them. He visited St Peter's Eastern Hill, became friendly with Hughes, and later praised that parish's outreach to the working classes.[42]

A Perth correspondent, who described his own churchmanship as moderate, replied in 1898 to the criticisms of Wheatley the Wesleyan in 'Ritualistic Bats and Moles' that those English churches with an advanced ceremonial such as St Alban's Holborn had a high level of social involvement. Slightly earlier, another correspondent who signed himself 'A Church of England Working Man' did not refer to specific English churches or clergy, but asked 'who is it that has gone out into the highways and byways of faith and disease but the so-called high church party . . .' and went on to claim that its clergy had 'held up the man of sorrows to struggling humanity'.[43]

The factors which helped to create the setting in which the Anglo-Catholic mission priest flourished were less apparent in Australian cities, least of all in Perth, which had nothing resembling the east of London's slums. But despite the absence of wealth and poverty known in England, and although the worst slums of its cities did not compare with a parish such as London's St George's-in-the-East, the myth of the slum mission priest who communicated effectively with the working classes was still invoked in Western Australia by the supporters of Anglo-Catholicism. Not only did it reflect the mythical status achieved by such figures; it represented one answer to the question as to what Anglicanism was doing for the working classes and the poor. It showed Anglo-Catholics grappling with the problems of contemporary society and, as such, was a counter to the claim that they were simply a group of reactionaries and antiquarians.

Both clergy under attack and correspondents defending them were quick to argue that their actions or doctrines were legal. As has already been pointed out, some of those who used this line of argument misunderstood the status of English canon and statute law in the colony; others privately or publicly seemed rather uncertain about it. Concepts of race underlay the arguments concerning legality brought forward by both opponents and supporters of Anglo-Catholicism in Perth. While opponents hinted that, by being devious, the clergy were failing a national ideal of truthfulness and their standing as gentlemen, F. J. Price presented a defence which sidestepped this suggestion. Responding in a sermon to the allegations made by Wheatley concerning the nature of Anglo-Catholicism he stated that, far from being an imitation of anything Roman, his own practice was simply undertaken in obedience to ecclesiastical law. A correspondent earlier that year had attacked the 'Protestants' in the Church of England as the real lawbreakers. They had failed to keep their churches open, offer the eucharist on all occasions prescribed by the Prayer Book, and hear confessions in accordance with the Communion Exhortation and the rubrics in the Visitation of the Sick. By signing himself 'Catholicus Anglicanus', he implied that the Anglo-Catholicism under attack was both truly English and therefore lawful. As for his opponents, they were not only lawbreakers, they were also unrepresentative of the true Englishman.[44]

But beyond the added issue of race and culture, and the assumption that English law of various kinds applied in Australia, the debate concerning Anglo-Catholicism in the Western Australian press showed that, in a broader sense than is suggested by the above comments, the concepts of lawfulness and authority had considerable significance. In 1899, when attempts to attack D. J. Garland and the Church Book Depot had failed, a terse comment in the *West Australian Church News* referred to charges of lawlessness 'from those who break almost every rubric in the Prayer Book themselves'. From the pulpit, Goldsmith defended his practices and teaching by an appeal to their lawfulness. A Roman Catholic correspondent referred to a sermon which he had recently heard

Goldsmith preach, in which the dean confessed his failure on a number of past occasions to observe some Prayer Book rubrics, when obedience to the rubrics was to be expected of him. In the same vein, in the debate over confession at the end of 1900, Goldsmith argued from the pulpit that the Prayer Book obliged him to hear confessions.[45]

While each side in this debate generally failed to acknowledge that the Prayer Book was a document that might be interpreted in more than one way, they both argued from positions which assumed a respect for authority and law. Owen Chadwick suggests that this in turn was part of a more general desire to identify and obey lawful authority, a theme which was a strong element in the Oxford Movement itself, but was also a concern which extended well beyond the church in the nineteenth century.[46] The search for authority certainly lay behind the Tractarian emphasis on the doctrine of apostolic succession, whose rejection by the critics of Anglo-Catholicism is noted elsewhere.[47] And in Western Australia, as elsewhere, people of all ranks still sought a Christian basis of authority, though individually they came to different conclusions. This quest was expressed by C. O. L. Riley in the 1897 diary entries, as he found that the hierarchy of truths which he once held was changing. An unidentified hearer of Goldsmith in 1898 had also been moved by the same drive to find a stable authority, though he came to a different conclusion from Riley or Goldsmith as to where it lay. He wrote to the press that he had forsaken the Anglicanism of his birth for Roman Catholicism because it persisted unchanging, 'the same yesterday, today and forever', and would persist in an undiminished vigour in the future, even when Anglican symbols of stability had collapsed and New Zealanders were sketching the ruins of St Paul's Cathedral from a broken arch of London Bridge.[48]

And in the future, Goldsmith himself was to continue to appeal to the need for order backed by lawful authority. The situations in which he would do this ranged from his claim that he wore cope and mitre because he was legally obliged to do so, to his address to the newly elected Bunbury town council in 1912, in which he envisaged the church as the source of order for the whole of society.[49]

Despite the criticism that Anglo-Catholicism was theatrical in character and appealed purely to the emotions and the senses, a number of contemporary statements also indicate that the restrained ceremonial which Goldsmith used in St George's cathedral succeeded in articulating standards of dignity and reverence which were acceptable as such, rather than as an expression of a particular churchmanship. Though Hillman had written scornfully in 1882 of the veiling of female confirmees, a correspondent only six years later could write of another confirmation: 'all present seemed to feel the influence of this solemn and impressive rite'. After describing the decoration of the cathedral, as well as its services at Christmas in 1892, another columnist commented, 'the idea of worship was prominent throughout'. If solemnity was an attitude which Victorians generally considered as being conducive to religious devotion, so was formality, and both were important ingredients in Victorian public life. Anglo-Catholics understood ceremonial of varying degrees to be an appropriate way of expressing the transcendance of God and preserving the worshipper from the dangers of a carelessly familiar mode of approach. In civil ceremony, formality dramatized the (ideal) social order. Perth people also regarded it as appropriate for a cathedral church as the seat of a bishop, quite apart from any questions of churchmanship: a columnist wrote approvingly of the 'imposing . . . pomp and circumstance' of the enthronement of C. O. L. Riley in the new cathedral, compared with the simplicity of Bishop Parry's in the old.[50]

Although some opponents of Anglo-Catholicism had contrasted its indulgence to emotionalism with the supposedly sober and restrained character of classical Anglican worship, others in Perth appear to have identified such sobriety and restraint with dullness. 'V. M.' referred to the 'hum drum style of church going' of 'the Protestants' at the cathedral in 1893 and the slowness of services as one of the principal reasons for unsatisfactory attendances.[51] For other writers, the characteristics which made a Christmas carol service acceptable included 'brightness', and it was the dean's attempts to 'make the worship of God a pleasure' which made 'Justice' defend him from the accusations by 'the old fogies' that they were being led to Rome.[52] 'Justice' commented that in order to attract a congregation 'the church nowadays must have an attractive service, one of the essentials of which is a good choir and good music, in fact a service that cheers'.[53] Not long after this comment, the troubled rector of Bunbury, W. F. Marshall, was defended by a correspondent who commented that it was the demands for a more attractive form of worship made by Anglicans themselves that led to the accusations of ritualism: 'they are so hard to get at and always craving for something new that the clergy are tempted to copy Rome who places her religion in so attractive a form before her people . . .'[54]

There is nothing to indicate that the writers of these comments identified themselves with Goldsmith's particular churchmanship. Behind the support for the cathedral services there were broader issues than this: feelings of reverence, approval of formality and a desire for high standards of music. These went beyond even the common Anglican tradition of comprehensiveness, to include ideals and qualities acknowledged and upheld by the Victorians at large. That there was this consensus is confirmed by the increasing attendances at the sung eucharists at Christmas and Easter, the very days when, by Goldsmith's own admission, 'many people go to church who seldom or never go at all',[55] the class of Anglican who had little personal involvement in churchmanship debates. To them, the mild ceremonial and sung eucharist of the cathedral was not perceived as offensively 'high', but as an acceptable expression of reverence.

But neither was their continuing presence on such days a sign of a general endorsement of Anglo-Catholic values. The low attendance figures at eucharists on saints' days and on a number of other occasions during the year and, in particular, the intensity of the debate concerning confession, both show that the more distinctive devotional and doctrinal attitudes of Anglo-Catholicism were not widely accepted or received without challenge. When the bitter correspondence, and the attacks by Hackett and the old colonist interests through the press, failed to dislodge Goldsmith and others like him from their positions, it was not so much because they had underestimated the Protestant strength in Western Australia's Anglicanism, but because the wider emphases of the Oxford Movement were in harmony with (and to some extent proceeded from) more widely accepted values.

Owen Chadwick has suggested that, in England, the increasingly rich decorative styles of Victorian churches reflected the increased material wealth generated by British empire trade.[56] To that extent, the richer setting of Perth's new cathedral, lending itself to a greater degree of ceremonial, was also a reflection of a taste for a less restrained style, having the increased wealth of the Perth community as a base as much as a commitment to a particular doctrinal tendency.

That the laity sought some degree of enrichment in symbolism and ceremonial is demonstrated by the presentation of a pastoral staff to Riley in 1898.[57] As early as 1891 a correspondent had asked why a staff should not be presented to Bishop Parry, when they were already used by Anglican bishops in England and America.[58] The staff was a symbol of a role rather than a doctrine (though it ultimately echoes the heightened emphasis placed on the episcopal office by the Oxford Movement), but the laity's desire that Riley should also be seen, staff in hand, points to the general acceptability of some increase in ceremonial and symbol.

Western Australian Anglicans certainly did not regard quasi-religious ceremonial as such as anathema: Anglicans of varying schools of churchmanship, including Bishop Riley and the dean, were strongly involved in the masonic community.[59] A Melbourne priest visiting Western Australia at the beginning of the century commented that Goldsmith and Riley were generally to be found at all major masonic functions. Later, as a bishop, Goldsmith was warmly welcomed by masonic groups in remote places, and on at least one occasion laid a church foundation stone with masonic ceremonies.[60] Nor was his involvement in the masonic community exceptional as far as his Anglo-Catholicism was concerned: Oliver Feetham of North Queensland, another definitely Anglo-Catholic prelate, was both a mason and an Oddfellow. The explicit rejection of masonry, more typical of a later generation of Anglo-Catholics, does not appear to have existed until after World War I.

There were also those who positively sought symbol and ceremony within worship because they were consciously committed to Anglo-Catholicism. While the anti-ritualists portrayed the Anglo-Catholic movement as a clerical conspiracy to which the laity were opposed, Riley's 1898 synod charge painted a more complex picture. As he defended his clergy, he stated that most who were accused of 'lawlessness' were acting within the framework of canon law, but added, 'it is quite as often, if not more often, the laity who urge on the Clergy to greater and greater ritual observance'. Along with the responses in correspondence by members of the laity defending Anglo-Catholic attitudes, Riley's statement acknowledges a degree of lay support for an increased ceremonial and for the Anglo-Catholic doctrine, and corrects the picture of an exclusively clerical high church plot, foisted on an unwilling laity.

While some of the most vocal critics of Anglo-Catholicism in the press were Western Australians of long standing such as the Stones and Forrests, E. R. Parker (born 1820, arrived 1830, died 1905) and James Cowan (1848–1937) who was connected with the Wittenoom family, Goldsmith received support from members of other significant families such as the Burts and the Lefroys.

Though Western Australians were not slow to blame the increased population brought by the gold rush for any changes they deemed to be undesirable, such as an 'epidemic' of property-related crime in 1896,[61] the new arrivals also had an impact on the life of the colony's churches. Among Anglicans who went west were men and women who were familiar with the influence of the Oxford Movement in the centres from which they came, and they added to the number of those prepared to accept or actively support its influence.

From the goldfields James Young, a former parishioner of St Peter's Eastern Hill, wrote delightedly to his Melbourne friends that at Coolgardie, under E. M. Collick, 'the service is as high in tone as circumstances will permit. At any rate, we have one point not in use at St Peter's when I left, i.e. altar lights . . . We have just started a surpliced choir, and hope soon to be able to render a full service . . .'[62] The choir of one of the most advanced churches in Sydney, Christ Church St Laurence, as well as that of St Peter's in Melbourne, was decimated by the Western Australian gold rush.[63] H. Pitts, once a curate of Goldsmith's in Perth, noted that Whitsunday at Marble Bar in 1901 was marked by one of the heartiest services he had ever celebrated in the north-west, the singing of his congregation being sustained by 'several old Perth and Melbourne men'. Later that same year, he described services on the first Sunday in Advent held at the Marble Bar Miners' Institute. Five men attended an early morning eucharist, but thirty came to Evensong; 'Mr. B . . . having lent his piano the service was very enjoyable. The chants were taken to Gregorian tones and the usual Advent hymns sung'.[64] Given that Gregorian chant was hardly common in Anglican churches anywhere in

Australia, Pitts had among his Marble Bar miners a handful of enthusiastic men who were already familiar with an Anglo-Catholic church.

The manager of the Church Book Depot, George Kidson, was another former parishioner of St Peter's Eastern Hill: in 1896 he was secretary of its men's club.[65] His later statement that the opponents of Anglo-Catholicism in Perth generally relied on descriptions of services of a kind not conducted anywhere in the country was accurate, because it sprang from his experience of the Oxford Movement on both sides of the continent. The cathedral's verger at the turn of the century, Albert Tarr, was also a new arrival from another centre where the Oxford Movement exerted a discernible if restrained influence, St David's cathedral in Hobart.[66]

In the domain of nationalism, which will be explored at greater length in the next chapter, the terminology used in the correspondence in the Perth press was certainly indicative of the extent to which the Western Australian population still regarded itself as English both in origin and identity. This is as true of those who signed themselves with such sobriquets as 'Catholicus Anglicanus' as it was of those who argued that their heritage as Englishmen was the liberty that had been won through the 'Glorious Reformation'.

But above all else, the debate over Anglo-Catholicism showed the extent to which sectarian bitterness continued to pervade the Western Australian community. In a colony in which the Anglican church had never enjoyed the priveleges which religious establishment brought to it in England, the vigour with which the nonconformist clergy, principally Congregationalist and Wesleyan, joined in the attack, demonstrated that the absence of privilege did not mean increased tolerance. Memories of their English experience could still be a driving force, something which was noted at the time with some puzzlement elsewhere by Australian Anglicans, who observed that the supposed equality of the denominations in the eyes of the state had produced the opposite effect from the anticipated one.

For Anglicans, too, the absence of establishment played an important role in the ongoing liveliness of the debate after the abolition of state aid in 1896. Opponents of Anglo-Catholicism in England still believed that the established status of Anglicanism offered the possibility of controlling ritualism: the problem was that those in authority refused to use the existing controls. In Western Australia a strident anti-ritualist critic commented that it was establishment that had enabled Anglicans of different churchmanship to subsist alongside one another in England until recently—the control which establishment implied meant that some degree of peace had been kept. But if establishment were a necessary mechanism for the containment of Anglo-Catholicism, its absence might signifiy the possibility of anarchy. Such a fear charactcrizes the apocalyptic tone of some of the Western Australian correspondence.

The largely working-class identity of Roman Catholicism in Australia, and especially its identification with the Irish community, was a complicating factor. In Australia, in the absence of a Roman Catholic gentry, such as had persisted in England (despite its impoverishment), sectarian divisions corresponded to a large extent with class ones. In the eyes of the opponents of ritualism in Australia, a 'Romanizing' of the Church of England would give it some resemblance to the church most of all associated with the working classes. It would form at once a betrayal of class and nationality as well as of religion. It is a tribute to the extent to which the opponents of Anglo-Catholicism were dependent on the images and terminology of their English counterparts that they generally pictured Roman Catholics as continental Europeans, and not as Irish—though, at the time of the debate, there were few of the former in Australia. In Western Australia the significant contribution of Winthrop Hackett shows how much the tensions of Ireland were a contributing factor. Elsewhere, in equivalent Melbourne debates, a leading role was likewise played by another individual with strong Northern Irish connections, Digby Berry. The occasional hostile correspondent would also invoke imagery which drew on Ireland's political and religious situation.

And although the opponents of Anglo-Catholicism relied heavily on their English conterparts for their imagery and their arguments—they were almost totally derivative in this regard—the colonial situation could still give such arguments a new edge. The recently created colonies were well aware that they depended on the well-being of the total system for their survival. To those who believed that the commercial wealth of Britain grew out of her Protestantism, Anglo-Catholicism was a threat to the colonies in their reliance on British prosperity. This element of anti-ritualist polemic could transplant well from Britain and take good root in colonial soil.

However, the controversy over confession in 1900 was the last such extended attack on Anglo-Catholicism in the Western Australian press. The ensuing silence is partly explained by the absence in Perth of other controversial aspects of Anglo-Catholicism which began to appear in Adelaide, Melbourne and Sydney between 1890 and 1910. But it was also a sign of some level of acceptance of the Oxford Movement, prompted in part by the degree to which it reflected more widely accepted values. The population growth caused by the gold rush had also brought with it new supporters of the Oxford Movement, modifying the influence of the ancient colonists and other critics. The way was also opening for the episcopal bench to reflect the influence of the Oxford Movement more and more, and Goldsmith's election to Bunbury in 1904 was the most obvious sign of this in Western Australia.

— SEVEN —

# Nationalism, Autonomy and Churchmanship: Perth Synod 1899 and General Synod 1900

In 1899, in the Perth diocesan synod, and in 1900, in General Synod, Goldsmith introduced motions proposing an alteration to the title of the Anglican church in Australia, then known as the Church of England in Australia and Tasmania. Though verbatim reports of the General Synod debates over this proposal have not survived, some of the sources quoted below indicate that several titles were proposed. Some described it as a province; other references to the need to avoid confusion with Charles Strong's Australian Church, formed after his expulsion from the Presbyterian Church of Victoria, are evidence of the proposals that stressed the national adjective; and the comment of R. P. Dodd shows that at least one alternative was a compound containing the term Catholic. Such a compound was still being urged from some quarters later in the decade: in 1909, at the Church Congress held in Perth, Archdeacon Crossley of Melbourne urged the title 'The Holy Catholic and Apostolic Church of Australia or Australasia'.[1]

If Goldsmith's churchmanship already seemed to be a radical kind of commitment, there were those who saw this new and different engagement as little short of revolutionary. In Perth in 1899 the rector of Guildford thought it incongruous that Goldsmith, an Englishman, should be urging a case on the grounds of Australian nationalism: 'had the motion been moved by an Australian it would have been considered revolutionary'.[2] Though Goldsmith argued that his motions should be supported on the grounds of nationalism, the ensuing debates and voting show that support did not generally correspond with Australian birth, or opposition with British origins: imperialist sentiment played an important role in their failure. Many of his opponents identified his case as a challenge to an understanding of the Church of England and the empire as integral to one another. The debates in Perth and Sydney therefore provided significant evidence of national, as well as Anglican, self-understanding in Australia at the time. But churchmanship also underlay support and opposition to Goldsmith's motions. The more pronounced churchmanship divisions in the discussion of proposals for a constitution for the Church of England in Australia, which took place before World War I, were foreshadowed in these earlier debates. They are significant, not only as evidence of the existence of such divisions at a slightly earlier time, but they also help us to see more clearly the way in which churchmanship was interwoven with issues of national and cultural identity.

In this chapter the arguments put forward in 1899 and 1900 will be examined in relation to the voting patterns and national origins of clergy and laity. We will then look at the underlying currents of churchmanship, allowing us to make a further examination of the part played in the debate by nationalist and imperialist sentiments.

Goldsmith was not the first to regard the current title as inappropriate. Interestingly, earlier suggestions all seem to have been made by Anglicans identified as high churchmen, sympathetic to, or influenced by, the Oxford Movement—the New South Wales chief justice, Sir Alfred Stephen (1802–94), Bishop Short of Adelaide and A. E. Selwyn, dean of Newcastle (1823–99), who proposed a motion at General Synod in 1886.[3] But Goldsmith's motion was pursued with consistency, over a decade: it was finally repeated, in a modified form, at the General Synod of 1910.

Goldsmith's motion in the Perth synod in 1899 anticipated an identically worded resolution at General Synod the following year, and an analysis of the debate in Perth shows significant trends which recur at General Synod. The motion sought an alteration in the name and title of the church in Australia so as 'to identify it more closely . . . with the history, development and national life of this Continent; and to prevent it from seeming to future generations to be exotic in character and sentiment'.⁴ In the earlier Perth discussion, despite the seemingly nationalist tone of the motion itself, Goldsmith only appealed to 'the growing nationalist sentiment' as he concluded the speech in which he proposed it. He claimed that this sentiment would be obvious to new arrivals from England: they were invited 'to mark the symptoms around them of a self-contained nation and church'. An independent Australian church would 'form a home for millions of Christians in this great Continent', and become 'the spiritual home of the Australian people'.⁵

Despite Goldsmith's appeal to national sentiment, the debate did not proceed on such clear national lines. Though a higher percentage of the laity than the clergy were of Australian birth, they provided much of the opposition. At General Synod, on the second day of debate, only one layman spoke for the motion, compared with three laymen who spoke against it.⁶ On the other hand, some of the strongest supporters were clergy born and trained in England. While Melbourne and Sydney had a higher proportion of Australian born clergy than dioceses such as Perth, some dioceses had very few such men, largely because of social and educational factors.⁷ In Perth in the 1899 debate, D. J. Garland commented that only two of the diocesan clergy were born in Western Australia.⁸ Press reports at the time noted the contrast in the voting patterns of clergy and laity. The *Western Mail* gave the laity's vote as the reason for the failure of Goldsmith's motion at General Synod, but reported that the majority of bishops and clerical representatives voted in its favour.⁹ The *Church Times* was specific in noting the national origin of the clerical supporters: 'those of the clergy who specially favoured it were the ones who had come here from England'.¹⁰

The negligible number of Australian clergy in the Perth synod of 1899 makes it difficult to use it as evidence of trends among the Australian-born clergy. In commenting on the wider debate on autonomy, John Davis recently suggested that, generally speaking, Australian-born clergy may have been greater supporters of moves for an autonomous church than the laity, quoting the views of Stephen Hart as a young man at the Ballarat Church Congress in 1898.¹¹ However, Keith Rayner identified the leaders of the autonomy movement as the English-born clergy.¹² And the English involvement drew comment, as we have already seen from the response of the rector of Guildford. Puzzlement at

English clergy support for the autonomy movement was certainly expressed in later discussion: in 1912 the Governor of Tasmania could not comprehend any 'bishop of the English Church' supporting an autonomy movement.[13] The editor of the *Age* saw an ironic twist in Goldsmith's motion: despite any such change in title, the church itself would continue to be led by a hierarchy and clergy who were mainly English-born. The change of title was simply a meaningless cosmetic alteration.[14]

And there was certainly a gap between the emerging Australian identity, to which Goldsmith had appealed at the Perth synod, and the historical and cultural background of Anglicanism which he had promoted so far. In 1899 he asked, 'Was the name of Australia never to be an inspiration; were they never to have a history of their own in this Continent?'[15] His earlier references to the Church of England as the 'English' church, and to the early Christian history of England as 'our past history' in his 1888 synod sermon, were understandable enough from a man who had been in Australia for barely six months;[16] but even in his 1899 speech of proposal, he (perhaps unconsciously) revealed his own deeper continuing identification when he introduced a quotation of the opening words of *Magna Carta* with the phrase 'in our own national history'.[17] Not only early in his career in Perth, but in 1899, he treated early English history as the inheritance of Perth Anglicans in various lectures that he gave.[18] At a deeper level, the history of Australia was not yet his, however convenient a peg the nationalist sentiment might be on which to hang an appeal for an Australian Anglicanism.

In 1899 in Perth the rector of Guildford also expressed a counter-claim that recurred in other speeches, both there and in Sydney at General Synod the following year:

> He believed there was in the heart of every Australian born Churchman a strong sentiment clinging round the name of the Church of England just as dear to him as the name attached to his own colonial birth right. He did not suppose that if a referendum were taken the Australians today would support the name of the Church of England being changed to the name of the Australian Church.[19]

Two speakers in the Perth debate, one a layman, and another a cleric, referred to a negative response among laity in their parishes.

W. A. Murphy of St Paul's Carr Street, claimed that 'the majority of parishioners . . . viewed the proposition not only with the greatest repugnance, but with the greatest alarm . . .', while Everingham stated that members of the Guildford vestry were unanimous in rejecting the motion. These comments foreshadowed the pattern of voting in General Synod in the following year. And to that extent, despite the fact that committees and elected bodies are often notoriously unrepresentative, the General Synod vote reflected something of the mind of the wider Anglican community in Australia. Church papers which broadly supported Goldsmith's position attributed the motion's defeat to the 'lack of education on the part of the people', and a recognition of the laity's resistance seems to have been behind the comment that 'the time is not yet ripe for any decided move'.[20]

In the Perth synod, beyond the rallying cry of nationalism, Goldsmith gave considerably more space to argument on historical and theological grounds. Goldsmith argued that it was a scriptural principle, first enunciated in the New Testament epistles, and later expanded in many other documents of the patristic period, that churches were designated by a geographically appropriate local name. The custom was therefore both ancient ('primitive') and Catholic, two terms which invoked the authority bases appealed to by Tractarians and Anglo-Catholics in other debates.[21] As he invoked the past, Goldsmith appealed to those of a quite different churchmanship from his own. He quoted the opening words of *Magna Carta* as though it consciously sprang from a Victorian evolutionary view of the history of churches and nations. This was consistent with a largely Whig interpretation of English constitutional history, and contrasted with the Tractarian or Anglo-Catholic appeal to antiquity. He also appealed to a Protestant sensibility by stating that what he sought 'was really an assertion of the leading principle of the Reformation'.[22] He described the principle for which he argued as the opposite of 'aggressive Papal custom', whose 'policy of centralization was completely against the sufferance of local names', against which 'they should always contend'. When 'he hoped they always should be associated with the Reformation', he was greeted with a round of applause, and another round greeted his rejection of any attempts to treat the primacy of the Archbishop of Canterbury as a quasi-papacy: 'they wanted no second Pope in the world. They did not desire to have a papacy among them in any shape or form'.[23]

These grounds were neither unusual, nor original. The particular line of anti-papal polemic adopted—that Roman and papal were synonymous with innovative, and therefore the opposite of primitive and Catholic— had been a stock-in-trade of Anglican controversial writing since the sixteenth century. The use of anti-papal language to describe the relationship between the see of Canterbury and the wider Anglican communion was also not uncommon, and it resurfaced in part of the description of General Synod by the Australian correspondent of the *Church Times*, even though Goldsmith did not make a statement in this vein at General Synod.[24]

Another clerical supporter, Archdeacon Barton-Parkes, coupled an attack on the 'monstrous' way in which the Colonial Clergy Act of 1874 prevented Australian clergy from functioning in England with an approving reference to the 'good many' colonial bishops who had recently refused to take the oath of allegiance to the Archbishop of Canterbury 'on account of what they considered to be a papal system'.[25] When he immediately followed this denunciation of centralized ecclesiastical systems with the assertion that 'they were not a new race, but were for all practical purposes a nation within themselves', this combination of national independence and defiance of church centralization elicited yet another round of applause from his hearers.

Goldsmith appealed to a British, reformed heritage which was also regarded as Catholic, and to a concept of a national church based on episcopal authority. This latter was consistent with the understanding of episcopal authority promoted by the Tractarians and their successors, but Goldsmith did not spell out the ancestry or associations of his theology. Another cleric, C. E. C. Lefroy, who seconded his motion, presented arguments more visibly inspired by the Oxford Movement, and also referred to specific situations in which that movement had been influential. In doing so, he brought into the open one of the significant factors behind the autonomy movement—not the nationalism on to which Goldsmith latched, but churchmanship. Lefroy emphasized that it was desirable that the church should be free from any kind of state regulation of her internal life. He contrasted the legal independence of some other parts of the Anglican communion with the situation of the church in England, and clearly saw her established state as a source of limitations: 'at home she was still subject to State control. But many people at home were now working hard to get some freedom for the Church at home to govern and legislate for herself'.[26] His reference to those who were 'working hard to get some freedom' could refer to more than just Anglo-Catholics labouring under the threat of hostile legislation. The Lincoln Judgement and the increasing use by the bishops of their right to veto prosecutions under the Public Worship Regulation Act were equally part of this movement. Approval of some degree of state control was generally favoured by low churchmen. A very different attitude towards current movements in the English church was characteristic of Field Flowers Goe in Melbourne the previous year. He deprecated the cries in favour of disestablishment that were coming from some quarters in England, and blamed the Anglo-Catholics for provoking them.[27]

A different turn to this line of argument was provided by another high churchman, F. J. Price, the rector of Highgate. He suggested that 'a not inconsiderable number' of English migrants came to Western Australia bearing 'prejudices against the Church of England as "the Establishment"'. However, in Australia, they

> were attracted by the freedom of the daughter Church, and, learning for the first time her truly Catholic, adaptive and expansive character, were led to look upon the old mother church in a different way, and reading her history in different light, learnt to love even Her . . . [28]

In Price, as in Lefroy, higher churchmanship coincided with some criticism of Anglicanism's established status in England, rather than with the vision of its established status as a protective bulwark. In referring to those parts of the Anglican communion that enjoyed 'independence of English State control', Lefroy singled out the Church of South Africa for particular and favourable comment. The case of Bishop Colenso had been significant in its life, and Lefroy claimed that the Colenso case had also strengthened the Church of England in her resolve to assert her own 'inherent right to self-government'.[29] (Part of the judgement which ended the case found that, in colonies with an independent legislature, bishops could not be appointed by the crown through letters patent—by implication, it was a matter for the church to decide, free from any direction by the state.) Lefroy almost certainly knew of another South African legal case, that of *Merriman v. Williams* (1882) in which the Privy Council ruled that Bishop Merriman of Grahamstown could not oblige his high-church dean to abide by English judgements on ritual—Bishop Riley's wife was Merriman's niece.[30] If such cases encouraged high churchmen to regard the South African church as a model, low churchmen saw it as a cautionary example: in 1910 the Primate described it as an example of the 'perils of reckless haste' in constitutional revision.[31]

The clergy who supported Goldsmith's 1899 motion—D. J. Garland, C. E. C. Lefroy, F. Barton-Parkes and R. H. Moore—were all influenced, though to varying degrees, by the Oxford Movement. Churchmanship underlay some of the opposition among both laity and clergy, though it was not necessarily explicit in open debate. Goldsmith himself commented on the less amiable tone of one opponent, William Rowley of Cottesloe.[32] Rowley's churchmanship became obvious later in the same synod in his attempts to attack the *West Australian Church News* and its editor, D. J. Garland, in an incident that has been described elsewhere.[33] As well as Rowley's obvious opposition, the response of the Reverend T. McClemans shows that others linked the dean's proposal with his churchmanship. Having suggested that Anglicans in Africa still referred to themselves as members of the Church of England, McClemans continued: 'as to the Church of America, he did not think the Dean had any love for its title. It was called the Protestant Episcopal Church of America. (Laughter.)'[34] And Goldsmith himself, in introducing his speech, was visibly anxious to dispel some such suspicion: 'nor was the question in any sense a party one'.[35] A year later, after the same motion had been defeated in General Synod, the individual whom the *Morning Herald* would only identify as 'a prominent churchman' stated that the proposed change of title was designed to neutralize the effect of any English legislation which might seek to contain Anglo-Catholicism.[36] And while Bishop Riley dismissed this and other allegations that he made, Goldsmith's own qualification of his proposal shows that 'Prominent Churchman' was not alone in that way of thinking.

As if to confirm that the matter was one of churchmanship and not just national sentiment, in addition to the *West Australian Church News*, other journals which belonged in a high church stable made positive comments on Goldsmith's 1899 motion. One was the *Mitre*, then edited by E. S. Hughes while he was still a curate at St Peter's Eastern Hill: it stressed the nationalist aspect of the proposed change of title. The *London Church Review* put more emphasis on the theological implications: by describing the use of the current title as an encouragement to heresy, it echoed Goldsmith's assertion that it was in accordance with Catholic practice and ancient tradition that churches should be described by a geographical name.[37] Though the *West Australian Church News* was careful to emphasize the breadth of interest generated by the proposed motion for General Synod, the Anglican journals whose support it quoted were all from the same stable. What they did show was that Goldsmith had sought as wide a coverage as possible for his proposal.[38]

Just before General Synod, support for the principle of the motion was also expressed by several bishops, none of them low churchmen. From beyond Australia, the Archbishop of Cape Town responded warmly. A more qualified comment came from James Moorhouse, Bishop of Manchester and a former Bishop of Melbourne. The Bishop of Adelaide, 'Harmer the charmer', expressed support for 'a better name'. Bishop Camidge of Bathurst gave a qualified response: he approved of 'the principle of a national Church having the name of the nation in which it exists', but expressed some reluctance at change, and anticipated legal difficulties.[39]

The most significant item of press coverage was a leader in the highly influential London *Church Times*, a weekly whose sympathy for Anglo-Catholics was well known. In an editorial entitled 'The Church and the Churches' published in the month before Australia's General Synod, it began by addressing those who had sought to argue against the use of local geographical names by the branches of the Anglican communion in different parts of the Empire:

> It has come before us of late in the form of objections to our often-made statement, that to speak of the Church of England in Australia, or Canada, or anywhere else is an absurdity. The truth is that reference to the Church of England in any other country, whether colonial or foreign, is against Catholic tradition, and implies a geographical impossibility . . .[40]

The writer did not limit his argument exclusively to the Australian situation, but the title 'Church of England in Australia and Tasmania' was a definite object of attack. Such titles might indeed occur in state documents, both in England and her colonies, but the editorial condemned this usage as a proof of the ignorance of legislators and the errors of some ecclesiastics. The terminology of documents of church and state alike needed to be corrected—in the light of the Oxford Movement's renewed awareness of the church and the basis of her authority. He described the individual diocese as a manifestation of the church in all its fulness, even though it would generally be one of several in a larger unit, a national church. Each diocese and each bishop was one among equals.

His emphasis on the notional equality of dioceses and of national churches went hand in hand with a quite traditionally British anti-papalism. Like others who have already been mentioned, he feared that a quasi-papal system could grow from the bond of dependence between the Church of England and the colonial churches. Acknowledging the autonomy of the national churches was one way of preventing such a development. Far from being the opposite of catholicity, nationalism was synonymous with the true meaning of that term. This equation deprived Rome of her claim to represent true catholicity and condemned her internationalism as a deviation from the primitive norm. At the same time, Anglicans who espoused such a view of catholicity, rooted in a federation of national Anglican churches, could hardly be accused of being deliberate or unwitting agents of the pope:

> A properly constituted local, provincial or national Church has to consider in making canons and rules for discipline and worship, not the wishes of the Church from which it sprang, but the doctrine and discipline of the Church Catholic, the Church of all ages and climes. The Church of England has no more right to impose its peculiar rules or ideas upon the Church of Australia, or of Tasmania, than the Church of Rome has upon the Church of England. People who desire to maintain the phrase 'Church of England in Canada' are really supporting the imperial policy of the Roman Curia. They are Romanists in disguise, Italians masquerading as Anglicans. If their contention be true, and if the mother Church has right of control over a daughter Church, not of the same province, for all time, then the action of the Church of England in the sixteenth century was schismatic and unjustifiable . . .[41]

The opening lines of this same paragraph also make it clear that any alteration of the designation of the Anglican church in different parts of the Empire was no mere change in nomenclature, but was understood to involve a legal independence from England for such churches, both civil and canonical. The writer, and those of a like mind, believed that the process referred to, by which each such 'national' church would establish its own body of canon law, would end any appeal to English courts that opponents of ritualism might cherish, particularly to the Privy Council. The leader's suggestion that the newer 'national' churches should base their own 'canons and rules for discipline and worship' on the 'doctrine and discipline of the Church Catholic' and not on the 'Church from which [they] sprang',[42] implicitly contrasted the law concerning liturgical practices in England at the time with another, ideal, standard—though scholarship eventually found that it had never been embodied in any one text or document, contrary to the suggestions of the *Church Times* writer, and others. Meanwhile, such a contrast would have sounded ominous to any colonial low churchman, especially in the light of the most recent liturgical decision in the Church of England—that of the archbishops against the processional use of incense and lights. Those who agreed with the *Church Times* leader might well be expected to ignore the Privy Council judgements of more recent years, and promote the very usages that were still illegal in England. Resistance was imperative.

Backed as they were by a carefully orchestrated campaign, the supporters of the motion might have seemed reasonable enough in hoping for the motion's success at General Synod. The poor general opinion then current concerning the leadership qualities of the President of Synod, Saumarez Smith, the Primate and Archbishop of Sydney, may well have increased such sanguine expectations.

Smith bore the brunt of much criticism in private and public. The *Adelaide Church News* referred to his poor leadership at General Synod in 1900, and at a safer distance, the *Church Times* described him as 'somewhat vacillating in his moods . . . the Primate does not make an ideal leader'.[43] In private correspondence with Randall Davidson, first of all as

Bishop of Rochester, then as Archbishop of Canterbury, Bishop Montgomery of Tasmania was far more scathing. He once described him as 'our dear old log of a Primate'. After his first experience of a meeting under Smith's chairmanship in 1891, he wrote:

> He seems to have no ideas beyond those of an Evangelical clergyman in a suburban parish. He is very kind and good tempered—but he has absolutely no dignity. I have never seen a Synod so disgracefully managed—never once did he speak or ask any questions, so as to make us raise our ideas or indeed give us any ideas at all. Where does his strength lie?[44]

By 1897 he claimed that Smith's 'natural incompetence to lead or take large views' had lost him the confidence of all the Australian bishops. More complaints of the lack of leadership in Melbourne as well as Sydney preceded the General Synod of 1900, and Montgomery savaged the Primate again when the synod was over as being 'obtuse'.[45]

When it came to Goldsmith's motion, Smith was far from obtuse and log-like. In his primatial address to the synod, he spared no effort to give the motion a decided setback. He singled it out for comment and expressed his serious reservations in a well-balanced mixture of appeals to colonial insecurity, loyalty to the Empire in the face of federation, and fear of extreme churchmanship. He made a calculated and successful appeal to the emotions of his hearers, rousing his audience to cheering when he rhetorically asked whether the proposed change was not 'needless'; and the pace, once set, was maintained. Bursts of loud applause greeted his statement that the current title was 'as satisfactory as we could wish for', and again when he reminded his hearers that it was the title of the 'church to which we belong, and which we so highly prize'.[46]

Smith argued that for Australian Anglicans, the current title formed 'an indication of the continuity of their ecclesiastical inheritance'. A secure identity with a familiar and identifiable past would be the result of its preservation. He wound up his condemnation of the motion to a crescendo and brought his whole presidential address to a close which was greeted with 'prolonged applause', by referring to the continuing evolution of the concepts of federation and empire, which he contrasted with 'a wider federation and a higher idea of empire'. Although he described this ultimate federation and empire as being fulfilled in God, it must have been difficult for his listeners, caught in the fervour of combined loyalty to British Empire and English church, not to hear other resonances in this peroration. It came close to envisaging God as the ultimate imperialist and federationist on the one hand, against whose empire were pitted other, smaller sectional interests, whether of the colonies of the past, now being transcended in federation, or of national churches—the churches of Goldsmith's proposal. Smith's speech implied that real loyalty to church, federation and empire would not express itself in favour of a national church.

At the heart of his 'distinctive objections' lay churchmanship, referred to in only thinly veiled terms. He criticized what he described as the 'misappropriation' of the term Catholic by the Roman church, but stated that those Anglicans who emphasized it risked 'arrogant exclusiveness'—a warning against the high church stream, whose critics were reminded to beware of 'vapid vagueness'. But earlier in his address he had identified 'unnecessary exclusiveness' as one of the risks of a change of title: 'might not the alteration be provocative of strife as laying them open to a charge of unnecessary exclusiveness?'[47] He thus identified the source of the motion as an arrogantly exclusive high church circle, and branded its promotion as a party-motivated act.

In proposing his motion in Sydney, Goldsmith altered the balance of the arguments which he had presented in the Perth synod the previous year, heightening his appeal to national sentiment and omitting the reference he had made in 1899 to precedents in scripture and the use of the early church. He took up Barton-Parkes' sense of humiliation at the exclusive clauses of the 1874 Colonial Clergy Act. As an English ordinand, its restrictions did not apply to Goldsmith himself, but synod members responded to his criticism of the act with a round of applause. A suggestion made by F. J. Price in Perth the previous year also found a place in his revised defence: 'the name "Church of England" carried with it an odour of "establishment" which repelled'.[48] He pointed out that episcopal authority was no longer conferred in the colonies by letters patent, but made no reference to the Colenso case by name, thus keeping at bay the spectre of the church in Africa and its suggestions of extreme churchmanship. To allay fears and insecurities played on in the Primate's address, he asserted: 'his proposal to change the name did not mean that they were going to cut the cable, or that any difference would be made in the relations of the Church here with the Church in the old country. They only wanted to show what they really were'.[49]

That this was a reassuring tactic, rather than a statement of his real intent, is suggested by a claim he made earlier in the speech, that 'legal ties having been dissolved, the Imperial Parliament had now no control whatever over the Church in Australia'.[50] In his view, much of the 'cable' had already been cut, and his motion, if carried, would make clear what he understood to be the present position.

The uneasy mixture of churchmanship tensions skilfully stirred by Saumarez Smith and diplomatically avoided by Goldsmith simmered under the surface of the debate. In response to suggestions for an alternative title, which included the national Church of Australia, the Catholic Church of Australia and the Church of the Provinces of Australia and Tasmania, R. P. Dodd, an Adelaide cleric, 'certainly objected to the church being called Anglo-Catholic, for then some people would want to be called Protestant'.[51]

Goldsmith's motion did not founder on the rocks of churchmanship alone. There was certainly no support at all from prominent low churchmen. But high churchmen were far from united in their responses to it, as is shown by the failure of Archdeacons Potter of Melbourne and Whitington of Hobart to support the motion at General Synod. On the other hand, a broad churchman such as Riley supported it, and though he was no stranger to anxieties about churchmanship, he was reported by the Melbourne *Argus* as being puzzled as to why it had been 'so violently received'.[52]

The associations suggested by the current title were a significant factor. The title evoked a complex of ideas: Anglican minds associated it with the Empire and thus with a concept of universality; and at the same time, it stressed a particular national inheritance. To Australians at that time, the attractiveness and importance of membership of the empire was only magnified, rather than diminished, by distance. In the debate at General Synod 'imperial sentiment', rather than logic, prevailed, as a writer for the *Church Times* noted.[53] Similarly, as the responses to Smith's primatial charge show, the specifically British inheritance which the title evoked was important to Australian Anglicans.

At the height of patriotic imperial fever in England following the jubilee of 1897, two prominent churchmen made statements which vividly convey the extent to which some Anglicans saw the Church of England as coterminous with the boundaries of the British Empire, and envisaged the civilizing mission of empire and church as identical. Mandell Creighton (1843–1901), distinguished medieval historian, Bishop of Peterborough, then of London, wrote in a letter to another Anglican priest: 'the question of the future of the world is the existence of Anglo-Saxon civilization on a religious basis . . .' [54] In the same year Frederick Temple (1821–1902), the Archbishop of Canterbury who officiated in his old age at the coronation of Edward VII, addressed the archdiocese of Canterbury in 1898 in these words:

> It has pleased God to break up the Church into fragments, and apparently to give a different mission to each part . . . It seems clear that we have a special call to a special work. Our immediate work, no doubt, is to evangelize the world, for we have more opportunities of doing so than any other nation.[55]

Such sentiments were not unique to English bishops, nor were they regarded as unacceptable by Australian Anglicans, who expressed similar sentiments themselves. In Western Australia in 1878, the following statement greeted the meeting of the second Lambeth Conference: 'To the English people has been given "The earth for an inheritance, and the uttermost parts of the earth for a possession"; and upon the Anglican Church devolves vast duties and vast responsibilities . . .'[56] In Melbourne, following the Lambeth Conference of 1897, a year specially chosen and celebrated by that body as the 1300th anniversary of the landing of St Augustine of Canterbury in Kent in 597, the *Church of England Messenger* provided the following overt identification of Anglicanism with Empire:

> It is clear that the Church abroad, as well as at home, is coterminous with the State, and that English-speaking races still accept the command to 'Go forth into all the world, and preach the Gospel to every creature.'
>
> The visit of the Anglican bishops has been well-timed to coincide with that of so many representatives from distant colonies to celebrate the 60th anniversary of Queen Victoria's reign. It has helped to impress upon Englishmen the fact that the Church is coterminous with the Empire . . .[57]

Its opening claim was particularly remarkable, given that since at least 1850 Anglicanism had not enjoyed established status in Australia, and that other denominations constantly reminded Anglicans that they were now one among equals. It may have been an ambiguous way of expressing the point of view which concludes the extract—that the spread of Anglicanism was as wide as the boundaries of the Empire. It certainly reflected an assumption accepted by many Anglicans in different parts of the Empire—that they still constituted an 'establishment' even if there were no recognition of this in colonial legislation. Whatever its writer really intended, the statement shows that some Anglicans regarded Anglicanism in the light of the universalism that was part of the imperial political concept. Those who espoused such a view might easily be persuaded to regard Goldsmith's motion as a narrowing of the imperial vision—despite the strongly nationalistic way in which the imperial vision itself was often expressed. The reference in the passage to 'the English-speaking races' was significant in this respect. It identified the Church of England's mission with the calling of a racial group. To the writer, the coterminousness of empire, ruling race and church was such that he clearly understood Anglicanism to be as 'British' as the Empire—to be, in fact, the British church of the British race, a combination that occurs elsewhere in Australian and other sources.

Many other statements show that Anglicans in Australia regarded Anglicanism as an integral component of the Empire. At a reception to Bishop Riley in Fremantle a week after his enthronement, Archdeacon Watkins described the Anglican communion as 'the Church of the British Empire, and . . . the Church of the English speaking people of the world'.[58] Even when Anglicans acknowledged that their church possessed no real established status in the colonies, the identification of church with race and empire persisted. When the Governor and the Volunteers attended a Church Parade at St George's cathedral on Easter Day 1897, the *West Australian Church News* saw this as proof that while 'the State recognizes no particular form of religion, the heart of the colony adheres to the ancient national church of the British race'.[59] The Church of England was the 'English' church: when Bishop Parry joined Goldsmith in naming the canons' stalls for the new cathedral after saints of the Anglo-Saxon church, they were seeking to provide models for

Western Australians as they established 'a fresh branch of the English Church'.[60] Goldsmith himself, when he preached to synod in his first year as dean, had described Anglicanism as the English Church, and on the same occasion, and elsewhere, used 'national' to refer to England.[61]

Given the threads that linked British race, nation, empire and church, this combination of themes was bound to recur in the discussions over Goldsmith's motion concerning the name of the church. The clearest opposition to the motion was expressed in a combination of these terms. In a private letter to the SPG, James Fisher, who was to become Perth's acting diocesan secretary in 1901, wrote of his opposition to Goldsmith's original motion in 1899. He certainly feared that the motion would provoke the withdrawal of financial support from England, but concluded:

> in seeking to oppose the motion I have only the welfare of the Church at heart, and I do not think that any change of name could identify that Church more closely with the national life of Australia than the name which is associated not only with the national life of the United Kingdom, but with the national life of the Empire itself . . .[62]

W. A. Murphy, an Irish-born member of the Perth synod, opposing the dean's motion, linked the use of the adjective 'national' to describe the Church of England with the British Empire and Australia's place within it. Anglicanism could never claim to be the national religion in any Australia whose future was independent of the Empire, because 'the only claim the Australian colonies, or their Churches in the Australian colonies could have to be called the national Church of the Empire was based on the fact that she was part and parcel of that Empire (Applause)'.[63] Given this premise, he logically feared a change because it would weaken the imperial ties. His apprehension was stirred by the dean's concluding remarks, in which he

> expressed the hope that the day would be far distant when these colonies would separate from the mother country but warned them to be prepared for that day, and to be there with their national Church to take the place of the Church of England in the Australian colonies, which separated from the mother country . . .[64]

For Murphy, to change the title of the church was in some sense to bring closer the feared day of independence.

T. McClemans, like Murphy, of Irish extraction, also opposed the motion on grounds whose logic is formally confused, but whose direction is still clear. He criticized the dean for having omitted to define the term 'national':

> The question they had to consider was whether they were members of the Australian nation. Was there an Australian nation, or were they members of the great British nation?
> The DEAN: Empire.
> The Rev. T. McClemans said that if they were members of the British or English nation, the title of their Church was as good as they could have . . .[65]

Whether McClemans envisaged Australians as members of an empire or a race, like Murphy, he sensed the loss or diminution of status in a change of title: in his case, their identity as imperialists as well as members of a race was under threat. Another example of a logical contradiction involving the same terminology occurred in General Synod when the Adelaide cleric, R. P. Dodd, agreed that the Church of England was regarded by the 'populace' as 'somewhat exotic in character', but claimed at the same time that an alteration in title was undesirable, as 'the church could not be more national than at present'.[66]

It was Goldsmith's seconder in 1899, C. E. C. Lefroy, who was more sensitive to these interrelated issues than the dean himself; he at least sought to allay potential fears which might have been aroused in those who identified the English component in the title of the church with both empire and race. In concluding his speech, he drew on the language of both race and empire in suggesting that Goldsmith's proposal was part of 'a great development of national Churches, and that those national Churches could do much to hold together the empire, and also to restore the lost unity of all Anglo-Saxon Christianity as one branch of the Catholic Church of Christ'.[67]

Lefroy did not specify exactly how such a reunion might come about. It seems likely that he had in mind the possibility that whereas in England the established status of the Anglican communion had been a source of difficulty in ensuring good relations between the churches, the absence of any establishment in the colonies would create a more favourable ground for *rapprochement*. However, his suggestions were not enough on their own to quell such fears.

A comment in a letter of H. H. Montgomery to Randall Davidson shows how the climax of the federation movement and the approach of General Synod in 1900 combined to stir the emotions of the bishops (and presumably the other members of that body) to a sense of new imperial vision. It created an atmosphere in which feelings, rather than logic, prevailed. Lamenting the quality of leadership in Sydney and Melbourne, he wrote: 'men are so ready to do some great thing, roused by Federation and Imperialism, that I really do not know what we might not do'. And although elsewhere in the same letter he was referring to the possibilities which might open up as a result of the mission jubilee that was to precede General Synod in Sydney that year, his words capture the fever of the period, a fever that had gripped the church:

> I have wonderful things to tell you here: My heart rejoices—these are great times and one feels the stir of an Imperial Christianity. Thank God—it is good to live in these days. One feels almost afraid to enter the new century: I am sure it contains some great and new gift—and we may be too timid to take it, or too stupid to make full use of it . . .[68]

Given such an atmosphere, it is not surprising that at the synod itself, Frederick Whitington of Hobart, a high churchman who supported Goldsmith's motion in principle, felt bound to vote against it 'on the ground that, in the current state of the imperial sentiment, it might, if carried, be misconstrued'.[69] And the Australian correspondent of the *Church Times* paid tribute to the strength of this sentiment in his post-mortem of the synod, when he wrote that 'the imperialistic tide is strong upon us, and anything which tends to weaken our connexion with the motherland is looked upon just now with suspicion . . .'[70] Such 'sentimental' grounds continued to be urged successfully and strongly in subsequent synods.[71]

It is appropriate to ask what was the nature of support for autonomy, and what Goldsmith's intention was in proposing this motion. That no distinctly low churchmen supported the motion is clear, as is the high churchmanship of many of those who favoured the motion, and of the journals that supported it. Was it therefore purely a question of churchmanship? And was the appeal to nationalism simply a front?

Only a decade later C. O. L. Riley, a supporter of the autonomy movement, responded with indignation at the opinions of counsel in 1911 concerning the Australian church's legal status. He protested at the Australian church's obligation to accept liturgical texts and legal decisions from England, in whose formulation she was prevented from having any part. A church that did not have the freedom to manage its own affairs could hardly play an effective role in the life of the nation: this understanding also motivated St Clair Donaldson of Brisbane in the first decade of the century to support moves for autonomy.[72] To that extent, such English-born Anglicans were sincere in appealing to national sentiment in the church. That an autonomous church in Australia would be made stronger through having to account for all aspects of its own life was an argument put forward in the 1899 Perth synod by F. W. R. Holmes and D. J. Garland.[73] Nor was Riley alone among broad churchmen in supporting autonomy moves: another strong supporter of such action in North Queensland, Bishop Frodsham, was identified by a contemporary not as an Anglo-Catholic (the classification into which Sydney placed him) but as a pragmatist.[74]

Goldsmith's pleading on the ground of the church's future place in the national life was almost certainly motivated by a similar and genuine conviction. But it seems ingenuous to ignore the impact on him of the events that took place as a result of the controversy over Anglo-Catholicism during his ministry as a junior priest in England, and his own profile as the most prominent high churchman in his diocese, one who had already been involved in promoting controversial liturgical usages, regarded as 'advanced' and ritualistic' by his opponents. Goldsmith himself had been ordained in Rochester diocese, in the same year that Arthur Tooth of St James' Hatcham became the first priest to be imprisoned under the provisions of the Public Worship Regulation Act; and until two years before he left for Australia, such sentences were being carried out. Though there is no direct reference to the Public Worship Regulation Act in any of the debates concerning Goldsmith's motions, C. E. C. Lefroy spoke of the desirability of freedom from state control for the Church of England, and referred approvingly to those who worked for it—and it is difficult to dissociate these comments completely from the attempts to contain Anglo-Catholicism through the Public

Worship Regulation Act and various decisions of the Privy Council, even though these comments also have a broader frame of reference. Goldsmith's own liturgical usages in Perth cathedral placed him clearly on the side of those who did not conform to a number of English judgements on ceremonial. For him, and those around him who sought to cultivate a similar style of churchmanship, there was every reason to seek an autonomous church—it would be free from any possible restraint imposed by decisions of English ecclesiastical courts. To that extent the operative force behind the motions was not nationalism conceived for its own sake.

The anonymous 'Prominent Churchman' of the Perth *Morning Herald* was explicit in understanding Goldsmith's proposals as a means of rendering English law ineffective, although he obviously believed at the time of writing that this operated through an ecclesiastical, not a civil, jurisdiction, whereas Goldsmith's supporters would have feared the opposite: 'the attempt to change the name of the church . . . was only an effort to take the church out of the jurisdictions of York and Canterbury, so that the priests might be free to carry on their ritualistic practices without interference from the church authorities in England'.[75]

An added incentive for an autonomous church was the confused understanding of the legal situation. The legal confusion which English clergy sometimes complained of was not immediately banished in Australia merely by geographical distance from England. Genuine uncertainty existed in Australia in the decade leading up to Federation as to the precise relationship between English statute and canon law and the Church of England in Australia. A variety of opinions were expressed as to which, if any, body of canon law was binding on the church in Australia. In 1881 the Bishop of Ballarat had moved a motion that the church in Australia was not bound by the canons and constitutions of 1603–04, a motion that was criticized as improper by the president, Hale of Brisbane. Until 1910, when Archdeacon Whitington produced a lengthy appendix on canon law which appeared with the synod report, it continued to appear as an ongoing subject of concern.[76]

When it came to statute law, which was particularly significant to the church as an owner of property, Bishop Riley confessed to the 1899 Perth synod that he found the position of the diocese a source of concern, because

> with regard to its connection with the Church at home, we have not yet found out how far English statute law which relates to the Church is in force here. Some tell me it is in force, others say it is not. I wish we could have the question settled, for only then shall we be able to put ourselves in a satisfactory position . . .[77]

If it were possible to establish that the Anglican communion in Australia was an independent, national church, a Gordian knot of uncertainties might be removed at a single stroke.

Like other Australian Anglicans at this time, Goldsmith was unaware of the full legal implications of the title 'Church of England in Australia and Tasmania' both in relation to property, and to Privy Council judgements, implications which became apparent a decade later. He seems to have believed (or at least to have hoped) that the church in Australia was already unfettered by any English legislation: he referred to the 'Imperial Parliament' having no control over the church in Australia because legal ties had been dissolved, presumably through Federation. And if this were the point of view from which he originally presented his motions, he shared a belief in the existence of a larger degree of autonomy with at least two other of Australia's most learned archbishops in the first decade of the century, St Clair Donaldson of Brisbane and Lowther Clarke of Melbourne. Their view was soon to be contradicted. To many others besides Riley the 1911 opinions came, as Bishop Hart of Wangaratta put it, like a 'bombshell'.[78]

At General Synod in 1910 Goldsmith attempted for the last time to put forward a motion, whose content included the plea, familiar by then, for 'a more appropriate designation than that at present in use', but accompanied by a second clause that sought recognition for Australian Anglicanism 'as an independent National Church . . . with such limitations as constitutionally bind every true branch of the Catholic Church . . .' Though the second clause was withdrawn, 'the motion was lost on the vote of the lay representatives'.[79] And when the legal position of the Australian church was made clear, Goldsmith addressed his own synod in Bunbury, reiterating the points of view that he had already expressed, without adding to their substance.[80]

In between this last motion of Goldsmith's, and his earlier ones, lay a decade of moves for, and opposition to, autonomy for the Anglican communion in Australia. Before the beginning of World War I, some Anglicans stated that in this debate, participants took their position largely on the basis of churchmanship. Though he was not prepared to comment on whether this point of view was well founded, the Bishop of Ballarat described it as 'widely entertained'. In a debate in the 1912 Melbourne synod over whether the current legal nexus should be maintained, one speaker said that opposition to the autonomy movement grew out of a fear that in the absence of the Privy Council as a court of appeal, ritualism might move out of control.[81] Other elements in the debate repeated arguments that had appeared when Goldsmith's motions were rejected: moves for autonomy were understood to call imperial loyalties into question. And, again, the voting of the laity was more conservative that that of the clergy: the clergy voted for and against in almost equal numbers, but eighty-three laity voted against, compared with only twenty-one for the motion. At an episcopal level, low church bishops led the resistance. By 1905 St Clair Donaldson had written to Randall Davidson that opposition to autonomy on the part of Sydney, Bendigo and Gippsland at the meeting of Australian bishops had centred around a desire to maintain some link with the Privy Council. Wright, Saumarez Smith's successor, continued to see the autonomy movement along the same lines, and in 1911 branded it as motivated 'by a wish for ritual liberty at any cost'.[82]

The laity continued to maintain a generally more conservative stance over autonomy moves than the clergy. In addition to the lay vote against Goldsmith's 1910 motion, and the lay vote at the Melbourne synod in 1911, a motion introduced by Cumbrae Stewart and Bishop Frodsham in 1909 seeking the establishment of an autonomous Queensland province—the most daring single attempt of the period to work through the autonomy issue—was met with suspicion by the laity.[83] The climax of such moves, seeking parliamentary legislation 'to obtain such freedom from the government of the Church of England by law established as shall enable her to adapt herself to Australian needs' was defeated in

1912 through a strong lay vote against, while the clergy voted almost two to one in favour.[84] By this time the apparent contrast between laity and clergy was regarded as reflecting churchmanship differences, as much as ones of national origin.[85] Sydney played a leading role. Before the end of the nineteenth century a number of its Anglicans had come to regard its low churchmanship as a distinguishing mark. They envisaged the diocese as an isolated defender of particular standards, threatened by those whose approach was different, as Montgomery commented to Randall Davidson.[86]

Outsiders sympathetic to other traditions, as well as anxious Sydney low churchmen, regarded the smaller and newer dioceses as having the more advanced churchmanship, while regarding Sydney and Melbourne as less advanced.[87] And while Sydney regarded the Queensland dioceses particularly as breeding grounds for Anglo-Catholicism, they were suspicious of others as well. Wright's determination to stave off the establishment of new dioceses in Western Australia for as long as possible, much to the frustration of Riley in his desire to be the first archbishop, was most likely motivated by the same fear—that with more country dioceses would come even more bishops bearing the imprint of the Oxford Movement, as actually happened with the appointment of Gerard Trower to the North-West, and Golding-Bird to Kalgoorlie. It certainly sought to ensure that the number of representatives in General Synod was in proportion to the total Anglican population of that diocese, and that smaller dioceses would not be awarded equal voting rights with their larger neighbours, a principle that finally came to be adopted in 1916.

The English bishops in eastern Australia who strongly championed the movement for an autonomous church—Webber and Frodsham to a lesser extent, but St Clair Donaldson and Lowther Clarke in particular—were more distinguished men than Goldsmith, and of less pronounced churchmanship (the allegations of nervous Sydneysiders notwithstanding). But the association of support for the autonomy movement with the English clergy, rather than the Australian laity, and the fear that a distinct churchmanship lay behind it, was a combination that was not created in the first decade of the century, but already existed as a discernible combination of issues when Goldsmith put forward his motions in 1899 and 1900. And though it lies outside the scope of this study, it remains for some scholar to investigate whether some kind of imperial loyalty continued to be invoked by the opponents of the autonomy movement, as happened at the turn of the century, and successfully, despite the rise of nationalism and the federation movement.

— EIGHT —

## *A*n Episcopal Mendicant: Goldsmith, Bunbury and the North-West: 1904–1910

Goldsmith's election as first Bishop of Bunbury, his consecration on 17 July 1904 and his enthronement on the following afternoon,[1] mark a turning point in his career which is a suitable one from which to view the rest of his life. In terms of Western Australian Anglicanism, it marked the way in which its perspectives were shifting. If Goldsmith had seemed, from some angles, to be some kind of radical, it was now a kind of radicalism that was more acceptable. And if Riley had already sought to modify the impact of the Catholic tide by prescribing the use of the less controversial ceremonial while eschewing the rest, a pragmatist might have speculated, with that in mind, as to whether Riley was exercising another kind of control by accepting this most distinguished local proponent of the Oxford Movement on to the bench of bishops; the naughty ecclesiastical schoolboy was being turned into the dispenser of discipline.

Goldsmith's election elicited comment from the *West Australian Church News* that it was 'no foregone conclusion', and, from the secular press, that the dean was 'no party man'.[2] The statements of the *West Australian* and *Morning Herald* are chiefly remarkable in that they represent the reverse of the position taken almost a decade before by the first paper. Hackett's editorial prior to the election of Parry's successor, and the ensuing debate in Perth synod, had clearly identified the dean as just that—a party man. Hackett himself was at least consistent enough to stay away from the enthronement, presenting an apology through Riley, and an offering of £50, not to the diocese, but towards the cost of Bishopscourt, which had still to be built.[3] Sir John Forrest was another notable figure whose absence was commented on when Goldsmith was received in Bunbury prior to the enthronement.[4]

In addition to this clear enough volte-face by the press, Riley's own statements concerning Goldsmith following his election affirm the existence of a degree of harmony and co-operation between the two men which is denied by Riley's own diaries:

> Bishop Riley remarked that if all the clergy throughout the world had acted as Dean Goldsmith had acted in matters where his private opinion was not altogether in consonance with that of his Bishop, much of the trouble that had arisen in the Church would never have occurred. Many times Dean Goldsmith had forgone his own wishes and his own ideas because his Bishop had asked him to do so. (Applause.)[5]

Another contradiction between public and private accounts also needs to be mentioned. The *West Australian Church News* description of the election seems designed to suggest that the election was the outcome of a popular vote, and indicated a spontaneous choice by the members of Perth synod, while in Bunbury, Riley described Goldsmith as a bishop 'whose people had chosen him for themselves'.[6] However, Wilfrid Henn's notes for a study of Goldsmith also contain the following significant notation:

> Bp Riley told electors 'I want (this election) to be carried out as in the sight of God.' [but I have been told that Bp. Riley knew just what man he wanted elected, i.e. F. W. G. — W. E. H. ][7]

Although Henn cloaked his source in a respectable anonymity, it may well have been his father, Percy Umfreville Henn, who returned to the Perth diocese just after Goldsmith's election and, although not an Anglo-Catholic, was sufficently sympathetic to, and in close contact with, Western Australian clergy who were supporters of the Oxford Movement's ideals.

The contrast between the public attitudes towards Goldsmith within a decade, moving from disapproval to approval, is accounted for by factors that I have analysed elsewhere.[8] The most significant of these, all

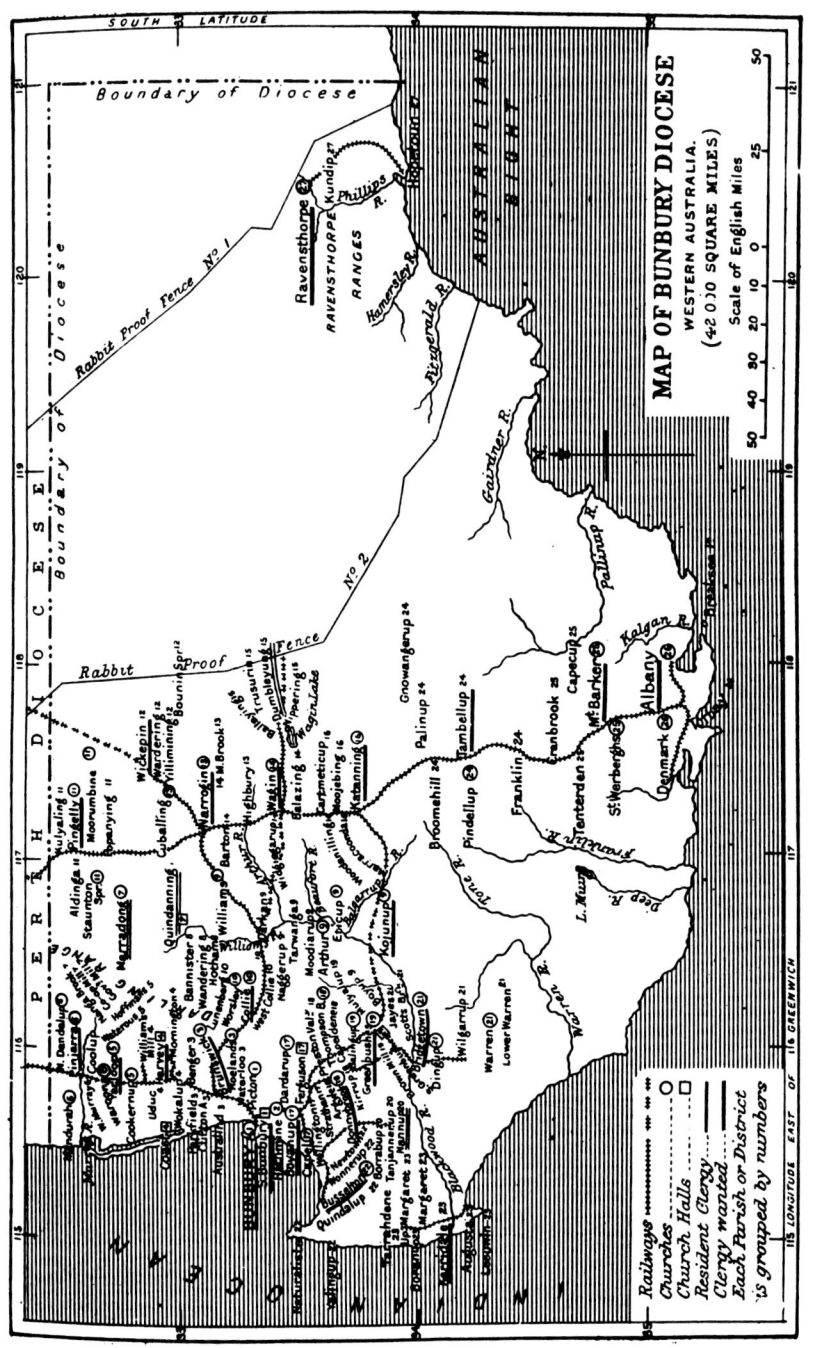

Bunbury and the South-West

consequences of the gold rush, were the dilution of the influence of the ancient colonists, the increased number of Anglicans favourably disposed towards the impact of the Oxford Movement from other places, and the growth of Perth and its transformation from a market town to a city centre, to an urban society, moreover, whose members expected a greater degree of formality and sophistication in all areas of its life, including its ecclesiastical life.

The contrast in public and private attitudes at the time—between Riley's frustrations expressed in his diary, and the public declarations of harmony; between Riley's apparent manipulation of the election, and the suggestions of impartiality in the *West Australian Church News*—may be accounted for by other factors again. Quite apart from the common tendency of leaders in large public institutions to wish to present an appearance of unanimity, and the commitment of Christian churches (in theory) to peace and harmony, there were two other elements.

One was Riley's clear desire to avoid any kind of public conflict. His own distaste for ceremonial had already been expressed in private. But when questioned by a low church priest from Victoria visiting Western Australia as to why he insisted that all the clergy use the eastward position to celebrate the eucharist, he replied 'To avoid questions'.[9] Riley's desire to maintain an appearance of harmony and avoid public dispute may well have imparted an added note of frustration to his private outpourings in his diary.

The other was a broader desire on the part of Western Australia's gentry, the 'ancient colonists', to maintain their controlling role by affirming their belief in social harmony, and playing down or suppressing evidence of its opposite, in what Tom Stannage has described as the quest for internal peace. Keeping his own personal distaste for Goldsmith well hidden in public as he laid the foundation stone of Bishopscourt, in the speech he made to mark the occasion, Sir John Forrest placed a heavy emphasis on general harmony.[10]

Riley had a personal reason for expressing some satisfaction in Goldsmith's election. It marked the first step towards the realization of his ambition to become the first Archbishop of Perth, a process for which the existence of three other dioceses was essential.[11] Was there any alternative form of church government in a state such as Western

Australia, with a thinly spread and widely scattered population? In Riley's eyes, the urgency of this question was not just an administrative one. Before the new century had begun, the Bishop of Adelaide, J. R. Harmer, had suggested the creation of a province of South Australia and Western Australia.[12] In 1899 Riley had objected to Harmer's proposal—it was illogical, he said, to join Perth in its isolation to a unit embracing Victoria, Tasmania and South Australia, and soon the West would have its own province.[13] The general tone of frustration that dominates his later correspondence over the establishment of the diocese of Kalgoorlie, the last element to fall into place before his scheme could be effected, and his increasing annoyance at the reticence of the Primate, are abundant witnesses to this personal urgency.[14]

A sense of satisfaction in the event of Goldsmith's consecration, rather than in the man himself, is clear in Riley's correspondence with H. H. Montgomery at the Society for the Propagation of the Gospel headquarters in London, in which he described it as 'splendid' and of great value as an 'object lesson'. A note of interstate hostility crept into his contemptuous comments about the way in which it exposed the ignorance of ecclesiastical matters by Victorians, even greater than that of Western Australians, which was in itself considerable.[15] But to the highest echelon of Australia's Anglican hierarchy Goldsmith's consecration seems to have mattered little if at all. It was performed by the requisite minimum of three bishops. The Primate, Saumarez Smith, sent a proxy, G. H. Stanton of Newcastle. The other co-consecrator was the ageing Dean of Newcastle, Bishop Stretch, who as vicar of Maldon provided the original for Mr Thistlethwaite of Barambogie in Henry Handel Richardson's *Ultima Thule*.

The establishment of the diocese of Bunbury proceeded from more than Riley's ambition. Only one other writer, S. Marshall, has attempted to explain its establishment in any degree of detail and her account places an understandable emphasis on the effects of the population increase following the gold rush.[16] While this is undoubtedly correct, there were other elements in the process.

In 1891 R. Hesketh Jones, deputy chairman of the Great Southern Railway Company, wrote to the SPG, predicting that half of the state's population would soon move to the south-west, and urged the establishment of a bishop at Katanning. Parry replied that Albany and not Katanning should be the centre of any southern diocese.[17]

Before the turn of the century, attention seemed to focus more on the goldfields and on the north-west. As early as 1889 the possibility of a missionary diocese was envisaged, combining the north-west with the Northern Territory, and discussions took place between Bishop Parry and Bishop Kennion of Adelaide.[18] Elsewhere, Parry referred to the way in which, in Queensland's north, Dawes was functioning at Rockhampton, and suggested that an archdeaconry be established in the north as a prelude to acquiring full diocesan status.[19] In the interregnum that followed Parry's death David Garland claimed that the Australian bench of bishops concurred with the concept of a northern missionary diocese that crossed colonial boundaries, and that the Primate would present a detailed map and proposal to the English missionary societies for approval and support during a forthcoming visit to England. The diocese was to be for 'aliens and aborigines'; it was also composed of the land that offered the greatest difficulties for concentrated European settlement.[20]

Riley's early experience in the state made him critical in public and private of the treatment of the aboriginal population, and part of his anxiety was registered in a letter in 1896 to E. S. Clairs, in which he stated: 'my visit north has oppressed me with the thought of our shortcomings—absolutely nothing is done for the thousands of aboriginals—and I don't know what can be done—there ought to be a new diocese . . .'[21] This concern was repeated later in correspondence to the SPG, and was entirely appropriate, since there were more Aboriginal people in the diocese of Perth than in any other Australian diocese.[22]

In 1897 he began to press for the creation of an assistant bishopric, and in 1899 a fund for that purpose was established.[23] In private correspondence Riley stated that such an appointment would only be a prelude to the establishment of a separate diocese, but the failure to raise sufficient funds for see capital within Western Australia itself helped to delay this. It was thus essential that the project be subsidized from England, but the Colonial Bishoprics Council was forbidden by the terms of its constitution from contributing towards the creation of a suffragan bishopric, while the two major missionary societies were reluctant to subsidize it. In 1903 they placed further pressure on Riley to divide the diocese in return for funding. In the end, the missionary societies stipulated a division as a condition of their grants towards the see capital.24

At first it appeared that the new diocese would be centred on the goldfields, not the south-west. In 1897 Riley had appointed Frederick Barton-Parkes as archdeacon of Coolgardie as a prelude to a goldfields see, and both Riley and Barton-Parkes corresponded with the SPG over this intention. The archdeacon, perhaps hoping to become the new bishop, wrote that Coolgardie would provide £250 annually towards the new bishopric. A columnist in the *Bunbury Herald* wrote that, early in 1903, Anglicans in the state's south-west were not expecting to be in the centre of a new diocese, a comment which is substantiated in Riley's own correspondence with H. H. Montgomery. That year, when agreement had been reached over the division of the diocese of Perth, he wrote of the change in plans; the division was not to encompass the goldfields, 'as expected'. Elsewhere, in correspondence with the Primate, he expressed his disappointment at having to retain them. By giving the bishop of the new diocese a missionary jurisdiction over the north-west, he would be free at least of that much—which he complained of as a burden to himself, but shrugged off as no burden to another:

> a trip to the N. West takes at least two months and the additional five hours to come up from Bunbury or in the South is a mere nothing . . . I am convinced that no Bishop at home or even in the settled parts of Australia has ever had to face the difficulties which have confronted me in this diocese for nine years . . .25

The change in direction was not only encouraged by the economic and parochial stability of the south-west compared with the suddenly populous but widespread goldfields, with their lack of amenities and their generally poor communities, as noted by Boyce and Marshall, but it was also politically motivated. As early as 1900, in a letter to Montgomery marked 'confidential, not for publication', he observed that the goldfields were seeking independent status from the rest of the colony, and that he would no longer back a goldfields bishopric, lest the church appear in the eyes of the government to be pro-secessionist. This political sensitivity to the position of the church in the eyes of the state government was echoed over other issues elsewhere in his correspondence.26

Goldsmith's consecration did not represent total divorce from activity in previous spheres of involvement in Perth. His resignation from Perth was not effective until 31 August 1904, and in the meantime he returned to Perth after his enthronement, and took a number of the cathedral services. In addition, his management of the orphanage lasted until 1906, when it came to an end with the arrival of his successor as dean, H. G. D. Latham.

Before the consecration Riley corresponded with Randall Davidson about the procedures necessary to obtain a D.D. for Goldsmith. Not only was it in keeping with his episcopal office—Riley also stressed that the conferring of a doctoral degree by Goldsmith's old university would be a matter of some kudos for the province that he sought to establish. The degree was not conferred until 1905.[27] And in Bunbury, from his inception as a bishop, he also took unto himself the title of dean of the procathedral of St Paul, while the incumbent of St Paul's continued to hold the title of rector of Bunbury.[28]

Even the choice of Bunbury as the see city of the south-west diocese was not a foregone conclusion. Representations were made from Albany, whose attractiveness had already been recognized and, in June, Goldsmith visited the town on a fact-finding tour to establish whether it would form 'headquarters that would best serve the interests of the whole diocese'.[29] The expansion of trade which led to C. Y. O'Connor's development of Fremantle harbour may well have made Albany's prospects look less attractive and highlighted the future potential of Bunbury, which claimed to be the fourth busiest port in Australia before World War I.[30]

The Bunbury of 1904 in which Goldsmith was enthroned was a small town of three thousand people. Major employers were the port and the railways which transported the steadily increasing volume of timber, coal and agricultural products, particularly wool and wheat.[31] The crippling effects of a strike in the timber industry in 1907 showed the close interdependence which existed between different groups in the township. The centre of Bunbury was in the northern part of the township, and its houses became more and more dispersed as one moved towards the south, an area that would be increasingly the home of working people, as the town grew before World War I.

An aerial view of Bunbury, c. 1899
The town centre as Goldsmith first saw it, with St Paul's in the foreground to the right

Its tiny Anglican church of St Paul, whose site had been surveyed by Sir John Forrest when he was a teenager, may have been adequate for the original town's Anglican worshippers, but as Goldsmith's episcopate continued, it was found to be increasingly inadequate for diocesan functions. In their history of Bunbury, A. J. Barker and Maxine Laurie misunderstood the significance of the Anglican statistics for the town in the colony's Blue Books, which list the total number of Anglicans baptized, but are in no way an attempt to record worshipping numbers. Estimates of the number of worshipping Anglicans are found in the statistics of the Perth diocesan yearbooks before 1904 and show that of the total number of registered communicants, regular services saw about one in ten communicating at the eucharist at any given time. A regular record of the total number present at services was not maintained, making it impossible for the modern historian to estimate the extent of non-communicating attendance.[32]

Predictably, the first years of Goldsmith's episcopate saw the consolidation of the relatively small beginnings, and also laying foundations for future growth. When he began his episcopate, the diocese of Bunbury comprised 9 parishes, 2 parochial districts and 6 mission districts, served by 15 clergy, and contained a total Anglican population of 17,250, of whom 914 communicated at Easter in 1903. Nominal Anglicans made up almost 50 per cent of the total population of the area. In the north-west, one parish and two mission districts were staffed by 3 clergy (2 priests and a deacon), and there, of 1,999 Anglicans, 54 had communicated at Easter.[33]

On the eve of the inauguration of the new diocese, Frederick Barton-Parkes had written to the Primate expressing trepidation over its dependence on the statute law of the original Perth diocese; he claimed that in this respect, the Perth synod act which allowed the new diocese to come into being was *ultra vires*.[34] Riley entered into a short and testy correspondence with both Barton-Parkes and the Primate. Whether it was because of Barton-Parkes' concerns or not, in 1904, at the first synod over which he presided, Goldsmith initiated a process which continued over several years, by which Bunbury formulated its own legislation.

Goldsmith also sought to reach out to those who lived in the remoter areas of the diocese. He inaugurated an appeal for a motor van run by one of the clergy which would be equipped with a travelling library and a magic lantern display. He emphasized the need for more clergy, promising to seek a solution by visiting England in the following year. In addition, he stressed the needs of the north-west, with its huge area and tiny staff of clergy and lay-readers. And while the north-west remained under his missionary jurisdiction he would find his energies and resources divided. Relief would only come with the establishment of an independent bishopric.

Goldsmith's origins in a professional middle class, strongly bound into the public school tradition, as well as the Catholic identity of Anglicanism which the Oxford Movement stressed, made him perceive the maintenance of Anglican pre-eminence as a highly important ground for swift expansion, both in the north-west and in the southern countryside. This became clear following his first visit to the north-west, between 1 and 23 October 1904, and took in Shark's Bay, Carnarvon, Onslow, Cossack, Roebourne and Port Hedland.[35]

For his wider English public, he reported that the isolation created an atmosphere of happy inter-denominational co-operation, which in the absence of any Protestant institutions in the north-west at that time, meant good relations between Anglicans and Roman Catholics. He praised the work of the Spanish Father Nicholas at Broome, and the hospitality of the nuns at Roebourne, who sent him 'a most magnificent cake'.[36] Privately, the following year, he pleaded with the Archbishop of Canterbury, Randall Davidson, to exert whatever pressure he could on the missionary societies in order to speed up the establishment of a north-west diocese, and gave as his reason the possibility that others would move in if the Anglicans were slow on the uptake.[37] Elsewhere, writing to the SPG of the presence of Seventh Day Adventist evangelists in parts of the south-west, he argued that 'the first body to occupy the country has tremendous advantages'.[38] And while some others, including Riley, and H. Pitts, a former curate of Goldsmith's who went to the north-west, could write of Roman Catholic mission work in a highly complimentary way,[39] Goldsmith's private anxiety was shared by the first Bishop of the North-West, Gerard Trower. He expressed irritation that Protestant denominations which had come into the north-west only after the formation of the Anglican diocese, were already 'making great efforts to oust the church'.[40]

The itinerary showed a predictable enough concentration on the European community—he attended the races at Roebourne and conducted a masonic service, as well as confirming, and visiting schools and hospitals. In addition he attended a corroboree, but his comment on Aboriginal prisoners at Roebourne does not suggest that their condition stirred any depths of compassion in him:

> there were about sixty prisoners, mostly Aboriginals and Malays, mostly in for murder or cattle-spearing. They are most humanely treated, well fed, and well clothed. The Aborigines, it is true, are on the chain, but great care is taken that they shall not be galled; and though one's British sentiment is against the chain, I do not see what alternative is possible, if these poor criminals—whom confinement would kill—are to work in the open. The Chief-gaoler is a Churchman, an enthusiast in his work, and the true friend of the prisoners . . .[41]

The neutral tone of his description contrasts strongly with the searching, almost angry one of a text in the Sydney *Bulletin* three years earlier which

Aboriginal prisoners at Roebourne, *Bulletin*, 11 May 1901, p. 14
The tone of Goldsmith's description of Aboriginal prisoners in the north-west contrasts with the anger of the *Bulletin* at the scene reproduced in its pages.

accompanied a photograph of the same abuses which Goldsmith witnessed.

Some sense of the need in this area did ultimately register, because just before Christmas he applied to the SPG for an annual grant of £150 to fund 'a Mission to the Natives in the North West of Australia', and hoped that he could persuade E. M. Collick to join him. Collick had already achieved almost legendary success in transferring the compassion of the Anglo-Catholic slum mission priest from London's east-enders to the despised Aboriginal people of the goldfields.[42] Goldsmith's desire to obtain the services of Collick was understandable. By 1900 his impact was such that the term Collick was already well established among goldfields Aboriginal people as the colloquial term for a cleric, and David Garland had already written of him as the first Anglican cleric who had taken an interest in the Aboriginal people 'without raising any opposition to it'.[43]

Collick did not respond to any invitation from Goldsmith (he did not leave the goldfields until 1924) but Goldsmith's initiative at least stood him in good stead with the SPG, because the following year Goldsmith sailed for England to recruit clergy and raise funds, and arrived to face an unanticipated storm over the Aboriginal situation in the north-west. It made Aboriginal mission work even more of a priority in order to appease public indignation, and at the same time effectively jeopardized the likelihood of a bishop's being appointed for some time to come.

The storm was provided by the Roth Report, an investigation into the treatment of Aborigines in the north-west, commissioned by the Western Australian government from W. E. Roth, the Queensland State Protector of Aborigines. The report found evidence of serious abuses: the use of neck chains on Aboriginal prisoners, including women and children; the payment of police for Aboriginal witnesses on a per capita basis in court cases, which encouraged the forcible bringing in of the largest number of witnesses possible; and the use of Aborigines for forced labour without payment of any kind.[44]

The report attracted leaders in major English newspapers. *The Times* referred to the 'almost medieval cruelty' involved, and 'callous indifference to the sufferings of an inferior race'. The House of Lords debated the report from a position of high moral ground. In a lengthy and bombastic speech the Archbishop of Canterbury expressed the pious hope that 'the statements which this Report contains are unique among modern records of administrative work in any portion of the British empire'.[45] He comforted himself with the consolation that it had been proved 'a thousand times in India and elsewhere' that the British race had 'some peculiar gift for dealing with the extraordinarily difficult problem of government of races other than our own'—which made the present blot on the imperial copybook all the more unpardonable.

What did reflect on Goldsmith, who was not named in Davidson's speech, was the archbishop's reference to the exemplary work, not of any Anglicans, but of the Roman Catholic Father Nicholas, and his assurance that

> as far as the Church of England is concerned . . . steps will be taken to send out men *really competent* to investigate these matters for themselves, to try to bring some elements of civilization into the condition of the aboriginal tribes, and what is still more important, to raise the standard of the sense of responsibility among the white people.[46]

In the face of expressions such as those of the Secretary of State for Foreign Affairs, the Marquess of Landsdowne, who referred to the feelings of 'deep indignation' and 'humiliation' at these affronts to the laws of humanity, which he believed to be more rarely breached 'under British rule than under any civilized Power',[47] Bishop Montgomery called on Goldsmith to comment publicly at a meeting at Exeter Hall on 18 May on the claims made in the report. The *Church Times,* while careful not to hold Goldsmith in any way responsible, regarded the Report as evidence of the pressing need for a north-west bishopric which, it assured readers, was more likely to be located at Broome or Roebourne than at Carnarvon. A later issue described Goldsmith's appearance at an SPG meeting. Here he pointed out that Riley had attempted to remedy abuses of which he had been aware on arrival in the West, but had failed because his evidence was inadequate in the eyes of the law. He stressed the problems and temptations facing well-intentioned Europeans as a result of their isolation in the north-west, and concluded that 'until a separate missionary diocese can be formed for that north-western part of Western Australia, it is impossible that things can be satisfactory . . .'[48]

In contrast to the pomposity and fatuous prurience of Davidson, who stated that he preferred not to quote 'what has happened when . . . pearl fishers land and supply drink to the natives, what drink is exchanged for, and the scenes that follow',[49] one of Goldsmith's north-west clergy, W. Sharp of Carnarvon, wrote with disarming directness:

> Many people I hear were shocked when they heard of the treatment of the natives in Dr Roth's report. If they understood the situation they would not be shocked at all, and if they were placed in the same surroundings as some of the people in the pearling boats at Broome, and at Marble Bar, they would probably have yielded to the same temptations . . . What has been done openly further north of this district is being done secretly in all our large cities, such as London and Paris.[50]

While Goldsmith stated—if only from sheer embarrassment—that he was aware of even deeper indignation in Australia than in England at the disclosures in the report,[51] the debate in the House of Lords concluded that it was the responsibility of the people of (Western) Australia to demonstrate that they were worthy upholders of the British ideals of justice and freedom. This expectation was combined with a parallel belief by the missionary societies that Australian Anglicans should show some serious financial commitment of their own to mission. Thus Goldsmith had to face the fact that there were decreasing prospects, in the short term, for viable funding for a north-west bishopric. Yet this was the very time when its imperative need seemed to be highlighted.

He assured the SPG that, since his arrival in England, he had already engaged one priest who was to be appointed to Onslow, with strict instructions to make mission among the natives his priority;[52] and Riley assured the *Church Times* that 'we are now trying to send a Bishop to the North, to spend his whole time among the natives'.[53] Goldsmith received little encouragement from Davidson, whom he asked to place pressure on the missionary societies for funding for the proposed north-west see. Davidson's reply was polite but remote.[54]

Perhaps because of Davidson's aloofness, and also knowing that the SPG's Standing Committee had decided to postpone the question of the north-west bishopric until it saw some clear initiative from the Australian end, Bishop H. H. Montgomery, the SPG secretary, privately wrote to the Primate of Australia, Saumarez Smith. Smith was preparing for General Synod later that same year. Montgomery expressed his own hope that 'if we struck while the iron was hot', a north-west see might be established. He was aware of the degree to which the Anglican Church in Australia had become increasingly self-supporting, but also included the detailed figures which caused the SPG to hesitate before it made additional grants. He suggested that if Smith were to make an appeal for the north-west into a priority and attracted a good initial response, this would reopen the way for further English subsidies. At the same time, he wrote to Goldsmith, urging him to raise as much support for his cause as possible at General Synod.[55]

Montgomery's private initiative grew from the inside knowledge of Australian conditions which he possessed from his period as Bishop of Tasmania. This included a visit to Western Australia to lead an appeal for the fund which became the basis of Bunbury's see capital. But despite this apparently timely warning, Smith did not make the north-west into any kind of high priority. According to Riley, he was simply not interested.[56] At his own synod in Perth later that year, Riley attempted to make the most of the heat generated by the whole issue to stir the consciences and pockets of his laity, by reminding them that the mission to the Aboriginal population was one of the purposes behind the attempt to establish a north-west diocese.⁵⁷

An ill wind seemed to blow over the north-west on Goldsmith's return, despite his apparent good intentions of removing 'the reproach lying against the Church in the matter of the Aborigines'.⁵⁸ At the beginning of 1906 a breakthrough appeared close. The opportunity arose of taking over, at a cost of £378, what he described in his correspondence with Montgomery as an 'undenominational' mission at Sunday Island run by a Mr Hadley. Goldsmith even hoped to run a missionary lugger among the pearlers—a novel enough approach, had it eventuated. But by mid-August the following year the negotiations had fallen through, Goldsmith having withdrawn after becoming convinced that the mission's situation had in many ways been misrepresented.⁵⁹ What his correspondence with Montgomery did not indicate was that this abandoned project involved dealing with one of the north-west's more eccentric figures. Montague Sidney Hadley, who eventually succeeded to a peerage following the death of his older brother, had originally been a partner with Harry Hunter in running cattle, collecting trochus and *bêche-de-mer*, pearling, and selling Aboriginal divers whom they captured and held in labour pools on the Lacapedes. It was claimed that his complete change of direction was a result of an apparition. An unsuccessful attempt to found a mission on the Forrest River in north Kimberley was followed by his more successful venture commenced in 1899 among members of the Bard tribe, who eventually allowed him to undergo a complete initiation as a tribal member. His relaxed standards contrasted with those of other nearby missions, and he did nothing to interfere with men from Beagle Bay and Disaster Bay when they came during the wet season to conduct initiation ceremonies that were frowned on elsewhere.⁶⁰ Was Goldsmith deterred by this openness to Aboriginal culture?

Whatever may have been the real cause for the withdrawal from this project, a ten-week visit in 1906 beginning on 15 June took Goldsmith to Carnarvon, Onslow, Cossack, Port Hedland, Broome, Derby—and from thence on a camping tour of more remote centres, and to Marble Bar and Roebourne. Death must have appeared an uncomfortably close companion in the north: dutring his visit to Derby the magistrate, Dr McQueen, collapsed and died on the verandah of the Institute as a congregation of almost sixty gathered for a Sunday evensong.[61] At the beginning of the next year Goldsmith wrote to Montgomery that W. A. G. Buchanan, a priest who had been at Marble Bar, 'was invalided south, and died shortly afterwards'.[62] Climate and isolation took their toll in due course on Archdeacon Brooks, who arrived in 1906 and was sent to Broome, but by the end of 1909 his health too had been seriously affected.[63] In an essay on the church in Australia written at the end of his life, Goldsmith expressed a commonly held view of the north: it was an area hardly fit for European habitation. The physical problems experienced by his skeleton staff could only have encouraged him in making this conclusion.[64]

Well might Goldsmith write: 'Oh! for a new Diocese there, and a bishop on the spot',[65] but by 1907 there may have been a sense of relief: £5,000 of the £10,000 necessary for an endowment fund had been promised, and he had been able to consecrate the new St George's church at Carnarvon.[66]

The importuning of the Australian bench of bishops by Goldsmith and his supporters resulted in a letter from that body addressed to the Australian church's members, encouraging their financial support for the north-west's see fund. Meanwhile, Montgomery showed where his sympathies lay when he wrote to Goldsmith that he believed 'there is no Diocese which has a heavier burden than yours',[67] and promised that the Society itself would offer further help with funds which it received from the Congress.

Montgomery's words could only have encouraged Goldsmith to believe that an answer to major funding problems was at hand. But in the face of the intense competition from other causes at the Pan-Anglican Congress, this was to be over-optimistic. Although Riley spoke at the opening meeting on 5 October, the needs of the north-west were balanced against appeals from the Church Missionary Society, the Universities' Mission to Central Africa, and missionary dioceses in China, Japan and Korea, to name only a few.[68] Goldsmith's supporters in England anticipated the event more realistically:

> Next year a new disease is going to be prevalent in Merrie England. Its name is 'Pan-Anglicanitis'. The microbes will be wearing gaiters; the blood-sucking will be refined—nay, even pleasant to the sufferer—but it will be unprecedented; the

only method of escape will be 'six months on the Continent'. The solemn declarations at Lambeth, preceded by the floods of oratory in June, will be, we believe, only a mere incident in the real campaign! The Episcopal invasion will mean business; the Right Reverend Fathers are coming to us with a tremendous call: 'Your money or your life!'[69]

Prodded by Riley's impatience and ambition, the church in Australia continued to limp onwards, until it made up the sum necessary for the see capital. Goldsmith felt that, at the degree of distance that separated him from the north-west, he was hardly a bishop 'in fact', and 'scarcely more than in theory'.[70] Although George Halford, with his experience of North Queensland, was also suggested as a possible incumbent for the new see, in 1910 Goldsmith was able to hand over the north-west to Gerard Trower, a former rector of Christ Church Saint Laurence in Sydney, who had gone to Nyasaland as Bishop of Likoma, where he established a large network of native schools, and presided over the completion of a vast anthill-clay brick cathedral.[71] His African experience was expected to qualify him for the evangelization of the Aboriginal people, which his commissary described as being 'so near to Bishop Trower's heart'.[72]

Goldsmith was limited by distance and resources rather than just a failure of vision. Even at the beginning of the century Howard Pitts, a priest responsible for Roebourne and Broome, reported spending much of his time in visiting pastoralists and miners and envisaged the north-west as an isolated corner of the Empire which would soon be well known, but also planned to evangelize the Japanese community as part of his mission.[73] Goldsmith's appointee, Archdeacon Brooks, took up some of this vision. At the Church Congress of 1909 Canon Stephen's statement that 'Christian and heathen' were mutually repulsive contrasted strongly with the words of Brooks, who was greeted with applause when he spoke of evangelizing the 'coloured brethren'. He was supported by Archdeacon Whitington of Hobart, who envisaged the north-west bishopric as one for the conversion of Japanese, Malays and others.[74] Trower inherited the crippling limitations. Close to his heart though Aboriginal evangelization might have been, in a letter to Montgomery he realistically listed his priorities, putting the scattered Europeans in the first place. After his first year he agreed with Montgomery's description of the north-west as 'the toughest ecclesiastical billet going'.[75]

For Goldsmith, the sand which provoked his almost despairing comment on his first visit to the north-west was a symbol of his work—much human effort, appearing like a tiny intermittent stream, dying in a trickle. By contrast, the inhabitants of the south-west sometimes described their corner of Western Australia as the garden of the state, a description that was certainly true of the orchard country with its undulating hills stretching from Donnybrook through to Bridgetown and Nannup, and the imposing timber forests of jarrah and karri running along close to the coast south of Mandurah, and inland through Manjimup and further east. Early in 1908 Goldsmith described most of the population of the diocese as 'farmers and fruitgrowers', and in addition there were miners in two towns—Greenbushes with tin, and Collie with its coal.[76] English readers of the *Bunbury Occasional Papers* could teasingly ask of its strange place-names '*Where* exactly are Looptheloop, and Stiremup, and Plumjelly, and the other sweetly-named places of which we read . . . ?'[77] But if the north-west imposed an impossible burden on Goldsmith's store of hopefulness, the south-west was a more manageable, but still demanding, unit, which required consolidation in the existing parishes and planning for expansion.

1905 was marked by several serious initiatives. Beyond the immediate domestic matter of a permanent dwelling—Bishopscourt was ready for occupation by the end of August[78]— Goldsmith's visit to England resulted in much more than a defence of the church in the face of the allegations of the Roth Report. He had organized the Bunbury Guild of Aid, a permanent committee to organize fund raising and promote the diocese in England, its leading figures being members of the Frewer family: George Ernest acted as its clerical warden and as editor of its journal, the *Bunbury Occasional Papers*; a sister-in-law, Ellen Frewer, was its secretary who subsequently organized many of the fund-raising activities. According to his itinerary in the *Bunbury Occasional Papers*, in four months, Goldsmith delivered 57 sermons, and gave 28 addresses on mission and the needs of the diocese. On his return he was able to report that as a result, in addition to the fourteen clergy who already held office in the south-west, he was expecting another six priests, and five or six candidates for holy orders to join the diocese either immediately or in the near future.[79] For the parishes, he encouraged the development of branches of the Church of England Men's Society, the Girls' Friendly Society, and the Mothers' Union.[80] Not surprisingly, just before Christmas, he was 'laid up' for a month.[81]

In February 1906 he was able to commence an experiment in bringing Anglicanism to the bush. Instead of purchasing a travelling van, as originally intended, he obtained a large buggy and a pair of horses. In addition to the library and magic lantern that were originally planned, it was also equipped with a font. Its driver, a deacon attached to the parish of Katanning, W. C. C. Caton, travelled south east and east of the railway line which ran between Albany and Perth, moving among the more dispersed settlers and animal hunters.[82]

During Lent that year Goldsmith visited five of the larger parishes (Albany, Katanning, Wagin, Bunbury and Collie), staying in each for a week, teaching and taking daily services. At Collie he played a harmonium at open-air services before services in the parish church. On Good Friday he was back in the cathedral, preaching the Three Hours' Devotion for its first observance there.[83] It was probably as much a result of his presence and the resultant increased degree of organization as of deepening piety among Anglicans that he was able to note a 66 per cent increase that year in the number of those confirmed—151.[84]

Increasingly as he considered the south-west from 1907 onwards, his attention was occupied by the effects of the dispersal and settlement of the population brought to the state by the gold rushes of the end of the previous century. Before 1896, male migrants considerably outnumbered female migrants, but between 1896 and 1900 the trend was reversed, and almost twice as many women as men came to Western Australia. Spouses came to join displaced diggers as they found work in both metropolitan and agricultural areas.[85] A letter by Goldsmith of 2 March 1907, published in the *Bunbury Occasional Papers,* was the first of many occasions on which he noted the increase in population, mainly settlers with little means, most of which were bound up in the land they came to develop and the equipment they needed to do this.[86] Eight new railways were under way, and the one between Wagin and Dumbleyung was already open. The railway lines, employing men to whom he wanted to offer some ministry, and the land which they opened up, became a constant burden of his correspondence to the SPG for some time to come.[87]

1907 was also a year in which the wider economy had a definite impact on the diocese. Despite the depressed market for wheat in Perth and Fremantle that year, railway lines continued to extend through the countryside. He confessed to Montgomery that the impact of a long and extended strike in the sawmills had forced him to spend beyond his intended budget, and that new tariffs were increasing the cost of living by almost a third.[88] In order to see the extent of the new settlement, he had undertaken a 951-mile trip in February, at the height of summer, during which he performed various ecclesiastical functions for 256 Anglicans scattered between Katanning and the Frankland district, and was introduced to 'squeaker' (jay) pie for dinner, and kid for supper. In his charge to the diocesan synod in September he repeated his concern about the expanding population, and the church's need to make adequate provision, to which he added relations between the church and working people and the reunion of the churches. As well as an increase of 70 per cent in male candidates for confirmation throughout the diocese,[89] in one parish in the previous twelve months, three brick or stone churches had been consecrated—St Mary's Dardanup, St George's Boyanup, and All Saints Donnybrook.[90]

In the midst of all of this, Goldsmith's constant travelling was already sufficiently conspicuous to prompt one anonymous wag to write the following lines:

*If your [sic] travelling in the country be it down or be it up*
*At Collie or Katanning Doodlekine or Cookernup,*
*At Narrowgin [sic] or Bridgetown or Dongarra or elsewhere,*
*It's a sovereign to a gooseberry, you will find his Lordship there.*

*You might seek secluded hamlets far from the haunts of men,*
*Out in lonely forests build yourself a gloomy hermit's den,*
*You'd have scarcely time to settle to your circumstances strange,*
*When "me Lud the bishop" would be found somewhere within your range.*

*Umbiquitous [sic] is scarce the word to designate the haste*
*With which the Bishop moves along, he doth no moment waste,*
*He's here and there and everywhere, just as a bishop should,*
*Who loves his church and flock, and, aye, delights in doing good.*[91]

By April 1908, on his way to England for the Lambeth Conference and the Pan-Anglican Congress, he could report that diocesan clergy had doubled in number in three and a half years, that seven churches, five halls and six residences had been built, and parish contributions to the extension of the church within the diocese had risen from £26 in his first year to £566. He arrived in England on the *Asturias* on 27 April.[92] The Pan-Anglican Congress ran between 15 and 24 June, and the Lambeth Conference extended over July into the first week of August.

While in England, he repeated his pattern of an exhausting round of sermons and addresses on behalf of the diocese: 93 sermons and 25 addresses between May and October. As a result, more branches of the Bunbury Guild of Aid were formed, and there were two new additions to the diocesan staff: one, a student from Burgh College, and the other, Theophilus Greatorex, vicar of St James the Less Westminster, who went to Pinjarra. After the dramatic and predominantly crimson interior of this church, designed by the prominent High Victorian architect George E. Street as a memorial to Bishop Monk of Gloucester, the small brick building on the edge of the Murray River at Pinjarra must have seemed another world, but Greatorex fulfilled one of Goldsmith's greatest desires in his diocese of hunters, timber hewers and tillers of the land—he was 'reputed to be *persona grata* with men', a former captain of Harrow's First Eleven, now going out to 'play the game' at the bounds of Greater Britain, where a new empire might be created in the South Seas.[93]

1909 was in some ways a prelude to a breakthrough. At the end of its first quarter he wrote optimistically to Montgomery, 'I am convinced that we are rapidly developing into what will be a great, important, populous state which will have considerable influence . . .'[94] Even allowing for the need to impress his contacts in England with the urgency of his needs, there is still no good reason to question the optimistic, almost nationalistic, tone of such a statement. Rather, it was this kind of conviction that made him impatient to organize and staff diocesan structures to keep pace with the anticipated expansion.

Collections and donations from the bishop's time in England amounted to almost £450, though £130 of this was from the Pan-Anglican Thank-Offering. He had ordained two priests on his return in Advent, and expected to ordain another that year. There was a third addition to the diocesan staff as a result of the previous year's trip: G. S. Stubbs, from the Anglo-Catholic parish of St Matthias Malvern Link. A new brick church at Thomson's Brook was opened on St Patrick's day, renovations to the interior of St John's Collie were completed, and communities at Kojonup, Cuballing, Popannying, Yarloop, Margaret River and Bridgetown were busy raising funds to build churches there.[95]

Particular issues close to his heart received greater priority. At the end of March, 'Field Place', next to Bishopscourt, became the home of the new Bunbury Girls' Grammar School, presided over by a Miss L. Friend. Even though it was only small, with 9 boarders and 22 day pupils, it was a beginning for Anglican education in the south-west, in a township which had only two other primary schools—a government school (now occupied by the State Tourist Bureau), and a convent school.[96] Later in the year, in September, Goldsmith gave addresses on education at the seventh Anglican Church Congress, held in Perth. One of a series of meetings that had been taking place in state capitals since the 1880s, it brought together speakers on a wide variety of issues seen to be of concern to Australian Anglicans.[97] At that conference T. M. Robinson also presented a paper on the religious life, possibly reinforcing Goldsmith's own intention of establishing a Bush Brotherhood, which hope had already been raised in 1908, and dashed when Western Australia was not designated as the object of the Pan-Anglican Thank-Offering. It resurfaced as a topic at clergy conferences at Katanning and Pinjarra.[98]

And if ministry to the Aboriginal communities of the north-west had been an issue, at least in theory, in the earlier years of the decade, issues of race and culture in connection with that area were also raised at the Congress. On the one hand, the kind of socialism embraced by Canon Reginald Stephen (subsequently Bishop of Tasmania and Newcastle), did not prevent him from suggesting that it was a 'fatal mistake' to introduce 'the highest interests of Christianity' to 'a heathen population'. Christian and non-Christian were diametrically opposed, 'repulsive' to one another. Against this narrow identity of race, culture and religion, Archdeacon Whitington of Hobart saw a future north-west diocese as an opportunity for mission to the Japanese, Malays and others working in the area. But it was Goldsmith's archdeacon, Brooks, who received a round of applause for a speech in which he reminded his hearers that Jesus was a 'coloured man', and that their lives and actions should demonstrate in the clearest possible way their belief in God and in a common humanity.[99]

Another highlight of the year was the visit to the diocese of H. S. Woollcombe, the Travelling Secretary of the Church of England Men's Society. His visits to Pinjarra, Greenbushes, Bunbury, Brunswick, Collie, Wagin, Katanning and Albany were described in terms which stressed the church's desire to appeal to men, an emphasis which was particularly understandable in the light of prevailing circumstances.[100] Despite the number of men whose families had moved on to the land with them, there was a heavy masculine emphasis in a society which was devoid of many of the comforts of a more sophisticated city lifestyle, and there was also an increasing number of new communities that were exclusively or almost exclusively male, mainly among the timber fellers and railway workers. In contrast to the very practical questions that needed equally practical answers, a curious sidelight is thrown by an entry in Melbourne's *Victorian Churchman*, a conservative evangelical journal, which referred to plans for a historic pageant in Bunbury in winter, featuring episodes of early British church history. The *Bunbury Occasional Papers* make no reference to this event. Whatever the outcome of preparations involving a choir and orchestra, it was likely that Goldsmith intended that such an educational entertainment should reinforce a sense of the English heritage of the town's Anglican community. Predictably, later that year, the *Victorian Churchman*, which envisaged one of its roles as that of a watchdog to sniff out ritualism in any guise, no matter how deceptive, carried a note that explained its interest in such proceedings even in far away Western Australia. Pageants were ritualist in sympathy. Presumably its editor felt that Bunbury Anglicans loyal to the reformation's principles needed to be warned that even seemingly innocent activities might mask a deviation from Protestant orthodoxy.[101]

By the beginning of 1910 Goldsmith could count 25 clergy in the diocese, and since his first year, eleven new churches, five mission halls, and six clergy houses had been built, and five rectories and one church had been rebuilt or enlarged. Eight new churches were under way. Beyond a Brotherhood, there was one other consideration which he deemed essential—a new cathedral, to replace 'the present undignified little Church which serves (most inadequately) as a Pro-Cathedral'; in later references he estimated that St Paul's held about 250 worshippers, and this estimate seems to have been generous according to other accounts. An appeal in June 1914 referred to it being 'packed' with two hundred people, and described its shortcomings:

> Probably a severe storm would wreck the roof; the walls are of very inferior brick, and are eaten through in many places. The vestry is a badly annexed wooden patch on the brick, and very small. Somebody years ago filled the East window with 'glazier' or some 'transfer' of horrible pattern, now worn through by sunlight . . .[102]

He went on to speak of a building which would cost £20,000, and noted that at the 1909 synod, a collection of £66 had been contributed towards it. A full design would cost £1,000 alone. He did not seem to notice, or perhaps he forced himself to ignore, the discrepancy between the giving and the vision. He would be successful in getting the Brotherhood, but the cathedral was beyond him.

— NINE —

# From 'A Nation in the Mill' to 'England's Green and Pleasant Land': 1910–1932

The end to missionary responsibility for the north-west, which came with the arrival of Bishop Trower, was described by Goldsmith as an 'inexpressible relief', and understandably so.[1] Even this sense of relief over the north-west was tempered as, by 1912, Trower was making allegations of 'untruthfulness and dishonesty' against Bunbury, claiming that money that should have been part of the north-west's grant from the SPG had been withheld by them.[2]

Meanwhile, the release, which freed him to concentrate on the needs of the south-west, came just in time. By the middle of 1910 he wrote to England:

> The stream is absolutely dry, and we have Four New Districts (Agricultural) most urgently requiring a Priest, besides Three Timber Mills, literally crowded with many hundreds of rough and reckless men . . . We have no money for new work, when we terribly need Seven more Priests.[3]

Elsewhere he wrote of what he described as the 'unprecedented growth' of farming and timber exports, with six new timber mills, including those at Nannup and Marrinup, and the rapid taking up of land for wheat production in districts such as Wickepin and Dumbleyung, as land continued to be opened up by the railways. At synod in September, he delivered the same message, and referred to the increase in British migrants as well as those who continued to come from elsewhere within Australia. As always, he sensed that the church had to move in immediately among the new settlers.[4]

With the rising population in the diocese, confirmation numbers had increased by 150 per cent on the figures of six years before. He confirmed 244 candidates, and singled out for comment the fact that 'about 37 per cent were men and boys',[5] manifesting his continuing concern to reach the men who formed a large part of the south-west's working population; at the following synod he commented on the high proportion of adults he had confirmed, though the proportion of males to females had dropped somewhat.[6] Comparative figures for clergy numbers, buildings, and for giving within the diocese over a period of five years all showed substantial increases, but the need for a fitting cathedral continued to frustrate him.[7] 1910 also saw the resignation of the rector of Bunbury, Harry Darling. His replacement at the pro-cathedral was the rotund 'Porky' Adams from Lancashire, whose churchmanship seems to have been more consonant with the bishop's own, as altar lights were restored and a daily eucharist commenced at St Paul's during his time.[8]

1911 saw the accession to the British throne of George V, but to the bishop of this remote corner of the empire the year was chiefly satisfying as the year of the long-awaited inauguration of the Brotherhood of Saint Boniface on 11 July. It began with four members: Mazzini Tron, who was a new arrival from England, two others, Gerald Stubbs and A. D. Webb already being diocesan clergy, and the other was its only Australian member, Frederick William Spargo. At the last moment, after arrangements seemed to have been finalized for locating them at Kojonup, they took up temporary headquarters at Williams.[9] There had been enough delays without waiting further for a permanent home.

The eventual alleviation of the irritation caused by the lack of an adequate cathedral also seemd to be in sight; by July a Cathedral Building Committee had been formed and was canvassed in the local press.[10] While his synod charge that year drew attention to the widespread social unrest in England,[11] in Bunbury itself there was an extensive strike by waterside workers. Local press reports made no reference to the bishop's having played any part in bringing about a reconciliation between the parties involved, but the compilers of the *Bunbury Occasional Papers* (presumably drawing on Goldsmith's own correspondence with his brother-in-law's family) described him as joining with the member for Bunbury and the local Traders' Association in trying to negotiate a compromise.[12]

Goldsmith continued to appeal for financial support from outside the diocese. Privately and publicly he quoted figures on British migration, which showed that the Australian intake of British settlers exceeded that of Canada or the United States together by almost 150 per cent. For his English readers, he described how

> Lancashire and Yorkshire have been pouring men and women into the country. As I stood at 3.00 a. m. on Narrogin railway platform recently, just after the arrival of a White Star ship, I could have fancied myself in a North Western or Great Northern station, while I listened to the talk of about 150 new arrivals investigating their unwonted surroundings. Away they go, penetrating further and further into the bush, clearing every year more land for cultivation, and consequently increasing the already huge area of our unwieldy parishes.[13]

In the bishop's eyes the new railways, the increasing timber trade and agricultural development demanded at least six new priests for the diocese. Already existing churches—St Peter's Brunswick, and St Andrew's Katanning—and rectories at Wagin and Yarloop were enlarged, and churches were in progress at Cuballing and Wickepin, and were contemplated for Wellington Mills and Boyup.[14]

The arrival of two of Goldsmith's relatives added to the existing family involvement in the diocese represented by the administration of the Guild of Aid by the Frewers. At the Girls Grammar School next door to Bishopscourt Miss Friend was followed as principal by Miss Bertha Harcourt. At synod that year Goldsmith described her as 'a gentlewoman of wide general culture, an enthusiastic teacher, and a loyal colleague'; but a report in 1913 makes it clear that she 'got results'—two students took the first and second prizes in a national essay competition, others obtained distinctions in *Alliance Francaise* examinations and in music— she was obviously training good gentlewomen for the empire's future.[15] But the other family member, John Frewer, who was appointed as domestic chaplain and private secretary, also came in response to signs that the bishop's health was being overtaxed. Goldsmith had been advised by his doctor to cancel some of his appointments.[16] As well as lightening the burden of administration, Goldsmith saw his nephew as another priest whose previous experience (in his case, among the wharfies of Skirbeck, Lincoln's dockland) prepared him for working among labouring men in the diocese. Shortly after arrival, he was described as assisting Adams at

Bunbury Grammar School staff and children, 1911

the pro-cathedral, and working 'amongst the lumpers, railwaymen and other parishioners of the cathedral Parish'.[17] Another impending arrival, A. J. Ridge, who was expected to join the Brotherhood, was regarded as a likely candidate for the diocese because he had previously worked 'largely among big lads near Woolwich'.[18]

1912 marked the bishop's third and last visit to England as diocesan, arriving on 15 February and leaving on 29 October. Here he described the growing Australia and the demands put on her by her rapid development as 'a Nation in the Mill'.[19] Again he conducted appeals according to the now-familiar pattern all over England, preaching 115 sermons and addressing 46 meetings; on his return, he was described at a public reception as 'a sort of wandering beggar'.[20] In response to his assessment of the need for at least eight additional clergy, seven new clergy came to the diocese, including three with previous Australian experience.[21] Without ever having met the bishop, Monica Wills offered to build a permanent home for the Brotherhood at Williams. A parishioner of the well-known Anglo-Catholic shrine, All Saints Margaret Street, also offered the means for the building of a substantial church in a mining town, All Saints Collie.

As well as promoting the ecclesiastical needs of the diocese, Goldsmith became a spokesman for the state, noting that 'people from the Eastern States' were unwilling or unable to give accurate information about Western Australia:

A general view of Bunbury, c. 1920
The town centre as it was when Goldsmith left Bunbury

> A great many have an idea that we do not want immigrants here at all. I always told individuals and audiences that what we wanted especially was men who were ready to go into the country rather than into the towns. I was able to give advice to a good many intending immigrants, and I have already received letters from promising young men since I came back who will probably settle somewhere in the South-West in the course of the next few months . . .[22]

Speaking on another occasion just after his return from England, he reaffirmed his belief that the waves of migrants would continue and that, with cheaper travel, 'they would see their acres filled up more and more rapidly'.[23] In the decade leading up to 1913, Western Australia had taken in 54,777 immigrants from Great Britain, and Goldsmith himself commented on the increased promotion of the state amongst potential migrants as a result of the presence of Newton Moore as Agent-General in London. Moore had been Bunbury's mayor at the time of the bishop's enthronement, and some evidence suggests that he planned an intense migration scheme as a stepping stone for his own political career.[24] As a part of Bunbury's establishment at the time of Goldsmith's election, Moore may well have felt inclined to share some of his hopes for the future of the state with the bishop during his time in London. But even without this, statistics from the *Diocesan Yearbook* pointed to continuing growth, adding further fuel to fire the bishop's optimistic vision of a prosperous future in a well-populated diocese.[25]

The year before the outbreak of World War I saw the first and only conference of all the Bush Brotherhoods in Brisbane, at which Harold Harper, then warden of the Brotherhood of St Boniface, was conspicuous in advocating the brotherhood ideal as one of religious community, an approach which reflected Goldsmith's particular hope for his own foundation's future. As the year drew to an end the completed House of Grace at Williams was blessed on 5 November.[26] In another part of the diocese, near Pinjarra, the Rhodesian Rhodes Scholar Kingsley Fairbridge, now a diocesan lay reader and synodsman, who had founded, when he was only an undergraduate, the Rhodes Emigration Society in order to promote the mass emigration of English slum children, had established Fairbridge Farm, with about forty boys.[27]

The episcopal visitations to the remote corners continued: the *Bunbury Occasional Paper* for June 1913 gave a lengthy account of a trip made by car across the diocese in mid-summer to Ravensthorpe, then a copper-mining area facing a serious slump. At synod, the usual report was made of new churches and halls built, existing buildings enlarged, and new churches contemplated, and more well-meaning noises about the desirability of a cathedral were heard from its Building Committee. As well as seeking funds for the projected cathedral, the bishop estimated that another £5,000 was needed to provide the Grammar School adequately for its future.[28] Through the *Bunbury Occasional Papers* and his ongoing correspondence with the SPG, Goldsmith urged the need for more clergy: he had need for six more and could finance five. With the building of the transcontinental railway, 'an immense army of hewers and millworkers are now in our forests, and is increasing every month . . .'[29]

The creation in 1914 of Kalgoorlie, the last of the state's country dioceses, completed Riley's scheme for a province and necessitated the calling of a special synod in Bunbury at the end of April in order to pass the legislation necessary for its enactment. Riley noted that J. C. Wright, who had succeeded Saumarez Smith as Primate in 1910, having seemingly inherited his predecessor's indifference to the smaller rural dioceses, was unwilling to allow the inclusion of the north-east diocese within the province (it did not have sufficient staff to make a quorum for a synod of its own). Wright had already blocked the formation of a Western province in 1911, and by 1914 the tone of Riley's correspondence verged on the hysterical, as he feared yet more objections.[30]

Just before the outbreak of war, two men whose impact on Anglicanism in the countryside was made on Goldsmith's return to England commenced their priestly work in the diocese. One was Arnold Fryer, whom Goldsmith ordained after he had studied at the House of Grace; he was to become the archetypal Anglo-Catholic priest of the diocese under Cecil Wilson, Goldsmith's successor. At Fryer's ordination he licensed another priest newly arrived from England, Edward Elsey, who entered the Brotherhood, and was elected to succeed Cyril Golding-Bird as second Bishop of Kalgoorlie in 1919.[31]

The war increased the urgency of Goldsmith's appeals for funds, and multiplied the areas of concern as uncertainties loomed over the stability and continuity of many institutions on which the diocese depended directly or indirectly. At the end of 1914 Goldsmith wrote to his English supporters of the closing of the timber mills and the drop in the export trade through Bunbury's port from two shiploads daily to one per month. As well as writing to H. H. Montgomery of the general dislocation of industry brought about by the war, he wrote of the effect of drought in 1914, which caused a rise in unemployment and prices.[32] Disruption also occurred at the House of Grace. Extensions were built to accommodate new members, but existing members were to join the Forces, and others who had stated their intention of joining likewise rechannelled their energies into the war effort.[33]

Apart from its brief meeting to ratify the legislation to enable the formation of the province, synod was not called together that year, but at synod in 1915 Goldsmith was able to report that there were 31 clergy in the diocese in spite of the war.[34] In their home adjacent to Bishopscourt, the Grammar School's life descended to a nadir. Many children were employed by their parents during the fruit-picking season and then an outbreak of smallpox led to the withdrawal of many other pupils.[35] The war overshadowed another note of personal loss that year when his father, who had been senile and in poor health for several years, died at Eastbourne, in the presence of his other son, Herbert Symonds Goldsmith, who had married only the year before.[36] The full clerical roll reported for 1915 gave the impression that the diocese was weathering the austerities imposed by the war remarkably well. One of the original Brothers of St Boniface, Mazzini Tron, then rector of Dwellingup, left as a chaplain, but there were four priests and one deacon then at the House of Grace. J. D. Grogan, a deacon at Collie, joined the army medical corps. To English friends, Goldsmith still wrote in frustration of the permanent thorn in his flesh, the lack of a cathedral, as services for a parish mission in Bunbury every night for three weeks attracted numbers of worshippers too great to fit into the tiny pro-cathedral:

> We are driven out into a *hall*—fancy oh ye worshippers in the glorious Churches of the Old Country—into a *hall* for worship. And here locally, what can we do? Our timber industry is closed, there is no shipping, our lumpers are idle, our railways doing very little, our business people and store-keepers, of course, suffer in consequence.37

At the 1915 synod, he commented that the existing Cathedral Building Committee consisted entirely of synod members, and that a more broadly constituted executive committee with real power to act—and to choose a site—was needed before any action was likely to take place.38

As a compensation, he could look with some satisfaction on the effect of the Bunbury parish mission on the local devotional life. At the pro-cathedral there were 184 communicants at Easter that year, almost double the number five years previously. In the evenings, during the course of the mission, there were processions to various parts of the town with cross, banner, lights, and choir and clergy singing the Litany; short addresses were given, and hymns sung from the *Mirfield Mission Hymnbook*, a product of the Community of the Resurrection. Six women parishioners collected £200 within a week, sufficient to provide a year's stipend for a second priest on the cathedral staff. After the mission its conductor, Father Walter Scott of the Brisbane parish of Toowong, conducted a three-day clergy retreat at the Grammar School.39 To Goldsmith, the effect of the mission must have proved that traditional Catholic methods could work in a remote Australian centre. He ordained two more deacons, one of whom replaced Mazzini Tron at Dwellingup. And at Collie, All Saints had been completed, and was consecrated on 3 November 1915: it had cost £2,000.40

But 1916 saw the war making deeper inroads. Goldsmith wrote to H. H. Montgomery of the enrolment of whole branches of the Church of England Men's Society, which he had been so eager to promote as a way of reaching working men; and of how the war had taken 'many hundreds of our best young men'.41 Goldsmith's comments concerning the impact of the war on male involvement in church organizations is hardly surprising. A random study of about half the members of the 11th Battalion, the first unit to be organized in Western Australia, shows that almost 70 per cent of its members were from the rural areas of the state. More than half the battalion were Anglican—58 per cent, as against a figure of 36 per cent for the proportion of Anglicans among males aged 20 years and over in the population. Of another unit, the 10th Light Horse, 28 per cent of its members were Western Australians.[42]

The war made inroads on his special project, the Brotherhood. Alan Thompson, Arthur White, and Harold Harper all left the Brotherhood House to go to the front, leaving Edward Elsey, John Frewer and a postulant alone to maintain its work. And it took up Goldsmith's time, taking him outside the diocese. As Archbishop Riley visited the European and Middle Eastern fronts as a senior chaplain, Goldsmith was called on to provide episcopal ministrations in Perth.

To the 1916 synod he described the war effort of those still at home as a matter of increased or renewed discipline and devotion, and implied that like a number of others, he had taken a pledge of total abstinence until the war should end.[43] And it was to this synod that he described the next step in his desire for a cathedral, the purchase of the site on Brent Tor (where the present cathedral stands), a site which he claimed was entirely suitable for the future growth of Bunbury. The site was purchased from George Rose, who also gave a small piece of land in Parkfield Street.[44]

But this public statement concealed a large degree of disappointment. As far back as 1912, had Nora Noyes not specified that her gift had to be used for the erection of a church in a mining town, Goldsmith might well have been able to build a cathedral, instead of All Saints Collie, which, as it was, exacerbated rivalry between Collie and Bunbury.[45] In 1915 Goldsmith had shown a preference, not for the Brent Tor site, but one close by on Bury Hill, which would need levelling by about sixteen feet to be brought to the same height, and which would constitute a 'commanding position' for a 'stately cathedral'.[46] A report on the site was made, and at least one sketch showed the scale on which it was hoped to build—the nave of the cathedral on this site was to accommodate 750, a chapel in the east would hold 189, and another in the west, 140, with room for another 289 elsewhere.[47] The site was owned by Edwin Rose, whose home, Bury Hill House, was near by. Rose offered it (supposedly at a reduced rate), to the diocese, but the price was considered by the Diocesan Council and Trustees to be too high. According to one source, when votes were evenly distributed between each site, William Balston, who had been elected by synod for several successive years as one of the two wardens on the cathedral council, cast the vote against the Bury Hill site, much to the bishop's dismay.[48]

Jack Hands, who later became mayor of Bunbury, soon made a deposit on the Bury Hill site on behalf of the Roman Catholic community.[49] According to A. E. Morris, the bishop was subsequently 'quick to buy', or rather encourage the purchase of the Brent Tor site, owned by George Rose.[50] But privately Goldsmith told George Clarke, then mayor of Bunbury, a member of the pro-cathedral vestry and near neighbour, whose house faced Bishopscourt from the other side of Cross Street, that he was not satisfied to build on Brent Tor, behind a new Roman Catholic cathedral, which would dominate the skyline from Victoria Street, the old township's main thoroughfare, and be easily accessible from the centre of the town.[51]

In Goldsmith's time as now, any building on Brent Tor would have been invisible from the old centre. Cross Street, which runs up the south side of the cathedral site, was not then a surfaced road, and ended at Bishopscourt, only part of the way up the hill; the present Parkfield Street, the southern boundary of the site, did not exist, being known only as 'the cutting at the Cross Street end'. Canon Adams, who preferred the Bury Hill site, threatened to leave all his estate to the Mission to Seamen if Brent Tor were used as a cathedral site—and fulfilled his threat when Goldsmith's second successor, Bishop Knight, finally presided over the decision to build there.[52]

The failure even to commence the building of an adequate cathedral was the immediate cause which led to Goldsmith's decision to resign, a decision which he made public on 29 November 1916, and explained in a letter dated 9 December.[53] But beyond the immediate disappointment over the cathedral site, the war had visibly aged him. His statement that the diocese needed to be placed under the direction of a younger man was realistic enough, though the election of Cecil Wilson was hardly to conform to this ideal.⁵⁴ In the final pages of an essay on the Anglican episcopacy in Australia, written within the last three years of his life, he described those aspects of the work of an Australian country bishop which had not even a remote equivalent in the experience of an English bishop, in a way which was clearly autobiographical.⁵⁵ To Montgomery he wrote more succinctly of the same thing:

> I am as ready for <u>work</u> as I ever was, but I find that thirteen years of almost incessant travelling—and very much of it nowadays has to be done in all-night journeys often under conditions inseparable from a 'mixed goods' train—begins at last to unfit one for immediate exertion. I have for some time been trying to solve the problem of my duty under the circumstances, when the unexpected offer of work in London came, and as it seemed to me, was the intended answer to my perplexities . . . ⁵⁶

In his second statement concerning his resignation, he described himself as a loser 'in dignity and financially'; he had in fact received an invitation from Sir Spencer Maryon-Wilson, whom he had tutored when a curate at Charlton, inviting him to accept the living of St John's Hampstead, in succession to Canon Deane, who had gone to All Saints Ennismore Gardens, to replace W. R. Inge, who in turn had gone to St Paul's Cathedral where he became known as the 'gloomy dean'.⁵⁷

His last weeks in the diocese included a visit to the Brotherhood House just after Christmas, which must have had something of the atmosphere of a parting family picnic, since he brought Bertha Harcourt and her aide, Miss Birch, with him. There were also gifts of books and of vestments, including the first chasuble worn in the state. On New Year's day four clergy joined the party at the House of Grace.⁵⁸ But he returned to Williams, this time to confirm, on the weekend of 5–6 February 1917, and later that week, when a farewell social was held on Thursday evening in Bunbury at the Bedford Hall, which was packed to the doors, his beloved brothers were there to see the bishop receive a presentation of £100.⁵⁹

His last Sunday in the pro-cathedral was Quinquagesima Sunday. The next day, at 6.30 a.m., he celebrated his last eucharist there and administered to fifty communicants. At the railway station a considerable crowd gathered, and he steamed out to cheers of good will.⁶⁰ In spite of later intentions to the contrary, he was never to see Bunbury again. Behind him he left eighteen new churches, a doubling in the number of clergy who were there when he first arrived, and several new parishes.

Before leaving Australia from Sydney to cross the Pacific to Vancouver on SS *Dimboola*, and thence by rail to New York, and on to Liverpool, he cabled his final message:

> My daily prayers and farewell message to my Diocese: Philippians 1, vv. 8–11. ('For God is my record, how greatly I long after you all in the bowels of Jesus Christ. And this I pray, that your love may abound yet more and more in knowledge and in all judgement; that ye may approve all things that are excellent; that ye may be sincere and without offence till the day of Christ; being filled with the fruits of righteousness, which are by Jesus Christ, unto the glory and praise of God.')[61]

By 9 May the Brotherhood House had received the news that the bishop had arrived safely in England.[62]

*B*efore following him back to England, it is appropriate to comment on the way in which the issues of churchmanship took their place in his life as a diocesan. Later and always sympathetic assessors of his overall ministry and character described him as firm in his own convictions while tolerant of others. Hawtrey suggested that in the diocese of Bunbury he confronted an even more self-consciously Protestant Anglican community than in Perth.[63]

Seven years before Goldsmith's election, considerable dissatisfaction over the incumbency of W. F. Marshall (Rector of Bunbury 1892–97) led to volatile public meetings at which impassioned denunciations of him as a ritualist were made. A description of one such occasion in the press was headed 'A Disgraceful Scene'. Marshall's ritual consisted in the use of altar lights, reverencing the altar and making the sign of the cross.[64]

These accusations also masked other more significant areas of dissension: tension between the Bunbury community, which seems to have regarded his attention to the outcentres, which gave him their unashamed support, as a form of neglect; and the belief that he was improperly appropriating collections for his own use—he was in fact taking the Easter offertories, which in England were traditionally the incumbent's.[65] But the hostility of Thomas Hayward throughout Marshall's ministry and the gradual alienation of W. H. Timperley, both of whom had been significant figures in the town's life for several decades, indicate that the conflict also involved a generation gap in which Marshall and his churchmanship were on one side and senior members of the community on the other, all the time manipulated by Marshall's predecessor as Rector of Bunbury, Joseph Withers.[66] To this extent, it was a small-town equivalent of the disapproval meted out to Goldsmith in his Perth days by some of the 'ancient colonists' who had been formed in a different kind of piety, an element that has already been discussed.[67] Indeed, at one point during the Bunbury conflict when Thomas Hayward assumed a less prominent role in church affairs, a pseudonymous correspondent even claimed that church meetings in Bunbury were being 'stacked' in the same way as those recently held at St George's cathedral.[68]

It was possibly to appease the ill will that Marshall's incumbency had generated, as much as anything else, that his successor, Harry Darling, did away with altar lights.[69] But even then, there were signs that Anglo-Catholicism already had its supporters in Bunbury. A correspondent in the Perth press who wrote under the name of 'An English Catholic' and gave his address as Bunbury, warned another south-west correspondent, 'Watchman', that even his vigilance 'will not be able to keep it out of Bunbury much longer'.[70]

If Perth taught Goldsmith not to appoint a dean to Bunbury, lest he be subject to a repetition of his own relationship with Riley, it may also have taught him to modify the forthrightness with which he put forward his own position. As a bishop, he certainly showed as much desire in his public statements as Riley to avoid taking sides over churchmanship: at the 1910 synod he affirmed the need for a unified church, characterized by diversity in unity—'Catholic and evangelical are not two, but one'. Suspicion needed to be avoided over non-essentials—'We must not magnify trifles'.[71] But his own churchmanship was certainly questioned. In the 1907 synod a speaker from the floor asked why the term 'altar', and not 'communion table' was used, to which Goldsmith replied by reference to the language of the Epistle to the Hebrews: the Holy Communion is a representation of the sacrifice of Christ on the Cross, and 'We have an altar here'.[72]

In England the traditional episcopal vesture of cope and mitre was attacked by anti-ritualists in spite of the fact that the use of the cope had survived in some cathedrals, severely diminished, but with a greater degree of continuity than most other ceremonial usages; and the mitre even appeared on the heads of some Anglican prelates in Ireland and North America in the eighteenth century.[73] The Church Association's *Ritualistic Clergy List,* which included Goldsmith among its catalogue of subversive clergy, was illustrated with a frontispiece showing a map of Britain, surrounded by ritualistic threats, one of which was a bishop in mitre and cope.[74] His ceremonial caution in the opening years of his episcopate may have reflected not only a respect for some local opposition to Anglo-Catholicism, but also an awareness of the sensitivity which his brethren in England still had to show, despite the abating of the height of anti-ritualist animosity preceding the 1900 election, with its attacks on the bishops. And from further back in time, there was a reserve engendered during his early years as a priest in England during the prosecutions under the Public Worship Regulation Act.

In 1909 a layman, whom Goldsmith did not publicly identify, presented him with the episcopal vesture. His policy on its use was a cautious one, which suggests that he anticipated some opposition or had learnt from his Perth experiences. He informed synod that year that he would use cope and mitre as a matter of course only in the pro-cathedral. Elsewhere, he would only wear them with the unanimous consent of churchwardens and vestry. But the explanation that he offered his synod still had overtones of the legal battles over ritual of the previous century. He told them that a recent report by a committee of the Upper House of the Convocation of Canterbury on the Ornaments Rubric and the 1604 Canons had found that cope and mitre were a 'practically continuous tradition', and that he was 'bidden', that is, legally obliged, to use them: 'I feel that if I demand canonical obedience from the clergy, I must render willing obedience myself to the ordinances of the Church in accordance with my ordination vows'.[75] In 1911 he repeated his claim that the vesture was obligatory, and reassured his listeners that not only the occupants of major English sees, such as Canterbury, York, Durham and London, wore cope and mitre,but other Australian bishops, including Brisbane, Adelaide and Rockhampton.[76]

Ceremonial at the pro-cathedral was modified, though only cautiously, under Darling's successor, Canon Adams. Altar lights were reintroduced in Advent 1912, and a daily eucharist began on Palm Sunday of 1913; the only other centre in the diocese to have a daily eucharist was the House of Grace.77 Given that the altar lights did not reappear until eight years after his arrival in Bunbury, Goldsmith could hardly be accused of pushing his own brand of churchmanship in the cathedral. The Bunbury press which had reported the turbulent meetings in Marshall's time were silent over these matters. If parishioners were uneasy, they did not resort to the correspondence columns. All-embracing public criticism of any kind of ceremonial no longer came from within Anglican ranks, but from outside. In 1912 a nonconformist cleric in Bunbury described 'the gospel of form and ceremony' as one of several 'false gospels'. It is not clear whether the main object of his censure was Roman Catholic or Anglican liturgy, but his strictures were sufficiently broad to apply to the Anglican rite, even when performed with a restrained ceremonial.78

F. W. Goldsmith in cope and mitre, from *Church Chronicle*, 29 February 1912

Although no service registers have survived from this period which provide a detailed record of communicant attendances, those figures that do survive through the reports of parochial meetings indicate that while the total annual communicant figures at the cathedral continued to rise throughout Goldsmith's episcopate, the daily eucharist was attended by a very few worshippers.

A description of the ordination of Fryer and Thompson in 1914 refers to the use of Merbecke's plainsong for the ordinary, a usage which was not new to the pro-cathedral, but its reference to an introit and gradual is too ambiguous to make it clear as to whether this refers to congregational hymns, or the use of plainchant propers from the Roman rite.[79]

In some Australian churches whose Anglo-Catholic identity was quite pronounced, such as St Peter's Eastern Hill, Melbourne, the war was marked by a noticeable increase in the attendances at requiems and the offering of prayer for the war dead. Goldsmith does not appear to have made special use of the war period in which to urge the desirability of prayer for the departed. What he did note was a deeper general devotion, an observation which was made by the leaders of all major churches during the period: 'the war is certainly exercising a good influence on many people, more particularly in leading them to prayer. Our eucharists and other Intercessory services have been specially well attended . . .'[80] The rise in communicant numbers in Bunbury during the war period was thus a response to the urgency of the moment.

The mission conducted by Walter Scott in 1915 did result in an apparent upsurge of devotion in the town. The bishop himself, who had been 'doubtful' about the reception which might have greeted the mission's outdoor evening processions and the short outdoor services held at prominent points in town such as the Rose Hotel intersection, was pleased to note that everywhere the processions went, male bystanders removed their hats.[81]

As was the common practice of Anglo-Catholic missioners, Scott chose ascetic and spiritual subjects for his major addresses, 'first principles', such as the vision of God as the purpose of life, the barriers to that vision formed by sin, the centrality of a personal relationship with God, and the life of prayer. The mission's core was a call to holiness of living, not a didactic explanation of a particular doctrinal system or liturgical style. However, Scott and the other missioners (W. Elsey and A. E. White of the Brotherhood, and Father Fryer) advertised their availability to hear confessions. Some of the tangible results—the raising of funds for an extra stipend, an increase in adults preparing for confirmation—can hardly be said to reflect a particular churchmanship, but others suggested a definite response to the Oxford Movement's emphasis on worship as a deliberate and formal offering, involving outward and visible signs: a 'Fellowship of the Sanctuary' was founded to care for the requirements of the altar; a 'St Cecilia's Choir' was formed to sing the liturgy on the Prayerbook Calendar's holy days; and the writer in the *Church Standard* makes Bunbury sound like the continental village whose devout peasants were often held up by Anglo-Catholic writers as a devotional model: 'At St David's the devotional spirit of the people was wonderfully developed by the morning prayer meetings, and many people may be seen now going into Church on their way to market to pray their "mysteries".'[82]

The statement made later by the same writer, that as a consequence of the Mission, 'the Holy Eucharist is made the principal Sunday Service', describes the achievement of a definite aim of most clergy generally influenced by the Oxford Movement and of Anglo-Catholics in particular—the removal of matins (morning prayer) from the dominant place in Sunday morning worship. While Goldsmith had cherished this aim since his Perth days, its actual attainment in 1916 is a reflection of the more general impact of the Oxford Movement with the passing of time, rather than an indication of a deeper commitment to its standards on the part of Bunbury Anglicans compared with those of Perth.

Not long after Goldsmith's attempt during the 1894 interregnum to give the sung eucharist a more central place at the cathedral by celebrating *before* matins, which ended with a return to the status quo of the fortnightly celebration after matins, that indefatigable Anglo-Catholic Carnarvon cleric, William Sharp, complained, 'it is a thousand pities that the Eucharist cannot be made the chief service on every Sunday in the diocese'.[83] He lamented the difficulty he encountered in trying to explain the reason for Carnarvon's weekly sung eucharist to those from the many other places in the Perth diocese where matins was the norm. A year later he referred to newcomers to Carnarvon, familiar with 11.00 a.m. matins, as 'prejudiced against the Blessed Sacrament being the great service of the day'.[84] At this stage, one of the most basic long-term principles of the Oxford Movement was still struggling to make headway. In England, though there were a number of explicitly Anglo-Catholic parishes where the eucharist had already overtaken matins, many clergy of strongly Catholic convictions still felt obliged to compromise and defer to custom. At Brede, Goldsmith's brother-in-law, George Ernest Frewer, had maintained matins in its central position until his retirement in 1916, the year that Bunbury's pro-cathedral had opted for a central position for the eucharist. And when G. E. Frewer's son succeeded him as rector and initiated the change his father had always wished to make, there were complaints. But even as Bunbury in all its remoteness was changing, in England, the Parish and People movement, which would bring this change to many English parishes, was in its infancy.[85]

In Bunbury a more explicit presentation of issues of churchmanship took place with the holding of a 'Churchmens Conference' after diocesan synod in 1916.[86] Its two sessions, one in the afternoon and one in the evening, were attended by about 70 and 120 people respectively. Liturgical matters were raised: 'worship' was listed as one of the topics. Dr Prins, who appears elsewhere as a devout Anglo-Catholic, spoke on the centrality of the eucharist, urging its celebration with 'full ceremonial', that is, high mass with incense, and an increase in the use of penance as a preparation for reception. The description of the conference implies the existence of a body within the pro-cathedral parish who did not agree with such views, but represents them as being silent at this point.

Though vestments were introduced at St Paul's during the episcopate of Cecil Wilson, Goldsmith's successor, it appears that the body which silently resisted suggestions such as those put forward by Dr Prins were finally representative of the impact of the Oxford Movement on pro-cathedral parishioners. Incense and the ceremonial of high mass were not incorporated into its liturgical tradition, while the regular use of incense in Bunbury began at St David's South Bunbury, under Father John Foley-Whaling, who left the parish in 1928. By this time St David's, a poor and strongly working-class parish, regarded its churchmanship as in advance of that of the pro-cathedral while at a later date the class division between the two parishes was so deep as to emerge in a strong current of ill feeling when an attempt was made to merge the two parishes to form the congregation of the new cathedral, completed in 1962. The liturgical pattern developed at St David's before the Depression, and maintained strongly for some time after, helped to ensure that the use of vestments and the daily celebration were not seen at the pro-cathedral as a sign of extreme churchmanship.

During Goldsmith's time the other major centre in the diocese, Albany, was the home of a similarly restrained liturgical tradition, accompanied by a high church theology under its rector, Archdeacon Louch, whose churchmanship was clear well before his move to Albany.[87] But it was not until A. E. White, a former member of the Brotherhood of St Boniface, became rector of Albany, that an unmistakeably Anglo-Catholic approach was manifested. White introduced incense, and vigorously promoted confession, something for which he had already been particularly noted as a mission conductor.[88]

While the devotional tone of the diocese was described for English readers in the *Bunbury Occasional Papers* in a way which left the Anglo-Catholic intentions of its bishop in no doubt, the tone of devotional life in many parishes is probably better represented by the comments of Edward Elsey shortly after his arrival in Western Australia. He described the pro-cathedral as 'the most dismal and depressing Church you can possibly imagine, of course made as nice as possible, but really impossible . . .' The parish church at Williams was in a 'tumbledown condition', its altar lights

> made out of round salmon tins and round tobacco tins gilded over . . . In Church life here there is a lot of dead wood about in the shape of ignorance and prejudice. Candles on the altar are out of the question in most places. But there are very distinct signs of progress. The children who come to the Holy Eucharist are evidently well instructed, while those who have been lately confirmed are making a start in the matter of kneeling . . .[89]

The attitude of 'ignorance and prejudice' which formed an obstacle to altar lights, by then one of the commonest of the Church Union's 'six points' in English churches, shows that a real gap existed between the bishop's churchmanship and the practice of many of the laity of the diocese.

Though the bulk of the evidence of advanced Anglo-Catholic practices at the House of Grace is presented in a detailed examination of the Brotherhood in a later chapter, it is still appropriate at this point to observe that Goldsmith's establishment of the Brotherhood fulfilled a number of purposes, one being the creation of a centre which could be staffed and organized on principles which the bishop himself held. It also offered considerable security for their expression, since its buildings were extra-parochial, and were not subject to any restrictions which hostile vestry members might have imposed on attempts to introduce more 'advanced' practices in a parish church. Both its isolation and the general focus on the war effort at this time helped to disperse any unwanted attention. Instead of the spate of controversy which had erupted in 1898 and at the end of 1900 in Perth over what were primarily doctrinal manifestations of Anglo-Catholicism, total silence in the press greeted the emergence of the first centre in Western Australia to present its liturgical standards *in toto*. There was not a single anti-ritualist murmur.

A photograph of celebrations at the House in November 1914 shows the bishop, processing in cope and mitre, attended by two small cope-boys vested in cassocks and cottas. As the procession moved around the outside of the House for the blessing of various new additions, the brothers' horses 'came to see this strange, new sight, and stood with eyes open with wonder at what they saw. One white pony in particular (Tommy to wit) seemed to take a keen interest in what was going on'.[90] The response of the horses might equally have been that of many of the diocese's more isolated and ignorant parishioners, on whom Elsey had commented. Shortly after Goldsmith's return to England, the response of a returned serviceman visiting the House of Grace for evensong was recorded: he enjoyed the service, but didn't understand the 'gas attack' during the *Magnificat*.[91] Anglo-Catholic devotion was a real ingredient in the spirituality of some, but by no means all, of Bunbury's Anglicans. And the most advanced liturgical ways were confined to the Brotherhood House, while a gentler easing into the Oxford Movement's emphases took place in parishes.

Goldsmith took office as vicar of Hampstead on 17 May 1917. The parish was one in which the broader emphases of the Oxford Movement were apparent. It had a daily eucharist; but on Sunday, matins still held pride of place, and was followed by a eucharist which was sung on alternate Sundays. Goldsmith might well have felt that he was returning to a modified version of St George's cathedral. A plethora of men's and women's organizations—fifteen in all—was listed on the front page of the parish magazine; but to deal with this Goldsmith had a staff of three other clergy; in addition, he was the patron of three other parishes.[92]

Clergy returning to Britain from the colonies were sometimes slightingly referred to as 'returned empties', and could not assume at the end of a long ministry in the colonies that they would be welcomed with open arms on their return to 'the old country'. Rather, the reverse was supposed to be true: for several decades it had been pointed out that clergy going to the colonies ran a considerable risk of losing any likelihood of future preferment, and the general contempt with which colonial ordinations were regarded was evinced by the Colonial Clergy Act of 1874 which treated colonial ordinands as, at best, second-class clergy in the imperial church.[93] It was his connection with the Maryon-Wilsons, rather than any intrinsic consideration of him as a bishop, which brought him what was then regarded as a desirable parish.

His ability as an administrator had not diminished. A longstanding debt of £1,400 on the Parish Institute, which provided recreational and other facilities, was cleared, and a chapel which had been commenced in the time of a previous vicar, Brook Deedes, was completed. As in his earlier years as dean of Perth, he encouraged organizational life, paying especial attention at St John's to the development of various guilds within the parish.[94]

Although confession was not publicly advertised at St John's—contrary to the claims of editions of the *Church Union Tourists' Guide* issued during the 1920s—Goldsmith resumed his earlier advocacy of confession, referring discreetly to it from time to time in his monthly letter in the parish magazine in connection with preparation for confirmation and with Lenten discipline. As before, he continued to stress the pastoral function of the confessor as one who could help individuals burdened with particular perplexities and temptations.[95]

Perhaps encouraged by the circumstances of the war, and certainly in keeping with his earlier ministry in Perth, he also encouraged the observation of All Souls' day, first asking in 1917 for the names of those who might be commemorated, and then in 1918, commenting at greater length in the parish magazine. By 1919, parishioners were presenting him with sufficient names to justify the commemoration of the departed at three eucharists on All Souls' day and the following day, and then on the four Fridays of the month, one of which was devoted exclusively to the war dead. That same year, on Sunday evenings in November, while the memory of the war was still fresh, he preached on 'Death and the Life Beyond'.[96]

But beyond this, there were no signs of the introduction of an advanced liturgy; service registers record only those holy days listed in the calendar of the Book of Common Prayer, and no attempt was made to introduce any form of Marian devotion. Here he probably felt like his aging brother-in-law, who wrote in the introduction to a Marian tract, published in 1923, of how he had 'grown up—and grown old too—under certain Tractarian influences which are regarded in some quarters today as "old-fashioned"'.[97]

The circle of associations which Goldsmith had fostered when promoting the cause of the Bunbury diocese was to continue into his time of office at Hampstead. In his very first year as vicar, the clergy of four parishes which he had visited as Bishop of Bunbury were invited to preach at St John's; they included his retired brother-in-law, by then an honorary canon of Chichester Cathedral. St John's Hamptead became a natural visiting place for Western Australian prelates. In July 1920 both Cecil Wilson, his successor in Bunbury, and Edward Elsey, recently consecrated Bishop of Kalgoorlie, preached there, while other colonial prelates, such as the bishops of Willochra, Toronto and Dornakal, adorned the pews from time to time.[98]

Following Cecil Wilson's election, Goldsmith was invited to act as his commissary in England. In that capacity and on the Bishop of London's behalf, he made Joseph Craven, a new candidate for the Brotherhood, a deacon at St John's in January 1920.[99] In subsequent years he interviewed other potential clergy for the south-west, such as J. J. Moore, who had already worked in Kalgoorlie. And just after Goldsmith retired, D. L. Booth, whose own poor health made his membership of the Brotherhood of St Boniface only a short one, was also ordained deacon by Goldsmith in October 1926, at St Cyprian's Clarence Gate.[100]

On later reflection, some who knew Goldsmith's state of health, including a former Bunbury priest, E. W. Crane, believed that it was unwise of him to have returned to England, and particularly to a parish such as Hampstead, with its crisp, even sharp air.[101] In 1921 he suffered his first serious setback to his health with a persistent respiratory condition, and instead of conducting Lent in the parish, he was sent to recuperate at Mentone on the Riviera from 9 March to 27 April.[102] He became increasingly frail. Bishop Perrin, formerly of British Columbia, who had lived in the parish since his own retirement, referred to Goldsmith's persistence in spite of ill health, which led to his resignation, effective from Easter 1926.[103] Hampstead parishioners, whose insularity and conservatism made it necessary for Goldsmith to prompt them concerning their need to be generous and quick to offer seating to servicemen worshipping at church during the last years of the war,[104] were disappointed that they could no longer refer to their vicar as 'our' bishop.[105]

It may have been simply a matter of ecclesiastical convenience that in his retirement he should have performed ordinations at St Cyprian's Clarence Gate, a major work by Bucknall and Comper, with the screen in its Lady Chapel covered with women saints, its high altar, one of the largest in England, and its rood screen and rood loft, which had only been completed in 1924, all in English rather than Counter-Reformation style, and regarded as unique among London churches as showing what Anglo-Catholic liturgy demanded at the beginning of the century.[106] It was certainly consistent with one of the preoccupations of his retirement, worship at some of the grander Anglo-Catholic shrines. He could now indulge in something which had once been only a dream. After his last visit to England from Bunbury as diocesan, he had written nostalgically of the atmosphere of worship at places ranging from Southwell Minster, to his brother-in-law's church at Brede, to the recently built St Mary's Clumber Park, the private chapel of the Duke of Newcastle, complete with its confessionals.[107]

At first he retired to Streatham, where he was associated with the branch of the Church Union at St Peter's. But subsequently, Goldsmith and his wife moved to Maida Vale, so that he could be close to W. L. Pearson's breathtaking creation, St Augustine's, a centre associated with the Sisters of the Church, and a church which had attracted generous and wealthy patrons, its tabernacle door studded with diamonds and precious stones, its rood screen in Pearson's best High Victorian Gothic.[108] Meanwhile, the Goldsmiths spent their winters in Italy. He confessed to Crane that 'I seem to spend most of my time musing over old Australian days'.[109]

The kind of Australia he remembered more and more is suggested by his conclusion to a chapter on the episcopate in Australia which he contributed to an anthology edited by Kenneth Mackenzie and Claude Jenkins.[110] In a similar vein, to the Kalgoorlie Diocesan Association, he recalled how he had been the first priest to celebrate the eucharist there:

> He told the meeting that he had travelled to Kalgoorlie on a coach on which went up the first billiard marker. The billiard marker wished to make a wager with the Bishop that he, the marker, would be the first to get work. The Bishop would have won as he held the first service straight away in the billiard marker's room, some of the people sitting on the billiard table . . .[111]

For as long as he could, however, he did more than muse. In consultation with Archdeacon Burbidge, who visited England in 1926 to seek yet more funding for the struggling diocese, he established a small committee to promote diocesan interests.[112] At much the same time he formed an Association of Prayer for the Church in Australia, which published a list of subjects for intercession; its purpose—'To ask the prayers of the Faithful for the conversion of Australia to the fullness of the Catholic Faith. In Australia the Faith is being advanced under great difficulties . . .' Above this plea for urgent prayer was the quotation: 'There remaineth yet very much land to be possessed'.[113] Associated with him in this plea was Walter Scott, former bush brother and missioner, then vicar of St Gabriel's Warwick Square, a parish in which he presented a determined Anglo-Catholic front; and S. J. Barrett, vicar of St Anne's Rose Place, Liverpool, another dedicated Anglo-Catholic, but with no obvious Australian connections. The family circle maintained its Western Australian interest when John Frewer was elected Bishop of the North-West by the ageing and dying C. O. L. Riley in 1929, and the new bishop promptly asked his uncle to act as his English commissary.

Goldsmith had lived long enough to see the apparent triumph of Anglo-Catholicism, marked by the congresses of the 1920s, and a new generation of younger clergy, some of whom were increasingly confident in their use of the Roman rite, rather than the Prayer Book, and based their liturgy, and their churches, on continental baroque rather than English models. One of the younger clergy who followed the newer trends and favoured the ways of the Latin rite while still enjoying Goldsmith's blessing was Percy Maryon-Wilson. He was vicar of St Mary's Somerstown, a gifted linguist and classicist, and heir to the Maryon Wilson title; his father would have preferred him to follow a political career. At St Mary's a requiem for Russian Christians was offered in the presence of Nicolai, Russian Bishop of London, at which Goldsmith preached, and was photographed afterward in the slightly improbable combination of rochet and biretta. Later in the year he returned to confirm at St Mary's.[114]

Crane recalled his last encounter with Goldsmith in London, in which he showed the persistence of the strength of character which had earned the respect of his Hampstead parishioners:

> I discovered his objection to any suggestion of infirmity. We had walked down Regent Street after lunch, and when about to cross Picadilly Circus with its intricate dangers of 'one way traffic', I offered him my arm, but he firmly refused, saying: 'No thanks, my dear boy, I crossed these streets of London before you were born.' True; nevertheless I kept a 'sharp eye' until we reached the other side, where I saw him safely in his 'bus.[115]

He had become increasingly deaf, and came to avoid engagements as a result. In the summer of 1931 he wrote to Percy Maryon-Wilson, telling him that he had preached his last sermon on 3 May that year and had undergone a severe operation. 'He was too weak', he said, 'even to say Mass now'; he could 'only look on and pray for others'.[116] By the last year of his life the Goldsmiths had moved to Eastbourne, a move which, according to the obituary in the *Brede Parish Magazine*, was undertaken in order to bring his wife closer to the rest of her family in Brede.[117] As it was, his wife was unable to care adequately for him and he moved into a nursing home at St Leonards, where he died of heart failure on 7 July 1932.[118]

The funeral rite took place the following Monday, not at St John's, but at the more distinctly Anglo-Catholic St Jude's, whose vicar, Father Arundell, had also served at St John's Albany. Others present included Archdeacon Burbidge. who had just arrived from Australia, and the vicar of Brede, Cyril Charsley Frewer, John Frewer's brother, who then took the committal prayers at the Golders Green crematorium. The next day a requiem was offered at St John's; the celebrant, Percy Maryon-Wilson, later recalled that in the best Anglo-Catholic style, Goldsmith had requested 'from his deathbed' that he officiate. The ashes were then interred in the church grounds.[119]

His occupation of genteel West End London units and removal to the south coast after a long period of service in the colonies was no different from the ending of many colonial civil servants, to whose neighbours they must have been 'someone who was someone in the colonies'. Despite the upheaval of the war and the realization that something like an age separated life before it from what followed, the decade in which Goldsmith died was one in which there was enough to prevent Englishmen from realizing that the British empire was in its decline. The war had almost reinforced the sense of the permanence of the imperial spirit, and even if the old expansionism was no more, the ties of empire seemed strong. The fragility of the imperial future was far from obvious.

The bishop's retirement had been preceded by that of his brother Herbert Symons, a former Lieutenant Governor of the northern provinces of Nigeria. In this part of Africa the influence of the benignly paternalistic Frederick Lugard was being replaced by that of Ralph Furze, whose ex-service and public school recruits also had a sense of the permanence of the empire.[120] And to find something similar in his wife's family, Goldsmith only had to look at Cyril Frewer, who had succeeded his father as rector of Brede not long after returning from Zanzibar in order to marry, bringing with him a handful of furnishings which reminded him of his years as a Universities' Mission to Central Africa missionary at Weti, and making his home like that of many others, whose exotic decorations spelt out something of the extent of British rule.

In other parts of the empire an absent brother of Cyril's, George Delamarck, had left for Canada in 1909, and John was still in the remote fastnesses of Western Australia. In Goldsmith's old Bunbury diocese the imperial link seemed only stronger with the influx of British migrants, as he pointed out in his last published essay.[121] There was little to prevent him from having at least some satisfaction in the belief that he had helped to extend the Church of England and left the way open for a 'greater empire in the southern seas'.

— TEN —

# Doctrine and Devotion: a Theory of Spiritual Independence Reinforces its Opposite?

As the founding bishop of an infant rural diocese, Goldsmith was virtually precluded from having the time to produce theology that was in any sense original. But their very derivativeness means that his theological statements can form an important source from which we may establish which particular doctrines of the Oxford Movement were regarded by a colonial bishop as being the most significant.

'Amongst the great objects for which the Christian Church exists, two stand out pre-eminent. First and foremost is the call of the Church to recognize the most Holy Trinity by regular worship and adoration . . .'[1] In this statement, made in 1914 on one of the many occasions when he pleaded for funds for an adequate cathedral, Goldsmith went on to refer to the English heritage of buildings, sculpture, painting, embroidery and music. One practical outcome of this conviction was the urgency with which he sought more, and adequate, buildings for worship.[2] But this statement also forms a theological basis for the stress which he placed on liturgical observances and the accompanying devotional attitudes, for which the buildings in one sense formed a backdrop, and were at the same time a visible embodiment.

In affirming that the worship of the Trinity was the prime purpose of the Church's existence, the bishop was a typical Anglo-Catholic, as was also the case when he declared that the ultimate form of worship in this life was eucharistic. Early in Goldsmith's time as dean of Perth, the Congregationalist cleric E. T. Dunstan had directed 'every Protestant' to consider carefully the theological position that Goldsmith was likely to inculcate in schools.³ Dunstan drew attention to a passage from a recent sermon, in which the dean had criticized worshippers at the cathedral for attending evensong in larger numbers than at the morning eucharist because, he claimed, they mistakenly regarded the sermon as the central element in worship: 'why are there but few comparatively, who come to worship at the Eucharist, when the glory of music is added to the silent worship of the heart? Why but few at the daily services of the Church, where there is no Sermon?'⁴ He went on to affirm that the eucharist involved an emotional and sacrificial response, implying that listening to a sermon might involve neither of these—and further justified the priority of the eucharist by claiming that daily reception was an apostolic norm:

> It is the love and homage of the heart that God wants, issuing forth in psalm and hymn, in almsgiving, in (above all) the worship of the Eucharist. Come here, brethren, first to love, and above all to *give* to God, come as St Peter, St John and the Blessed Virgin *daily* came, to meet their risen Lord in the Sacrament of His Love.⁵

And while he failed to establish a daily eucharist at the cathedral in his time in Perth, the centrality of the eucharist in Goldsmith's liturgical theology received a practical expression in many aspects of his building programme and in his liturgical aims.

The questioning in the 1907 Bunbury synod of the terminology in which he expressed this conviction in his early years as a bishop has already been mentioned.⁶ The theological basis that underlay his response at that point was to reappear six years later, when he appealed to synod over the daily eucharists that were being offered in the pro-cathedral and at the House of Grace. In 1907 he had referred to the Epistle to the Hebrews, a source central to sacramentally minded Anglicans who, as early as the seventeenth century, had elaborated a concept of the eucharist as an earthly participation in the heavenly intercession of Christ as high priest. In the earlier statement he described the eucharist as a 'presentation of the Sacrifice of Christ on the Cross'.⁷ But in his later statement he also interpreted the daily eucharist via the Prayer Book Prayer of Consecration: as intercession in the eucharist could embrace the broadest scope, including the faithful departed ('those who from time to time are gathered into the great unseen world'), it was always (and by implication) most effective here because the eucharist was the pleading of 'the benefits of His Passion'. The prayers offered at the eucharist were also of eternal value, since a full awareness of the prayers of the faithful would eventually be revealed in the life of the world to come: 'some day you will know how often, not merely the Church corporately, but individual names and needs have been in the silent intercessions of that daily sacrifice . . .'[8]

His own experience of the isolation of the south-west may have united with the more widespread yearning of imperial colonists for the distant motherland to intensify his conviction as an Anglo-Catholic that, in the eucharist, the apparent separation effected by space and time were transcended. In encouraging members of the Guild of Aid in England to be faithful in attending the eucharist in order to pray for the topics of intercession listed in the *Bunbury Occasional Papers*, he added: 'May you at home, and we in Australia, realize more than ever how closely the Eucharist can unite those whom the ocean sunders . . .'[9] His wish paraphrased a Latin tag expressive of this aspect of Anglo-Catholic piety sometimes found embroidered on altar frontals, *Oceano divisi, eucharistia conjugimur*.

But while the isolation of Western Australia may have intensified his devotion, it did not alter his understanding of its basis. At the close of his life, in a foreword he wrote for a small book of meditations on the Prayer Book's readings for the eucharist, he reaffirmed the conviction he had enunciated in his early years in Perth, that the external expressions of worship were simply the outward signs of an inner life, and not ends in themselves. Books which encouraged meditation, he wrote, would

> help to clear away a popular misconception, viz. that Catholics in the Church of England are more interested in ceremonial than in the cultivation of the spiritual life. The Catholic religion is associated with Sacraments which must be celebrated with dignity and reverence, but only because they have been ordained by our Blessed Lord as helps to inward sanctity. Well we know their futility unless they are received with penitence, faith, and devotion![10]

His condemnation of any tendency to magnify ceremonial above spirituality or treat it as an end in itself was perhaps stimulated by the greater freedom with which Anglo-Catholics had come to express themselves, especially as the Congress movement continued to grow in strength before World War II.

One of the grounds of complaint against Goldsmith in Perth by Mr Justice Stone had been prayer for the departed. When Goldsmith's initial persistence in trying to establish an All Souls' day celebration at Perth cathedral is recalled, the omission of any reference to the offering of requiems for the fallen among his comments on the effect of the war on the worship of the diocese seems a peculiar lacuna, particularly in view of the way in which some more aggressively Anglo-Catholic centres elsewhere in Australia highlighted them at this time.

Instead, he expressed a concept of the unity of the church militant and the church triumphant in the context of less controversial memorials, at the same time voicing an understanding of the communion of saints which extended beyond those whose sanctity was of a heroic degree, to embrace men and women who had lived less extrovert but 'good' lives. A comment made in the aftermath of his 1912 visit to England well illustrates the breadth of this vision. He hoped that four gifts would 'all help us to realize the Communion of Saints'. They were Monica Wills' House of Grace for the bush brothers—'a delightful and appropriate name, which also associates it with the memory of a lover of mission work, now departed', 'a gift *In memoriam* George Carruthers Little' ('my late devoted and saintly commissary'), and one simply 'in memory of a Godmother'.[11] The last was the coming of A. E. White as a member of the Brotherhood to replace a friend from Keble College, H. G. Hornsby, who had drowned.

In 1913 he again associated an awareness of the communion of saints with a wide range of Christian experiences, including those which were embraced equally by all schools of Anglican churchmanship. He stated that prayer, meditation and the reading of scripture, as well as the sacramental life, all 'take us into a very real fellowship with Christ and His Saints'.[12] In the same address, he implied a wide range of devotional experiences when he referred to the 'thoughts, the example, the very Presence of the unseen' as influencing the faithful wherever they might be. At this point he may have been voicing, albeit unconsciously, something of the ground on which the communion of saints and the faithful departed occupied a significant place in his own, and in the devotional lives of other Victorian and Edwardian worshippers. The 'Presence of the unseen', truly a *mysterium tremendum et fascinans*, awe-inspiring and supra-rational, powerfully conjures up something of that sense of mystery which was beloved by Victorians, and which was an important element in Anglo-Catholic piety.[13]

To define the church in 1907 he invoked another frame of reference which had become as axiomatic for Tractarians and their Anglo-Catholic heirs as assertions of the centrality of the eucharist and appeals for daily mass attendance. He quoted Canon Reginald Stephen, then of Melbourne, subsequently Bishop of Tasmania, then of Newcastle, who defined the church as the extension of the Incarnation, describing the visible church as 'the Son of God Himself, everlastingly manifesting Himself among men in human form, the Body of Christ'.[14] An emphasis on the Incarnation in the theology of Anglo-Catholics acted as a counter to the traditional Evangelical stress on the Redemption and a substitutionary doctrine of the Atonement. As a sign of the potential for the sanctification of all material things, it was frequently used as a theological argument for justifying accessories of worship which might otherwise seem to have only a strongly aesthetic appeal.

Incarnational theology also formed a basis for the more or less radical positions on social issues promoted by a number of Anglo-Catholics. But Goldsmith himself did not embrace any such position. As a bishop, he certainly made statements in his synod charges in which he expressed sympathy for the unemployed in Australia, and deplored the conditions which led to unrest in England in 1910 and 1911, but his most practical suggestion in 1907 was to urge the formation of a Social Services Committee to report to synod and to make 'the voice of Christian morality heard'.[15] In synod in 1911 he could 'only hope and pray that the grace of God may moderate passion, banish selfishness, and end oppression wherever it exists'.[16] Such statements, in which he deplored the distress of the poor and hoped for a greater social harmony, did not contain anything to contradict the acceptance of control as a means of promoting social harmony. This latter attitude characterized his earlier attempts as Dean of Perth to pressure the government to prohibit boxing, and stringently supervise the conditions of female migrant workers. The later statements did not articulate social issues in terms of rights or the need for any kind of new order. Nor was his correspondence in 1912 with prospective English migrants inconsistent with the position which he had clearly articulated in his earlier years. And at the end of 1912 he preached a sermon in the presence of Bunbury's mayor and councillors in which he stressed the importance of order in society, which he understood to derive ultimately from a disciplined church, a position which clearly indicates that his stance had not substantially altered since his Perth days.[17]

The conservative influences which predominated in his earlier years may well have influenced him to adopt such a position. He passed through Oxford in the 1870s, the decade before Christian Socialism made itself so strongly felt in many sermons from the university's pulpits, that by 1883 the *Oxford Magazine* could comment that social questions were uppermost in the minds of university men, and that their ears were 'ringing . . . with the exceeding bitter cry of the outcast'.[18] He did not come under the influence of Henry Scott Holland, whom Gore regarded as the most broadly influential figure of the Christian Social Union; and when branches were eventually formed in Australia, these included the clergy of prominent high churches in Melbourne and Sydney such as St James King Street and St Peter's Eastern Hill.[19] But a branch did not spring up in Perth, even though the approach there, generally academic and intellectual, was a mild enough one that would hardly have threatened Goldsmith's conservatism.

His failure to develop a well-articulated social theology appears rather to stem from an innate conservatism of his own, of which there is other evidence in his theology as analysed below. Neither the characteristics of the parishes in which he worked in England, nor his own social substratum, entirely explain it. Certainly in Charlton its landed gentry still played a significant part in its society, and at Cheam, though the recently extended railway was having an impact on housing development, Goldsmith was not faced with the full extent of the impact of industrialization. On the other hand, in May 1906 Goldsmith's brother-in-law, George Frewer, though politically a conservative, invited as a guest to his parish one of the most aggressively socialist Anglo-Catholics, Charles Plomer Hopkins. There he delivered an address on the Order of St Paul, a unique Anglican religious community dedicated to promoting the spiritual and material welfare of seamen of the mercantile marine. Hopkins himself was involved in trade unions, strikes and demonstrations.[20] Yet another friend of the Frewer family, Frank Weston of Zanzibar, made strongly worded appeals for social justice, which reached a climax in his address at the 1923 Anglo-Catholic Congress, by which time Goldsmith himself had returned to England.[21]

If Goldsmith did not see some form of Christian socialism as a logical outcome of the doctrine of the Incarnation, he did tease out another characteristic theological emphasis of the Oxford Movement to its fullest extent in his Australian setting—its stress on episcopacy. In accounting for the authority of the church, in his first year in Perth he expressed the conviction that episcopacy was of the *esse,* and not simply the *bene esse* of the church. This position was one of the features that distinguished Tractarian and Anglo-Catholic theology from its antecedents in an earlier, seventeenth-century high church stream. In his sermon to the Perth synod of 1888, Goldsmith implied that Tractarian standards simply repeated existing and accepted Anglican norms when he claimed that Anglicanism had consistently refused

> on principle to recognize any ministry, but that which is derived through Episcopal ordination from God, as either regular or valid, she has been true to the Apostles' Fellowship, not from lack of charity, but because she knows she cannot be truly liberal in dispensing with an ordinance of God. 'For it is clear unto all men diligently reading the Holy Scripture and Ancient Authors, that from the Apostles' time there have been these orders of ministers in Christ's Church, Bishops, Priests and Deacons.'[22]

Certainly Goldsmith's long-term advocacy of autonomy and his championing of an alteration in the title for the church in Australia was consistent with his conviction that episcopacy was of the *esse* of the church. His last motion to promote this cause, made at General Synod in 1910 in the shadow of the impending judgement on the Australian church's legal status, referred to the Australian church's being 'with such limitations as constitutionally bind every true branch of the Catholic Church, an independent National Church, in communion with the Church of England . . .'[23] Such terms showed clearly that he understood the Australian church to be a fully constituted body.

In his Bunbury synod charge that same year, he made clear that the episcopate guaranteed and was the basis on which the Australian church could claim to possess the marks of the Catholic church in all its fullness.

Speaking of the ongoing pressure to establish a goldfields bishopric, he went on to speak of the consequences within the state and beyond:

> Steps will then be taken to create a province of Western Australia, of which the four dioceses will be the constituent parts. A group of parishes make a diocese. A group of dioceses make a province. A group of provinces form a National Church . . .[24]

As he described them, the church's structures depended for their fullness upon an episcopal presence. The following year he similarly referred to the hope that as a result of the establishment of the goldfields bishopric, Western Australia might soon be 'organized as a province of the Catholic Church'.[25] And although he never came to state the logical opposite, one could be excused for concluding from such statements that it was almost a case of 'no bishop, no church'. Certainly the positive form of Goldsmith's equation—that where a bishop is, there also is the church— was also held by others contemplating the whole issue of national churches, such as the author of the *Church Times* editorial which appeared a fortnight before Australia's General Synod in 1900. He wrote:

> Once formed, once in possession of the episcopate, once established, the Church in Crete, or Cyprus, or Alexandria, was the Church of that locality, and not known by the title of some other locality. It became a province or a diocese of the Church Universal, and as such, took its place as a constituent member of the whole body, with its own inherent rights, privileges and powers of other parts of the Church, and only in subordination to the whole Church as the Body of Christ on earth . . .[26]

In Goldsmith's motions at General Synod and in Perth, the Tractarian exaltation of the episcopal role was carried to one of its logical ends. The rejection of these motions took place on the grounds of what at the time was described as 'sentiment', sometimes prefixed by the adjective 'imperial', a frame of mind that could equally well be described as one of colonial insecurity. It did not necessarily indicate any substantial divergence from the high value placed on episcopacy by statements such as those of Goldsmith which have already been quoted, or disagreement as to the inherent completeness of autonomous national churches, as expressed in the *Church Times* editorial. It was in fact the supporters of autonomy (though not Goldsmith himself) who were to point out occasionally that there were dangers inherent in regarding the individual diocese or province as though it were a unit complete within itself.[27]

This stress on the episcopal office continued after Goldsmith's own elevation to the episcopate. One simple expression was the appearance in diocesan handbooks of an episcopal succession list showing the line of consecration beginning with William Grant Broughton, Australia's first Anglican prelate and the only one to have the title Bishop of Australia, and tracing its lineal descent until it devolved upon Goldsmith through his own three consecrators.[28]

When he preached at Goldsmith's consecration in 1904, Bishop Stretch, Dean and later Bishop of Newcastle, proffered a more guarded and less aggressive statement concerning episcopacy than that presented by Goldsmith in 1888. He left the question open as to whether government by bishops was an essential characteristic of historic Christianity, or a development that promoted good order; however, he noted that despite the eschewing of the actual title in the churches that had formally rejected episcopacy, there were nevertheless officials who fulfilled most of the episcopal functions.[29] Since the congregation contained many representatives of Perth's Protestant churches, Stretch may well have observed a diplomatic reserve in his statements on episcopacy, knowing that to some nonconformists, episcopacy was an offensive concept, irrespective of the churchmanship of Anglicans who upheld it. In Bunbury only a year later a Church of Christ cleric, T. H. Scambler, described episcopacy as 'heresy' and 'sin' in a correspondence in which he crossed swords with E. S. Clairs, then Rector of Pinjarra, who presented an old-fashioned high church defence of the apostolicity of the Church of England.[30] Stretch may equally have been protecting himself from criticism from some other Anglicans, since within the fold, opponents of the Oxford Movement identified its claims concerning episcopacy as marking a radical innovation: correspondents in the debates over Anglo-Catholicism in the Perth press described the doctrine of apostolic succession as un-Anglican and unscriptural.[31]

Goldsmith's conviction that episcopal order was an essential ingredient in church government, and a guarantee of historic continuity, was naturally a significant element in his understanding of inter-church relations both then and for the future, although he never offered a fully worked out rationale as to how his principles might be put effectively into practice. In his 1888 synod sermon, he expressed something of an optimism current among Anglicans elsewhere as he drew to a close by claiming that 'it seems almost certain that when the movement towards re-union comes we must be the centre of that movement', and that 'the future lies in our hands'.[32]

At this point he offered theological grounds for the central role he envisaged for Anglicanism. Basing his whole sermon on a text from the Acts of the Apostles, he used it to stress that unity in doctrine, ministry and sacramental life with apostolic standards had been maintained more consistently in Anglicanism than in any other communion. Here the Catholic and Apostolic faith remained 'untampered with' throughout the medieval period, to emerge in a purified form at the Reformation. Claims for a future universal role for Anglicanism coincided with a mood of imperial optimism concerning Britain's broader place in international affairs. Creighton and Temple based their vision of Anglicanism as the future of world Christianity on the assumption that Britain and her empire would likewise be the political world's future.

On another occasion, Goldsmith spoke of the central position occupied by Anglicanism as that of the church from which others had separated: 'we have never separated from any other Christian body—though we sometimes have been partly responsible for a separation'[33]—as though the disunity of Christendom was the result of other churches having initiated an American style independence movement, and consequently, their unnecessary divisions could all be corrected if they showed a readiness to return to the ever hopeful and patient bosom of an Anglican mother church.

Goldsmith envisaged the reunion of churches as taking place in the near future: if not in his own lifetime, then in that of the following generation. The projected unity would be fulfilled, not in 'a loose confederation of differing Sects—but in a Church, united, Evangelical, Catholic—"Jerusalem, as a city that is at unity in itself" '.[34]

On the one hand, it is absurd to try to suggest that when in 1888 he distinguished between 'the Church' and 'one or other of the many Christian communities',[35] Goldsmith's terminology anticipated the directions and nuances of some of the ecclesiological statements of Vatican II.

Rather, he would have rested such terminology on the 'branch' theory of the church as articulated by Pusey and other Tractarian theologians, who envisaged Anglicanism, Orthodoxy and Roman Catholicism as 'branches' of the Catholic church by virtue of their adherence to episcopal order, an ecclesiology which at the same time unchurched the churches of the Reformation. And closest to home for any dialogue that Goldsmith might anticipate, it unchurched those which sprang from English dissent from Anglicanism.

Goldsmith's vision of the future union assumed that episcopacy would be accepted by the non-episcopal communions, but avoided explaining how this was likely to come about by falling back on an appeal to Anglicans to 'wait and pray and work until God's good time comes, to bring together all His children in one united family'.[36] But that it was essential in his mind was shown when he invoked the articles of the 1888 Lambeth Quadrilateral as a minimum standard for 'home reunion'. The fourth of the principles for reunion—'the historic episcopate locally adapted in the methods of its administration to the varying needs of the nations and the people called of God into the unity of his church'—was in itself an indication of the degree to which the Oxford Movement's renewed emphasis on episcopacy had influenced Anglicanism as a whole. After listing all of the articles, Goldsmith added that they were 'principles on which the church takes a firm stand—principles which I hope and believe we shall never consent to modify or alter'.[37] Almost a decade later, in 1915, one of the longest statements in his synod charge that year was a comment on the Kikuyu controversy, in which he reiterated that the Church of England would be compromising essential principles if she were to admit nonconformists as communicants at Anglican altars without insisting on their being confirmed.[38]

Some of these statements suggest that Goldsmith was unaware of the degree to which the Oxford Movement's stress on episcopacy had developed beyond the position taken in earlier Anglicanism. He certainly lacked a historical perspective from which to view the influence of the Oxford Movement on the Anglican church in Australia in the past, and displayed this in an outline of church development which he wrote for English readers at the end of his life. When he came to the first bishops' conference of 1850, he expressed surprise at the 'emphatic desire' that their 'every act and purpose whould be consistent with Catholic tradition and custom', since they were 'all sturdy Evangelicals'(!)[39] He obviously did not know that, at the time, those who gave the conference a hostile reception identified all the bishops, save Perry, as being tainted with Tractarianism. The isolation of the west from the east during Goldsmith's time of office in Australia partly explains this lack of awareness. However, his assessment of the earlier Australian bishops was one that was shared by other contemporary Anglo-Catholics. The increasing preoccupation with ceremonial elaboration and correctness, and the strength of the Congress movement, made it easy and tempting for Anglo-Catholics to identify churchmanship with external signs, and to interpret their absence as evidence of a different stream.[40]

And even within the framework of his own arguments Goldsmith could be inconsistent. In 1888 he sought to contrast the harshness of Roman Catholic attitudes to other communions, as exemplified by Pius V's excommunication of Elizabeth I, with the moderation shown by Anglicanism: 'she was gentle withal'. He went on to quote from the Prayer Book Preface (Of Ceremonies, Why Some be Abolished, and Some Retained) to show that they had no intention of 'forsaking or rejecting' other (reformed) churches 'in these our doings', and concluded, 'if all had acted so, there would have been no rending of the Body of Christ'.[41]

The classical Anglicanism represented by the Prayer Book might be invoked to prove that Anglicanism did not seek to judge the reformed churches of the continent in the sixteenth century, but Goldsmith's stand was hardly anything other than a judgement of the churches that had emerged from English dissent, a judgement that weighed them in an Oxford Movement balance and found them wanting. Such statements as those already cited are in no way unusual among those of other contemporary bishops influenced by the Oxford Movement. But that his position reflected an innate personal conservatism, as well as being consistent with the Catholic inheritance with which he openly identified, is suggested by his responses to proposed Prayer Book revision.

The unrest over Anglo-Catholicism at the end of the nineteenth century was a significant factor, though not the only one, in the creation of a Royal Commission on Ecclesiastical Discipline in 1904. It concluded that there was widespread need for Prayer Book reform. The

Commission and the subsequent issuing of Royal Letters of Business and the formation of several committees by Convocation were steps along the path that led to the Prayer Book Measure of 1927–28, a progress interrupted by World War I.[42]

At his first synod in Perth in 1888 Goldsmith had commented on what he considered to be omissions in a number of trial services for occasional use which had been authorized by Australia's Anglican bishops. A certain youthful concern to make the most of any possibility for ceremonial of some kind, no matter how restrained, possibly lay behind his anxiety to ensure that the officiant at the consecration of a cemetery should perform a 'perambulation' of the grounds[43]—something he was careful to do later when he came to consecrate a cemetery in Bunbury.[44] But if there were an earlier enthusiasm for supplementation, if not revision, it had become muted by 1911. At his own diocesan synod that year he stated

> I confess to being very conservative in regard to Prayer Book revision. We are all in practical agreement about the book as it stands. Revision without liturgical experts is full of danger, and any action in this direction on the part of one branch of our Communion, more or less independently, is not without its risk. We do need services which are not in the Prayer Book, such as that for the consecration of a church . . . Probably the addition of a supplement, at any rate in the first instance, containing such additional services, would be the wisest course.[45]

Although there were to be Anglo-Catholic clergy in Australia at a later stage who hesitated to support any local process of revision lest it be used to restrict them, Goldsmith's hesitation in this area is perhaps made more remarkable by his otherwise strong urging of autonomy for Australian Anglicanism. Generally, the supporters of autonomy considered one of its outstanding benefits to be the potential it offered for carrying out Prayer Book revision free from dire consequences regarding property ownership. That such a view transcended churchmanship boundaries is shown by Riley's correspondence with Davidson in 1911, expressing impatience at the restriction on revision which was placed on the church in Australia by its legal position, a situation which brought further expression of irritation from him in the 1920s.[46]

Goldsmith's theological and liturgical conservatism is most clearly expressed in the stance he adopted over the status of the Athanasian

Creed and proposed revisions. The 1662 Prayer Book made its recitation obligatory on thirteen days, including Easter and Christmas. A desire for some modification was expressed by the last decade of the seventeenth century, and it remained a target in proposals for revision throughout the nineteenth century, especially in the 1870s. Argument focused on the so-called 'damnatory clauses', which introduce and end its statements concerning the Trinity. These clauses offered everlasting damnation as the only alternative to an orthodox belief in the Trinity, and were felt by critics to be a cause of both misunderstanding and offence. The solutions proffered at this time were repeated in debates in which Goldsmith became involved at the beginning of the present century.[47]

'Those damnatory clauses'
*Bulletin*, 19 October 1905, p. 16
While Goldsmith believed that the Church waited 'breathless for our utterance' on the status of the Athanasian Creed, many Australians seem to have taken rather a different point of view.

The debate re-emerged in England with the 1904 Royal Commission on Ecclesiastical Discipline, and in Australia in 1905 at General Synod, where the Archdeacon of Armidale moved that the damnatory clauses should be removed, claiming that they were a source of offence to many. It was resolved that 'constitutional means should be adopted for the omission of the rubric requiring its public recitation'.[48] Not surprisingly, cartoons that appeared in the Sydney *Bulletin* indicated that a more liberal point of view was widely held.[49]

From his distant viewpoint at Lambeth, Randall Davidson watched the expressions of Australian opinion with interest, seeing confirmation of his own belief concerning the general direction in which the wind was blowing in England. St Clair Donaldson, Archbishop of Brisbane, wrote to him noting that the vote was two to one in favour of the omission of the rubric that ordered the recitation of the Creed, and commented, 'certainly an overwhelming majority wanted some relief'.[50] Before General Synod met, the Primate, Saumarez Smith, conferred with Davidson on the subject, and Davidson later noted that any positive action was inhibited by the fear that any change in Prayer Book usage might entail legal challenges and property loss.[51]

At the 1908 Lambeth Conference the only speech that Goldsmith made during its course was devoted to the question of Prayer Book revision and the status of the Athanasian Creed, under the wider title of 'Prayer Book Adaptation and Enrichment'. Early in the discussion the Bishop of Chester quoted the Australian General Synod motion, describing the Athanasian Creed as an 'outrage to our conscience and reason and deepest religious convictions', while the Bishop of Bombay claimed that it was a purely intellectual statement, inadequate in the face of the need for a response of faith that involved feeling and will. Others proposed the retention of the text of the creed, accompanied by the removal of the rubric compelling its recitation.[52]

Goldsmith was not alone in voicing opposition to any alteration. Bishop Williams of St John's

'The Australian Synod sends home a grumble'
*Bulletin*, 19 October 1905, p. 17

Kaffraria, an Anglo-Catholic who inherited the staunch position of the leading Tractarians in the 1870s, identified this creed as a statement of truth, to which responses in terms of likes or dislikes were inappropriate. Sustained applause followed references to Pusey, Keble, Bright and Liddon in a speech by the aged Bishop King of Lincoln, for whom it was to be his last conference.[53] Moving along lines almost the opposite of those laid down by Williams, he suggested that a faith which included love and affection among its elements would not ultimately be troubled by what at first appeared difficult, unclear or limited. But he acknowledged that the 'mixed condition of our congregations' formed understandable grounds for hesitation of the Creed's public recitation.

Goldsmith's contribution to the discussion followed King's. As well as pleading on the grounds of continuity, he suggested that the damnatory clauses were described as such in error, and were more correctly 'monitory' clauses, whose purpose was not to enforce assent to a series of propositions, but to insist on the absolute necessity of right conduct and right worship. They were moral rather than theological in intention. He was forced to admit that they were 'severe' in character and tone, but quoted in his defence of the Creed another Tractarian, Dean Church, formerly of St Paul's: 'it is so severe, (because) the New Testament is severe'. As a practical solution he suggested a retranslation, accompanied by an explanatory statement. He allowed the desirability of making some alteration in the days on which it was to be recited, especially Christmas Day and Easter Day, when 'many people go to church who seldom or never go at any other time'—a concession which for him was liberal enough, given his broader general conservatism.[54]

But some of his argument also demonstrated a lack of awareness of a broad cross-section of the laity. He pointed out that at the General Synod the strongest opposition to the retention of the Creed came from the bishops, not from among the other clergy or the laity. More surprisingly, he said that in twenty years in Western Australia he had only met two worshipping Anglicans who had resisted or resented the recitation of the Athanasian Creed, and said that the laity's real objection centred not round its abstruseness or its authority, but on misunderstanding of the damnatory clauses. In his concluding words, he showed again that his own awareness of lay opinions was confined to the views of those who were least likely to question the Creed's appropriateness, and who were more likely to approach it à la Bishop King:

> We often exaggerate the opposition, which, where it exists, does not come as a rule... from the most faithful and the most earnest and the most hardworking sons of the Church. And we often fail to realize the immense conservative force in the Church which loves the Creed.

While he was undoubtedly correct in identifying the lovers of the Athanasian Creed with a conservative force, his vision of that force as something 'immense' was hardly consistent with the *Bulletin*'s cartoons. Nor was his anticipation of the results of any major alteration at all realistic:

> The alienation of such people caused by any rash statement which might be put forth by such an authority as this Conference, would, I am persuaded, precipitate the greatest crisis that the Church has experienced for centuries... I do know that the Church waits breathless for our utterance on this matter; and our responsibility is very heavy.[55]

Goldsmith was the only speaker to whom Davidson himself made a response, in this case providing a quite different interpretation of the position of earlier Lambeth Conferences to which Goldsmith had alluded. According to Davidson, their lack of action on the question was due to choices made by Benson and Temple. He added that he did not regard a new translation as a sufficient answer to the problem, and that while he himself experienced no difficulty with the Creed, greater consideration should be

A bullock driver's view of the Athanasian Creed
*Bulletin*, 16 November 1905, p. 16

given to the position of those who did not understand its status.[56] Perhaps Goldsmith's speech simply demonstrated to Davidson that obscure colonial prelates could be expected to be out of touch.

Davidson went on to appoint a committee to report on 'Prayer Book Adaptation and Enrichment', which in turn generated a series of sub-committees, including one on the Creed, presided over by Saumarez Smith of Sydney. Whether Davidson had forgotten Montgomery's earlier complaints of Smith's lack of leadership qualities, or whether they suited his current purpose, is not clear. Although Goldsmith was also a member of the subcommittee, its minutebook shows that he made no further contribution to the discussion. Davidson attended its second meeting, and advised that 'the views of the minority should find some expression', 'as there was considerable divergence of opinion'.[57] As it was, the committee eventually recommended the need for a new translation, but also attempted to address the question of the non-prescriptive authority that the conference possessed, given the number of autonomous member churches, by stating that the various branches of the Anglican communion were sufficiently competent to decide for themselves what was 'desirable and most likely to tend to the maintenance of the Catholic Faith in its integrity among the Clergy and People'. If Goldsmith had come to the conference hoping that its recommendations would call into question the viewpoint expressed on the Creed at Australia's General Synod, he went home disappointed.[58]

The crisis predicted by Goldsmith never came to pass. Instead, as liturgical questions continued to be discussed in England, the Athanasian Creed gradually receded from view while the issue of Sacramental Reservation came to occupy centre stage. And in Perth a year later, at the Australian Church Congress, Riley mentioned in his presidential address that Goldsmith and Nutter Thomas of Adelaide had served on 'a strong committee' which considered Prayer Book revision at Lambeth; but he did not provide any opportunity for discussion of liturgical revision in general or the Athanasian Creed in particular. Riley clearly did not sense any impending crisis comparable to the Reformation.[59]

Goldsmith's stance on the Creed was also consistent with a reactionary stream within Tractarianism and Anglo-Catholicism, perhaps first noticeable in Tractarian responses to German Biblical criticism. It continued in the general failure of Ango-Catholic theologians throughout the twentieth century to make any significant contribution to the dialogue between science and religion; their preferred concerns were liturgy and ecclesiastical history.[60] Goldsmith's 1913 synod address demonstrated a preference for nostalgia against any attempt to grapple with the modern world in its own terms. 'Indifference, carelessness, neglect' were products of 'a general unsettlement of old ways and customs, with the accompanying conceit begotten by modern scientific progress'. The air which Christians now breathed daily was 'poisoned', and the response he suggested was a largely anti-intellectual one—not to engage in a search for a way of purifying the air, but a degree of withdrawal.[61]

While such statements highlighted his conservative personality, some commitment on his part to the more radical implications of Oxford Movement theology also needs to be pointed out. The Tractarian understanding of the nature of the church and her authority left the established status of Anglicanism in England to be viewed as, at best, the consequence of particular historical situations in that country, and not an essential condition of her existence. Goldsmith himself gave vigorous expression to this in 1893 when Hackett, in the face of mounting pressures for the disestablishment of the Church of England in Wales, predicted that 'the Anglican Establishment, as well as the Scotch, is within measurable distance of its end', and that 'a brief period will see both the Anglican and Presbyterian Churches cease to be Churches by law established'.[62] Goldsmith's ire was roused by Hackett's description of disestablishment as 'quenching the candlestick of English Christianity', and thundered in response:

> How long shall we have to remind newspaper editors . . . that it is not establishment which makes a church, or lights the candle of Christianity, or preserves the church from being 'brought to the ground'.
>
> Perish 'establishment' in England, and everywhere else, if it is to obscure the spiritual character of the Church, or to lead people to imagine that the Church is founded on 'the authority of Parliament,' rather than on the word of Christ. Recognition by the State never made and never will unmake the Church.

Goldsmith's fiery delivery prompted a somewhat meek response from the editor, disclaiming that there was any intention of suggesting that disestablishment would result in Anglicanism's destruction as a church, or limit its 'activity and usefulness in spiritual concerns'.[63]

That Goldsmith also conceived of the church's authority as one which existed over clearly delineated spheres of life, in which any infringement by the state stood in need of rebuke, is clear from his attitude to proposals to enact colonial divorce legislation which would give greater recognition to divorce on the grounds of cruelty.[64] In an address given to the St George's Young Men's Society, he argued on scriptural grounds against any relaxation of divorce law: when Christ traced the indissolubility of marriage back to the creation of man and woman, He had moved beyond the imperfection of the Mosaic law which allowed divorce in limited circumstances. But as well as presenting a scriptural argument, and the statement that the Church of England only recognized divorce as separation *a mensa et toro,* Goldsmith described the proposed legislation as evidence of 'a strong tendency on the part of the civil authority to encroach beyond its province into the religious department onf the marriage estate'. He regarded it as acceptable for the state to legislate to 'safeguard' the marriage contract as he saw it, but also feared that a 'design' existed to destroy those safeguards.[65]

Later in the year at the diocesan synod he introduced a motion expressing sympathy with the church and especially the clergy in those colonies 'where the law relating to divorce had lately been brought into acute conflict with the law of Christ and His Church'. In doing so, he gave support to Bishop Parry, who had commented on divorce legislation in other colonies in his synod charge, stating that 'no human authority, whether of Church or State . . . can set the law (of Christ) aside'.[66] Goldsmith also rebutted a subsequent editorial in the *West Australian* criticizing Parry's position and suggesting more broadly that the clergy would often do better to be silent, because uninformed and unintelligent comments had already reduced their status in the eyes of the laity.[67] Far from agreeing that it was 'very unwise of them to whisper such things at the present time', Goldsmith urged that 'the Church's duty was to speak, and they must speak . . .'[68]

Goldsmith's last criticism of the state occurred in his 1910 synod charge, and the ground on which he offered his criticism was a failure in the practice of democratic principles. He commented on the results of the

Queensland referendum on religious instruction in schools, in which 'a majority larger than that which carried Federation in Queensland was in favour of the introduction of this teaching'. The language in which he criticized the action of parliamentarians has an unusually egalitarian flavour:

> By a referendum parliament practically says to the people, 'Tell us what you want with respect to this particualr matter and we will carry out your wishes.' A referendum can mean nothing else. It is therefore disappointing to find that a considerable number of members, professing democratic principles, should still oppose the expressed will of the people. The time for debate has passed. The will of the people should prevail.[69]

Even if the degree of his commitment to a theory of the church's relation to the state was only tested in a limited way, it is clear that Goldsmith accepted the most radical element of the inheritance which stemmed from Tractarianism. The church was no organ of the state; ultimately its authority was both independent and higher, a fact which created potential for conflict in which he was prepared to engage.

If anything, Tractarian reassertion of the claim that the church possessed a basis of authority independent of the state could easily turn into a claim concerning the priority of the one over the other. In his correspondence with Randall Davidson over the establishment of an independent north-west see, Goldsmith certainly envisaged the desirability of church institutions keeping abreast of those being established by the government. Harsh realities frustrated the realization of this idealistic hope for the north-west, but any theory of church and state running abreast of one another was hardly borne out by recent development in the more populous centres of the state, as Goldsmith acknowledged in his own comments concerning the difficulty the church experienced in providing a ministry to the increased population during the gold rushes before the close of the nineteenth century. But despite this absence of anything resembling a burden of proof, he addressed the mayor and councillors of Bunbury in 1912 following his return from England, emphasizing the need for order and discipline in life in general, and affirming the desirability of discipline in the church in particular, since the church was the source of order for society as a whole.[70]

𝓑ut a consistently unbending adherence to a theological conviction could lead to practical results which might be inconsistent with the ideals actually promoted by the same theory. This is particularly the case with his views about the nature of episcopacy, but is also true in the broader sense of other areas—the questions of staffing and funding.[71]

As his sermon to the 1888 Perth synod shows, the high view of episcopal authority which Goldsmith held was not something which emerged from his own election as a bishop, but was part of his doctrinal furniture from the beginning of his ministry in Western Australia. But, only slightly later, others around him saw the presence of a bishop as desirable or essential for the effective functioning of the church in different parts of the state. At Roebourne, H. Pitts wrote of the isolation of the families working on stations, and in the absence of 'every influence which makes for purity and peace', envisaged the church's hand being strengthened by the presence of a bishop.[72] On the Kalgoorlie goldfields, R. H. Moore saw the presence of a bishop as an answer to some of the financial problems of the struggling community there, as he should be able to use 'his influence both personal and that which naturally attaches to his office in bringing the comparatively leisured and wealthier members of the community to take some interest in the Church and to realize even a little their responsibilities towards it . . .'[73] Moore and Pitts were certainly influenced by the Oxford Movement, but their comments on the episcopal office all occur in the context of their expressing the need for a bishop in one of the areas that eventually became a see—in other words, their comments stemmed from immediate practical needs as much as from a particular theory about the nature of the church.

Goldsmith himself was certainly capable of drawing on such pragmatic arguments to move others to support and finance the establishment of new sees. He provided a more fleshed-out form of Pitts' line of reasoning when he appealed to Randall Davidson for support over the establishment of an independent north-west see: 'it is only by sending a Bishop to live on the spot, a man who can constantly guard and develop Christian effort, sustain the officers of the Government, organize mission work, and cheer and guide the clergy and other workers, that we can do our duty'.[74]

In encouraging the readers of the *Bunbury Occasional Papers* the next year, he led up to a similar appeal on behalf of the north-west by pointing to an increase in the clerical staff from 13 to 23 during his own episcopate and attributed an increase in the clerical staff of the diocese of Perth from 25 to 60 to the influence of the bishop which was 'great because his presence was felt', rather than to the natural growth caused by the gold rushes. In the north-west a bishop on the spot would help its people 'to the possession of all those blessings which Christianity affords, and which we believe are best provided under the fostering care of a Bishop of their own . . .'[75]

And in his last published work, he claimed that, in the second half of the nineteenth century, it was the appointment of bishops to a number of Australian centres, including Perth, which gave 'considerable impulse' to the life of the church. Though as a historical analysis this was a considerable oversimplification, it was consistent with his own belief concerning the establishment of sees in his own lifetime. Elsewhere in the same essay he added that, far from having upheld the traditional episcopal structure for pragmatic reasons, Australian Anglicans had never shown any sign of doubting that the authority held by the bishop was sacramentally based, another claim which reflects his own position, rather than representing the results of an informed awareness of Australian church history.[76]

As long as Goldsmith held to the view of episcopacy which he had articulated at the Perth synod of 1888, he was bound to agree to the establishment of new sees in Western Australian country centres, not simply on the kind of practical grounds given above, but because the church in its fullness could not exist without the presence of a bishop, while conversely, as he pointed out in his statement to the Bunbury synod in 1910, the creation of more dioceses brought the existence of a province closer and would in turn hasten the creation of a national church, the largest self-contained organism through which he understood the Catholic church to manifest itself.[77] While for Goldsmith the creation of new sees in the west meant that Anglicanism would be equipped on a provincial and national scale to show its Catholicity, Riley, the key mover in the operation towards the formation of a province, was motivated by pragmatic considerations and by his own ambition. Taking the pragmatic line, he wrote to the SPG that the establishment of a north-west bishopric was essential for the future success of any native mission work.[78]

But other comments indicated neither pragmatism nor commitment to a particular theology, but impatience and ambition. Along with his genuine concern for the native population there, Riley was anxious to be rid of the north-west at all costs. The burden it might place on another hardly mattered: although a proper tour of the north-west took at least two months, he dismissed the possibility that it would be any strain on Goldsmith, since 'the additional five hours it takes to come up from Bunbury or the South is a mere nothing'.[79]

The north-west bishopric was created in 1910, despite its inability to support enough staff to form a quorum for a synod of its own. But until three independent synods existed, the province which Riley sought in order to become its first archbishop still eluded him. Frustration as well as impatience made him write to the SPG of his wish to be 'rid of the Goldfields'.[80] The diocese of Kalgoorlie finally came into being in 1914, despite the decline in mining—Riley claimed that the transcontinental railway would rejuvenate the goldfields economy, but his personal ambition was betrayed by the increasing impatience he showed in correspondence over the forming of a province.[81] There are some uncomfortable parallels between Riley's insistence in setting up a province, despite the evidence that economic viability for some of its component dioceses was not possible, and a much more recent creation, that of the Province of South Australia under Thomas Reed. Again, ambition drove a would-be archbishop who had ample access to appropriate information to create a structure whose rural components could barely maintain themselves. Riley's creation of the province has been described by Boyce as 'premature' and undertaken with 'immoderate haste'.[82] Any failure on Goldsmith's part to object to the circumstances in which the diocese of the north-west was created is probably due to the freedom from responsibility which it offered him. However, the considerable degree of friction between Goldsmith and Riley before 1904 makes his apparent unquestioning acceptance of Riley's formation of the province of Western Australia seem all the more remarkable, unless he had substantial grounds of his own for agreement—grounds that were more than adequately provided by his theology. He saw a national church as the eventual outcome of provincial organization, while Riley looked forward to assuming the style of archbishop.

But while the presence of a bishop might in theory provide sacramental and hierarchical fullness, a bishop without clergy was in reality an impractical proposition, a head without limbs, as Trower discovered. And sees established in centres whose population produced few if any ordination candidates, instead of contributing to the autonomy of the church, could hardly forward the formation of an Australian Anglican identity, as their limited resources forced them to turn elsewhere for their clergy. Goldsmith's unquestioning commitment to a doctrine made him oblivious as to how an over-hasty setting-up of episcopal structures might bring the ecclesiastical ship close to running aground on the reefs of local circumstance.

In the north-west an alternative to the rapid establishment of a bishopric was possible. Though Anglicans had little tradition behind them that would have made it feasible to create some kind of 'archpriest'—a cleric who could perform some episcopal functions, such as confirmation, without having episcopal consecration—Parry's suggestion of maintaining the north-west as an archdeaconry would have been viable, as long as a bishop were willing to travel from Perth, or Bunbury. As it was, Riley was increasingly reluctant to extend himself in travelling, while the south-west could occupy all of Goldsmith's time.

And though the south-west was a more viable unit than the extreme north for the establishment and maintenance of a diocese, Goldsmith's theology and the piety that went with it could only be put into practice there as well by recourse to a strong dependence on England for various kinds of support. Thus, paradoxically, adherence to a theology which in many ways stressed the autonomy and independence of the life of Anglican churches could lead Bunbury in a quite different direction.

The piety which was associated with his theology depended on the regular presence of a priest to celebrate the eucharist. here it differed most markedly from that encouraged by Methodist, Baptist and Seventh Day Adventist communities, which could be largely if not completely supplied by the ministry of itinerant laity. It placed considerable stress on seasonal observances extended over an annual cycle, and its piety and teaching were best absorbed through long-term exposure. In place of the experience of a moment of conversion, its life was centred on frequently repeated liturgical actions, which had their fullest impact in substantial buildings equipped with a range of accessories which involved some degree of expense.

The circumstances of the isolated rural populations of his diocese were hardly ideal for such an exercise. The limited means of many of the population of the diocese meant that it was difficult, though not impossible, to raise funds for the stipends of clergy. And it was difficult, though not impossible, to teach a piety which depended on frequently repeated acts built around a yearly cycle to a population which contained a large itinerant and fluctuating element. When it came to liturgical standards, he was forced to acknowledge in a synod address that it was in spite of, and not because of, the kind of buildings that rural Anglicans were able to raise, that the 'beauty and dignity of Christian worship' could be seen.[83] For the fullest realization of his ideal, he could only bridge the gap between the limited means of the population and the cost of adequately equipped buildings, by turning to English resources for funding.

The area of staffing might seem to have offered more opportunities for flexibility, and for a lesser degree of dependence on Britain which would forward the autonomy which he advocated. He ordained a steady trickle of Australians to the priesthood. He tried to break away from the traditional parish pattern of ministry where this seemed necessary and possible. Reference has already been made to Caton's Katanning-based travelling mission, and the projected lugger for work among the northern pearlers. But in this area as well, the creation of the Brotherhood of St Boniface, which was his most radical attempt to depart from the conventional parish structure, was not so much a case of the evolution of an indigenous style of ministry as an attempt to transfer another model of ministry, which was still strongly English in its inspiration, to the bush setting.

This clash between ideals which were products of his theology and piety, and the setting in which he sought to put this into practice, was not unique to Goldsmith. In 1908 the *Church Times* had observed that in the face of the larger, older and more conservative dioceses of Sydney and Melbourne, it was the newer and smaller dioceses which had the more advanced churchmanship.[84] Rather, the rural location of many of the high church prelates who supported autonomy partly explains why their apparent numerical strength was not matched by a corresponding impact on the wider Anglican church in Australia, as they sought to move against what they saw as the inertia of the Sydney giant. And it may explain why their ideals were only slowly realized, as many of them were forced to turn to England for the same reasons as Goldsmith. Tractarianism and Anglo-Catholicism was thus giving birth to an offspring that, Janus-like, looked more than one way.[85]

— ELEVEN —

## Bunbury Diocese as an Anglo-Catholic Cause

There is a remarkable contrast between references to the diocese of Bunbury in publications for British readers and references to the diocese published for an Australian audience. And it does not matter whether the local publications were from within the diocese itself or from beyond it. With the exception of a description of the aims of the Bush Brotherhood of St Boniface and the few more discreetly worded comments quoted elsewhere from the *Church Standard* (a journal which originated in the amalgamation of earlier Sydney and Melbourne publications with a decidedly high church profile),[1] there is little if anything in print in Australia to identify the bishop or his diocese with a particular churchmanship. In the light of Riley's personal proclivities as far as churchmanship was concerned, it seems decidedly ironic that a journal such as the *Victorian Churchman* which claimed to be an evangelical watchdog, denounced Perth for allegedly ritualist tendencies, but was silent about Bunbury.[2] On the other hand, the *Bunbury Occasional Papers* presented to their English readers a picture of a diocese which, while decidedly Catholic, was not extreme. And an examination of the churches at which Goldsmith preached on his visits to England shows that many had a distinctly Catholic profile, or at least were staffed by sympathetic clergy who would have made common cause with Goldsmith.

But how do we account for this strong Anglo-Catholic emphasis in the British material, which forms another strand in the complicated web of churchmanship and nationality? Even before the establishment of the diocese of Bunbury and the publication of the *Bunbury Occasional Papers*, two passages in the *Perth Quarterly Magazine*, the equivalent publication of the Perth Committee which Parry had founded, would have suggested to its more Catholic-minded English readers that this far-flung and distant diocese might be an appropriate object for their generosity. The first was a note thanking English supporters for a number of items that suggested a particular churchmanship, including eucharistic stoles, crosses, and a copy of Vernon Staley's *The Catholic Religion*. The other passage, probably written by Goldsmith himself, described the newly consecrated St George's Carnarvon. It made it clear to the readers that it was a church equipped with eucharistic vestments, and also drew attention to the Catholic piety of its founders, expressed in the inscription on its altar—*oceano divisi, eucharistia conjugimur*.[3]

There is nothing in the early issues of the *Bunbury Occasional Papers* to suggest a deliberate wooing of an Anglo-Catholic clientele. But the definite position which their editor, George Frewer, took within his own parish makes it unlikely that this was due to any fear of alienating Anglicans of broad or low churchmanship. Rather, in the opening years there was little enough in the diocese to warrant description in unequivocally Catholic terms. An account of the newly opened All Saints Donnybrook in a Western Australian paper described the furnishings of the church in sufficient detail to make it obvious that the essentials for a restrained high church worship were all provided, but it did so without using a vocabulary that was exclusively Anglo-Catholic.[4] The *Occasional Papers* could sometimes use a terminology that was reminiscent of an older high church piety, rather than contemporary Anglo-Catholicism, or devotional ways that were as much those of the earliest Tractarians.[5] Equally, when the bishop himself expressed the hope that an awareness of the communion of saints might be deepened as a result of various gifts made during his English tour, he was expressing a piety which was as much in keeping with the general Victorian love of commemorating the dead through memorials, as it was with an earlier strand of high churchmanship.[6] Anglo-Catholics could read such passages as signs that the bishop was one of their own, but many of those used to more restrained Anglican liturgical standards might have found such expressions equally acceptable.

However, the editor of the *Occasional Papers* did not hesitate to include references to the first signs of a more explicit Catholic practice in the diocese—a layman's gift to the bishop of a cope and mitre.[7] As well as the signposts provided by the episcopal vesture, Anglo-Catholic readers of issues in 1911 would have recognized from the description of the aims of the Brotherhood of St Boniface that this body was to perform many of the functions associated in England with a male religious community such as the Community of the Resurrection or the Cowley Fathers. And it was in the lull just before the outbreak of war, and as more clergy of definitely Anglo-Catholic persuasion came to the diocese after Goldsmith's visit to England in 1912, that the tone of the journals becomes more explicit. The liturgy at a festival held in Pinjarra was described as a *missa cantata*, a term to which anti-ritualists objected, and for which there was no precedent in the Prayer Book.[8] Short articles from different hands used a more obvious Catholic terminology. A writer in 1913 referred to the eucharist as the Holy Sacrifice—a usage that also appears later on—and spoke of prayer being offered that the Holy Angels might guide the brothers in their journeying.[9] The same writer assumed that his readers would be familiar with (and approve of) those eucharistic devotions which were regarded as a sign of the most advanced and controversial Anglo-Catholic centres of the time, when he described an Australian sunset as 'God's Benediction of the Blessed Sacrament of Light'.[10] When this was written, benediction still had the hearty disapproval of some clergy who were otherwise regarded as Anglo-Catholic, a notable Australian example being John Oliver Feetham of North Queensland.[11] The most controversial of the terms for the eucharist, the mass, appeared in the next issue in another article concerning the Brotherhood,[12] and although this usage was unusual for the *Papers*, which generally preferred to refer to the Holy Eucharist, the publication of the article in which it appeared can only have been made on the assumption that the readers would not find it intrinsically offensive— and that they did not include evangelicals or uncompromising low churchmen.

The audience towards which Bunbury diocese was pitching its appeals in England was to that extent a definitely Catholic one. The descriptions of the blessing of the House of Grace, and of subsequent extensions, pointed out precisely those aspects that indicated the advanced churchmanship of this centre—its statue of the patron saint, the ringing of the Angelus and the observance of several offices not found in the Prayer Book, the bishop's vesture and attendants, in one article described as deacon and subdeacon, the singing of a hymn particularly associated with Anglo-Catholic mission functions, 'Faith of our Fathers'.[13] At the same time, short phrases of ecclesiastical Latin tags began to appear. In the last issue to appear before the outbreak of war, a list of subjects for prayer by members of the Guild of Aid included a thanksgiving for various clergy and laity who had recently died, and concluded with the traditional Latin rite formula, 'Grant unto them O Lord eternal rest, and let light perpetual shine upon them', which in the eyes of low churchmen and evangelicals constituted an unwarranted and illegal form of prayer for the departed.[14]

Wartime issues still contained passages such as an account of the ordination of Alan Thompson and Arnold Fryer, in which an otherwise restrained ceremonial—the candidates were vested only in stoles, the chasuble not being introduced in Bunbury ordination rites until the time of Bishop Wilson—was described from the point of view of a clearly Catholic piety, with 'the solemn laying on of hands in accordance with the rites of the Anglican branch of the Catholic Church' and the ordinary was sung 'beautifully' to 'Merbecke's plainsong music'.[15]

The same issue contained an advertisement which appealed explicitly to an audience whose piety was Anglo-Catholic. It promoted a volume of 'delightful' litanies and other prayers from Saints Basil and Chrysostom specially suitable for use in wartime translated by one Miss Etheldred Hewlett of Barming. It gave as a sample of her obviously tasteful wares her intercession for 'the humble beasts who with us bear the burden and heat of the day, and offer their guileless lives for the well-being of their countries'.[16] She was obviously no animal liberationist.

Later issues were even more explicit. Early in 1915 the bishop listed as among the diocese's special needs the most important was 'a really good Catholic Priest for the Brotherhood . . .'[17] In the same issue, a contribution by the newly arrived Edward Elsey, with its stress on the lack of even minimum ceremonial fittings such as altar lights in some places, and its statement that much improvement was possible if only funds were available, was designed to pull on Anglo-Catholic purse-strings. Its title, 'Impressions of a Pommy', was at once its author's justification and a defence. As an Englishman used to quite different minimum standards, the situation which he described was a shock to him; at the same time, any Australian into whose hands the *Occasional Papers* might fall might be persuaded to regard the negative tone and findings as nothing more than what one might expect from a 'new chum' fresh from the 'old country'.

However, of all the evidences of Catholic piety in the *Occasional Papers*, the most interesting are references to St Boniface, patron of the diocese, whose name, Bunbury, was held to be a contraction of Boniface-Bury. Earlier issues had made passing mention of his example as a missionary and as an Englishman who should inspire the men of the English church who came to join the staff of the diocese.[18] The war provoked both Goldsmith and Frewer to draw a contrast between the demands of the Gospel to which Boniface the Englishman had converted Germany, with the present German position. Boniface was part of the historical inheritance of Germany and was a central figure in its evangelization, but the current actions of Germany were a repudiation of the whole of that tradition and its real spirit. After quoting from a description by Goldsmith of Fulda, the site of a large bronze statue of the saint, George Frewer concluded

> Will Fulda, on 'the Anniversary Day of the Martyrdom', June 5th, be remembering this year her debt to the English St. Boniface? 'The Apostle of Germany.' How strange it all sounds, does it not? The holy teachings of St. Boniface being rejected for those of Berhardi; hymns of hate replacing the messages of the Gospel of Peace; methods of murder and poison substituted for the chivalry of manly warfare. O Boniface, Saint of God, *Ora pro Nobis!*[19]

Here a distinct feature of Anglo-Catholic piety, the invocation of the saints, was combined with a strongly nationalist wartime sentiment. And although it was to an English audience, and not an Australian one, that Goldsmith and Frewer offered these points for consideration, they still indicate that a theological and devotional focus which was normally used by Anglo-Catholics as part of an accommodation, or even celebration of European, supra-national allegiances, could be modified so as to appeal to a more insular and patriotic sentiment. This patriotic redirection might also have diminished the sense of discomfort felt by other Anglicans at such a direct expression of Catholic devotion, though it certainly would still have been unacceptable to most evangelicals and low churchmen. According to their more prominent bishops in England during World War I, many of the laity were disturbed and angered by the erroneous theology which they claimed to lie behind prayer offered for those who died in battle.[20]

In themselves, the passages referred to above, particularly the later ones, show that an appeal was being made for support from an audience that adhered to a quite distinguishable theological position. But they also contrast with the terminology used in material produced for Western Australian readers in both the church's own journals and through the wider press. The more narrowly Anglican and ecclesiastically oriented readership of the *Bunbury Occasional Papers* does not account entirely for this conservative contrast: the Perth secular press had not been averse to publishing material relating to Anglican churchmanship at considerable length until the beginning of the present century. Reasons for a modification of the earlier hostility towards Anglo-Catholicism have already been discussed.[21]

The description of the ordination of Thompson and Fryer in the *Bunbury Occasional Papers* which reproduces an article from Bunbury's *Southern Times* certainly indicates the extent to which the reporter had picked up the 'correct' terminology—or had he been given a prepared statement?[22] But it was also typical of the limits that are evident in documents other than those that derive from specifically Anglo-Catholic sources. What it described was a piety expressed in a service which was devoid of any of the distinctive features of Anglo-Catholic ceremonial, and the English terms that it used for the eucharistic ministers had already made occasional appearances in the *West Australian* and the *Western Mail* before 1900. The few references to the Brotherhood's life in the *West Australian* or the *West Australian Church News*, most of which occur during Wilson's episcopate, stressed the rural location and demanding nature of its work, not those features, such as the use of a number of monastic daily prayers, which might give the impression that its life approximated in some way to that of a religious community.[23]

In this period, prayers invoking the saints, and references to such devotional practices as the Angelus, do not appear in the *West Australian Church News*, sympathetic to the Anglo-Catholic cause though it was. It was far more concerned to present the broader issues of sacramental theology and devotion. Only in the late 1920s, after the appointment of

John Foley-Whaling to South Bunbury and the arrival of the sisters of St Elizabeth of Hungary, did it regularly carry descriptions of ceremonial and vesture in a way which assumed that an audience within the state was edified by liturgical minutiae or 'man-millinery'.[24]

Goldsmith's appeal in the *Occasional Papers* for a Catholic priest for the Brotherhood used the term as though it defined a particular kind of Anglican cleric, and was not necessarily applicable to all Anglican clergy. Though Goldsmith himself elsewhere defended its use to describe the whole Anglican communion, and by inference all of her clergy, the more exclusive sense would have been regarded as an improper narrowing of its meaning by such men as Riley. In those documents in which he referred to churchmanship, C. O. L. Riley never spoke of Catholics, but of ritualists or high churchmen, the former particularly in a pejorative context.[25] It was in the *Defender,* the journal of the Australian Church Union, that pleas for young Catholic priests to offer their services to the Brotherhood would appear again.[26]

The contrast between the delight of the *Occasional Papers* in the few Catholic externals which were visible in the new diocese and the silence of the Perth press over such matters is only partly explained by the obscurity of Williams, the site of the Brotherhood's House of Grace. Goldsmith's use of cope and mitre was hardly inconspicuous, especially when Trower, another convinced Anglo-Catholic, joined the province; and Mrs Noyes' gift made possible the building of All Saints at Collie, which received attention in the daily press.

Riley's desire to avoid any kind of ceremonial extremes in his diocese in order to 'avoid questions'—that is, discussion that would promote divisions on the basis of churchmanship—has already been noted. To this reticence of Riley's, and Hackett's distaste for Anglo-Catholicism, must be attributed some of the silence over the more obviously Catholic appearance of the south-west. Significantly, on the consecration of All Saints Collie, the one occasion when Riley was involved in a major ceremony in the diocese under Goldsmith, he was consistent enough to 'avoid questions' by allowing Frewer and Elsey to vest him in cope and mitre instead of the rochet and chimere which he otherwise always wore.[27]

That the increasingly Catholic tone of the *Occasional Papers* was part of an attempt by Goldsmith to appeal to a consciously Anglo-Catholic audience in England, which was perceived to be lacking in (Western) Australia, is also confirmed by one of his retirement projects, his establishment of the 'Association of Prayer for the Church in Australia'. In its appeal to members, it stressed the 'great difficulties' faced at the time in Australia.[28] The Association's prayer lists clearly implied that in the light of their more fortunate circumstances, both in their means and the fullness with which they expressed their particular position, it was the business of Anglo-Catholics in Britain to support their less privileged counterparts at the other end of the Empire.

The other evidence of an appeal to a consciously Catholic stream in England lies in the very churches in which Goldsmith appealed for funds and clergy for the diocese. As his commissary, his brother-in-law organized many of his preaching engagements. G. E. Frewer circulated printed handbills which advertised the impending visit and invited clergy who were prepared to offer their pulpits to notify him.[29]

Apart from Brede, six other parishes had clear Frewer connections: the parish church of Hitcham (Bucks.) where George Frewer, G. E. Frewer's father, was rector; the Eton mission church of St Mary the Virgin Hackney Wick; St John's Upper St-Leonard's-on-Sea, where G. H. Frewer had earlier served a curacy; Sts Peter and Paul Fenstanton, G. H. Frewer's own parish, and St Swithin's Lincoln, whose rector, Bernard Hancock, had been G. E. Frewer's curate at Horncastle, before the latter accepted the parish of Brede.

Centres in which G. E. Frewer preached or took missions—Beckley, St Barnabas Bexhill, St Saviour's Eastbourne, All Saints Hastings, St Barnabas Hove, Christ Church St-Leonard-on-Sea, Rye and Westfield— also appear in his brother-in-law's itineriaries.[30] To that extent, Goldsmith's preachments also reflected Fewer's own connections, particularly as a member of the organization of mission priests, *Novate Novale*.

Six other centres were connected with Goldsmith's family or his personal career before he left England—Merchant Taylors' School, by then relocated at Charterhouse; parish churches at Charlton, Cheam and Halling; All Saints Highgate, the parish of an aunt who had married into

F. W. Goldsmith and family group in the garden at 'Hillside', Brede, 1912
Back row, l. to r., the Reverend Cyril Charsley Frewer, Eva Clara Frewer, née Jacob, his wife, Miss Amoore, the Reverend George Herbert Frewer, Rector of Fenstanton, Mrs Edith Goldsmith, née Frewer; seated, l. to r., Ellen Elizabeth Frewer, the Reverend George Ernest Frewer, Vicar of Brede, Louise Charsley Frewer, his wife and patron of the parish, the Right Reverend Frederick William Goldsmith, Alice Maud Frewer; seated on ground, Dorothy (Dolly) Frewer

the Low family of publishers;[31] and St Jude's Bradford, whose incumbent, C. G. Swann, was a cousin.[32]

His entrée to seven other churches came through clergy currently in Bunbury diocese, or clergy whom Goldsmith had met or worked with in Western Australia: Emmanuel Church Didsbury (Manchester), St James the Less Westminster, St George's Camberwell, St Peter's Keighley, St John's Cleckheaton, and parish churches at Barming and Fletching.

But the lowest common denominator linking the largest number of churches in which Goldsmith preached was neither staff associations nor family links, but churchmanship, which was a significant element not only in many of the centres to which George Frewer himself had the entree, but to many others as well.

Out of the one hundred and sixty-two centres in which Goldsmith preached on his visits to England, the churchmanship of one hundred and four can be accurately described by drawing on contemporary parish records, Church Union membership lists and a variety of controviersial material from the churchmanship battles of the period. Of the one hundred and four centres, only nine had a distinctly low churchmanship. He had entry to two of those centres through his own clergy who had served their curacies in them: the Emmanuel Church Didsbury, through J. E. Stansfield, and St John's Woolwich, through W. J. Parish. On one occasion, his contacts were with the low-church parish in a particular centre, and not its distinctly Anglo-Catholic equivalent—when he went to Henley-on-Thames in 1905, he preached at Holy Trinity, not St Mary's. At Harrogate, where St Wilfrid's had become the Anglo-Catholic centre by 1912, the comparative wealth of Christ Church, a centre with a surpliced choir but a conservative evangelical preaching tradition, explains the bishop's appearance there.

The remaining ninety-five centres demonstrate the many different ways in which the influence of the Oxford Movement manifested itself. In twenty-six centres its influence was general, and given very little expression through ceremonial. But of sixty-nine other centres thirty-four had a definitely Anglo-Catholic identity, even though they did not use the most controversial of the Church Union's 'six points', vestments and incense. Such centres were identified as Anglo-Catholic by the contemporary critics of ritualism, who identified the Anglo-Catholic movement as a movement with a doctrinal and devotional thrust, and not merely a ceremonial one, especially where the eucharist and the revival of confession were concerned.

Three of Goldsmith's clergy came from parishes of this kind. In the case of St Faith's Stepney, from which Edward Elsey came to join the Brotherhood of St Boniface, the evidence of his own churchmanship in private documents illuminates our understanding of the parish, The *Church Times* had welcomed the establishment of St Faith's, a daughter church of St Dunstan's, as creating 'a fresh centre where the Catholic faith of Christ will be taught with all truth and sincerity'. According to the *Ritualistic Clergy List* it did not use either vestments or incense, but the *Church Times* had listed features which suggested its complexion well enough—its high altar and alabaster super-altar provided with lights, cross and Arundel Society prints of the Crucifixion, Sts John, Jerome, Giles and Blaise, its main Sunday liturgy a 'high celebration'. Elsey's own diaries from his time in charge of St Faith's confirm that the liturgical restraint was not a matter of doctrinal or devotional hesitancy—they list regular weekly appointments for hearing confessions. No wonder he found the Williams parish church, as he described it, barely adequate.

From further north, J. E. Stansfield came to Bunbury after Goldsmith's 1905 visit: his father, a Church Union member, was the first incumbent (1882-1921) of St Peter's Keighley, then the most Catholic parish in its locality in the predominantly evangelical diocese of Bradford. Goldsmith preached at St Peter's in 1908 and 1912. Its location in an unattractive working-class area of the town made it an unlikely source for major financial support. Goldsmith's appearances would partly have stemmed from a sense of Anglo-Catholic solidarity—but also because he may not have been particularly welcome in the other centres of the area.

At St John's Cleckheaton, where Goldsmith also preached in 1912, the vicar, W. Burbidge, had already served in Australia as a member of the first of the bush brotherhoods, the Brotherhood of St Andrew. The parish had an unambiguous tradition for some time before his appointment, even though vestments were not introduced until after he had come to Bunbury. Burbidge himself had associations with what was perhaps the oldest centre with a strong Catholic tradition in the north—Leeds, where he served a curacy at All Souls' before joining the Brotherhood of St Andrew.[33]

The final group of parishes in which Goldsmith preached was formed by thirty-five centres in which the most controversial of the liturgical 'points'—vestments, and often incense as well—were in use. Their wide distribution invite us to see Goldsmith as more than a 'church taster' merely seeking to make a comfortable pilgrimage to the best-known south coast Anglo-Catholic shrines. It ranged from St Deniol's Hawarden, and St Mary's Bath to St Matthias' Malvern Link, and Sts Mary and Chad in Staffordshire's Longton, taking in the Worksop Priory, St Cuthbert's College and St Mary's Clumber Park in Nottinghamshire, and All Saints Leamington, in Warwickshire. Its northern limit was reached at St Cuthbert's Hebburn-on-Tyne, where Tom Groser was a curate before joining the Brotherhood of St Boniface. Here Goldsmith addressed a meeting, though he did not preach.

Among such parishes located in the south of England, only three could be considered to belong to the well known centres of 'London, Brighton and South Coast religion' which had developed an almost legendary fame or notoriety as a result of surviving the hostility of anti-ritualist protests, or hostile bishops.[34] One was St Stephen's Lewisham, which Goldsmith first visited in 1891 when the incumbent was still Rhodes Bristow, a member of the Society of the Holy Cross, who had survived the displeasure of Bishop Thorold over his introduction of vestments and incense; another was St Matthias' Stoke Newington, a centre where the use of incense and vestments as early as 1865 provoked rioting. Of the south coast Anglo-Catholic centres, the most notable one in which Goldsmith preached was Christ Church St-Leonard's-on-Sea, to which his brother-in-law provided the entrée.

The hope of some generous patronage, and not churchmanship alone, certainly would have attracted him to seek an invitation to a centre such as All Saints Margaret Street, whose lavish High Victorian Gothic interior by William Butterfield matched the means of many of its congregation. By the time he visited it, the frescoes painted by William Dyce were being replaced by J. N. Comper with copies on boards, but light still scintillated across ceramic murals, coloured mosaics, marbles, naturalistic sculpture and patterns in inlaid mastic. Even its much humbler predecessor was the worshipping home for at least two women of means who founded religious communities, the Honorable Georgina Hoare and Harriet

Brownlow Byron.³⁵ A similar possibility of funding as much as a common churchmanship would have attracted him to the Woodward School of St Cuthbert's College, the nearby Worksop Priory and St Mary's Clumber Park, built as a wedding present for its patron, the Duke of Newcastle, and provided by its designer, G. F. Bodley, with a confessional.

But the Catholicity of a church was sometimes the only rationale for Goldsmith's appearance there—even if sometimes it might also have been likely that Goldsmith's own position made him unacceptable in the low church or churches of a centre where there was more than one Anglican church. Dorking was just such a centre: the self-conscious position of St Paul's was such that the son of a servant on the staff of the vicarage at this time has suggested that Goldsmith would not have been permitted to preach there—hence his appearance at St Martin's, where the Cowley Fathers conducted a mission concentrating on communicant life and confession a decade before Goldsmith's visit. And only its Catholicity could explain his appearance at All Saints Southend, in 1905 and 1908. Its associations were promising enough to an Anglo-Catholic: its patron was Keble College and the building itself was designed by G. E. Street. But a local religious census carried out in 1903 showed it to be the least supported of the Anglican churches in the vicinity: its morning attendance of 184 and evening attendance of 137 had to compare with figures from four other churches ranging between 237 and 403 in the morning and 176 and 383 in the evening. By 1910 it was celebrating the feasts of Corpus Christi and the Assumption, had Stations of the Cross during Lent, and a daily eucharist.

Lastly, his inherent cautiousness did not inhibit him in England from visiting two parishes that thumbed their noses in almost every possible way at the Church of England's establishment, and at other kinds of establishment as well, parishes that were part of what many other Anglicans regarded as an extreme fringe of Anglo-Catholicism, a kind of Anglican underworld.

The first was St Giles South Mymms, where Goldsmith preached in 1908 and 1912. The parish also had a local branch of the Bunbury Guild of Aid; its secretary, a Miss Whitty, lived in the larger nearby centre of Barnet.³⁶ The earlier history of South Mymms could almost be described as paradigmatic. A Tractarian had been appointed as its vicar in 1852 and approached G. E. Street to provide plans for a restoration of St Giles', but Street's plans were initially rejected by the laity of the parish. The tide turned after two other incumbents performed faithful ministrations. Street's plans were put into effect in 1872 and further additions made in the last decade of the century. For a period of time extending a little longer than the first half of this century, the key figure in the Anglo-Catholic identity of the parish was Allen Hay, a former curate of Plaistow in London's east end, the supposed Anglo-Catholic mecca. He became vicar in 1898. Hay came fired up for the Anglo-Catholic cause, inheriting a parish in which incense was already in use, and where there was a sung eucharist on Sundays, which came to completely displace matins before World War I. Hay remained until his death in 1954, his immobility partly (if not completely) due to his association with the curious figure of W. H. Mathew, an *episcopus vagans* who lived in a cottage in South Mymms which Hay provided for him.[37]

The presence and actions of bishops such as Mathew over several decades was of sufficient concern to the Anglican hierarchy to be the object of a resolution at the 1920 Lambeth Conference. It repudiated the validity of the orders of the clergy they ordained, and denied any ecclesial reality to their churches.[38] Mathew had been consecrated in 1908 by four continental Old Catholic bishops, who understood that he was to act as the head of a sizeable Old Catholic movement in England. In the same year he founded an Order of Corporate Reunion, claiming that he was reviving Dr F. G. Lee's organization of the same name. Through it, he offered re-ordination and even consecration to Anglican incumbents, which would supplement any defects that resulted from their Anglican orders and prepare them for the time when Western Christendom would reunite with Rome.[39] Mathew performed such conditional acts (sometimes referred to as 'bedroom ordinations') in his cottage though, unlike some of his other contemporaries, he does not appear to have charged for such services. When he died in 1919, seven years after Goldsmith's last visit to South Mymms, several Anglican clergy seized Mathew's ordination register and systematically erased their names from it, fearful that any disclosure of its contents might jeopardize their future careers.

Despite Mathew's 'bedroom ordinations', Hay encouraged him to appear at St Giles' church in full episcopal vesture and to take part in ceremonies to which no Anglican bishop then on the English bench would have consented, such as processions with the Blessed Sacrament through the village. Hay was only saved by Mathew's death from being seriously disciplined by the Bishop of London, Winnington Ingram, as a result of their association, and Peter Anson regarded it as possible on the basis of correspondence between Hay and Mathew that Hay himself had received episcopal orders at Hay's hands, though no documentary evidence exists.[40] Isolated in his parish as a result, his ongoing activities were characteristic of a number of other priests who saw in the Congress movement the apogee of Anglicanism. He continued to invite men he regarded as heroes of the faith to preach at South Mymms, and would sit during their sermons on a specially placed chair at the front of the nave, taking snuff all the while. At least once in his declining years he forgot to invite one of the heroes whose presence he subsequently advertised.

The second such centre was St Saviour's Hoxton, where Goldsmith preached twice in 1912, once at the morning high mass, and on the same day at the first evensong for the Annunciation of the Blessed Virgin. Its incumbent, E. E. Kilburn, had been a curate in the parish, and before his return as vicar he was associated with two other centres in which Goldsmith preached—St Ives Huntingdon, another fully fledged Anglo-Catholic centre, and the missionary college of St Paul's Burgh, of which he was the vice-principal from 1899 to 1903. Even when Goldsmith preached there, St Saviour's was far from the decorous Anglicanism of St John's Hoxton, where George Pownall, a former Dean of Perth, lived after returning to England. Its designer was James Brooks, a Church Union member and worshipper at St Matthias' Stoke Newington. Like St Matthias', it achieved some degree of notoriety during the period of the Public Worship Regulation Act. When Goldsmith visited it, it had not quite reached the flights of ultramontanism for which it was later well known, but was on its way. By 1920 Kilburn had totally superseded the use of the Prayer Book rite in English in the parish with the Roman rite in Latin. As a result of this and a variety of other related usages, Kilburn was subject to the increasing criticism and formal censure of Winnington Ingram. For Kilburn and similar ultramontane clergy, colonial prelates could serve a variety of uses, at worst, performing episcopal functions in the parish when the diocesan refused to do so. But while high profile appearances were made at St Saviour's by which such well-known bishops as Frank Weston, who once pontificated in the African language he customarily used in Zanzibar to cover his (rather surprising) lack of fluency in Tridentine Latin, there is no evidence to suggest that Goldsmith's appearance involved the performance of such exotic functions—though by comparison with the usage of the majority of Anglican churches at the time, a bishop in cope and mitre blessing incense in English, as he would have been expected to do at the morning liturgy, would have been exotic enough.

On his 1891 visit, when he had been Dean of Perth for only three years, Goldsmith preached at only three centres with an advanced ceremonial—St Stephen's Lewisham (for the Conversion of St Paul in 1892), Christ Church, and St John's at St Leonard's-on-Sea (for the first evensong of St Andrew, 1891). Several factors explain his visits to an increasing number and widening geographical range of parishes in which the full Anglo-Catholic ceremonial was used or which otherwise displayed other signs of strong Anglo-Catholic influence.

The 1900 election did not return the strongly Protestant government which Kensitites predicted and from which they hoped for new parliamentary legislation to put down Anglo-Catholicism.[41] If anything, the most concerted level of opposition was declining, and Anglo-Catholicism was beginning to move towards the apparent ascendancy indicated by the massive Congress gatherings of the 1920s and 1930s. The gradual movement up the churchmanship ladder seen over a period of time in many of the parishes which Goldsmith visited was also a part of the resulting sense of confidence felt by the heirs of the Tractarians. They had emerged victorious from critical encounters, and represented a force that was permanent.

If the Anglo-Catholic movement felt increasingly secure, Goldsmith also was more attractive as a visitor after 1904. For any committed Anglo-Catholic church, a bishop who would wear mitre and cope was far more of a marketable commodity as a visible demonstration of the cause than a colonial dean. Catholic-minded editors of parish magazines were quick to exploit the possibilities inherent in an episcopal visit and show loyalty to the cause: All Saints Leamington described Goldsmith as 'assisting pontifically' at a Sunday eucharist—readers knew that a bishop had visited and the parish showed it was up with the latest 'correct' Anglo-Catholic terminology.[42] And if some bishops were more diffident concerning ceremonial at the beginning of the century than they might otherwise have been in the wake of anti-ritualist allegations of active complicity (or at least failure to administer clerical discipline) made before the 1900 election, a colonial bishop was free from such pressure. Goldsmith could function in the way that Anglo-Catholics expected of a bishop, secure that his remote seat distanced him from any pressures the others might have feared or felt.

That a bishop who so acted was an attraction to Anglo-Catholics was certainly acknowledged by their opponents. The frontispiece of the Church Association's *Ritualistic Clergy List,* in which Goldsmith himself was named, included a bishop in cope and mitre among the ritualistic dangers illustrated around the borders of a map of England. An anti-ritualist Australian publication, the *Victorian Churchman*, referred to the Anglo-Catholic penchant for using fully vested bishops as an excuse for hitherto unknown processions, but when it came to specific instances, the only individuals it could name were English prelates such as Winnington Ingram, who was attacked for encouraging 'lawlessness' when he took part in a procession at All Saints Margaret Street, in which incense was used.[43]

And while Goldsmith himself ho doubt sought invitations to preach at celebrations for major feasts in the liturgical calendar because such days would bring a larger audience to hear of his diocese and its needs, Catholic-minded parishes were equally likely to jump at the opportunities offered by a compliant colonial prelate, who could bless incense, absolve and sing the final blessing at a solemn mass in the morning, or feature as the ceremonial climax of a figure-of-eight procession at evensong. At Mansfield in 1912 he preached at evensong on the patronal festival, and the local press regarded the procession for the feast as being as much worthy of note as his topical references to the sinking of the *Titanic,* in his view, a situation in which Englishmen displayed their capacity for self-control and the performance of their duty.[44]

Three Catholic parishes welcomed him for Marian feasts. For the Annunciation, the most significant of the Marian feasts retained in the Prayer Book, he was at St Silas' Pentonville, on its eve for the first evensong, and on the day itself he preached at St Stephen's Lewisham. For the Visitation, which in the Prayer Book is only a black-letter feast, he was at Longton with Father Murray, where his presence doubtless acted as an excuse to give an added degree of elaboration to the liturgy.

In accounting for this pattern of preachments with its increasing number of Anglo-Catholic centres, Goldsmith's own devotional preferences must not be overlooked. Reference has already been made to the nostalgia he expressed in Australia when he recalled the peaks to which worship could rise in England.[45] In the absence of any strongly developed centre in his diocese, it is hardly surprising that, while he was in England, he ensured that for the devotional climax of Lent, Holy Week and the Holy Week rites, he was at an Anglo-Catholic centre, St Deniol's Hawarden, on Maundy Thursday and Good Friday. Passion Sunday morning was spent with Father Kilburn at the increasingly exotic St Saviour's Hoxton.

But woven among these other strands was also a conviction that Anglo-Catholics had a mission to convert and transform the whole of Anglicanism, a conviction that the bishop himself occasionally voiced, and which possessed his brother-in-law, and some of those who heard Goldsmith, or heard of him. The clearest expression of his own conviction dated from his retirement period, in the intercession lists for the Association of Prayer for the Church in Australia, which sought 'the prayers of the Faithful for the conversion of Australia to the fulness of the Catholic Faith'.[46] The document described the situation in Australia as one that demanded some committed response from English Anglo-Catholics. Many of the intercession headings named dioceses in different parts of Australia where, by implication, the Catholic faith was advancing in spite of 'great difficulties': three were for concerns within the Bunbury diocese.

But much earlier in his Australian career, two years after his arrival in Perth, he had written to Mother Emily Ayckbowm in London inviting her to send members of the Community of the Sisters of the Church to staff the Perth orphanage. Here too he suggested that something needed to and could be done to improve the churchmanship of Western Australian Anglicans:

> The church tone of the place is by no means advanced but Australians are quick to merit the value of honest hard work, and real devotion, and persons of ordinary tact can not only be happy in their own work, but can also exercise considerable influence on those around . . .[47]

Though his long-term experience showed him that more than just the presence of hard-working Anglo-Catholics was needed before Australians would rally in numbers to the cause, the inference remains that he envisaged Anglo-Catholicism as a force emerging to dominate Anglicanism in Australia and Anglicanism in general. The strength with which he gave voice from his retirement to his ultimate hope for Australia was certainly consistent with the high tide of the movement in England represented by the Congresses.

The increasingly Catholic tone of the *Bunbury Occasional Papers* in the period after 1912 is partly due to the contributions from within the diocese of priests who were committed to the Anglo-Catholic movement, such as John Frewer and Edward Elsey, but other factors which may have contributed include the generally increased confidence of Anglo-Catholics in England and the degree of success which George Frewer himself met in converting the parish of Brede. He did this, even though his predecessor, the patriotic poet Augustus Aylward, was a low churchman who was the incumbent of the parish for over thirty years (1851–85) and enjoyed the support of the Frewen family who had occupied Brede Place as the local squires since 1708. Many of the signs of the change in the parish's churchmanship have been referred to already, but a tribute to the tactfulness with which George Frewer accomplished this is suggested by parish statistics. Communicant figures during George Frewer's incumbency show that not only was there an overall increase in the number of communicants in the village, but the percentage of the total population who were communicants was almost 8 per cent higher than the average for the deanery of Rye, of which Brede was a part.[48]

Frewer was possessed of a degree of tact but also of a missionary conviction that the future belonged to Anglo-Catholics, a conviction that was sharpened by the regular occurrence of Kensitite protests on the green that adjoined the church at Brede. He voiced it in a sermon preached at one of the great shrines of south-coast Anglo-Catholicism, St Bartholomew's Brighton. Towering above the slums that surrounded it, it stood higher than any cathedral in the country, but its interior equally drove the viewer to look upward, as its high altar stood on an extreme elevation of steps, as though to approach it the sacred ministers were truly ascending the mountain to enter into the cloud and speak face to face with God. This sense of the transcendant, the triumphant and the triumphalist was continued in the richly wrought Arts and Crafts style pulpit from which Frewer spoke, all of a piece with the ciborium, candlesticks, and high altar and rails, designed by Henry Wilson. It was a passionate and eloquent symbol of what Anglo-Catholicism aspired to, and an appropriate setting for Frewer's message. He based his sermon on Deuteronomy 7: 22, a text that referred to the gradual occupation of the Promised Land by the Israelites. Frewer interpreted it as speaking of a temporary co-existence of Catholic and Protestant, which must eventually end because the church, which Israel analogically represented, could only belong to one of them. Protestantism was a 'strange, weird, alien thing' with chameleon-like qualities, still in need of ongoing support from Catholics for a little longer in the fight with the 'lions of Rationalism and Infidelity and aggressive Atheism'. But after that,

> The capture of Canaan in the name of the Lord involves fighting. It is a sad but inevitable necessity. We would fain, would we not, enter into our rightful inheritance peacefully. But it may not be. It is a campaign of gradual, but none the less persistent, extermination, to which we are called and pledged.[49]

The audience to which Goldsmith appealed was also committed to some extent to a belief in Anglo-Catholicism as the Anglicanism of the future, and this is particularly true of parishes such as South Mymms and St Saviour's Hoxton. Because they only represent a small cross-section of the total from which Goldsmith sought support, they do not constitute irrefutable evidence of ultramontane connections or exotic tendencies on his part, so much as their own dissatisfaction with the English episcopate of the time. However they explained the refusal of English bishops to endorse their idiosyncrasies, the tensions between such parishes and their diocesan bishops (and often their provincial archbishops as well) made it easy for them to believe that the Catholicity of Anglicanism was more pronounced at the periphery of the British empire in its

St George's Brede, 1928
The church as Goldsmith would have seen it in his last years. 'Hillside', the cottage in which the two unmarried Frewer sisters lived, and centre of much of the fundraising of the Bunbury Guild of Aid, is visible to the left.

colonies than at its centre, and fuelled their support for colonial missions. The giving of St Saviour's Hoxton, to Bunbury in 1913 certainly suggests this: its offering of £2 4s 1d might seem small enough, but out of thirty parishes that year whose collections for Bunbury are recorded, only one other raised more—Brede, the home of the Guild of Aid.[50]

The best evidence, however, that a sense of Anglo-Catholic mission possessed his listeners and his readers is provided by the gifts which enabled the two most extensive single building programmes of his episcopate. The first occurred as a response to his appearance at All Saints Margaret Street in October 1912, just before his return to Australia, when he spoke of the need for more adequate churches in the mining communities within his diocese, such as Greenbushes, Collie and Ravensthorpe. He might well have expected a generous response in this, the most opulent of Butterfield's churches, which continued to attract wealthy patrons, and he was not disappointed. A little more than a fortnight after his visit to All Saints, he wrote that 'a member of the congregation' had offered to build a church at Collie, on the condition that it should be a basilica dedicated under the title of All Saints, as a memorial to a departed relative.[51] There seems to have been some confusion over the condition of the gift, namely the identity of the donor. In his 1913 synod charge, the bishop referred to her wish to remain anonymous, but she had already been identified in the *Bunbury Occasional Papers* a year earlier as Mrs Noyes.[52] According to a contemporary report, the building was completed at a cost of £2,000.[53]

The other building project was a permanent home for the members of the Brotherhood of St Boniface. As with the endowment of All Saints, Goldsmith at first wrote of the gift without identifying the donor. In this case, the donor had not been in any direct contact with the bishop, but learnt at second hand of the brothers' temporary accommodation in a rented farmhouse, and wrote, offering to build a permanent residence.[54] She may well have become aware of the Brotherhood and its needs through a contact Goldsmith had with the parish of Holy Trinity Knowle, an Anglo-Catholic centre in Bristol, close to her home. A subsequent issue of the *Occasional Papers* identified her as a Mrs Wills and specified the sum given—£1,000.[55] She was Monica Wills, later Dame Monica, the second daughter of Sir Philip Cunliffe-Own, KCB, KCMG, and wife of Henry Herbert Wills, a grandson of one of the two brothers who founded the tobacco company of W. D. and H. O. Wills. Neither she nor her husband had any children; on his death in 1922 her husband left an estate worth £2,750,000. Their childlessness may explain their generous giving in a number of areas—he built a large retirement home and hospital in the Bristol suburb of Clifton, called St Monica's—but Monica Wills was well known as a supporter of Anglo-Catholic causes. In England the organizations to which she made gifts included the Oratory of the Good Shepherd, an organization whose rule still binds together a number of Catholic clergy in the Anglican church. In 1920, when John Oliver Feetham approached her seeking support for schools in his diocese, she apologized for being unable to offer him more than £500 immediately, but her husband subsequently made him a bequest of £8,000.[56]

By 1914, when there were four brothers, two novices and a postulant living at the house, extensions became necessary, and Monica Wills provided another £300, which made it possible to build three more rooms for brothers, and to extend the chapel.[57] Her interest in Bunbury persisted beyond the Brotherhood of St Boniface: Bishop Wilson, Goldsmith's successor, was advised to approach her. When John Foley-Whaling attempted to establish a Benedictine community at Brunswick in 1929, she offered to pay his passage to England so that he could spend some time living at the Benedictine house at Nashdom, a course of action advised by Bishop Frere and supported by Bishop Wilson, but rejected by Foley-Whaling himself.[58]

Substantial patronage from Anglo-Catholic donors thus made possible the two buildings whose settings were the most conducive for fostering the mysteriological piety that Goldsmith favoured. It was probably partly as a tribute to the Englishness of its readers that the *Bunbury Occasional Papers* placed maximum stress on those elements in the new buildings which could be linked with what was decidedly English in origin. A description of the blessing of the foundation stone of All Saints Collie, asked

> What more appropriate day could be chosen than May 19th, the feast of St Dunstan in our English Kalendar? The very name of Dunstan—Hill stone—speaks of the Church which will rise on the crest of the highest spot in Collie. St. Dunstan too, it was, as history tells us, who laid at Glastonbury the foundation of a church more beautiful than that which existed.[59]

Consecration of All Saints Collie, 1915
The two bishops in cope and mitre are Goldsmith and, surprisingly, Riley—the only occasion on which he vested in this way.

The laying of the foundation stone in the western mining town was thus linked with a saint of the Anglo-Saxon church, a part of their heritage to which Anglicans often turned as they claimed that their church shared the essentials of the faith with Rome without having been subject to her jurisdiction. And it was linked with Glastonbury, the site associated in British legend with the coming of Christianity to Britain with Joseph of Arimathaea. Western Australia was to be linked with a particularly British past, just as the present patrons were English. Readers were also assured that the church would be conducive to real devotion, 'beautiful and inspiring for the worship of God—a gift which would inspire the kind of piety of which the donor and the bishop (and readers of the *Occasional Papers*) approved.

This invocation of the quintessentially English and of all that was not continental bears at least two interpretations. Conceptually, it linked the new Collie church with the Anglo-Saxon element in British history, and thus to the well-springs of the British, as much as the ecclesiastical past. And the imperial rallying cry of World War I may have made such an

Exterior, All Saints Collie, 1923
*West Australian Church News*, September 1923, p. 14

The Chapel of the House of Grace, Williams
Note the stalls arranged on each side of the chapel in which the brothers would sit, choir-wise, like a monastic community. Four riddel posts, topped with sconces for candles, stand at each corner of the altar, and between them run curtains, forming what Dearmer and others promoted as a characteristically 'English' altar. The altarpiece is a triptych, a colour print reproduction of an old master painting; other such prints decorate the walls. A statue of St Boniface, raising his hand in blessing, is just visible to the right.

identification between the colonial offspring and the remote British antiquity all the more pointed. But it could also offset the strikingly un-English visual suggestions of the building, and pre-empt any hint that its continental outline—it ended in a basilican apse at its west end, to which a campanile was added in 1928—was prophetic of the ultimate identity of Anglo-Catholicism. For unlike some other brick and stone churches in the diocese whose first descriptions stressed their English features and associations, its form hardly filled the landscape with an outline to comfort those British migrants seeking solace in the familiar.

Instead, these comments almost ignored the extent to which the building and its interior were to reflect the stress on the international. This stress, never entirely absent from Anglo-Catholicism, was to find a greater degree of expression after World War I in the increasing number of churches built in England in continental neo-Baroque style. The *Occasional Papers* noted in passing that All Saints was to be in the Romanesque style, not the revival Gothic by now associated with all shades of churchmanship, and seen as particularly glorious in its English manifestation. When completed, its altar was fitted not with the two lights claimed by Percy Dearmer to be particularly characteristic of English use,[60] but with a set of six candlesticks and matching crucifix, thought at the time to be of continental baroque silver on wood, thus making it approximate instead to a Latin rite altar, except for the absence of perhaps the most controversial current fitting for an Anglican church—a tabernacle.

In describing the enlarged chapel of the House of Grace, an even greater stress was laid on a combination of piety and churchmanship articulated in nationalistic terms. The original chapel's cramped conditions made 'dignified ceremonial' impossible but, in the extended chapel, 'the Old English use at our dignified English Altar was most impressive, and it was a great joy to many of our visitors to take part in a service so beautiful'.[61] Discerning readers were expected to conclude that the new chapel would attract many visitors in the future, who would go away convinced at once of the appropriateness of a Catholic performance of the liturgy, and that its dignity was consistent with both the English character and the liturgy's claims to represent an inheritance from the best elements of antiquity. And since readers had little reason to question that the future of the world might be anything other than British and imperial, such descriptions acted as a reassurance that, at the circumference of the empire, Anglo-Catholic standards were gradually being planted even in the remotest corners of a continent whose future was destined also for greatness, because it was British.

— T W E L V E —

# Bringing Monasticism to the Bush: the Brotherhood of St Boniface

On the morning of 11 July 1911, in the Williams parish church, Goldsmith admitted four men as the members of the Bush Brotherhood of St Boniface, the first such brotherhood to be established in Western Australia. Of the original members, A. D. Webb and G. S. Stubbs were priests and Mazzini Tron and F. W. Spargo were laymen, the former being a candidate for ordination.

The term 'bush brotherhood' suggests a distinctly Australian experiment which sprang out of a response to rural conditions. But despite the Australian suggestions of the term, the strongest inspiration for the group lay not in the bush brotherhood movement which had arisen in eastern Australia in the previous fourteen years (a movement which in itself had strongly British overtones), but in the revival of regular religious community life which was taking place in the Church of England in Britain. The English clergy whom it attracted—men such as Elsey, Frewer, Groser, Harper, Stubbs, Webb and White—were definitely Catholic in character, and the ethos of the Brotherhood was thus the product of a kind of spirituality with which they were familiar in England, as well as of the bishop's own conviction that he had a vocation to establish a religious community.

Bishop Dawes of Rockhampton, founder of Australia's first bush brotherhood at Longreach in Queensland, later spoke of that organization as though it were an original and unique experiment which eventually formed a model for other ventures,[1] but this claim demands qualification.

Though a full exploration of the origins and use in Anglican circles of the term 'brotherhood' has yet to be conducted, any suggestion that it was unique to Australia is called into question by its use by 1905 (if not earlier) to describe groups of clergy working under the auspices of the SPG in the dioceses of Cawnpore, Trichinopoly and Tokyo—dioceses as widely separated from Australia as they were from one another.[2]

And if Dawes was the first to use the term brotherhood to an Australian body that achieved some degree of permanence, he was by no means the first cleric in Australia to conceive of such a structure. Until other evidence to the contrary is produced, a claim can fairly be made that such an organization was first conceived of by Goldsmith, even though he did not use the brotherhood terminology in describing it. In 1889 at the Sydney Church Congress he delivered a paper in which he considered alternative models to the customary English parish structures for the more efficient running of parishes in Australia, both urban and rural. Concerning the rural scene he asked, 'should not large and scattered country districts be worked from a centre by a College of Priests, if not pledged, at any rate habituated to obedience to a Superior?' After describing the situation that obtained in many bush parishes, he sketched his ideal. Each member of such a house would 'go forth to his district, not scouring through the bush on the Lord's Day, but spending a week (more or less) in each neighbourhood'.[3] Although Goldsmith presented monetary savings as a significant attraction of such a scheme, when viewed in conjunction with the life that was actually lived in the House of Grace at Williams, the references in this paper to 'religious life' and clergy living 'in Community' reveal the driving force behind this proposal. The life that he described in this paper was the life of the Brotherhood of St Boniface in embryonic form.

It is difficult to avoid seeing this embryonic scheme and Goldsmith's influence behind the use of the term brotherhood in 1893, four years later, by Bishop Parry. He referred to the presence in the parishes of Northam and Beverley of two 'lay brothers' from Burgh College who were performing a variety of liturgical and pastoral functions in return 'merely for board, lodging and clothing', and envisaged a diocesan 'church brotherhood' made up of a number of such men.⁴ Though this seems to be the only occasion on which Parry used the term, in the previous ten years he had already raised the possibility of inducting single men from English missionary colleges to come and do such work.⁵ The comments of B. G. Richardson quoted below show that the idea and the terminology survived Bishop Parry's death.

In the same year that Dawes launched the Brotherhood of St Andrew, the term brotherhood surfaced again in correspondence between the Society for the Propagation of the Gospel and C. O. L. Riley concerning the provision of clergy for the goldfields. Although the proposal does not seem to have come to anything, Riley hoped that the SPG's Irish branch might provide a group of between four and six clergy who would work at Coolgardie under the direction of Archdeacon Barton-Parkes. A house and stipends of £100 per annum would be provided, and the men would return to Ireland after a period of several years service.⁶ A similar concept of a five-year 'foreign service order' on the part of Bishop Webber of Brisbane was a factor behind the formation of the first Queensland brotherhoods.⁷

These Western Australian proposals which precede Goldsmith's foundation both share a common feature with the bush brotherhoods which sprang up in New South Wales and Queensland—they were conceived as a way of solving a staffing problem in situations that were both difficult and remarkably different from those of British parishes. That the quasi-community suggestions of the term 'brotherhood' might simply act as a mask for a cheap source of manpower with little real organization and no defined outlook was explicitly acknowledged by some of those who were involved with the life of bush brotherhoods.⁸ When the Community of St Barnabas was reformed after nearly closing down altogether, the *Church Commonwealth* said that the existence of 'plenty of bush, but no brotherhood' was often regarded as a major teething problem for bush brotherhoods. Some of the worst examples of such failing occurred in South Australia. The six-year life of the Brotherhood of Saint Aidan (1915–21) which had been founded by Bishop Nutter Thomas of Adelaide was partly due to the absence of any genuine common life; most notorious was the Brotherhood of St Stephen, founded by Bishop Richard Thomas of Willochra, some of whose underpaid and often unpaid members met neither one another nor their bishop.⁹

The gap between needs and available resources imparted a sense of desperate urgency to the agendas of most rural bishops, and in periods when they faced many difficulties, other Western Australian prelates such as Trower and Elsey wrote of the possibility of having their own brotherhoods, as though they were some kind of instant cure-all and, even as late as 1949, Hawtrey was writing of the brotherhood concept as if it were a viable answer to the problems of ministry in the north of the state.[10]

When discussion of the organizational and philosophical models for the eastern states' brotherhoods did occur, the life of religious communities was not necessarily the model that was specified, and it was sometimes even denied. Appealing for funds with which to build a Mission House at Longreach, Bishop Dawes himself spoke of the centre as being 'upon the lines of the Oxford House, in Bethnal Green, London, and adapted to conditions of mission work in the vast western Bush of Central Queensland'.[11] Oxford House, a settlement founded from Keble College, was Catholic in inspiration, but was not so much a community as a clergy house staffed by curates under the direction of a senior priest.[12] Dawes also spoke of the Brotherhood as offering proof that 'the Catholic faith is living still, and life-giving; and that the old Church of our fathers can adopt her ancient methods to successfully grappling with modern means'.[13] But if this were intended as a claim that the brotherhood represented an adaptation of community life, it was an ambiguous one: Dawes' words could equally well be understood as referring to the adaptation of parochial structures to the conditions of the bush.

Charles Matthews, whose *Parson in the Australian Bush* provided many British readers with their first awareness of the brotherhoods, explicitly denied that the founders of brotherhoods in Queensland and New South Wales had any intention of establishing 'religious communities in the strict sense of the word', and described them as 'a thing *sui generis*'.[14] However, in a passage which immediately preceded this one, Matthews also identified the reason why any parallels with community life might well have been deliberately played down: 'the immense prejudice against anything really Catholic', which was something 'fatal . . . to effective work and prevented any measure of local support'.[15] His point was proved by outcries in the *Watchman*, a conservative Protestant journal, directed against 'Anglican Monks for the Bush'.[16] Of the eastern states brotherhoods, one alone, the Brotherhood of St Barnabas in North Queensland, described itself as a community. Yet in explaining what this meant in his parting address to the North Queensland diocese, Bishop Frodsham affirmed that the key to the concept of community was neither 'permanent vows nor asceticism, poverty and celibacy, nor in a special cultivation of the interior life', and instead identified it as 'nothing more than the doing of things in common, that is, the surrender of the principle of individualism'.[17] Though Frodsham's definition of the essentials of the community was taken from Father Herbert Kelly, the founder of the Society of the Sacred Mission, there was some advantage in offering a definition of community which avoided naming precisely those things to which conservative Protestant critics objected.

Goldsmith's Brotherhood of St Boniface was certainly an attempt to deal with problems of staffing and manpower that were regarded as peculiar to the Australian bush. The area to be covered by the brotherood, its 'territory', stretched from the Frankland River to Wandering in the north and from Boyupbrook in the west to the Great Southern railway line, and beyond the railway line to Broomehill and Palinup, an area almost 150 by 100 miles, or alternately, covering eight million acres. A sense of desperate situations provoking desperate remedies continued as the Brotherhood's territory was altered in less than a decade to take in 'a few thousand square miles of territory, in an Easterly direction'.[18]

In explaining the Brotherhood's *raison d'être* to English readers, the *Bunbury Occasional Papers,* in a passage which assumed that single men, but not married clergy, would work in the bush, pointed to the size of bush parishes and their scattered populations as posing a problem for 'one Priest living alone'.[19] Similarly, the commercial press explained that the Brotherhood would 'supply the spiritual needs of settlers scattered over wide and thinly populated areas'.[20] Edward Elsey, a member of the Brotherhood until his election as Bishop of Kalgoorlie in 1919, repeated the same grounds, and stressed the debilitating effects of isolation in the bush on a single cleric.[21]

Reference has already been made to Parry's proposal to create a body of deacon-schoolmasters even though it meant lowering the academic standards accepted in England, and to Riley's hope for a goldfields brotherhood. Before Goldsmith's foundation of the Brotherhood of St Boniface, however, other suggestions were offered and other attempts made by Western Australian Anglicans to address the problems of ministry in the countryside. In 1895 E. S. Clairs, then in the rural depths of Northam, repeated Parry's suggestion, referring to the possibility of 'a band of itinerating clergy, either as assistants to the rectors of the parishes or missionary curates unter the Bishop' or alternatively to a Methodist-style 'circuit system'. The latter was also advocated by another correspondent who signed himself 'Progress'.[22] E. H. Myerson, an ex-Sydney lay-reader of Anglo-Catholic persuasion, urged that the laity could be drawn on more effectively, pleading for a greater use of lay-readers.[23]

Though it was not a response to Myerson so much as a reflection of the practice of a number of other Australian bishops, Goldsmith himself later treated the function of lay-reader as an important element in the preparation for ordination of local candidates. The lengthy periods of time for which some men remained in the diaconate in Bunbury under Goldsmith is more likely a reflection of a desire to further test their vocation or extend their education, rather than an attempt to create a diaconate of the kind envisaged by Parry. However, W. C. C. Caton's mission, in which he drove a buggy equipped with a magic-lantern display and a small lending library around an area centred on Katanning, was one attempt to provide a form of ministry which operated beyond traditional parish lines, and it is unfortunate that the only reference to its discontinuance does not elaborate on why it was regarded as unsuccessful.[24] Lack of funds likewise prevented another even more unusual suggestion—a ministry to the pearlers of the north-west by means of a mission lugger—from becoming a reality.[25]

If the establishment of the Brotherhood of St Boniface was explained as an attempt to create a ministry adapted to local conditions, what is quite unclear is any strong association with the brotherhoods which existed in the east, apart from the use of the common term. In 1909, readers of the *Bunbury Occasional Papers* were advised to read Charles Matthews' *A Parson in the Australian Bush*.[26] In the same year Archdeacon A. T. Robinson, then the head of the Brotherhood of St Andrew, delivered an address on 'The Revival of Community Life' in Perth at the Church held there, but an encounter between Goldsmith and Robinson at that time is the only definite link that can be posited between the bishop and those involved in the New South Wales and Queensland brotherhoods: Goldsmith's motions at General Synod were not seconded by any of the bishops or other founders of brotherhoods.[27] Certainly, a former member of the Brotherhood of St Andrew came to the diocese as Rector of Katanning, but Goldsmith first met him during his 1912 visit to England, after the Brotherhood of St Boniface had been founded. Walter Scott, another former member of the Brotherhood of St Andrew, came to the diocese as the chief missioner for the pro-cathedral parish mission, but that was not until 1915. Neither of these men was asked to spend any time giving the new brotherhood the benefit of his experience elsewhere.

The most peculiar confirmation of Goldsmith's isolation from the other brotherhood experiments lies in his incorrect enumeration of the number of existing brotherhoods. In his synod charge in 1911, he referred to the Brotherhood of St Boniface as the fourth in existence, whereas it was the fifth. He listed the Brotherhood of St Andrew, the Western Brotherhood or Brotherhood of St Paul and the Brotherhood of the Good Shepherd.[28] That the Community of St Barnabas should have been omitted from this list is even more peculiar in view of Goldsmith's own interest in communities and the occasional claims that the St Boniface Brotherhood was in some sense a community, since the Community of St Barnabas was the only other brotherhood which described itself as such. The same incorrect number of brotherhoods and the lack of awareness of the North Queensland brotherhood were repeated in other sources, which probably depended on Goldsmith himself, and even appears in a recent local history of the Williams district.[29] But this apparent ignorance was not a uniquely Western Australian phenomenon, though it was perhaps imposed by isolation rather than being a deliberate product of desire: the other brotherhoods had each been founded as independent ventures without seeking support from their predecessors, and to that extent the independence of the Western Australian venture fitted into a larger and more common pattern.

Goldsmith also intended to do more than create a temporary organization to deal with a difficult area of work, let alone a cheap labour supply. In contrast to some of those involved in the brotherhoods of Queensland and New South Wales who saw the brotherhoods as an interim device created to convert mission districts into stable parishes, he told the Bunbury synod in 1913: 'I desire that all of us should realize that this enterprise is a serious, far-reaching, and a permanent one, and as such claims the keenest sympathy'.[30]

Though it performed pastoral work in the same way as existing bush brotherhoods, its life was explained in terms normally used of a stable religious community. When the House of Grace was blessed in 1913, an article in the *Church Standard* (the closest thing Australia had at the time to a national high church journal) made this claim quite explicitly, describing the Western Australian Brotherhood as differing from other brotherhoods precisely in being a community:

> Why all this fuss?—one might ask. Have not other brotherhoods had houses opened? . . . In the Brotherhood of St Boniface a great step has been taken. The Brotherhood of St Boniface stands for the community ideal. The brothers have made the act of self renunciation, which Dr Workman (in his book on 'The Evolution of the Monastic Ideal') says is the essence of the life of a Regular.[31]

The unidentified writer went on to claim that the members of the Brotherhood fulfilled all the conditions which were regarded as essential for a community by Father Herbert Kelly, who had also been invoked by Bishop Frodsham. He further claimed that those who drew up the rule (of the Brotherhood) 'intended its adherents to be bound by the traditional evangelical counsels of poverty, chastity and obedience', and described them as such. What the writer did not mention was that the rule of the Brotherhood had been drawn up only that same year. But the creation of the Rule in 1913 is less likely to indicate any basic change in Goldsmith's understanding of the nature of the community, so much as a necessary way of clarifying this for future members. In *The Lure of the Golden West*, Tom Groser alluded to teething problems in the first two years which he related to the absence of a 'vow of service binding the Brothers to any definite period of work'. Goldsmith may well have assumed that the first members all understood the Brotherhood to be a permanent community, even though this had not been spelt out in a formal rule.[32] The *Church Standard* writer concluded, 'They do not claim to be monks, they do claim to be regulars. One sees the need for a Community in a country like Australia . . . Whatever the future may bring, the step has been taken. A religious community now exists in the Australian Church'.[33]

## Brotherhood of St. Boniface,

### DIOCESE OF BUNBURY.

**The Object.**

The object of the Brotherhood of St. Boniface is the service of Christ and the building up of the Kingdom of Heaven in Western Australia.

**The Rule.**

1. Holy Eucharist in the Brotherhood Chapel daily, whenever possible.
2. Regular recitation of Mattins, Sext, Evensong and Compline.
3. Daily meditation.
   (Brothers away from home are expected to observe the rule of devotion as far as is practicable )
4. Pecuniary self-denial.
5. Abstinence from marriage or any engagement to marry.
6. Cheerful obedience to the Visitor, and to the Warden and Chapter of the Brotherhood.

**The Duration of Vows.**

The vows of the Brotherhood are made for three years; but during that period they can only be dispensed by the Bishop for sufficient cause. They may be renewed at the end of that period.

A page from *Constitution and Rule of the Brotherhood of St Boniface*
The terminology used for items 4, 5 and 6 barely disguises their essential nature: the three traditional religious vows of poverty, chastity and obedience.

That such an understanding of the Brotherhood of St Boniface was held by some of its members and was not simply an unwarranted assumption made by an overly zealous Anglo-Catholic correspondent is clear from a paper by H. H. Harper, then warden of the Brotherhood. Entitled 'The Brotherhood Ideal—the possibility of the Community Life for the Brotherhoods', it was delivered in 1913 at the only conference of representatives of brotherhoods to meet before World War I.[34] Against Harper, Father Kempe of the Brotherhood of the Good Shepherd argued that a community life was a possible fruit of the brotherhood movement, but was not an absolute prerequisite for any of the groups.

Harper stressed that a rule accepted and lived in community made continuous intercession possible.[35] At this point Harper appears to have combined two ideals which had the bishop's imprimatur. In 1914 he committed the Brotherhood to taking part in a scheme for 'perpetual intercession for the extension of the kingdom' devised by the SPG.[36] Earlier in the year, in a description of the blessing of extensions to the House of Grace, its writer stressed that 'whatever else the House of Grace stood for, those who designed it meant it to be a House of Prayer'.[37] And almost a year before that, in another article on the Brotherhood of St Boniface, the writer pointed out that each brotherhood had its 'own special underlying spirit. We are trying to make ours a brotherhood of prayer'.[38]

Significant though such statements are in expressing the community ideal which the Brotherhood was meant to realize, an equally important source of evidence is formed by extant records of the day-to-day life at the House of Grace. A continuous daily record beginning in 1916 has survived.[39] It lists consistently all eucharistic celebrations at the house, together with the celebrant's name and the number of those present, including communicants. In addition, it consistently lists the date of return of each member from absence from the house, whether for a relatively short period or for the longer trips which lasted for almost four weeks while brothers visited particular areas in the Brotherhood's territory. Departures are less consistently recorded.

While the record only commences in 1916, this highlights rather than detracts from its significance: it shows the Brotherhood adhering to the practices it regarded as essential to the life of a community at a time when its numbers were depleted as four members left for the battle front.[40] In 1910 it had been suggested that at least one brother (and preferably two) would always be at home while others travelled, and that every three months the whole community would be gathered together. Edward Elsey referred to this model in a passage that has already been quoted, but added the following qualification:

> Now owing to the fewness of the numbers, the remaining brothers are each travelling two months out of every three instead of as originally in alternate months, but the month at home at the House of Grace makes up for it. There is the ordered healthy life; all centring round the chapel and the chapel services . . .[41]

The Brotherhood Diary shows that, apart from the time of diocesan synod and the diocesan farewell to the bishop on his retirement from Bunbury, the pattern was carefully adhered to. Chapter meetings, at which all members of the Brotherhood were to be present, are recorded as taking place with clockwork-like regularity.[42] These entries confirm Tom Groser's claim that chapter meetings at quarterly reunions were a 'permanent institution'.[43] Entries between 27 April and 3 May show that the House was full, and also from 31 May until 2 June. Then, except for Thompson and Leach the cook, its members went on short trips, but were all at home by 7 June in time to join after breakfast 'in organized search party for child lost in the bush the previous afternoon'. From 27 July the company was again complete for at least a week, but by 11 August Elsey appears as the only celebrant listed until the end of the month, when Frewer and Thompson returned from trips in the eastern and western parts of the Brotherhood territory.[44]

During those periods when two out of three brothers were absent from the House, the communicant figures make it clear that the brother who remained in the House maintained a daily eucharist and the recitation of the daily offices which the Brotherhood Rule made obligatory. In these services he was joined by S. M. Cumming, a student who stayed at the House for most of 1916 to test his vocation. Leach the cook also acted as a server for several larger liturgical functions.[45] Many entries throughout the year record the celebration of the daily eucharist; the celebrant's name was always recorded and he was usually assisted by one (unnamed) communicant, presumably either Cumming or Leach.

Entries made for episcopal visits show that the Brotherhood sought to reproduce the kind of liturgical life which was the norm in a religious community in England. On 30 January 1916 pontifical high mass (described as such in the Diary) was celebrated in the presence of thirteen worshippers, of whom nine communicated. On Sunday 30 July there was a similar celebration at which eight out of nine communicated; this was a day before the quarterly chapter meeting for which the bishop was present as Visitor.

More interesting are two other entries. The first was for the annual celebration of the Brotherhood Festival on 7 November, when eleven of fourteen worshippers communicated at an early morning eucharist, which was followed later in the morning by a pontifical high mass. The diary shows that while the others were present, there were only three communicants—the three sacred ministers. A similar non-communicating high mass took place on 2 January 1917; on the previous day the Diary records that four other clergy had arrived and were staying at the House. Both of these non-communicating celebrations took place late in the morning, by which time it would be assumed that worshippers were no longer fasting, and therefore should not communicate.

What is equally interesting in terms of an attempt to approximate to the patterns of worship of a stable community is the entry for Good Friday in 1917, shortly after Goldsmith's departure.[46] The service times include six of the seven monastic offices, in addition to which there was a children's service after a 3.15 p.m. 'breakfast', and the evening office was followed by the popular Victorian musical devotion, 'The Story of the Cross'.

While the rule of the community made the recitation of the office of sext at midday an obligation,[47] an article describing the annual Brotherhood festival in 1914 clearly refers to another practice common in religious houses, the ringing of the Angelus, and a bell was rung at the end of the evening before the recitation of compline, the final office of the day.[48]

A final evidence of deliberate concern to reproduce as faithfully as possible an already existing and familiar pattern of worship is provided by a description of the Brotherhood festival in 1916. English donors had presented a thurible to the house, and its first day of use provoked the writer to record evocatively the way in which, for those caught up in the Anglo-Catholic movement, ritual was no end in intself, but part of a mode of worship which stimulated the emotions:

> The unaccompanied singing, the quiet and unobtrusive, yet correct ritual . . . all combined to uplift the hearts of those present, and to invest their pleading of the Holy Sacrifice with a deep intensity, and to enable them to worship the Lord in what was surely the beauty of holiness . . .[49]

In the light of these different attempts to reproduce the features of a settled religious community, it hardly seems surprising that even before the Brotherhood was established, the work it was envisaged as undertaking was the work currently being performed by the more stable male religious communities in the Church of England. The Community of St John the Evangelist, the Society of the Sacred Mission and the Community of the Resurrection all prepared candidates for ordination and conducted retreats and missions. At the 1909 Bunbury synod, as though the proposed Brotherhood were part of the same movement, Goldsmith himself listed the provision of 'opportunities of instruction and training for candidates for Holy Orders' as its first priority. The visiting of the bush was given second place. Another summary of their work again placed first the training of candidates for holy orders, followed by the conduct of retreats for clergy and laity, and mentioned pastoral work in the backblocks last.[50]

When the Society for the Propagation of Christian Knowledge made a £35 grant towards the housing of the brothers, it understood that their centre 'would also serve in a manner as a Theological College'.[51] In 1914 when Mazzini Tron, then a deacon awaiting ordination as a priest, and Arnold Fryer, preparing for his deaconing, were being lectured regularly at the House of Grace by H. H. Harper and A. E. White, the latter teaching almost daily, the *Bunbury Occasional Papers* commented, 'As we say to ourselves, "Quite like a University now"'.[52] Though he never materialized, it was envisaged that when a Mr Ridge arrived from St Nicholas' Plumstead, he would be sent to the House of Grace to train. John Davy Grogan was described as 'going to reside for a time' at the House of Grace in preparation for ordination, and Charles Dunn, for 'several months'.[53] It was presumably at the House that J. G. Thompson studied in preparation for his Australian College of Theology ThL.

No syllabus of the instruction given at the House of Grace has survived. However, the remains of its small but specialized library which contained works of the most recent and thorough scholarship such as Hammond's *Liturgies Eastern and Western* and Brightman's *The English Rite* suggest a concentration on Anglo-Catholic theology, English ecclesiastical history and liturgical studies. A volume by Sparrow-Simpson entitled *Non-Communicating Attendance* was presumably on hand in case

House of Grace, Williams, 1914
The home of the Brotherhood of St Boniface after extensions to the building

the need arose to defend the non-communicating masses which were held in the Brotherhood's chapel from time to time.[54]

When it came to the conduct of retreats, the inauguration of the Brotherhood was accompanied by a quiet day for the clergy which must have offered an added incentive to bring some of them from Perth to such a remote centre. Entries in the Brotherhood Diary show regular appearances year by year for a time of retreat on the part of W. Sharp, who travelled the even greater distance from Carnarvon, where he kept the Anglo-Catholic flag flying in that remote outpost until 1922. Before the June 1915 ordination White conducted a retreat for candidates at the House. A couple of months earlier White and Elsey joined Scott in conducting the mission in Bunbury itself.[55]

Many of the actual activities of the brothers, as well as the expectations voiced even before the Brotherhood was founded, would be less deserving of comment, were it not for the isolated location in which all of this took place. Certainly this offered some protection. Despite the assertion that the brothers did not claim to be monks, geography rather than diplomatically worded statements concerning their ideals saved them from diatribes similar to those in Sydney's *Watchman* directed at members of the Brotherhood of the Good Shepherd. But when the expectations and many features of this experiment are viewed in the context of the setting, it is difficult not to regard it at first as both a remarkable and an impractical one.

However, at the same time, the intention of establishing a community which was expected to perform functions characteristic of a religious house in a more densely settled area may have seemed far from unrealistic. The Brotherhood was founded precisely at the time when the south-west was seeing a steady increase in population. As well as men who had joined the gold rushes, later bringing their families and settling on the land, there was the new and increasing wave of British migrants. It was upon these grounds that Goldsmith based his appeal in his 1909 synod charge. In the area in which he proposed that the Brotherhood should serve, he pointed out that 'settlement is increasing rapidly every year', and recent regional studies of centres within the Brotherhood territory show that his comments were amply justified.[56] In 1911 the bishop wrote in a similar vein, but with a greater sense of urgency, describing northern English migrants 'pouring into the country', and he quoted statistics from the Australian High Commissioner's office in London.[57] Also, within weeks of the foundation of the Brotherhood, an article in the *Southern Times* made similar comments, and related the foundation of the Brotherhood to the increase in population, as much as (if not more than) the isolation of existing settlers.[58] In London in 1912 Goldsmith saw the evidence of Newton Moore's campaign to promote migration to Western Australia, and may well have been aware of Moore's personal interest in that campaign.

At the time, the Brotherhood's inception had less of the appearance of an impractical venture than a far-sighted provision for the not-too-distant future in which the Brotherhood territory and the diocese as a whole would house a population whose Anglicans would seek retreats and produce young men with vocations for the brothers to train as the next generation of Bunbury clergy. Just before the outbreak of World War I, the *Occasional Papers* noted that Goldsmith was in touch with 'four or five Clergy and a layman' who anticipated joining the Brotherhood, and a reference in Groser's *Lure of the Golden West* shows that the war ended any prospect that these men might materialize.[59] In 1911 Goldsmith could hardly foresee the effect of the conflict, and the way in which economic conditions in the wider world at its conclusion would alter the steady growth he anticipated.

Such a background for its foundation also explains why the Brotherhood did not opt for survival by moving out of its original territory into 'mission districts'—those which as yet could not provide a regular stipend for a permanent pastor. R. A. F. Webb, surveying the demise of the Brotherhood from the distance of half a century, suggested that this was a strategic and fatal error.[60] Webb's suggestion assumes that the provision of ministry in such areas was a *raison d'être* of the Brotherhood of St Boniface, as it was for some of the brotherhoods elsewhere. But if the creation of a stable community was one of Goldsmith's aims, the Brotherhood's dogged perseverance at Williams was a matter of faithfulness to the original vision and a holding on in hope of eventual fulfilment, impractical as this turned out to be.

After Goldsmith's retirement, the opportunity for some kind of extension beyond the original territory did arise when a Brotherhood of St Margaret was formed to minister to Anglicans in the areas south of Busselton in 1926. The possibility of combining the two brotherhoods was suggested but it was never taken up.[61] That the Brotherhood sought to maintain its original vision during this time is all the more likely, given that its warden from 1919 until its closure in 1929 was Goldsmith's nephew, John Frewer, whose election as Bishop of the North-West effectively spelt the end of the Brotherhood.

The foundation of the Brotherhood was also the fruit of a long-term interest in religious communities on Goldsmith's part. His Oxford undergraduate days would at least have exposed him to the sight of members of Anglican religious communities: by then, the Cowley Fathers (more properly, the Society of St John the Evangelist) had been established by Richard M. Benson for over a decade, and of the three women's communities in Oxford, members of the Community of the Holy and Undivided Trinity had considerable freedom of movement which included attending university lectures.[62]

He can only have been encouraged to believe that community life was becoming both an important force and a permanent feature of Anglican church life by the trend visible in England throughout his lifetime, where the community movement showed a remarkable growth between 1850 and 1900. The doyen of anti-ritualist writers, Walter Walsh, took gloomy joy in demonstrating how much the Church of England had been 'Romanized' by pointing out that at the end of the nineteenth century the number of women in Anglican communities exceeded those in religious houses in England before their supression under Henry VIII.[63] Something of this strength was registered in the parishes in which Goldsmith preached on his visits to England. In twelve of these parishes, members of communities had houses or carried out their work, and were often at parish eucharists, along with those among whom they worked.[64] He was also familiar with some of their institutions. In Highgate in 1905 he preached at the diocesan penitentiary, which was run by the sisters of the Community of St John the Baptist. And W. H. Cleaver, the rector of Christ Church St Leonard's, another parish which he visited several times, had been the priest-warden to the Community of the Sisters of the Church ever since their mother house had been established in Kilburn in 1871.[65]

The general pattern of experience of religious communities in Australian Anglicanism followed the English one: women's communities were founded first and had greater stability. Goldsmith himself showed an awareness of this in 1896 when he replied in Perth synod to B. G. Richardson who resurrected Parry's suggestion of forming a brotherhood to train lay readers. Goldsmith responded that 'nearly all attempts to establish brotherhoods and societies elsewhere had resulted in failure', and that 'the men always waited for the clergy', while 'the former [= sisterhoods] depended on themselves'.[66] In Australia the Community of the Holy Name was founded in Melbourne in 1888 and the Society of the Sacred Advent in Brisbane in 1892; at the same time the Sisters of the Church began to establish houses in Australia.[67]

In 1896 Goldsmith may have made his qualification concerning male communities in the knowledge that there were no such communities anywhere in Australia. But he is more likely to have had in mind the experience of male communities in England. With the exception of the Cowley Fathers in Oxford, male community evolution was marked by the predominance of eccentric individuals and irregularities in discipline, a fact acknowledged by other Anglo-Catholics. A cutting in one of George

Frewer's journals referred to the 'harmless raving' of 'the eccentric but amiable "Father Ignatius"'.[68] Joseph Lester Lynne, otherwise known as Father Ignatius, made the first attempts to revive the Benedictine life among Anglicans but was rejected by Bishop Wilberforce of Oxford as 'sacrificing the kernel for the shell' in his concentration on externals—despite a real spirituality. And when Goldsmith was a curate in Charlton, not far from Greenwich, he was close to another community, the Community of St Augustine, in which individualism predominated over order. According to Anson, their lavishly furnished house in Walworth was 'best described as a residential club for religious eccentrics'.[69] Their outdoor processions during Holy Week caused a sensation in the area. Beyond obtaining attention from the general public, they were in frequent conflict with bishops over discipline. A young curate with Catholic sympathies would have found an abundance of cautionary material in them for any future ventures of his own. Such bodies were fictionalized by Compton Mackenzie in an episode in his novel *The Altar Steps*, but the problematic nature of the experiment in male community living that formed part of his story had a real basis in the experience of some late nineteenth-century groups.

Even though they were not conceived as traditional religious communities, the emergence of five bush brotherhoods in Australia between 1897 and 1911—the Brotherhoods of St Andrew (Longreach) in 1897, St Paul (Western Queensland) in 1901, St Barnabas (North Queensland) in 1902, the Good Shepherd (Dubbo) in 1903 and Goldsmith's own Brotherhood of St Boniface—reflected many aspects of the gradual change in the fortunes of male communities in English Anglicanism. In most English eyes, the handful of male communities had as much of the quality of an experiment as the brotherhoods did for Australian Anglicans.[70] As well as the existing Cowley Fathers, two other communities emerged in England in the 1890s which were characterized by stability, the use of the Prayer Book rather than other (medieval or contemporary Roman Catholic) liturgical sources and a positive attitude towards episcopal authority—the Community of the Resurrection and the Society of the Sacred Mission. In their original austere (and ugly) home off the Iffley Road, the Cowley Fathers under Father Benson used only the unadorned Prayer Book text.[71] The newer Community of the

Resurrection, founded in 1892, centred its worship on the Prayer Book eucharist and offices, emphasizing its Englishness by using the Sarum Breviary as the source for its little hours, and its members wore only the cassock, eschewing any of the distinctive clothing which aroused the suspicion of earlier bishops. The constitution of the Society of the Sacred Mission, founded in 1894, emphasized its obedience to diocesan bishops.[72]

The avoidance of a distinctive habit and a hesitancy concerning life-vows were points at which the Australian brotherhoods resembled some English communities. Members of the various bush brotherhoods including the Brotherhood of St Boniface wore the traditional Anglican priest's cassock, not the cowled habit of the orders of friars. Members of the Brotherhood of St Boniface were distinguished by a purple girdle, but it does not appear to have contained the customary knots representing the evangelical counsels.[73]

For some time Anglican bishops had been reluctant or refused to allow the taking of permanent vows by community members, male or female, because they did not believe that they possessed any authority to dispense individuals from such vows if the need later arose. Though the position of many English bishops towards this issue gradually altered, the Australian brotherhood practice of making a commitment which was to be renewed or terminated over a period of three to five years meant that the question of legal dispensation from life-vows was not raised. The absence of any clear statement of commitment at the commencement of the Brotherhood of St Boniface, such as the 1913 rule eventually provided, seems to have been the result of administrative carelessness. However, the openness of the contractual relationship which is suggested in the *Southern Times* in its description of the earliest conditions of membership may also register a degree of hesitancy lest conservative Protestant opinion be offended by any suggestion of vows.[74]

As stability emerged in male community life in England, so warmer responses came from the bench of bishops: in 1894 Bishop Festing of St Albans ordained Father Andrew, the first priest who had already taken vows to be ordained in England since the Reformation; in 1898 Charles Gore, a member of the Community of the Resurrection, became Bishop of Worcester, and at the Lambeth Conference in the previous year the subject of the relationship between religious communities and the episcopate was discussed, a discussion which Bishop Riley pointed out in advance to his own synod in Perth.[75]

That Goldsmith as a diocesan bishop founded the Brotherhood of St Boniface thus reflected the changing English trend in community life. But he and the other Australian bishops who founded brotherhoods were also responding to realities within their own scene. In Australia, for its future to be secure, any kind of community needed the active co-operation of the diocesan: in the case of Goldsmith, he definitely wanted the Brotherhood to have a future, as he saw the brotherhood movement as an essential part of the Australian church. And generally, despite occasional large gifts to Australian brotherhoods which could bestow a measure of independence, such as were presented to the Brotherhood of St Paul, the Brotherhood of the Good Shepherd and the Community of St Barnabas by wealthy patrons, bishops generally founded brotherhoods in order to protect them, as well as to guarantee some control over their life.[76]

In a brief correspondence in 1907 in reply to the suggestion that all the existing Australian brotherhoods should be amalgamated and placed under the authority of a single bishop who would have been an extra-diocesan, Randall Davidson recognized that Australian bishops would be sensitive to questions of control and the independence of brotherhoods, especially when it was even suggested that an amalgamated brotherhood should be headed by an English suffragan, the Bishop of Dorking![77] Certainly, control was an aspect of Goldsmith's relation with the Brotherhood as its Rule defined his functions as visitor to the community. All regulations made or altered by chapter of community had to be approved by him; he was to hear and decide all cases of discipline; hindrance of any enquiry conducted by him as visitor could result in instant expulsion from the community, and in all cases of appeal, any decision which he made was to be regarded as final.[78] But such sweeping powers also meant that he was finally accountable for the Brotherhood—hence any critic of the community needed to beware of him.

In 1927 such a critic reviewed Tom Groser's *The Lure of the Golden West* and its description of the Brotherhood:

> The reader gets the impression that, good as the Bush Brotherhood work is, and though it seems to be worked on what may be called Catholic lines, it

suffers from amateurishness. This is doubtless due to the fact that the Brotherhood rule only binds a man for a short period, and that the brethren have very little training for their difficult task. Such a work should be in the hands of a contingent of men, say, of the SSM or the CR Religious Orders, subject to discipline. The impression is obtained, after reading certain episodes in this book, that if some of the Brethren are as amateurish in the Confessional as they are in the kitchen, there is little hope for the movement . . .[79]

By comparison with entry into the stable religious communities in England, men came to all the Australian brotherhoods without any common systematic preparation, and there was likewise no structured initiation through which they passed before being plunged into the demanding pastoral routines of their territories. The critic was perhaps unaware that at this point he had identified two major weaknesses of all the brotherhoods, but he had also underestimated the individualism and tenaciousness of many of the English recruits, and was unaware that in those brotherhoods where a team of supportive men already existed, this was often enough to make the difference between long-term survival or defeat for the 'new chums'. Most of all, the critic perhaps stung Goldsmith into responding because he had identified what was a common weakness of all the brotherhoods, but he lacked the first-hand experience which might explain what made the crucial difference in those brotherhoods which survived.

Goldsmith's reply sprang from a paternal feeling towards his own foundation, but also showed a remarkable, almost aggressive identification with the Australian church. The writer had 'slightingly' alleged that the Brotherhood suffered from 'amateurishness', but had produced no examples. Goldsmith implied that Anglicans at home were quick to criticize the church in Australia, but that neither had they responded to calls for help from Australia nor were they automatically equipped to understand the Australian situation. 'Repeated appeals to English Communities' had 'failed'. The best training the brothers had was one 'which is impossible in England—viz, a knowledge of the Australian temperament, and the conditions of Bush life and work'. Finally, the writer had underestimated the quality of the men involved: the Brotherhood's wardens were 'men inspired by love of our Blessed Lord, of His Church, and of the souls of men, that I have never seen exceeded'.[80]

Goldsmith's personal investment in the Brotherhood is indicated by a persistence in pursuing the project despite initial frustrations. In his 1909 synod charge, he referred to it as 'One project which I desire very keenly to see carried out in the immediate future, if God wills . . . '[81] But it is clear from a letter written in 1912 while he was still in England that he had envisaged it as early as 1908.[82]

By spring of 1909 he had already been in touch with one definite candidate, and two others who were considering joining the community. By the end of next summer, as he questioned how much longer A. D. Webb, then stationed at Williams, was to do the work of the Brotherhood, it was with a sense of frustration that a venture which had been under consideration for some time was now subject to some doubt.[83] The question of housing proved to be problematic even before the Brotherhood began life in its temporary home in Williams at 'Barroworn'. It was originally envisaged that it would be located at Kojonup, and even after Williams was chosen instead, it was still suggested that a second house would be built, 'probably at Kojonup'.[84]

The way in which he dealt with a crisis in its early development also displayed the bishop's personal commitment to the Brotherhood. He appointed his nephew John Frewer as his domestic chaplain in 1911, when the strain of the diocese on his health was becoming evident. But when the first warden of the House, A. D. Webb, was obliged to resign because of illness, Frewer was immediately sent to act as warden for six months pending the arrival of H. H. Harper, who had promised during Goldsmith's 1912 visit to England to join the Brotherhood. Frewer's presence at the Brotherhood centre ensured that the basic patterns of worship and visiting would continue uninterrupted.[85]

Above all else, the best evidence of the part played in the Brotherhood by the bishop's own piety is provided by a description of Goldsmith at the House of Grace (which is also the fullest surviving contemporary personal description of the bishop in any context) by Tom Groser:

> Nothing pleased the good bishop more than to be able to visit the Brotherhood, and spend a few quiet days with the Brothers in their own home at their quarterly reunions and chapter meetings; to pontificate in the services at the Altar, fully and becomingly vested; to take part in the various offices through the day, sung to Gregorian settings; to make various excursions through the Bush with

one of the Brethren in a 'sulky' to some neighbouring centre; to preside at the Quarterly Chapter Meetings and build 'castles in the air' as to future developments; or—most pleasing of all—to take his part in the daily routine of housework, cooking and washing up the dishes, which was invariably succeeded by a comfortable resort to 'my lady Nicotine' under the cool shelter afforded by the spacious verandah of the House of Grace, where more 'castles' would be built.[86]

There are thus good grounds for concluding that, moved by the Anglo-Catholic piety whose current strength was already visible in the upsurge of religious community life in England, Goldsmith understood himself to have a vocation as founder and nurturer of a kind of community which would remain a permanent feature of the (Western) Australian church's life. An experience of Anglo-Catholic piety also characterized the most important early members of the Brotherhood. Tom Groser came to the Brotherhood from a curacy at Hebburn-on-Tyne, a parish with the externals of Anglo-Catholic worship, as well as the teaching of Anglo-Catholic doctrine; Elsey came from the more restrained St Faith's Stepney; A. E. White had been trained at Mirfield, the Community of the Resurrection's major centre; and John Frewer had the definite Anglo-Catholic background of his father's parish, and of St Nicholas' Skirbeck, his first appointment after his ordination.

It is also significant that on returning to England in 1912, when Groser, White and Harper had all committed themselves to join the Brotherhood, Goldsmith referred to them as 'three new men for the Brotherhood who had had a good training, and men who were determined to devote their life to the work . . . '[87] Though Goldsmith himself may well have presented the Brotherhood to them as a lifelong commitment, their own experience of English community life would equally have led such men to assume that this was a normal, indeed essential, condition of community life; and the Anglo-Catholic piety which they embraced would only have acted as an added incentive to accepting such an interpretation of the Brotherhood's purpose, even though it had not yet been enshrined in a formal rule.

It was not only the bishop who had 'pipe-dreams', but some of the brothers themselves. An account of life at the House of Grace from just before the outbreak of World War I suggests that within the community there was a division between those who saw the Brotherhood primarily as an instrument for addressing pastoral needs as 'large tracts of country were being opened up' and those who anticipated more:

> We talked of many things for some time . . . Until at length the Bishop brought the subject round to the future of the Brotherhood, and men told of the dreams they had dreamt, and the visions they had seen as they jogged along behind Ginger and Tobias. But to some it seemed that these were idle tales; there was pressing work to be done in the immediate future.[88]

Though the war intervened dramatically enough, war service itself did not necessarily bring an end to a concept of the Brotherhood as a stable community for the dreamers. White and Groser attended the annual chapter meeting in 1918, although they appear to have been treated as visitors, rather than as members.[89] Tom Groser had left the Brotherhood, not as a response to the war effort, but to act as curate to his aging father at Midland. Elsey and Frewer continued to share the dream.

England may have been a fertile recruiting source for men fully formed in the Anglo-Catholic piety which Goldsmith saw as the future of the Anglican church, but it was also his intention that the Brotherhood would be as much an Australian body as it would be a permanent one. It is perhaps a tribute to Goldsmith's powers of persuasion that when not one Australian had so far joined the existing brotherhoods, he should have an Australian as a foundation member. But when he reported the foundation of the Brotherhood to the 1911 synod, it was almost with a sense of puzzlement that he pointed this out, and asked, 'Are there not some more Australians who will consecrate their bushmanship and their other gifts to the service of God and His Church?'[90]

The predominantly English membership of the Brotherhood of St Boniface was thus characteristic of the brotherhoods as a whole. When the first brotherhood, the Brotherhood of St Andrew, closed in 1917, it had been composed entirely of English clergy. But that there were other possibilities is indicated by the markedly different history of the Brotherhood of the Good Shepherd. From its inception it began a campaign of promotion in Sydney schools in the hope that in the future its membership would be recruited from among Australians. On one occasion when Bishop Long of Bathurst appealed to an Australian audience, five men immediately offered themselves.[91] Goldsmith's hope for an

Australian membership for his own brotherhood continued after he retired to England through concerned appeals in Australia for new recruits. A 'Brotherhood Week' was held in Perth in 1922, and advertisements appeared in journals whose readers were of a sympathetic churchmanship—the *Church Standard* and the *Defender*.[92]

A discreet silence surrounds the short term served by Frederick William Spargo, a layman who was never subsequently ordained.[93] There is nothing to indicate whether he was alienated by the English-formed Anglo-Catholic piety which was a common bond between the bishop and most other members of the group, or whether he found the work unbearably demanding. But despite a variety of appeals, Spargo's membership remained the only example of Australian involvement in the Brotherhood, despite R. A. F. Webb's mistaken statement that only eleven out of a total of twenty-one members were English.[94] On a broader front, an article in the *West Australian Church News* could not understand why few Australians seemed to be entering religious communities.[95]

However, the factors which explain the predominance of English members across all the brotherhoods at this time form a way of accounting for the paucity of Australian recruits.[96] Though men of broad churchmanship constituted some of the recruits to the different brotherhoods, the brotherhoods as a whole were identified (particularly by low churchmen and evangelicals) as a high church exercise. In the case of the Brotherhood of St Boniface, the Anglo-Catholic piety and advanced ceremonial which had formed several of its members in England was in marked contrast to the restrained norms of all but a few Australian parishes. Its concern to maintain the same churchmanship was clear enough in the advertisement in the *Defender* which appealed for Catholic priests to join the Brotherhood.

When he asked why there was only one Australian member, Goldsmith described the work as 'strenuous', and demanding 'considerable' sacrifice. As passages quoted elsewhere from the *West Australian* show, clerical work in rural areas of Australia was identified by Australians as arduous and with few obvious attractions. When the *West Australian Church News* carried advance notice of the 'Brotherhood Week' to be held in Perth, its account of the work concentrated on its sheer arduousness.[97] But English promotion of the brotherhoods emphasized the work as a form of adventure which could appeal to the 'muscular' traditions encouraged by the public schools, as well as creating a sense of the excitement of the exotic at the ends of the empire.

Writing in the *Mission Field*, Henry Adams, the Rector of Bunbury's pro-cathedral, described the hardships in terms which suggested a boy's novel by R. M. Ballantyne:

> Throughout this country the brothers will travel, driving in sulkies, or riding on horseback, under the blazing sun, and often in winter through torrents of rain; often they will drive for miles without seeing any human being or habitation, the only signs of life being an occasional kangaroo or iguana running across the track, or green parrots flying shrieking through the air. In the night-time, either in pitch darkness or under the marvellous star-lit canopy of heaven, he will pass many miles amidst an incessant chorus of frogs . . . [98]

Adams was hardly original in approaching brotherhood life in this way. It was also typical of the often-quoted appeal of Bishop Frodsham in 1908 in which he asked for men who would 'ride like cowboys' and 'preach like apostles'.[99] That same year Frederick Campion of the Brotherhood of the Good Shepherd covered the same grounds, claiming that the

> system of the brotherhood should make its high appeal to the right spirit of adventure. The life of a clergyman in Australia is full of adventure. This spirit should be appealed to in the public schools, and mothers also should tell their sons that if they wished a life of adventure there was nothing grander than the missionary life.[100]

The concept of the missionary life as one of adventure had to contend with the view that saw the mission field as one for men who would be regarded as second-rate at home. It may have appeared less a matter of adventure to A. D. Webb, the first warden of the Brotherhood, of whom Goldsmith wrote to Montgomery that he feared for his health because he had been 'recently in hospital from exposure to the winter rains. Their long journeys involve real hardship in the winter season'.[101]

At the close of the *Lure of the Golden West* Groser appealed to English readers by invoking the imperial theme. Increased migration to Western Australia would solve 'a great Empire problem' by filling the empty spaces of the continent at a time when other eyes were casting longing glances at them; it would assist 'in the building up of a new British nation in the southern seas'.[102] Although here he was primarily seeking migrants to settle the land rather than recruits for the Brotherhood, the grounds of imperial outreach and British responsibility appeared in appeals for other brotherhoods as well. When he sought financial support for the Brotherhood of St Barnabas, Bishop Montgomery, sounding like Riley or Goldsmith, reminded his readers that English investors who profited from the colonies had a responsibility 'to their countrymen who are building up the British Empire overseas'.[103] Bishop Frodsham was even more deft in weaving together the themes of empire, nationalism and religion, as he stated (of the Brotherhood of St Barnabas) that

> I think that this Bush Brotherhood is connected with the subject of immigration and colonization, inasmuch as the British race owes its stability, not so much to possessions as to the character of the British, and that character is founded mainly on the Christian religion . . .[104]

At the Australian end in 1921, the *Church Standard* admitted that the life of a member of the Brotherhood was undoubtedly 'hard' but that it was rich in what would now be called 'job satisfaction'—'full of joy and encouragement'.[105] Earlier it had thrown down a more idealistic gauntlet, when it described the Brotherhood as a community which, as such, presented a challenge to the prevalent mood of materialism in Australia, which was 'not so much a professed creed as the working hypothesis of a man's life'. But it went on to identify what may have been a real reason why Australians did not join, when it claimed that

> if the Australian Church is to attract to her ministry her best sons, she must do so either by offering higher salaries than the business houses can offer or by appealing to the highest in Australia's best sons, and offering them absolutely nothing.[106]

In 1911 the annual stipend of each brother was £25, little enough even when lodgings and meals were accounted for, yet regarded as sufficient by those Englishmen who joined the Brotherhood, and could be accepted in a spirit of self-sacrifice which was almost romantic in tone. This was certainly true of A. E. White, who offered himself as a replacement for Harold Grist Hornsby, a friend from Keble College, who had drowned before he could fulfil his vocation as a brother, and whose friends raised enough money to pay a brother's stipend for the next five years.[107]

While Englishmen exposed to Anglo-Catholic asceticism at home could also treat the denials imposed by brotherhood life as part of an adventure, to the native born the work of the brotherhood truly did offer nothing. Within a short time of the *Church Standard*'s appeal, concepts of self-sacrifice were to be enshrined in the national consciousness of Australians as a result of military action, and although religious imagery was to be used on many occasions to interpret the significance of death in war, the Australian image of both the adventurer and the sacrificial victim was to be firmly linked with an action of the state.

To conclude, the Brotherhood's foundation in an Anglo-Catholic piety which had only shallow roots in local soil, was a reason for the dearth of prospective members. And equally, the firm commitment to a permanent and stable residence, which was a basic ingredient in the community life as revived by Anglo-Catholics in England, finally could not be combined with the kind of flexibility which was demanded in a ministry centred on a rural parish or mission district. Despite appearing in 1911 as a far-sighted way of providing for future needs, it ultimately failed to provide enough of the mobility which was recognized as essential in earlier suggestions for some kind of itinerant ministry adapted to the needs of the bush. To that extent, Webb's analysis of the reasons for its failure were accurate. The desire to be faithful to standards which held good in the English setting unwittingly doomed the experiment from the moment of its birth.

— THIRTEEN —

## Resonances

Patterns that were established by Goldsmith as he played significant roles in the Anglican community in Western Australia—as dean, bishop and Anglo-Catholic leader—have continued to exert an influence much later in the century, and their resonances can be detected in many different areas.

The first of these is in the articulation of churchmanship at St George's Cathedral. It seems likely that the churchmanship debates last century and earlier this century encouraged many Anglicans in Australia and elsewhere to envisage their cathedrals as diocesan centres that should not be identified narrowly with any one kind of churchmanship, but as centres that could accommodate those of different traditions. Laudable though this aim might be, it has been far from easy to achieve in practice. In Melbourne, for example, the ongoing absence of eucharistic vestments from the cathedral reflects the long shadow cast by an earlier evangelical predominance, rather than the diversity that has increasingly characterised its life, notably since World War II. In the case of Perth's cathedral, it could be argued that if, throughout this century, it has at the very least functioned as a centre in which Oxford Movement influences were expressed in a restrained, if not more explicit, way, this was a reflection of the absence of a strongly articulated low church tradition in the diocese, rather than an attempt to alienate evangelicals. And while the maintenance of this profile reflects the values of other Anglicans, Goldsmith was in many ways its originator. While in Goldsmith's time it was perceived by critics as an Anglo-Catholic centre, it was still restrained by comparison with many other English centres, and parishes that were emerging in other Australian capital cities, such as St George's Goodwood or St Peter's Eastern Hill. By the 1930s, while a Victorian visitor, Athol Haesler, described its dean, R. H. Moore, as an Anglo-Catholic, the cathedral itself continued to express Oxford Movement influences in a rather restrained way. Vestments, altar lights, the reserved sacrament were by now among its uses, but incense, processions and Marian or eucharistic devotions were not. Haesler described the 'average tone' of Perth's churches as 'better than it is in Melbourne', but its Anglo-Catholicism was a small pond, in which the leading figures were prone to jealousy. He thought that it was Moore's membership of the Australian Church Union that kept the priests of the 'two greatest or most advanced Anglo-Catholic churches', Canon Collick at Fremantle and L. E. Webb at Midland Junction, from joining it, even though 'Webb actually has Reservation and Incense and Collick has 6 lights and vestments'.[1] St Paul's Carr Street emerged with a clear Anglo-Catholic profile shortly after Haesler's visit to the west. Meanwhile, instead of being an Anglo-Catholic centre, the cathedral remained the parish church for the Anglican residents of St George's Terrace and Mount Street. This middle-class identity dominated the cathedral, despite Moore's desire to expand its outreach to the working classes, and to undertake more social work. The appearance of any ceremonial beyond its restrained norm could cause amusing confusions in the press. When Moore threw the cathedral open to the Greek Orthodox community for the celebration of a requiem following the assassination of King Alexander of Yugoslavia in 1934, the *Church Standard* published the following, unconscious that it was painting a picture of extraordinarily muscular feats: 'As Fr Manessis in full robes entered the church, preceded by 2 Greek boys in albs . . . the Revd L. E. Webb, in the capacity of MC, handed the thurifer to Fr Manessis, who after approaching the high altar, censed the catafalque. Then he returned the thurifer to Fr Webb.'[2]

A restrained expression of Oxford Movement influences continued to be the cathedral's norm until the 1960s. With the exception of James Payne, the deans themselves were all moulded by the Oxford Movement, and Payne left his precentor, Arthur Grimshaw, to maintain the status quo, while Payne himself, a gifted communicator, placed the cathedral more and more on the city map as a church relating to the wider inner-urban community, through his effective networking in the city's business and professional organizations.

Dramatic changes took place during the 1960s under John Hazlewood. Building on Payne's work, he broadened its scope: the cathedral came to be identified as the city church for the communities associated with the arts. The extent of his ministry to the marginalized and addicted bewildered his successor, Vernon Cornish. And his ministry to the young, particularly through occasional liturgical happenings—the 'rock masses'—were backed up by public statements on a range of issues that had a larrikin, subversive tone that was not unknown among Anglo-Catholics elsewhere.

His introduction of a high mass as the principal Sunday liturgy, the appearance of statues of St George and our Lady (the latter a memorial to Bishop Frewer from the Society of Mary) and of icons that encouraged devotion to the saints, were among a number of signs that gave the cathedral an overtly Anglo-Catholic profile. In the light of the closure of St Paul's Carr Street and the failure of the church of the Holy Family at Yokine to fill the vacuum so created, the emergence of this profile is understandable, but it was one fraught with difficulty. The subsequent closure of St Mary's West Perth by Geoffrey Sambell in 1985, despite well-articulated protest, only helped to confirm the cathedral's role as a centre for Perth Anglo-Catholics, while at the same time, though unintentionally, blocking off a possible outlet. While the cathedral offered an impressive symbolic centre, and an architecturally sympathetic site for their devotions, it was shortsighted of Perth's Anglo-Catholics to envisage it as a permanent home. The representatives of the congregation on the cathedral chapter supported such an identity more than did those members who came from outside the congregation's ranks. John Hazlewood's critics would see him as a dean who would have been unlikely to encourage the emergence of another strong centre of this kind; and the cathedral's leading role for Perth Anglo-Catholics continued under David Robarts, who was elected partly on the strength of his churchmanship. In response to the claims made by some Anglo-Catholics that changes in the cathedral after David Robarts' resignation constituted a form of betrayal, it must be said that Perth's Anglo-

Catholics would have been serving their own cause far better had they established themselves firmly in a particular parish or parishes, in which they could exercise far more control over decision-making than was possible in the cathedral. For two and a half decades the cathedral was like a mesmerizing magnet that encouraged dependency, when initiative and planning in other directions would have been well in order. And while it no longer has a profile that could be described as a predominantly conservative Anglo-Catholic one, its worship, while designed not to exclude those of varying traditions, remains firmly within the tradition that the cathedral has represented throughout the century.[3]

The second significant area in which resonances from Goldsmith's era can be discerned up to the present is in that of the articulation of authority over the cathedral in the roles of dean and archbishop. When preaching at the consecration of John Hazlewood as Bishop of Ballarat in 1975, Geoffrey Sambell described the period in which they had occupied the offices of dean and archbishop of Perth as one of 'collisions and collusions'. On another occasion, during the interregnum following Hazlewood's departure, he kicked a stone as he walked past the cathedral, commenting sourly, 'I wish the bloody thing would fall down'. If it were possible to bring together those alive and those long dead, one suspects that Riley, Sambell and the present archbishop, Peter Carnley, would find much in common with one another over this issue, as would Goldsmith, Hazlewood and Robarts.

That autonomy should be removed in one way or another—that the role of dean should either be totally abolished, or else be replaced with that of a subdean—were both alternatives that were raised in response to Goldsmith and his successors. Riley wrote to Montgomery 'If I had not been away so much, I think I should endeavour to get Synod to do away with a Dean.—I don't believe a divided Authority at the Cathedral is a good principle on which to act . . .'[4] Riley altered the cathedral statute on Goldsmith's departure, making himself president of the cathedral chapter, and dean in any vacancy; other measures strengthened his authority over the cathedral.[5] Much later, shortly after the death of another dean, Ernest Foster, in 1925, Riley, now ageing and ill, stated that 'the Bishop should be in supreme control . . . In some Dioceses in Australia . . . there are Deans—but Deans only in name, and they do not control the Cathedral'.6 At the end of World War I, R. H. Moore, who was not to become dean until the end of 1929, just over a decade later, commented in private correspondence that there was no need to search either overseas or interstate for a replacement for H. F. Mercer, as the role (as Riley envisaged it) was really that of a subdean, and not the autonomous figure of an English cathedral.7

But Riley's view of authority and power-sharing was not upheld by others. On his death in 1929, another cathedral statute was framed, returning the presidency of the cathedral chapter to the dean, along with his role as the cathedral's executive officer. The diocesan administrator of the time, Cuthbert Hudleston, signed the new statute, complete with a clause to mollify the pride of any future prelates who might feel threatened like Riley: 'Nothing in this statute contained shall be construed to sanction an encroachment upon or to in any way prejudice the legal powers vested in the Archbishop as ordinary'.8 Both synod and chapter had concluded that a division of powers was preferable to an absolute concentration—even, or especially, in a bishop. Much more recently David Robarts questioned the wisdom of lessening the dean's autonomy and leaving only one 'strong man' in Perth's Anglican community, stating that the chapter itself continued to see the dean's role as part of a structure of checks and balances.9 But elements in the election of his successor could be interpreted as a sign that in practice, Perth Anglicans had concluded that the price to pay for such autonomy was too high, a level of friction that called the whole theory into question.

But in favour of the preservation of autonomy it can be said that this model has worked when those holding the offices of dean and bishop have been like-minded. Although I have been unable to locate a copy of the original cathedral statute that caused Riley and Goldsmith so much trouble, Parry found it no obstacle to his relations with Goldsmith or the cathedral; under the present statute, the same appears true of Peter Carnley and John Shepherd. The danger lies in the clash of two strong individuals—Riley and Goldsmith last century, or more recently, Carnley and Robarts. But there could also be less robust contenders who experienced difficulty, as did Ernest Foster: Foster came to Perth because of his already fragile health, while in his later years Riley became increasingly irascible as his own health deteriorated. At the height of tensions between them, Foster vacated the deanery, and it was believed that the stress of office contributed to his death in 1925. It has been said that in a setting in which the dean has autonomy, and is elected by the cathedral chapter, the bishop is bound to be frustrated, but that the bishop's influence can still be decisive in the election of a dean was demonstrated in the wake of David Robarts' resignation, when Peter Carnley refused to ratify the election of an English candidate, Canon David Painter, even though he had been nominated unanimously by the cathedral chapter, and the senior canon had already publicly announced to the cathedral congregation that chapter had been unanimous in nominating a candidate—though he was not at this point identified by name.

Each of the structures—an autonomous dean or a dependent subdean (or no dean at all)—has demonstrable weaknesses. But co-operation has occurred despite autonomy, while clashes have taken place despite modifications in the cathedral statute, which suggests that the core of the problem lies not so much in the structures as in the personalities of the individuals holding office at particular times.

Another area in which parallels can be drawn is the reporting of debates, and specifically, the conscious or unconscious tendency of those in authority, particularly the bishops, to produce accounts of debates that minimize the degree of tension or friction involved. The opening chapters of this study documented the introduction to Western Australia during the episcopate of Bishop Parry of a number of clergy committed to doctrines and ceremonial that had grown out of the Oxford Movement. Most were English born and trained, and those who were not either came from interstate, as did D. J. Garland and F. J. Price, or, like William Sharp, Charles Groser and R. H. Moore, from America and Ireland. Their doctrinal, liturgical and devotional attitudes met with strong opposition from some Anglicans born in Western Australia, particularly from 'ancient colonist' families. Disputes over churchmanship were carried on with a degree of virulence that overthrows any suggestion that, as a result of its isolation and consequent (supposed) homogeneity, Western Australia had escaped much sectarian rivalry which occurred in other colonies, an interpretation of the state's religious history offered by Frank Crowley, J. A. La Nauze and Geoffrey Bolton.[10] More recently, a consensus myth promoting a picture of homogeneity in other aspects of Western Australian society identifies it as a creation, in part, of dominant power groups and their interests.

On the surface, national origins might seem to account for such strong differences in this ecclesiastical debate. However, in accounting for its intensity, other factors have also to be reckoned with. The very isolation of the West may have been the factor that helped to engender a degree of insecurity that in turn encouraged the reaffirmation and strengthening of sectarian boundaries and an emphasis on differences from Western Australia's very beginning. Unlike Anglicanism in Victoria during the nineteenth century, it did not suffer any fear of melding into some kind of pan-Protestant union with nonconformity. The conservative evangelical stance of Bishop Mathew Hale (Bishop of Perth 1857–75) did not result in widespread concessions to dissent in country centres and, in private correspondence, Anglicans expressed a strong urge to retain their hegemony. Later in the century, a *West Australian* editorial pointed out that the new Anglican cathedral into which Goldsmith moved in his first months was distinguished in *not* being the result of the joint giving of various denominations in the colony.[11] It saw no obvious inconsistency in the fact that the cathedral was 'raised . . . almost altogether if not altogether by the offerings, unaided' of Anglicans, and the growing claims which it made concerning the total absence of 'sectarian strife and denominational hatred' from Australia.

Against this ideal picture, and allowing for the possibility of exaggeration by the correspondent who described the Anglican community of Perth as deeply divided in 1875,[12] there remains Lefroy's description of the reception of a priest strongly influenced by the Oxford Movement as a 'persecution',[13] and the hostile outpourings over almost a quarter of a century of that consistent opponent of Anglo-Catholicism, E. Parker, all of which led up to the outbursts of correspondence in 1898 and 1900.

In a community with such potential for division, the attractiveness to Riley of a consensus myth is easy to understand. And it may well have cast its shadow over the more recent debate concerning the ordination of women. The tension this issue engendered among Anglicans across Australia was unprecedented, but it is still possible to discern regional differences in the mode and effects of the debate. In Perth the absence of a strong conservative evangelical tradition meant that the dynamics of debate were diffferent from its Sydney or Melbourne equivalents. But it was no less heated, and all the more painful because the myth of consensus had appeared credible throughout much of the century, as long as those who were 'extreme' in any way acted on their convictions in quiet and unobtrusive corners. The mythical nature of consensus was exposed by wide differences, perceived at high levels in figures with high and public profiles. It is significant that neither David Robarts nor Peter Carnley, who were commonly identified as the leading figures with opposite points of view, were Western Australian in origin. Neither had been influenced in their formation, either consciously or unconsciously, by the shadow of the consensus myth propagated by Riley.

During the debate over the ordination of women, the doctrine of 'reception' was referred to from time to time, both in the wider Anglican world, and, for Western Australians, in Peter Carnley's synod charges. The term, considered on its own, focuses on a particular final outcome, acceptance, and if it implies a degree of testing, hardly suggests a high degree of tension, even though it might well imply a process that was gradual. In 1987, a year after he had ordained the first women deacons, Carnley stated that

> if a bishop in the exercise of his teaching office or if a theologian in the Church or a particular holy person expresses an opinion on some matter relating to faith and morals, or if a synod articulates the authoritative view of this Church, then it still has to be 'received' by the Church as a whole.[14]

But this was not to be interpreted to mean that there might be room for continuing debate over the issue of the ordination of women: it was the 'authoritative view of this Church . . . that the theological objections that have been raised are not sufficiently cogent or weighty' to prevent their ordination. 'Alternative views' might be held by some 'as a matter of conscience', but 'these are simply private opinions of particular individuals'.[15] This position was reiterated in 1990. In 1989 there was a more detailed acknowledgement of continuing disagreement. Those who resisted belonged in one of two groups, the first comprised of vocal critics, whose publications were said to be either unhelpful—or worse, sources of misinformation—and the second, of those whose uncertainties would dissolve once they had an actual experience of the ministry of ordained women.[16] Though it was possible, as his hearers were reminded in 1987, that Synods, like General Councils, might err, there was little if any suggestion that this might be the case with this issue; rather, the focus was set firmly on that point in the future towards which the church was felt to be moving in a positive evolution, guided by the Holy Spirit. In 1988 the term consensus was used to described this desired final point.[17]

It may not have been the intention of those who used terms such as 'reception' or 'consensus' to gloss over or mask the seriousness of the tensions that were felt, but it nevertheless had this effect. The reality was far from smooth, and the recourse to litigation was one evidence of this.

And this tactic forms another area in which a parallel may be drawn between the earlier debates and those nearly a century later.[18] Recourse to litigation had already marked the nineteenth-century debate over Anglo-Catholicism in England. There had been a variety of law cases before the creation of the Public Worship Regulation Act of 1874. And outside the narrow confines of the law courts the argument was fought in terms of legality or illegality. Many Australian critics of Anglo-Catholicism joined their English counterparts in denouncing its promoters as lawless, and, equally, a sophisticated level of historical research was brought to bear in defence of Catholic practice and teaching by their supporters.

In his 1990 synod charge, Peter Carnley referred to what he described as 'widespread reports' that the late David Penman had been restrained from ordaining women to the priesthood in Melbourne by threats of litigation. Carnley did not mention that, like Penman, he had been threatened with litigation by a prominent lawyer. In addition, there are others who have claimed that Carnley himself has threatened them with litigation over statements that he has considered to be defamatory, though this course has not in the end been undertaken. Those who opposed the ordination of women mounted two legal cases. The first of these, *Scandrett* v. *Dowling* in Sydney, centred on the Bishop of Canberra-Goulburn, Owen Dowling. But the second case, heard in Perth, sought to restrain Carnley from ordaining women in March 1991, and until such time as the General Synod had passed a canon authorizing the ordination of women to the priesthood. Those who mounted both these cases claim that they did so as a last resort, and they might well have hesitated in the face of the increasing reluctance of civil law courts to hand down judgements over religious issues in England and Australia in the last 120 years. The Public Worship Regulation Act had worked in favour of Anglo-Catholics by sheer counter-productivity, making them into martyrs, a process that did not go unnoticed by some of their critics at the time. It partly explains why when the possibility of creating new legislation to contain Anglo-Catholic practice and teaching was again raised at the end of the nineteenth century, it was not followed through.[19] More recently, in Australia in 1947, the bench in the so-called 'Red Book case' allowed that when issues of property and possible breach of trust were at stake, recourse to a civil court was available. In this action, Lomas Wylde, Bishop of Bathurst, featured as defendant, while the plaintiffs claimed that his authorization and use of a home-made edition of the 1928 eucharistic rite accompanied by additional commentary and rubrics constituted a breach of trust. However, members of the judiciary expressed serious concern that the case should ever have been brought to a civil court in the first place.[20] 'Reception' implied a relatively smooth evolution; litigation, entered into by both those in favour and those against, pointed to the shortcomings of this word, and the bitterness that the debate had generated.

In addition, beyond these specifically local issues, there are some parallels and comparisons that need to be drawn between the situation of Anglo-Catholicism in Western Australia and in other states. By 1900 the Western Australian experience of Anglo-Catholicism was developing along lines that distinguished its development from that of its counterparts in South Australia, Victoria and New South Wales, and provided some parallels with Queensland. In the first three states, its chief and most advanced centres were already, and remained, urban churches. But the appearance of vestments in country centres in Western Australia, and their absence at the same time from any urban centre was a distinctly different pattern. The transformation of Perth from a market town to a more sophisticated centre provided new wealth, but did not result in the transformation of an existing church as happened in Melbourne at Eastern Hill, or the building of a new one, as in the case of St George's Goodwood, in Adelaide.

In Perth, as the patterns of attendance in the service registers show, the aesthetic and formal values promoted by the Oxford Movement were sufficiently consistent with the standards appreciated by Anglicans at large, to ensure that this much of the Oxford Movement's impact was absorbed. But for any deeper involvement in Western Australia, Goldsmith's election to Bunbury effectively removed the priest most likely to foster a more explicitly Anglo-Catholic devotion, or attract and channel significant patronage. His election provided a broader support for the hitherto unfocused pockets of Anglo-Catholicism in rural areas.

In Perth the failure of any one parish to emerge as a strong Anglo-Catholic centre was partly due to C. O. L. Riley's personal predilections. By the beginning of this century his distaste for any kind of ceremonial was outweighed by his desire to avoid public controversy over the same issue. As a result, he devised his own middle path, insisting on the use of the eastward position, despite his personal dislike of it, and allowing the widespread use of altar lights, but discouraging other more advanced usages. His insistence on this kind of middle way, as though he were a kind of Western latter-day Elizabeth I finding a politic religious mean to create the greatest happiness for the greatest number of subjects, certainly did satisfy those Anglicans who sought some degree of ceremonial, without insisting on 'full Catholic privileges'. At the same time, it left a small stream who complained from time to time of the absence of any full ritual centre in the city.[21]

In these two respects—the rural presence of Anglo-Catholicism, and the higher churchmanship of the rural episcopate compared with that of the metropolitan diocese—the strongest parallel to the Western Australian phenomenon is found in Queensland. In the absence of specific dates for the introduction of various ceremonial features in Queensland rural centres, detailed comparisons are difficult to make. A survey of Anglo-Catholic growth in Queensland in an Anglo-Catholic journal in 1925 emphasized that Catholic teaching had preceded the appearance of the external usages for some time, a pattern which was equally true of Western Australia and other Australian states.[22]

Usages varied considerably among the scattered rural parishes of Queensland. Of the bush brotherhoods, the Community of St Barnabas insisted in the use of vestments in all churches served by its members, and a donor to that brotherhood during World War I saw its financial and organizational independence of the diocese as a bastion against possible episcopal infidelity. But among the other Queensland brotherhoods, members ranged from definite Anglo-Catholics, such as Walter Scott of the Brotherhood of St Andrew, to broader churchmen such as Hulton Sams, and usages varied accordingly. Also, on the episcopal bench in Queensland, some bishops, such as Gilbert White of Carpentaria, were strongly influenced by the Oxford Movement, without being Anglo-Catholic in their liturgical ways.[23] Lights and vestments appeared in the cathedral at Townsville during the episcopate of G. H. Frodsham.[24] Still, signs of Anglo-Catholic churchmanship such as the daily celebration introduced at All Saints Wickham Terrace in 1904, were still exceptional for Brisbane: Brisbane Anglicans before World War I were less likely to have been exposed to vestments than some of their rural conterparts, as equally were their Perth brethren, compared with their country cousins.[25] Compared with Bunbury, a Queensland rural diocese such as North Queensland under Frodsham achieved a greater degree of independence from British funding, due to its richer and broader economic resources; Gilbert White of Carpentaria largely relied on external funding for Carpentaria, but this largely came from within Australia. And just as Goldsmith accepted and ordained an increasing number of Australian candidates, so too did Frodsham.[26]

It was the very rural identity which Anglo-Catholicism took in Western Australia, beginning with Goldsmith's election to Bunbury, which is a key to at least part of the weakness of its influence within Western Australian Anglicanism as a whole. It is tempting to explain the long-term fragility in simple terms of nationalism—of a continuation of the lower churchmanship of the Australian born, in the pattern already detected in Goldsmith's time as Dean of Perth, and in the English birth and training of the majority of its clergy. However, this would be to overlook the extent to which some of the emphases and expressions of Anglo-

Catholicism could also be consistent with elements of nationalism. It would also ignore the part played by economic features in the initial establishment of the Bunbury diocese, and the extent to which changing economic factors would force the church into a continuing dependence on England, especially for its clergy, despite earlier hopes that an Australian clergy would emerge.

Any historian reflecting on the role played by the English origins and training of Bunbury clergy in shaping a heritage for Anglo-Catholicism in the diocese in the longer term needs to be careful to avoid the assumption that Goldsmith's Anglo-Catholicism and public school background, with its middle-class values and imperial loyalty, was bound to be diametrically opposed to the values of those born and bred in Australia and those qualities already regarded as characteristically Australian.

To this extent, his rural setting may have been an advantage in that, already, the images which were to assume national and mythological status for Australians were ones that drew on the rural experience. The formality and ceremonial of Goldsmith's Anglo-Catholicism may have

John Frewer on the roof of the House of Grace, Williams
An informal setting for a protégé of Goldsmith who was to influence Anglicanism in Western Australia long after that bishop's return to England

had more appeal to the men and women of the urban middle classes in any city in the empire, including Perth, than to the average country dweller, whose lifestyle was supposedly characterized by individuality, initiative, and a degree of informality and relaxedness. However, Goldsmith's pragmatic and thoroughly realistic preference for clergy who had previous Australian experience, or were gifted in communicating with working men, demonstrated that he was aware that, for a cleric to make an impact, he needed to rely on more than simply his professional accreditation and social status. His concern to find clergy who could communicate effectively with men was also consistent with the predominantly male values of Australian society, and proceeded from an awareness of this.

Most of all his formation of the Brotherhood seems to have been intended to promote a local adaptation of religious community values, but its break from the traditional British parochial structure, and its attempt to grapple with the distinctive features of sparse rural areas, cast its members into the mould of prized Australian values, by accident, if not by design. It is hardly an accident that descriptions in the *Bunbury Occasional Papers* of the 'tours of duty' undertaken by the brothers happen to be the contributions which possess the most obviously Australian flavour: in these vignettes the brothers come across as men isolated against the rural landscape, battling in their own way with the difficulties of the rural environment as much as any farmer, and especially with its distances, cast upon their own initiative. They are at once tales in which the Anglicanism of Bunbury diocese takes on an Australian flavour, and at the same time, they can be read as stories of British pluck and endurance, in which the doggedness of the sons of the empire shines out once more, as Englishmen create a greater Britain in the South Seas. Certainly some of the relatives of Goldsmith's clergy pictured them as isolated from the most basic benefits of civilization. Members of the Brotherhood of St Boniface were intrigued when a large and ungainly parcel arrived just before Christmas, addressed to Arnold Fryer, then a resident at the House of Grace. The removal of the wrappings revealed it to be a collapsible canvas bath![27] Goldsmith certainly believed, even though his own idea of it elsewhere was somewhat sketchily based on reading rather than first-hand experience, that the brotherhood movement as a whole was to play a significant role in the emerging Australian church, and he was genuinely puzzled that the brotherhood concept had not appealed to a single Australian in the West.

Significantly, in the context of the Australian obsession with the image of the rugged male, clear evidence survives that the bush brothers and other British clergy were tested to see whether they would show up as 'new chums'. At the end of a meal provided for Edward Elsey on an isolated property that he was visiting, the farm dogs were called in as the plates were put on the floor; the host claimed that this was what was done due to the absence of running water, water whose presence was revealed once Elsey passed the test by not flinching at the apparently primitive surroundings.[28]

Emphasis on masculine qualities did not cease with Goldsmith's retirement. Just before the Great Depression, the media emphasized the masculine profile of John Foley-Whaling, then working at St David's South Bunbury in an area dominated by dock and railway workers, a kind of rural equivalent to an East London setting, and one in which any such profile must have been a decided asset. When he preached at St John's Fremantle, he held its parishioners 'spellbound'. The *Mirror* waxed lyrical: '"What a Man!" A John Storm type pulsing with robust religion, with none of the apologetic creepy curate air about him . . .'[29]

But in all of these anecdotes the question of their real masculinity is posited of them as Englishmen, or as clergy in general; the only instances of any querying of the

The Right Reverend Edward Elsey, undated photograph
Episcopal attire, British humour and Australian informality

essential masculinity of Western Australian clergy as a result of their supposed Anglo-Catholicism occurs not in any of the stories concerning the Brothers of St Boniface, but in the more limited controversial field of an Australian evangelical journal with a consciously anti-ritualist stand, the *Victorian Churchman*. A Victorian, now living in rural Western Australia, objected to several ceremonial uses: a celebrant at the eucharist who took the eastward position and used liturgical colours. But the writer further hinted that the dissolving of the Protestant profile meant a confusing of gender roles: 'decorations of sashes and emblems, which makes the minister look like a show, or a toy man, which to me, take all the manly look away from him'.[30]

More broadly, in this connection, the brotherhood image in other parts of Australia was also characterized by the same potential for being 'read' simultaneously at more than one level. Sometimes it consciously appealed to be read in this way. When he was still a member of the Brotherhood of the Good Shepherd in New South Wales, Arthur Robin, later bishop of Adelaide, published an account of his work and lifestyle, entitled *The Sundowner*, and C. H. S. Matthews, a founding member of the New South Wales Brotherhood of the Good Shepherd, published a fictional work in 1914, *Bill, A Bushman*, which likewise drew on the same rural mythology and imagery.

During his visit to England in 1908 for the Lambeth Conference, G. H. Frodsham appealed in Oxford for 'a band of men that will preach like apostles, ride like cowboys, and having food and raiment, will therewith be content'.[31] He attracted men of public school background to go to Queensland's northern fastnesses, where Hulton Sams succeeded as 'the boxing parson' in combining the muscular Christianity of his public school tradition with an appeal to the Australian respect for rugged masculinity. This very appeal, frequently quoted as it was in the later Brotherhood anecdotes, was in itself a case of an image that could be read effectively in different contexts: Frodsham had in fact taken the phraseology from an American bishop, Whipple, but it held its drawing power for English public school boys and seemed eminently applicable to the rigours of the Australian bush.[32]

Given such instances of a dual appeal to British and Australian values, the concluding pages of the only systematic published account of the

Brotherhood of St Boniface, Tom Groser's *The Lure of the Golden West,* came as no surprise, with their appeal to British settlers to migrate and conquer the bush for the empire; at once, the rural setting is seen as quintessentially Australian, and at the same time a response to it is a response for the empire, and a contribution to its extension in the southern hemisphere.[33] Indeed, the whole work presents the Brotherhood of St Boniface, and the brotherhood idea in general, as a distinctive response by Anglicans to the conditions of the Australian bush, and its anecdotes concentrate on the isolation of bush people, and the simplicity or roughness of their circumstances.

Recently, in A. E. Williams' *West Anglican Way*, the short life of Goldsmith's Brotherhood of St Boniface is treated as a significant form of ministry to rural Anglicans, but not a whisper escapes the writer concerning its Anglo-Catholic basis. Here its story has been identified completely with the outback with which its members sought to blend, totally divorced from the churchmanship that was basic to its foundation and style of operation.

Yet there is a caution that needs to be observed here, even if muscular Christianity, the figure of the adventurer, and a particular masculine profile, underlie many of these texts. There were those for whom this does not seem to have been a dominant theme, even if it were part of their experience. The course of events for Mazzini Tron fulfilled all of the above elements: a young English ordination candidate, journeying to the ends of the empire to become a member of the Brotherhood of St Boniface, and subsequently distinguishing himself on the European battlefield in conspicuous acts of bravery. But subsequently he appears to have been reserved, almost secretive, about this period of his life: surviving parishioners of the Wolverhampton parish of St Chad in which he served from 1929 until 1955 were unaware of his Australian 'adventures'.[34]

And although it is on the periphery of Goldsmith's own personal impact, in the area in which the streams of Australian nationalism, masculine identity and Anglo-Catholic churchmanship meet, it is still appropriate to mention the indirect influence on many Western Australians of one of his protégés, the sometime member of the Brotherhood of St Boniface, A. E. White, who on returning to Western Australia from

Broken Hill as Rector of Albany, initiated the tradition of dawn services in 1929 at this point which, for many Australian servicemen, offered them their last view of the Australian coastline. A variety of sources, ranging from the headstone at White's grave at Herberton in Queensland to articles in the popular press, have claimed for him the distinction of creating the dawn service tradition nation-wide; the date for the first Albany dawn service by White is sometimes given as 1923, even though he held a clerical appointment interstate at that time.[35] White's Albany observance in 1929, a date confirmed by his son, appears to have been based on the 1928 Sydney cenotaph commemoration.[36] Beyond the question of the correct date for the inception of such a ceremony in Western Australia, what is significant is that White, an Anglo-Catholic imbued with a deep conviction concerning the significance of ceremonial and symbol, envisaged this commemoration as at once a patriotic and a religious event. In this he was very much one with another of Goldsmith's contemporaries and rivals, David Garland, who played a significant role in promoting the commoration of Anzac day in Queensland as an event that was at once religious and patriotic.[37]

More importantly, in connection with nationalism, though it may have been Goldsmith's incipient Anglo-Catholicism, coloured by his awareness of the ritual prosecutions in England during his time as a junior priest there, that gave real impetus to his expressions of support for autonomy for Australian Anglicans; an appeal on behalf of an autonomous Anglican church in Australia, untrammelled with the establishment connections of Anglicanism 'at home', was also an appeal that was consistent with perceived Australian values.

In the leader in a 1908 edition of the *Church Times*, which presumably relied on the opinion of that paper's Australian correspondent, it was stated that the concept of a church which enjoyed official recognition by the state was anathema 'to the average Australian: rightly or wrongly, he believes that the Church can do its best work without the help or trammels of official recognition'.[38] Those around Goldsmith seem to have been aware of such a sentiment, and Goldsmith's former curate, F. J. Price, suggested that the absence of such a status for Australia's Anglicanism caused English newcomers to look at it in a more favourable light.

Goldsmith's own appeal to Australian nationalism was hardly an excited or romantic one—unlike that of his acquaintance, Percy Wise, of St George's Goodwood, in Adelaide, who saw the colour and light of Catholic worship as being at one with the bright Australian light and wealth of natural colour.[39] Yet, between his test launching in 1899 of his motion proposing a name change and 1900, Goldsmith came to appeal once more to what he saw as the growing national sentiment, and asked whether Australia were always to be considered as having no history of her own. In this situation again, it was possible for Anglo-Catholic interests rooted in an English experience to appear to have an authentic Australian flavour. However, unlike the bush brotherhoods, the issue of autonomy was surrounded by intense political issues which led the motives of its proponents to be thoroughly questioned, and while the autonomy movement included significant figures such as St Clair Donaldson and Riley, whose motivation was far from any ritual one, it was in the interests of low churchmen wishing to stave off any possible 'cutting of the painter' to represent the movement as being motivated by a desire for liberty in ceremonial and other areas irrespective of the cost.

The flow of Australian candidates in, and to, dioceses such as Bunbury and North Queensland, indicate that while still more candidates for holy orders were needed than were coming forward, 'high jinks' alone could not be blamed for the shortfall, in the way that evangelical journals such as the *Victorian Churchman* were wont to do. Likewise, any question of the fragility of the Anglo-Catholic tradition in any one part of Australia cannot simply be accounted as evidence that this kind of Anglicanism was unacceptable to Australians as such.

Nor was the increasingly Anglo-Catholic emphasis which characterized at least the surface of the diocesan life after Goldsmith's departure rejected by all the laity, even if the presence of resistance to the more overt expressions of Anglo-Catholicism was hardly even hinted at by sources such as the *Bunbury Occasional Papers*. Comments in the Perth press concerning the apparent appeal of John Foley-Whaling have already been cited. When he arrived at St David's South Bunbury, his predecessor, C. S. Hardy, had already introduced the reserved sacrament, making this working-class centre the first Anglican parish in the state to have reservation.[40] To this foundation Foley-Whaling added all the accessories that he could possibly use in its cramped wooden church—incense and holy water, statues, and a set of remarkable wooden triangular candlesticks for the altar that were still being used in the early 1980s in the nearby parish of St Elizabeth of Hungary Carey Park.[41]

In Goldsmith's time the churchmanship that he promoted was obviously recognized and valued by those who were already familiar with it from 'home', as a former server 'in a good London church' wrote of his isolation in a letter that appeared in part of the *Bunbury Occasional Papers*.[42] Though its heading, 'By the Waters of Babylon' was obviously designed to maximize the degree to which it could tug at hearts and pursestrings in England, the situation and response described can hardly have been unique. Another Englishman, who normally walked forty miles to the nearest church to make his Christmas and Easter communion, found the distance lessened to sixteen miles through the building of a closer centre. Obviously brought up under the Oxford Movement's impact, he had originally walked his forty-mile journey on Saturday, and camped in the bush overnight so that he would only have a short distance to cover while he fasted.[43]

A simple gratitude for 'services rendered,' without any apparent reflection on churchmanship, characterized the response of a number of farmers and timber workers in remote districts in the following decade, as is evidenced by survivors from that period.[44] And something of the impact of Anglo-Catholic values is indicated by the fact that of those men who were born in the diocese and offered themselves for ordination between the period immediately after World War II until as late as 1975—Douglas Davies, Raymond Cheek, George Harvey, John McDonald, Graeme Manolas and David Murray—all acknowledge that the influence of Anglo-Catholic piety, and the example of older priests who identified themselves as Anglo-Catholic, were significant factors in their own formation as priests.[45]

Among the factors which led to the choice of the south-west for the location of the state's first rural diocese, its possession of a larger number of established parishes than the goldfields, and the current population trends, seemed to augur well for the future. In the face of the population that came to settle in the south-west in the aftermath of the gold rush, the rising tide of British migrants before World War I, and the

'A New Problem for the Bunbury Diocese'
*West Australian Church News*, 1 February 1924, p. 31
Part of the wave of working-class British migrants after World War I

opening up of the land with the development of a network of railways, Goldsmith's conclusion that the south-west was on the way to becoming a highly populated and prosperous centre was understandable enough. His establishment of the Brotherhood in 1911, with the intention that its members would train clergy and take retreats, and be more than just a labour force for reaching isolated settlers in the backblocks, was based on the assumption of a continued population growth that would provide the necessary support for such a *modus operandi*.

His private correspondence with the SPG, as well as his public statements, conveys no sense that a mission to a countryside populated largely by working people might be a task fraught in principle with great difficulty. Rural isolation, rather than inherited indifference to religious practice, was the enemy that Goldsmith most often identified in his own correspondence, in which he assumed that the provision of a ministry would generate an adequate response. In his mind, the influx of workers and their families might well have represented a potentially fertile field for the Anglo-Catholic sowing. He obviously believed that large numbers of them were still accessible to religious appeals, and probably saw the proof of this conviction in the number of men offering for baptism and confirmation in the early years of his episcopate, a fact which may have been due as much to the increased opportunities offered by the growing structures of the infant diocese. He may well have overestimated the degree to which it would be easy to win working people to the church. Anglo-Catholics had already claimed that it was as a result of the work of Anglo-Catholic clergy in London's east and south that the working classes were being won, and also saw their work as evidence that Anglo-Catholicism had a particular appeal to working people, a point of view that had already filtered through to Australian Anglo-Catholic circles elsewhere.[46]

It was not until his later years in England that he could refer to the 'great difficulties' under which the Catholic faith was advancing in Australia—perhaps as a conclusion drawn from his diocesan experience, after an initially quite different expectation. Any possibility of an ongoing migrant boom creating the basis for a populous, stable and prosperous society in which Anglicanism would flourish was destroyed for Goldsmith and his successors by World War I and its aftermath, with the economic slump that led into the Great Depression and World War II. Goldsmith had turned to Britain for finance and manpower because the capital of the first wave of settlers on the land was generally tied up with their property development, but instead of an eventual sequence of prosperity and increased population, population increases in the south-west rose and fell in response to external factors, and the 1920s brought a new wave of equally poor, if not poorer, British migrants to the south-west.[47] The economic circumstances of most of the population of the south-west remained a fragile base for the kind of Anglicanism which Goldsmith promoted. In many prominent English centres the backdrop for its sacramental theology was the suggestive atmosphere of richly endowed Gothic revival or neo-Baroque edifices, which a struggling rural community in Australia could not afford. One example of the continuing dependency on English support in Wilson's time that highlights such differences is the church built in Northcliffe. It was the consequence of a gift of £200 from the Sunday School of Christ Church Lancaster Gate: during the second half of the nineteenth century, Christ Church had been nicknamed 'the thousand pound church' from the collections raised on Hospital Sunday, and its pulpit was much sought after by colonial mission preachers.

Bunbury's Anglicanism was not alone in seeking further injections of English funding or turning to England for many of its clergy: Perth was still strongly dependent on England for clergy and to a lesser extent for money.[48] But if a rural diocese such as Bunbury were to be the Anglo-Catholic stronghold for Western Autralia, the greater vulnerability of its economy, compared with that of Perth's, was to leave its Anglo-Catholic core in a situation that was hardly conducive to security or stable growth from within.

Wilson was obliged to turn to England for his clergy at a time when the Anglo-Catholic wave was reaching its peak, visible to the wider public in the series of large congresses held in the 1920s and 1930s in an atmosphere of almost unrestrained triumphalism; seventy thousand registered to attend the Anglo-Catholic Congress of 1933.[49] Anglo-Catholic clergy and candidates seeking ordination were not in short supply, though a diocese whose economic conditions were as insecure as Bunbury's could not always be overly particular about those it accepted. The resultant link between his clergy's Anglo-Catholicism and their English origin was made by Bishop Wilson as he defended them, at the same time implying that he had no alternative to accepting their ministrations:

> God has supplied us with clergy who, owing to the Anglo-Catholic movement in England, their studies, training and friends, are largely Anglo-Catholic. We are training scarcely any priests ourselves, and if it were not for them, as far as we can see, half our parishes would be vacant . . .[50]

Wilson was not alone in commenting on the high proportion of diocesan clergy who identified themselves as Anglo-Catholic.[51] Part of Goldsmith's vision was reaching fruition, but the continuing British origin of the clergy left his hope of an Australian clergy unfulfilled.

Nor was it just that Bunbury's unstable economy made her unattractive to clergy who could really choose where they went, and left her open to staffing in some cases by men who were hard put to find employment elsewhere. The international economic conditions that impacted on the fragile infant structures of south-west society were reflected in the quality of the egg laid by the English clerical hen.[52] In England a decline in clergy incomes was accompanied by a lowering in the educational levels of men who came forward for the priesthood: Wilson had little choice but to accept Englishmen as ordination candidates for his diocese, but his daughter commented on the contrast between the scholarship of Arnold Fryer, one of Goldsmith's candidates from before World War I, and the respect with which he was held in Bunbury, and the clergy of the next decade, such as John Foley-Whaling and Joseph Moore, both of whom came to the diocese under Wilson.[53] Goldsmith's list of twenty-nine clergy in November 1914, of whom twelve were graduates of English and Canadian universities, six with MAs from Oxford and Cambridge, was an educational pinnacle for the diocese, not to be repeated; nor was the diocese to have a Dublin LLD as a parish priest after 1912.

Clergy such as Moore and Foley-Whaling represented not only a more militant Anglo-Catholicism, but appear to have been eccentric, even by English standards. Foley-Whaling, the recipient of a private income, at least was economically representative of the class from which Anglican clergy had often come in the past, but before ordination both he and Moore had trained at St Paul's Little Bardfield, a centre not formally recognized as a seminary or college, and whose particular brand of Anglo-Catholicism, as well as the kind of candidates it admitted, caused the Archbishop of Canterbury, Cosmo Gordon Lang, some concern.[54]

The continuing Englishness of the clergy, and their increasing Anglo-Catholicity, promoted at least some continuation of the identification made in the earlier debates during Goldsmith's time in Perth of the older Australian-born Anglicans as being generally lower than that of the more recently arrived English. In Goldsmith's time in Bunbury the daily eucharist and reintroduced altar lights did not prevent the pro-cathedral community from identifying itself as basically low church, as one member from Goldsmith's time recalled.[55] Another daughter of a prominent 'ancient colonist' family, the Bussells, who witnessed the birth and short life of the Brotherhood of St Margaret among the Margaret River settlements, commented that the appearance of cassocked clergy was generally taken for granted by the English migrants, but provoked derogatory comments about high churchmanship from the more established Australian-born landowners.[56] And Wilson's own reflection on the churchmanship of the continuing stream of English clergy who staffed the parishes was a prelude to an appeal to the laity to accept their Catholic emphases, a clear enough sign of resistance, although it makes no positive identification of Australian-born Anglicans as its source. Again, while Wilson's daughter regarded Foley-Whaling and Moore as odd, the Benedictine community which the former attempted to establish at Brunswick and other 'Romeward Features' brought forth a letter of complaint in the *West Australian Church News* from a correspondent who signed herself 'An Old Churchwoman'. The cause of her irritation is well represented by a description in the Western Australian provincial paper of the solemn blessing of the convent of St Elizabeth of Hungary in Bunbury in 1928 with its careful enumeration of liturgical functionaries from thurifers down to a 'holy water carrier', the archdeacon's 'white silk cope', the intoning of 'prayers, invocations and blessings' and the use of 'ancient plainsong' for antiphons. She can hardly have felt comforted by references to quiet days conducted for members of the Brotherhood of St Margaret, during which members made their vows to the bishop.[57]

Economic factors, though different ones, played a part in the continuing high proportion of English clergy in the diocese during the period after World War II. Even in the episcopate of Donald Redding (1951–57) and his successor Ralph Hawkins (1957–77) it was cheaper to pay for an English priest to come to the diocese as a migrant on an assisted passage than to finance the removal costs involved in bringing a priest from elsewhere in Australia.

There was another economic aspect which helped reinforce existing suggestions that national origins lay behind divisions in churchmanship. The failure of Goldsmith, or his successors, to find adequate local finance for the provision of buildings to convey their vision was only partly due to the siphoning off of the lion's share of gold rush profits to mine owners and shareholders, chiefly British, outside Australia. The complaint made by Bishop Wilson, that an absence of any sense of generosity towards the church on the part of those Western Australians who did make money, was an attitude which had also surfaced in Goldsmith's time, if not earlier. In the north-west, Bishop Trower denounced the 'moderate' giving of its wealthier settlers: they were there only 'to make money and to clear out'.[58] Representative of a similar attitude in the south-west was the response of Ernest Lee Steere to appeals for the chapel at Guildford Grammar School. Lee Steere's family owned extensive holdings around Boyupbrook, a part of the Brotherhood territory, and since he was not the only south-west Anglican to send members of his family to that school, his attitude can hardly have been atypical of responses to Goldsmith's appeals for generous funds for a cathedral and other buildings:

> I do not agree that it is necessary to have a 'gilt-edged' edifice to make one's devotions in, and am of the opinion that our prayers are heard from beneath a mulga tree just as much as in a magnificent edifice such as St Peter's in Rome *or* your own Chapel.[59]

Such a response represented an attitude that would hinder the attainment of Goldsmith's vision. The collection that marked the opening of Guildford Grammar chapel, amounting to £10, including £4 in threepences and £2 in sixpences, was likewise an indication of the extent to which the Western Australian country families were unlikely to produce patrons of the kind who lay behind the building or refurbishing of Anglo-Catholic churches in urban centres elsewhere in Australia, such as Isabell Hughes at Eastern Hill, or Priscilla Bickford at Goodwood.[60] As well as emigrant poverty, which could not build Western Australian equivalents of the kind of English churches that Goldsmith nostalgically remembered and yearned for, Western Australian wealth would not build in that way.

Building programmes did receive support from the smaller landowners, as well as settlers with even more limited means. Such was the case with the building of three brick or stone churches at Dardanup, Boyanup and Donnybrook between 1906 and 1907 in the small but fertile area east of Bunbury dominated by dairying, orchards and mixed farming. Goldsmith wrote that their construction reflected the giving of the local population.[61] The building of St Thomas' Brookhampton, near Donnybrook, reflected the generosity and piety of one family in particular, the Thomsons; and the prosperity of the orchard district between Donnybrook and Bridgetown formed a likelier setting from which such a

The Bishop's Chapel, Kalgoorlie
*West Australian Church News*, September 1923
Not one of Lee Steere's 'gilt-edged edifices'; a stark contrast to All Saints Collie, it was hardly the ideal setting for acts of worship that would express the ideals of Goldsmith and his supporters.

gift might emerge. The Bridgetown community, which included a member of the Thomson family, planned in 1908 to build a stone church at a cost of £2,000.[62] A background of well-endowed English middle-class piety certainly characterized H. G. Hinde, a prominent Donnybrook Anglican, son of a major-general and cousin of P. R. Edgerton, vicar of Bexley and founder of All Saints School, Bloxham. Many of the fittings of the Donnybrook church were gifts that came through his connections.[63] At Katanning the local MLA, F. H. Piesse, a synodsman and diocesan trustee, was also a generous contributor to the building of the church, hall and rectory.[64] Another MLA, H. W. Venn, was a generous contributor to St Mary's Dardanup, giving the land on which the church was built, as well as contributing towards the construction.[65]

But despite such gifts, the scale on which the people of the new country gave to the church could only be compared unfavourably with the endowments that were still being made by some of the faithful with means in England. At the annual general meeting of the Bunbury

Collapse of a church—Broome Hill
*West Australian Church News*, September 1923

pro-cathedral parish in 1905, the absence of generous bequests to the church in wills was noted.⁶⁶ The Lee Steere response concerning the Guildford Grammar chapel was certainly consistent with the already perceived tendency of 'ancient colonists' to prefer a lower churchmanship. But even before Goldsmith's arrival in the colony the more pronounced generosity of those born outside Western Australia when it came to church-building was also evident in the raising of funds for the new cathedral in Perth. The only significant Western Australian-born contributors towards its memorials before World War I were members of the Burt family.

Though to Goldsmith the Anglo-Catholic vision which he espoused was theologically based, he also consciously yearned, as he wrote from time to time, for the sympathetic settings for Anglo-Catholic liturgy and devotion offered by various well-endowed or well-patronized centres in England. To the extent that he seems more likely to have been able to develop such a centre by remaining in Perth and attracting local patronage, his move to the country ultimately meant that the likelihood of such an occurrence in the state was lessened even further. He can hardly be blamed for failing to understand the extent to which the Oxford Movement in England was linked with the cultural atmosphere of the wider Romantic movement. But the gap between the scale of the plans for a new cathedral as he envisaged it, and the level of financial response which occurred over several years, suggests that, despite his awareness of the limited resources of most of the new settlers, he had not fully realized the extent to which an equivalent of the more generous British ecclesiastical patrons would simply not be forthcoming in this new environment.

The straitened economic means of most of the population of the diocese again go part of the way to explaining why the two centres that gave clearest expression in the diocese to Anglo-Catholic ideals—the House of Grace, and All Saints Collie—were built almost entirely as a result of individual gifts by English and convinced Anglo-Catholic donors. At the time, worshippers appear to have generally regarded the presence of the House of Grace and its staff, and of the Collie church, as a welcome relief and answer to particular needs in a harsh and isolated environment. But their long-term history suggests that they represented a vision that was also to some extent exotic to those who were born there.

The fittings and layout of the Collie church certainly reflected the advanced Anglo-Catholic standards of its giver, and made it one of the few churches in the whole of Australia that approximated in this way to a 'good' Anglo-Catholic church in England. Its altar was placed so as to allow for the full ceremonial of high mass; on it stood a set of six silver candlesticks and crucifix. Shortly after Goldsmith's return to England the sanctuary walls were painted with a representation of the court of heaven. Each side of an enthroned Virgin and Child seated below an aura containing Christ the King, significant figures fan out—Goldsmith himself, with John Coleridge Patteson alongside him, are linked in a widening circle by figures such as Sir John Forrest, Aborigines, and even local miners equipped with their lamps. On the surface, its iconography certainly suggested that the Anglo-Catholic vision was at one with all that was best in the local soil.[67]

But the fate of the interior fittings shows that the vision did not proceed from or take deep root among Collie Anglicans, despite the miners who featured in the mural. The silver candlesticks and crucifix were removed in the 1950s by a rector whose churchmanship found them

Interior, All Saints Collie
*West Australian Church News*, September 1923
One of the few Western Australian centres to embody many of Goldsmith's ideals: prominent in the mural (centre left) is Goldsmith himself; other contemporary or near-contemporary figures who mingle with more traditional members of the court of heaven are the Melanesian bishop and martyr, John Coleridge Patteson (second from left), and figures of Aborigines and miners.

offensive, and were so roughly handled in their ignominious exile, thrust into a recess in the most striking Italianate external feature of the building, its campanile, as to be irreparably damaged. Much of the responsibility for this sordid incident must be laid at the feet of a particular cleric, but the lack of any public outcry in Collie over the abuse of such significant works indicates the extent to which they were peripheral to the concerns of Collie Anglicans, as well as of the town's citizens as a whole.

The Brotherhood, which had only one Australian member in its history, came to an end in 1929. Earlier in the same decade it had already been recognized that the life of a bush brother was an arduous and isolated one, with few obvious attractions—which, as much as anything else, accounts for the failure of the House to attract Australian-born recruits, despite the recruiting campaign by Elsey and Frewer in 1922, and appeals in the *Defender,* the Australian Church Union's official organ. Lacking the romantic vision and sense of vision that inspired some of the English recruits, and instead seeing the unattractiveness of the prospect at first hand, none of the locals responded.

The Brotherhood house, intended by Goldsmith to function as a clergy training centre, was a significant, indeed an essential, feature, if there were to be any likelihood of the formation of an established tradition in the diocese. That seminaries had already been established elsewhere in rural dioceses, and significantly, ones with much stabler economies—St John's Morpeth in the diocese of Newcastle, St Aidan's in Ballarat and St Columb's Hall in Wangaratta—showed what could be done; and they were a means by which diocesan traditions were reinforced.

But the standards of education which both Riley and Goldsmith regarded as necessary for the clergy if they were to fulfil effective leadership roles in both church and nation—a tertiary, and preferably university education—was the kind of education that could still only be afforded by men whose social background differed from that of most of the laity of the diocese. This was another point where the economic situation of many of the settlers was also part of a broader rural social and economic setting which, in its lack of sophistication and limited resources, was hardly favourable for the achievement of Goldsmith's ultimate vision.

The ambiguous situation of Anglo-Catholicism in Bunbury, and the more generally deceptive surface of rural Anglicanism in Western Australia, is represented by the episcopate that emerged after Goldsmith's retirement. As has already been pointed out by Robert Withycombe, Australian bishops had significantly more influence than their English counterparts in the appointment of clergy.[68] In a newly established diocese a bishop such as Goldsmith was in a remarkably strong position for a number of reasons, which included his right to appoint to parochial districts—that is, those areas which were envisaged as eventually becoming self-supporting parishes, but which as yet were unable to raise the whole stipend of a priest, and therefore had no right to nominate their clergy. Because the diocese continued after

Goldsmith's time to have a significant number of such districts, and the episcopate remained in the hands of men of Anglo-Catholic sympathy, the outward appearance of an Anglo-Catholic diocese could be maintained.

Of his six successors, all have continued to use Anglo-Catholic ceremonial. Wilson, though not growing up in an Anglo-Catholic background, was increasingly influenced by the Oxford Movement before he came to Bunbury, while Knight, Redding, Hawkins and Stanley Goldsworthy had all been identified in their ministry as parish clergy as priests in the Catholic tradition, and the present bishop, Hamish Jamieson, a New South Welshman, emerged from associations with some of the handful of Anglo-Catholic parishes of Sydney, and spent several years as a member of the Brotherhood of the Good Shepherd.

While rural bishops whose own origins are in the diocese in which they serve are rare, it is indicative of the degree that an explicit Anglo-Catholicism was atypical of Western Australian parishes as a whole, to note that only one of Bunbury's bishops, L. A. Knight, was a Western Australian. Of the other Australians, Redding and Goldsworthy were both Victorians. Hawkins, though Canadian by birth, was English by training, representing the end of the wave of clergy Western Australia derived from that fertile source, though he sought to continue to tap the familiar—and cheap—reservoir.

Around the state until Kalgoorlie merged again into Perth, the bench of bishops had a strong Anglo-Catholic flavour. The election to country sees of two men who had entered the Brotherhood of St Boniface under Goldsmith, Edward Elsey to Kalgoorlie in 1919, and John Frewer to the North-West as Gerald Trower's successor in 1929, in some ways typified the way in which a small but devoted core could give an impression of strength and exert an influence beyond their actual numbers. Their election was a reflection of trust in their experience of, and ability to handle, a tough rural environment, rather than a sign of a preference for Anglo-Catholics on the part of their electors. But that two committed English Anglo-Catholics emerged from a bush brotherhood into the dim glow of rural episcopacy was also generally a true enough reflection of the churchmanship and origin of the majority of men who had been encouraged by Goldsmith, and accepted the call to minister in the rural backwaters of the south-west, a response that combined some genuine zeal for an Anglo-Catholic mission with the call of the empire to help build its greater extension in the South Seas.

And within the wider Australian context, it was consistent with the way in which the alumni of other bush brotherhoods were also raised to the purple—Robin to Adelaide, Moline to Perth, Halse to Brisbane, Feetham to North Queensland, Wylde to Bathurst—placing them in the situation from which they, and their Anglo-Catholicism, exerted perhaps its greatest influence on the Anglican church in Australia, and certainly imparted, through the apparent preponderance of copes and mitres at diocesan and inter-diocesan functions, the impression that Australia was being converted to 'the Catholic faith in all its fullness'.

Lastly, one episode in Goldsmith's career still offers some direction for the Anglican Church of Australia in its future: his concern over its title, and his readiness to leave behind a title that was resonant with the national, cultural and historical heritage of a parent body 'to identify it more closely . . . with the history, development and national life of this Continent; and to prevent it from seeming to future generations to be exotic in character and sentiment'. While others thought such a proposal a revolutionary one, it is one that he did not hesitate to uphold. As contemporary analysts of that debate noticed, support for such a move often came from those who had only recently arrived from Britain. In the near future, as the specifically English resonances of the title Anglican lead to continuing questioning of its appropriateness in a multicultural and pluralistic society, those who favour its retention will do well to recall that a willingness to move beyond such terminology is as distinctively a British inheritance as the title itself.

# Glossary

**advanced**  (of churchmanship) used particularly in 19th and early 20th century texts to designate something (or someone) perceived as Anglo-Catholic

*Agnus Dei* (Lamb of God)  words of text said or sung as a pre-communion devotion, originally sung during the breaking of the consecrated bread

**alb**  white body length robe commonly worn for the celebration of the eucharist

*Asperges*  ceremonial sprinkling of the congregation with holy water as a sign of purification before high mass on Sunday, prescribed in the Roman Missal and used in many Anglo-Catholic churches

*Benedictus* (Blessed is He)  text said or sung as part of the prayer of consecration in the eucharist

**biretta**  hat worn both ceremonially and as part of street dress by Roman Catholic and Anglo-Catholic clergy, generally abandoned since the Second Vatican Council

**Caroline**  of the period of Charles I, often used in conjunction with high church Anglican theologians and devotional writers of the first half of the seventeenth century

**cassock**  modified coat, formerly commonly worn as street dress by clergy, and still in common ceremonial use, usually black, but in other colours for higher clergy—violet for bishops

**chasuble**  vestment worn by priest celebrating the eucharist, derived from Roman imperial street dress, sometimes highly decorated; originally circular in shape, but modified over a period of time

**chimere**  robe of black or scarlet worn by Anglican bishops and doctors of divinity as academic dress and on some other occasions

**churchmanship**  (Anglican) particular position in terms of the different theological, devotional and liturgical tendencies within Anglicanism, i.e. Anglo-Catholic, high, broad, low, evangelical

**ciborium**  vessel, usually of precious metal, containing wafer bread at the eucharist

**communion**  1. to make one's, to receive the consecrated bread and wine at the eucharist; 2. the liturgy of the eucharist (used in this sense particularly by Anglicans) 3. by extension, of a church or denomination, e.g., the Roman Catholic communion, the Anglican communion

**compline**  the last of the offices of prayer said in religious communities at the close of the day before going to bed; made familiar to Anglicans through its appearance in the 1928 Prayer Book

**cope**  ceremonial robe modified from the cloak, worn by clergy as a processional robe; it may be worn for baptisms, weddings, funerals and the offices

**cotta**  modified form of the surplice, using considerably less fabric, and usually with square instead of rounded neck and arms

**diocesan**  the bishop of a diocese

**dossal**  fabric, often embroidered, hung at the back of the altar in place of a reredos

**eastward position**  position taken by celebrant of eucharist at centre of altar with back to congregation; used in Anglican tradition to distinguish from northward position, traditionally identified with evangelical and low church clergy, presiding at the north end of the altar. Whether this position was to be identified with a sacrificial theology was debated.

*episcopus vagans, episcopi vagantes*  1. a bishop who has been consecrated in a clandestine or irregular way; 2. a regularly consecrated bishop who has subsequently been excommunicated, and is in communion with no other recognized body. In the 19th century various individuals claimed consecration often at the hands of bishops of small Eastern communions; the groups they sought to build up often appeared to exist solely for the sake of their episcopal leaders.

**eucharist**  the principal act of Christian worship, derived from the Last Supper of Jesus with His disciples, consisting of the reading (and frequently expounding) of scripture, congregational prayer and the consecration of bread and wine; from the Greek for 'to give thanks'

**frontal**  Decorative treatment of the front of an altar, most commonly in embroidered or painted fabric, either as a framed panel or a length of fabric completely covering the altar

**gradual**  psalm or portion of psalm said or sung at the eucharist before the reading of the Gospel

**high mass**  celebration of eucharist by priest or bishop assisted by a deacon and subdeacon, with a choir, thurifer and a number of servers

**introit**  psalm or portion of psalm said or sung at the beginning of the eucharist, originally sung as the clergy entered, hence the term (lit. 'entry'); also used of the opening hymn at a sung eucharist

**little hours**  the five short offices or services of prayer said during the day in religious communities—prime, terce, sext, none, compline—as distinct from the greater or longer offices of lauds and vespers

***Magnificat***  text and/or music of canticle said or sung at the main evening office (Roman Catholic vespers, Anglican evensong) from St Luke's Gospel (1:46b–55)

**mitre**  the distinctive liturgical head-dress of western bishops

**mixed chalice**  addition of a tiny amount of water to the wine at the offertory in the eucharist

**ordinary**  1. the fixed liturgical texts of the eucharist, as opposed to those that vary according to the particular celebration of the day or occasion—for example, the *Gloria, Sanctus* and *Benedictus, Agnus Dei*; 2. the individual, clerical or lay, who makes executive decisions concerning the liturgy in a church or chapel

**orphrey**  coloured panel, often embroidered or decorated in other ways, on vestments, banners or altar frontals

**reredos**  wooden or stone decorative treatment at back of altar; altarpiece

**riddel posts**  vertical posts at four corners of altar supporting curtains across back and sides of altar. Often surmounted by candles, sometimes carried by angels, they were regarded as distinctly English.

**rochet**  white linen vestment worn by bishops and some other ecclesiastical functionaries; the Anglican version is normally characterised by puffed sleeves, gathered at the wrists by scarlet bands

**rood screen**  screen at entrance to choir decorated with figure of Christ crucified, Our Lady and St John, or a plain cross without figure; from Anglo-Saxon rood = cross

**rubric**  direction in liturgical text, rule for liturgical conduct, originally written in red ink (*rubrus*) in manuscript

**sext**  one of the little hours (see above)

**suffragan**  assistant appointed by a diocesan bishop

**superfrontal**  horizontal length of material, often embroidered, masking the gap between the top of a frontal and the altar to which the frontal is attached

**thurible**  metal vessel, usually in the form of a lidded bowl suspended on chains, in which incense is liturgically burnt

**thurifer**  server who carries the thurible in a liturgy in which incense is used

# Notes

## Abbreviations

| | |
|---|---|
| BOP | *Bunbury Occasional Papers* |
| Henn Notes | Notes towards a biographical sketch of F. W. Goldsmith collected by the Reverend Percy Henn |
| *MH* | *Morning Herald* |
| *PQM* | *Perth Quarterly Magazine* |
| USPG CLR | United Society for the Propagation of the Gospel: Colonial Letters Received |
| USPG CLS | United Society for the Propagation of the Gospel: Colonial Letters Sent |
| *WA* | *West Australian* |
| *WACN* | *West Australian Church News* |
| *WAT* | *West Australian Times* |
| *WM* | *Western Mail* |

## Introduction

[1] J. R. Wollaston, *Bunbury Journal*, 2/5/1843, p. 82; 8/3/1850, in *Albany Journal*, p. 89.

[2] J. R. Wollaston to Augustus Short, 10/3/1850, in *Albany Journal*, p. 93.

[3] *Perth Gazette*, 4/11/1843, 18/3/1844, 10/5/1845. The satire which is reproduced in the first of these entries is discussed in S. L. Ollard, *A Short History of the Oxford Movement*, pp. 122–3.

[4] See A. Burton, *Church Beginnings in the West*, pp. 115–16, A. de Q. Robin, *Mathew Blagden Hale*, p. 144; *WAT*, 21/9/1875.

[5] Concerning Pownall, see A. Burton, *Church Beginnings*, p. 62; on Johnson, see A. de Q. Robin, *Mathew Blagden Hale*, pp. 143–4. For his obituary, see *WA*, 13/6/1898, p. 5.

[6] See A. A. Robertson, Mitres, Gaiters and Hoods, PROWA, MN 614, Acc 3568A/7, pp. 22–3.

[7] A Pioneer Sister, *Perth College*, pp. 6–7.

8 Robertson, Mitres, Gaiters and Hoods, p. 5. Bishop Charles Gore, who had been a prominent figure in the Christian Social Union, appears to have influenced Le Fanu, judging from Le Fanu's own comments in the Perth press on Gore following his death.
9 Burton, Church Beginnings, pp. 43, 62, 115–16.
10 J. Scarfe, 'The Diocese of Adelaide (and the West)', in Colonial Tractarians, ed. Brian Porter, pp. 75–104.
11 A. E. Williams, West Anglican Way, pp. 227–36.
12 C. L. M. Hawtrey, The Availing Struggle, p. 135.
13 Hawtrey, ibid., pp. 134–5, 119.
14 P. Boyce, 'The First Archbishop', pp. 58, 59.
15 W. E. Henn, entry for Frederick William Goldsmith, ADB, ix, pp. 42–3.
16 Williams, West Anglican Way, p. 293.
17 'Tocsin', in WA, 30/9/1898, p. 7, offers some specific statistics for the late 19th century in Perth.
18 Major works by those close to its originators are R. W. Church, The Oxford Movement, and S. L. Ollard, A Short History the Oxford Movement; for modern accounts, see O. Chadwick, The Victorian Church, i, pp. 167–231; G. Rowell, The Vision Glorious.
19 Different positions on the Tractarians and liturgy are presented by Louis Weil, 'The Oxford Movement', pp. 118–23, and 'The Tractarian Liturgical Inheritance Reassessed', p. 110 ff; and Horton Davies, Worship and Theology In England from Watts and Wesley to Maurice, p. 271, and Worship and Theology In England from Newman to Martineau, pp. 120–1.
20 See pp. 29–30.
21 On the surplice riots, see O. Chadwick, The Victorian Church, i, pp. 215–16; on the St George's riots, see L. Ellsworth, Charles Lowder . . . , pp. 40–54 and more generally, O. Chadwick, ibid., i, pp. 495–501; for the Public Worship Regulation Act, see J. Bentley, Ritualism and Politics in Victorian Britain, pp. 46–108; and on the later agitation before the 1900 election, see G. I. T. Machin, 'The Last Victorian Anti-Ritualist Campaign', pp. 277–302.
22 Eucharistic vestments, incense, the mixed chalice, the eastward position, altar lights and wafer bread. For an attempt to make a head-count of the Anglo-Catholic clergy in England at the end of the nineteenth century, in which use of the 'six points' was treated as a significant indicator, see J. E. B. Munson, 'The Oxford Movement by the End of the 19th Century', pp. 382–95.
23 For a somewhat hostile assessment of Anglo-Catholicism this century, see W. S. F. Pickering, Anglo-Catholicism; Francis Penhale (ed.), The Anglican Church Today: Catholics in Crisis is a more sympathetic anthology of essays. Readers seeking a remarkably perceptive recent study of Anglo-Catholicism should consult J. Shelton Reed's Glorious Battle.

## 1: Figure in the Shadows

1 H. H. Parry, Diary, 27/4/1888, PROWA, MN 134, Acc 1223A/7.
2 Lyall Hunt, entry on James Winthrop Hackett, ADB, ix, pp. 150–3. See also C. T. Stannage, The People of Perth, pp. 324–5. I am indebted to Professor Geoffrey

Bolton for suggesting that Hackett's Church of Ireland background coloured his editorial comments on Goldsmith. On Irish Prayer Book revision and the suspicion of Tractarian and ritualist tendencies, see J. G. Cuming, *A History of Anglican Liturgy*, 2nd edn, pp. 159-60.

[3] *WM*, 5/5/1888, p. 16.
[4] C. O. L. Riley, Diary, 21/1/1897, PROWA, MN 369, Acc 1921A/8.
[5] *WM*, 5/5/1888, p. 20.
[6] L. J. Blake, entry on Sir Samuel Wilson, *ADB*, vi, pp. 418-19.
[7] *WM*, 5/5/1888, p. 20.
[8] ibid. This may be compared with the reminiscences of one of Goldsmith's cathedral curates, F. J. Price, in *WA*, 16/10/1897, p. 5.
[9] *WM*, 5/5/1888, p. 20.
[10] ibid.
[11] ibid.
[12] Merchant Taylors' School Register, entry, Frederick William Goldsmith; F. W. M. Draper, *Four Centuries of Merchant Taylors' School, 1561-1961*, p. 127.
[13] Death certificate of F. W. Goldsmith senior.
[14] *WACN*, September 1932, p. 9.
[15] See pp. 201 and 207; for a paper on education which he delivered during his episcopate, see 'The Principles of the Church in Education', in Official *Proceedings of the Church Congress held at Perth, Western Australia, 25th to 30th October, 1909* (hereafter *Church Congress Proceedings*, Perth, 1909), pp. 152-8.
[16] Certificate in Kent Archives Office, DRb/A1 1876 with ordination documents. For the parish of St Clement's, see H. P. Clunn, *The Face of London*, pp. 121-4.
[17] Merchant Taylors' School Register, entry, Frederick William Goldsmith.
[18] N. Pevsner, *The Buildings of England: London*, ii, p. 183.
[19] See F. M. L. Thompson, *Hampstead, Building a Borough 1650-1964*, pp. 27, 28, 52-3.
[20] ibid., p. 436.
[21] Quoted in D. J. Olsen, *The Growth of Victorian London*, p. 232.
[22] ibid. For census figures indicating the rate of population growth during the 19th century, see Thompson, *Hampstead*, p. 435.
[23] Thompson, ibid., pp. 381, 420, and pp. 387-8 for the Anglican predominance in Hampstead.
[24] See pp. 188-90, 195-6, .
[25] Draper, ibid., pp. 1-11.
[26] Merchant Taylors' School Archaeological Society, *Merchant Taylors School: Its Origin, History and Present Surroundings*, p. 65.
[27] Draper, *Four Centuries*, pp. 159, 181-5.
[28] Merchant Taylors' School Archaeological Society, *Merchant Taylors School*, p. 63; Draper, *Four Centuries*, pp. 184-5, 195, 166-72, 177.
[29] *WM*, 21/8/1896, p. 2, and 18/8/1894, p. 12.
[30] Merchant Taylors' School Archaeological Society, *Merchant Taylors' School*, pp. 65-6.
[31] Draper, *Four Centuries*, pp. 75-101.
[32] John Chandos, *Boys Together*, p. 270.
[33] *Merchant Taylors' School Register*, entry, Frederick William Goldsmith; and T*he Historical Register of the University of Oxford*, p. 695.

34 C. Y. Fell, St John's College Ms. 343, p. 43.
35 *The Encyclopaedia of Oxford,* pp. 403, 406.
36 Prys Morgan, Jonkers under Bellamy, typescript of a paper read to the Essay Society of St John's College, St John's College Library, p. 29.
37 ibid., p. 25; see also Prys Morgan, 'Bellamy and his Fellows', pp. 126–8.
38 *The Encyclopaedia of Oxford*, p. 405.
39 ibid., p. 406.
40 Morgan, Jonkers under Bellamy, p. 15; see also V. H. H. Green, *Religion in Oxford and Cambridge,* pp. 297 ff, on the state of theological teaching in the colleges at the time.
41 Ordination papers, September 1876, Kent Archives Office, DRb/A1, 1876.
42 *The Encyclopaedia of Oxford*, p. 405; see also Geoffrey Faber, *Oxford Apostles*, pp. 407–9.
43 Green, *Religion at Oxford*, p. 275.
44 Morgan, 'Bellamy and His Fellows', pp. 126–8.
45 Morgan, Jonkers under Bellamy, p. 38.
46 Dom Anselm Hughes, *The Rivers of the Flood,* p. 41.
47 Green, *Religion at Oxford*, p. 319.
48 Ordination documents, Kent Archives Office, DRb/A1 1876.
49 See Thompson, *Hampstead,* p. 283.
50 On Sir Thomas Maryon-Wilson, see Thompson, ibid., pp. 165, 208; the *Si Quis* is among the ordination documents, Kent Archives Office, DRb/A1 1876.
51 Letters Testimonial addressed to T. L. Claughton, Kent Archives Office, DRb/A1 1876; for Claughton's churchmanship, see entry in *DNB*, xxii (Supplement), pp. 454–5.
52 An account of the case that pays considerable attention to media reporting is Joyce Coombs, *Judgement on Hatcham,* pp. 16–133. The most detailed recent treatment of the Act is James Bentley, *Ritualism and Politics in Victorian Britain,* especially pp. 46–120.
53 See especially comments by the editor directed against H. R. Baker, of St Michael's Woolwich, in *Kentish Independent,* 29/4/1876; and *Kentish Mercury*, 10/7/1875, p. 4, where the anti-ritualist party is described as the 'true church party'.
54 *Kentish Mercury*, 10/7/1875, p. 4; and J. C. Miller, *'Subjection; No, Not for an Hour:' A Warning to Protestant Christians, in Behalf of the 'Truth of the Gospel', as now imperilled by the Romish Doctrines and Practices of the Tractarian Heresy.*
55 G. E. Frewer, Journal, i.
56 C. H. Simpkinson, *The Life and Work of Bishop Thorold,* p. 70.
57 ibid., pp. 41, 70.
58 ibid., pp. 87, 119, 78–80.
59 P. Anson, *The Call of the Cloister,* pp. 93–101.
60 *Crockford's Clerical Directory,* 1897, p. 1306, and J. G. Smith, *Charlton,* ii, p. 152.
61 See Pevsner, *The Buildings of England, London*, ii, p. 160.
62 Described in J. G. Smith, *Charlton,* p. 309, with a photograph from a 1909 issue of *Country Life,* showing the chapel as Goldsmith would have known it; for the subsequent history of the frontals, see p. 125.
63 ibid., pp. 117–19.

64 These are housed at the Greenwich Borough Local History Library, Woodlands, Blackheath.
65 See *An Alphabetical List of the Signatures to a Remonstrance Addressed to the Archbishops and Bishops of the Church of England on occasion of the Report of the Judicial Committee of the Privy Council in re Herbert vs. Purchas*, p. 76; concerning the petition, see Cuming, *A History of Anglican Liturgy*, p. 156.
66 *Kentish Mercury*, 25/9/1875.
67 For George Frewer's clerical career, see *Crockford's Clerical Directory*, 1897, p. 492. George Frewer joined the college staff as a mathematics master in 1844, only eight years after the subject had first appeared in the college's curriculum.
68 Anson, *The Call of the Cloister*, pp. 80, 110.
69 ibid., p. 291, and S. L. Ollard, *A Short History of the Oxford Movement*, p. 172.
70 See Anson, *The Call of the Cloister*, p. 285, for the Sisters of St Thomas; a description by a near contemporary of Goldsmith's is W. E. Sherwood, *Oxford Yesterday*, pp. 18–19.
71 G. W. E. Russell, *Edmund King*, p. 59.
72 *Crockford's Clerical Directory*, 1897, p. 1130.
73 *WA*, 3/5/1888, p. 3.
74 W. Henn, Notes, C2; the primary copy at Cheam has subsequently disappeared.
75 *Alphabetical List*, p. 67.
76 Full service registers only begin in 1933. Occasional magazines from 1872 onwrads survive, giving details of worshipping patterns and parish growth, but there are significant gaps in Goldsmith's time.
77 *Church Times*, 17/2/1888, cutting in G. E. Frewer, Journal, i; but *Crockford's Clerical Directory* in 1880, in the entry for Joshua Nalson, gives the population as 838 (p. 720), compared with 2000 in the 1886 edition (p. 463): had Goldsmith's predecessor failed to provide current figures in 1880?
78 *Crockford's Clerical Directory*, 1880, p. 720.
79 Handbill, and also a cutting from the *Church Times*, 17/2/1888, in G. E. Frewer, Journal, i. The procession is only referred to in the parish register.
80 It was criticised for its sympathy with a society of Anglo-Catholic clergy, the Society of the Holy Cross, in W. Walsh, *The Secret History of the Oxford Movement*, pp. 121, 137. Such links led to the formation of a corresponding body, the Church of England Working Men's Protestant Union—see Lambeth Conference Papers, 1888, vol. 29, fo 36–7.
81 G. E. Frewer, Journal, i: undated cuttings from Halling Parish magazine; Frewer's addresses in Lent are listed in St John's parish register.
82 *English Church Union Directory*, 1888, p. 151, where Goldsmith is listed as a member of the Rochester and Chatham branch. This annual publication was published at the beginning of each year—hence my conclusion that he joined in 1887.
83 G. E. Frewer, correspondence of 13/2/1888 concerning a proposed mission at Addington, Surrey, in Journal, i.
84 *WM*, 28/1/1888, p. 16.
85 Figures from extract from *Church Times*, 17/2/1888, in G. E. Frewer, Journal, i.
86 G. E. Frewer, Journal, i.
87 C. H. Simpkinson, *Bishop Thorold*, pp. 143, 146, 180, 182.
88 H. H. Parry, Diary, 28/1/1888, 'acknowledging his letter and announcing the

selection of the Rev. F. Goldsmith as our new Dean . . .', PROWA, MN 134, Acc 1223A/7.

[89] *WAT*, 5/3/1875, p. 5, and H. Laurence to A. C. Tait, 2/1/1876, A. C. Tait, Correspondence Official and Foreign, vol. 226, fo 221.

[90] Canon Tucker to C. O. L. Riley, 22/2/1895, USPG CLS vol 140, fo 150.

[91] For his appointment as his father's coadjutor, see A. C. Tait, Correspondence, Domestic and Foreign, vol. 169, fos 42–8; concerning his expectation of succeeding his father, and the colonial intrigue that accompanied this, see vol. 194, fos 364, 382–405.

[92] Some details of Parry's life including his early responses to Anglo-Catholicism are contained in summaries in Parry Papers, PROWA, MN 134, Acc 1223A, which are taken from originals in the West Indies. On St Alban's Holborn at this time, see Bentley, *Ritualism and Politics,* pp. 17–18.

[93] She is referred to in the Community's reports and chapter minutes for 1886 and subsequent years.

[94] H. H. Parry, Diary, 25/5/1886, PROWA, MN 134, Acc 1223A/5.

[95] H. H. Parry, Diary, 9/6/1886, 10/6/1886, 22/6/1886, 22/7/1886, PROWA, MN 134, Acc 1223A/5.

[96] James Allen, Notebook on Ecclesiastical Matters, PROWA *1249A.

[97] Thomas Sidney, St John Beverley and Ernest. Another son, Noel, who had enrolled at St John's College was killed in World War I. For Thomas's Anglo-Catholic background, see p. 307.

[98] *Southern Times*, 31/10/1895.

[99] *WACN*, November 1927, p. 9. This obituary described Louch as a high churchman, sympathetic to the Anglo-Catholic movement.

[100] *English Church Union Directory*, 1890, p. 428.

[101] *WM*, 10/9/1892, p. 19.


## 2: Throwing Down the Gauntlet

[1] C. T. Stannage, *The People of Perth*, pp. 193–205.

[2] F. K. Crowley, *Forrest 1847–91, Apprenticeship to Premiership*, p. 547.

[3] For the date of the last service—5 August 1888—see entry and comments in St George's Cathedral Service Register 1888–91, PROWA, MN 614, Acc 2778A/32; on the unfinished state of the new building, see *WM*, 28/7/1888, p. 16, and *Perth Diocesan Yearbook*, 1888, p. 9; and on its opening, *WM*, 11/8/1888, p. 20.

[4] See *Perth Diocesan Yearbook,* 1889, pp. 14–16, which gives statistical summaries, and refers to organizations and activities in the parishes of Swan, Beverley, Gingin, Fremantle and Northam.

[5] *PQM,* June 1888, p. 11 and August 1888, p. 13; *WM*, 4/5/1889, p. 15—figures had doubled; *PQM,* July 1890, pp. 162–3; MSGV i, 21/4/1890, PROWA, MN 614, Acc 2778A/1.

[6] For its patrons, see *WM*, 7/7/1888, p. 20, and 28/7/1888, p. 24; for its activities, see *WM*, 24/11/1888, p. 20; 2/3/1889, p. 12; 27/4/1889 p. 16; 4/5/1889, p. 20; 6/7/1889, p. 16; 21/9/1889, p. 16.

[7] Concerning membership problems, see *WM*, 11/10/1890, p. 16; 18 /10/1890, p. 5; Goldsmith's address on marriage is given in *WM*, 31/5/1890, p. 4.

[8] *WM*, 7/7/1888.

9 *PQM,* August 1888, p. 13; *WM,* 28/7/1888, p. 20; 4/8/1888, p. 5.
10 See the editorial in *WM,* 15/2/1890, p. 15, referring to Goldsmith exposing the 'inexcusable laxity under which female immigrants are brought to this colony'; his original letter appears in *WM,* 15/2/1890, p. 5. *WM,* 7/2/1891, p. 14, records a petition presented by the dean to the Colonial Secretary; see also a letter by Goldsmith, *WM,* 7/3/l891, p. 6.
11 *WM,* 30/4/1897, p. 17. A useful presentation of aspects of social service 'delivery' by the churches of Perth in this period is found in E. Willis, 'Protestants and the Dispossessed in Western Australia, 1890–l9l0', pp. 31–44.
12 *WM,* 22/4/1893, p. 2.
13 *WM,* 20/9/1890, p. 15; *WA,* 23/9/1890, p. 3. He was still intending to establish the home in 1893—see *WM,* 21/10/1893, p. 22.
14 *WM,* 8/12/1888, p. 20.
15 *WM,* 31/5/1890, p. 4, records Goldsmith as speaking of 'the greatest social glory of the Anglo-Saxon race, the beauty and purity of its home life . . .'
16 For the founding of the Anglican society, see *WM,* 12/10/1889, p. 13, and 26/101889, p. 16; Hackett's support is recorded in the first of these entries.
17 *WM,* 25/2/1893, pp. 6, 19–20; 4/3/1893, p. 17; 3/6/1893, pp. 17, 18.
18 For the Methodist community in Perth, see Stannage, *The People of Perth,* pp. 150–1, 304–5. Concerning their outreach among the working classes in England, see K. S. Inglis, *The Churches and the Working Classes,* pp. 91–100.
19 For boxing in Perth, see Stannage, *The People of Perth,* p. 315. For Goldsmith's involvement, see *WM,* 10/2/1894, pp. 3, 6, 23. See also Brian Stoddart, 'Sport and Society', in *A New History of Western Australia,* ed. C. T. Stannage, pp. 665–6.
20 Concerning betting in Perth, see Stannage, *The People of Perth,* pp. 311, 315, and Stoddart, *Sport and Society,* p. 666. For Goldsmith's statements, see *WM,* 22/12/1888, p. 16, and 17/9/1892, p. 5; editorial comments criticizing the dean and other clergy are found in *WM,* 22/12/1888, p. 15; and 17/9/1892, p. 17.
21 Compare Goldsmith's correspondence in *WM,* 7/3/1891, p. 6, with the editorial on p. 13.
22 *WA,* 13/3/1893, p. 3.
23 This sermon is quoted below; see pp. 237, 240.
24 *Perth Diocesan Yearbook,* 1888, Appendix j, p. xxiii, 'Sermon preached in St George's Cathedral, Perth, at the Meeting of the Synod of 1888, by the Rev. F. Goldsmith, Dean of Perth, W. A.'
25 *WM,* 9/2/1895, p. 2.
26 *WM,* 14/7/1888, p. 20; cathedral AGM printed report in MSGV i, PROWA, MN 614, Acc 2778A/1.
27 *WM,* 25/8/1888, p. 20, 16/3/1889, p. 16.
28 1889 cathedral AGM printed report in MSGV 1, PROWA, MN 614, Acc 2778A/1.
29 Entries in St George's Cathedral Service Registers, PROWA, MN 614, Acc 2778A/32 and 33 for Good Friday 1889, 1890, 1892; see also entries for 4 November and 2 December 1893. These last two do not appear to be related to any special day or season.
30 St George's Cathedral Service Registers, PROWA, MN 614, Acc 2778A/33.
31 See Cyril Frewer, correspondence with Moreton Frewen, 10/10/1916, G. E. Frewer, Journal, viii.
32 *WM,* 9/6/1888, p. 20, 22/2/1890, p. 16.

33 See service times for the new cathedral in *WM*, 11/8/1888; service registers and *WM*, 22/12/1888, p. 20, show celebrations at 7.00, 8.00 and 12.00 for Christmas 1888; but the pattern of four or five eucharists for Christmas and Easter at 6.00, 7.00, 8.00, 10.00 and 12.00 established in 1890 eventually became the norm.
34 G. E. Frewer, Journal, i.
35 Although my source for these points is a copy of *The Church Union Tourists' Guide*, London, 1898, p. 476, English Church Union Archives, and dates from just after the period in question, there is no evidence to suggest that Goldsmith waited for some time after his arrival to introduce them. They were part of his usage from the beginning.
36 Between 1882 and 1894 the number of churches using them in England rose from 581 to 4765 according to O. Chadwick, *The Victorian Church*, ii, p. 319; Nigel Yates, *Buildings, Faith and Worship*, p. 144, claims that 4.8% of churches in England and Wales used them in 1882, compared with 18% by 1903.
37 H. H. Parry, Diary, 8, 13 and 17/4/1892, PROWA, MN 134, Acc 1223A/8.
38 *WM*, 10/8/1889, p. 12.
39 Chadwick, *The Victorian Church*, ii, pp. 296–400; G. E. Frewer, Journal, i.
40 A. Hillman, *Diary*, 10/2/1878, pp. 28–9.
41 *WM*, 29/12/1888, p. 16, and compare *WM*, 31/12/1892, p. 18.
42 The *Agnus Dei* even featured in the enthronement of Bishop Riley—see *WM*, 9/2/1895, p. 10. On the *Agnus Dei* and the Lincoln Judgement, see G. J. Cuming, *A History of Anglican Liturgy*, p. 157.
43 *WM*, 31/12/1892, p. 18; *PQM*, July 1890, p. 162. The latter refers to the singing of Bright's hymn, 'And now O Father, mindful of the love', in addition to the *O Salutaris*.
44 On its rarity in England, see Peter Anson, *The Call of the Cloister*, p. 336, n. 1; see also for Australian responses p. 261, and H. J. Harrison and J. M. Truran, *St George's Goodwood 1880–1980*, pp. 49–50, on the clash between Bishop Nutter Thomas of Adelaide and Canon Wise of Goodwood on this issue.
45 *WM*, 9/2/1895, p. 10.
46 *WAT*, 21/5/1875, p. 21.
47 Yates, *Buildings, Faith and Worship*, p. 169; see also pp. 129, 154–5.
48 Yates, ibid., pp. 156–9.
49 The original screen is clearly referred to in *WA*, 18/10/1890, p. 14, in a description of the decoration of the cathedral for the Foundation Day service; see also a photograph of the cathedral interior in the 1890s, in the Old Deanery, Perth; *WM*, 21/1/1905, p. 27, also reproduces a painting of the cathedral interior by Gertrude Ford, of which the original is in the Old Deanery, Perth. On the arrangement of the interior and especially the screen as a sign of growing professional awareness, see Yates, *Buildings, Faith and Worship*, pp. 161, 173–4.
50 See C. L. Eastlake, *A History of the Gothic Revival*, p. 244; Yates, ibid., p. 154, refers to instances of the installation of stone altars without adverse comment before 1840.
51 The frontals were the work of women of the Frewer family. On the cathedral opening, see *WM*, 11/8/1888, pp. 5, 20; on frontals, see *WM*, 31/12/1892, p. 18; 23/4/1892, p. 5, and the 1894 cathedral AGM printed report in MSGV 2, PROWA, MN 614, Acc 2778A/2. The revival of this decorative way of emphasizing the altar dates back to the first decade of Tractarianism, but in the last two decades of the

century a committed Anglo–Catholic such as G. E. Frewer could still comment on the gift of frontals, even though priests of more central churchmanship were also using them.

52 G. E. Frewer, Journal, ii, undated cutting, 1890.

53 Entry for 21/12/1892 in MSGV ii, PROWA, MN 614, Acc 2778A/2 on expenditure of £5 for the chapel.

54 On the fittings of the chapel, see *WM*, 18/11/1898, p. 37. The only ilustration known to me is the Gertrude Ford painting. On Comper and 'English' altars, see Yates, *Buildings, Faith and Worship*, p. 171.

55 *Argus*, 19/2/1906, p. 4.

56 *WM*, 11/8/1888, p. 16.

57 On the windows, see *WM*, 15/12/1888, p. 20; on the naming of the canons' stalls, see *WM*, 17/11/1888, p. 9.

58 *WM*, 15/12/1888, p. 20. One of these windows is now in St Alban's Highgate. I have not located the other window.

59 1892 Cathedral AGM printed report in MSGV ii, PROWA, MN 614, Acc 2778A/2.

60 In Goldsmith's time a debate took place over the vesting of women as well as men: see *WM*, 21/6/1895, p. 17, for editorial comment, and pp. 5, 23, 26 for correspondence.

61 See Yates, *Buildings, Faith and Worship*, pp. 137–9, and on their later prevalence, Chadwick, *The Victorian Church*, ii, p. 318.

62 *PQM*, July 1890, p. 173f.

63 Hillman, *Diary*, 8/10/1882, p. 738.

64 *WM*, 10/11/1888, p. 16; A. de Q. Robin, *Charles Perry*, p. 160; Hillman, *Diary*, 10/12/1882, p. 770.

65 G. E. Frewer, Journal, i; the ceremonies were introduced in 1888, but the origin of the palms was given in 1889.

66 The numbers of communicants—1895—29 at 8.00 a.m; 25 at 8.00, 19 at 12.00; 1898—9 at 7.00, 31 at 8.00; 1900—15 at 8.00; 32 at 11.00—Cathedral Service Registers, PROWA, MN 614, Acc 2778A/33 and 34.

67 *WM*, 15/4/1898, p. 38, refers to the continuous observance of this devotion since 1888; for the Brede parallels, see G. E. Frewer, Journal, i.

68 G. Rowell, *The Vision Glorious*, p. 129.

69 See 'A St Peterite' (= L. Brockelbank), *Canon Hughes*, p. 22; Harrison and Truran, *St George's Goodwood 1880–1980*, p. 23; L. C. Rodd, *John Hope of Christ Church St Laurence*, p. 37; and D. Hilliard, 'South Australian Anglicanism', p. 44.

70 C. O. L. Riley, 6/12/1895, Letterbook 1866–1900, fo 202, PROWA, MN 614, Acc 2467A/178.

71 Before 1888 Joseph Gegg had held services at Wanneroo south every second Sunday afternoon and James Allen maintained a continuous ministry from St John's Mission room to those who lived around Freshwater Bay, now Claremont—*Diocesan Yearbook*, 1882, Appendix G, p. xlviii.

72 Stannage, *The People of Perth*, p. 246.

73 For the first service on this site, see *WM*, 20/10/1888, p. 20; for the church's opening, *WM*, 15/6/1889, p. 13.

74 *WM*, 31/12/1892, p. 18; 1894 Cathedral AGM printed report in MSGV ii, PROWA, MN 614, Acc 2778A/2 refers to the gift of two handsome frontals, and the fact that at evensongs, the enlarged church was almost full.

75 *WM*, 30/12/1893, p. 21.

76 *WM*, 23/4/1892, p. 5. For an Anglo-Catholic manual containing a Passion Litany, see R. F. Littledale and J. E. Vaux, *The Priest's Prayer Book . . . with a Brief Pontifical*: it ran through many printings into the twentieth century.

77 Stannage, *The People of Perth*, p. 246.

78 *WM*, 18/8/1888, p. 20; and 16/4/1892 on the appointment of J. E. Harston, a priest who mainly worked in the East Perth area.

79 'The Dean was celebrant, assisted by the Rev. J. E. Harston . . .' *WM*, 31/12/1892, p. 18.

80 Communicant records for St Bartholomew's have only survived from 1893 onwards. Christmas communicants in the years 1893–98 range from 11 in 1897 to 29 in 1894—PROWA, MN 614, Acc 2467A/323.

81 *WM*, 30/6/1888, p. 20, and *Perth Diocesan Yearbook*, 1888, pp. 8–9.

82 Stannage, *The People of Perth*, p. 246.

83 *WM*, 30/6/1888, p. 20; compare *Perth Diocesan Yearbook*, 1882, Appendix G, p. xlviii, with *WM*, 14/7/1888, p. 20, and *WM*, 30/6/1894, p. 21.

84 On the congregational preference for said psalms see *WM*, 22/4/1893, p. 22, and *WA*, 29/5/1893, p. 6; compare *WACN*, February 1927, p. 24. Its popularity is indicated in the 1894 cathedral AGM printed report in MSGV ii, PROWA, MN 614, Acc 2778A/2. According to the *Statistical Register of the Colony of W. A. . . . 1899*, it seated 120.

85 1897 Cathedral AGM report in MSGV ii, PROWA, MN 614, Acc 2778A/2.

86 1893 Cathedral AGM report, printed insert, MSGV ii, PROWA, MN 614, Acc 2778A/2. *WM*, 22/4/1893, p. 20, refers to the status of the outcentres as a question 'now agitating the Anglican community of Perth', indicating that some tension was involved.

87 H. H. Parry, Diary, 1/5/1893, PROWA, MN 134, Acc 1223A/8.


*3: Reaction and Response*

1 *WM*, 13/6/1891, pp. 6, 15.

2 *WM*, 21/10/1893, p. 10.

3 He had been choirmaster at Christ Church Brunswick under C. Bardin and was a curate at Holy Trinity, Balaclava, and St Mary's North Melbourne.

4 *WM*, 27/7/1893, p. 3.

5 *WA*, 25/5/1893, p. 6.

6 R. Twopeny, *Town Life in Australia*, pp. 121–2; A. Hillman, *Diary*, 6/6/1880, p. 373.

7 *WM*, 19/10/1889, p. 15.

8 *WM*, 5/5/1888, p. 20.

9 *Western Australian Parliamentary Debates, New Series*, v, 1893, p. 784.

10 *WA*, 29/9/1894, p. 4.

11 *WM*, 9/2/1895, p. 2.

12 F. K. Crowley, 'Church and State', pp. 228–9.

13 See *Western Australian Parliamentary Debates, New Series*, iii, 1893, p. 642.

14 *West Australian Catholic Record*, 8/6/1893.

15 *PQM*, January 1889, p. 14, April 1889, p. 20, and October 1889, pp. 79–80. The managers of the school were listed as Goldsmith, James Allen and a Mr Harwood.

16 1890 Cathedral AGM printed report in MSGV i, PROWA, MN 614, Acc 2778A/1.
17 1892 Cathedral AGM printed report in MSGV ii, PROWA, MN 614, Acc 2778A/2; see also the report of the 1892 synod in *WM*, 10/9/1892, p. 20. Though it is not stated explicitly, the context implies that the three church schools referred to were assisted schools.
18 *WM*, 14/4/1894, p. 23.
19 1889 Cathedral AGM printed report in MSGV i, PROWA, MN 614, Acc 2778A/1.
20 *Western Australian Parliamentary Debates, New Series*, iii, 1893, p. 1059.
21 *WM*, 26/5/1894, p. 14.
22 *WM*, 6/10/1894, p. 4.
23 'Of all it least lies with the Catholic body to seek to restore in Australia what they tore down in the land they have left'—*WM*, 2/6/1894, p. 6.
24 *WM*, 26/4/1894, p. 14.
25 See the editorial in *WM*, 18/10/1890, p. 13, and Groser's comments on the incident in *WM*, 10/9/1892, p. 20.
26 *WM*, 23/8/1890, p. 4.
27 *WM*, 17/3/1894, p. 23, 10/9/1892, p. 20, 26/5/1894, p. 14. The relevant clause from the New South Wales Act was quoted by Goldsmith in correspondence in *WM*, 2/6/1892.
28 See such a complaint over a country school headmaster who gave his children a holiday on the visit of Bishop Parry to Geraldton, *WM*, 2/4/1892, p. 17.
29 *WA*, 7/10/1893, p. 3.
30 *WM*, 17/9/1892, p. 16, 10/6/1893, p. 22.
31 *WM*, 17/9/1892, p. 26.
32 Dunstan's correspondence in *WM*, 10/6/1893, p. 22; the sermon is quoted on p. 13.
33 G. I. T. Machin, *Politics and the Churches in Great Britain, 1869–1921*, p. 101.
34 G. I. T. Machin, 'The Last Victorian Anti-Ritualist Campaign', p. 281.
35 Machin, *Politics and the Churches*, pp. 94, 298–9.
36 For Garland's speech, referring to his own experience of the NSW Act, see *WM*, 10/9/1892, p. 20; also correspondence in *WM*, 29/7/1892, p. 6.
37 *WM*, 17/10/1892, p. 26.
38 *WM*, 22/7/1893, p. 13.
39 E. T. Dunstan in *WA*, 22/3/1894, p. 3; also 23/3/1894, p. 6.
40 *Western Australian Parliamentary Debates, New Series*, v, 1893, p. 784.
41 ibid., iii, pp. 640 ff; compare this with ii, 1892, pp. 555–7.
42 ibid., i, 1891, p. 259.
43 *WM*, 14/3/1891, p. 13.
44 *Western Australian Parliamentary Debates, New Series*, i, 1891, p. 259; ibid., iii, 1893, pp. 640, 642.
45 *WM*, 6/10/1894, p. 4.
46 *WM*, 17/10/1894, p. 23.
47 *Western Australian Parliamentary Debates, New Series*, iii, 1893, p. 644.
48 See H. H. Parry, Diary, 5/7/1888, 5/7/1889, 7/7/1890, 21/5/1891, PROWA, MN 134, Acc 1223A/7–8. After allowing the dean leave of almost a year in 1891, he planned a welcome on his return, which was muted as a result of the drowning of his son—see MBSGV ii, entry for 26/2/1892, PROWA, MN 614, Acc 2778A/2.
49 *WM*, 18/11/1893, p. 12, 25/11/1893, p. 10.

50 *WM*, 13/12/1893, p. 4.
51 *WM*, 16/12/1893, p. 12.
52 ibid.
53 ibid., p. 13.
54 ibid.
55 Woodruffe was one of the two 'lay brothers' trained at Burgh to whom Parry referred when he speculated about the establishment of a 'brotherhood' in the diocese—see p. 286. Woodruffe later claimed in correspondence that it was due to Goldsmith's influence that he came from England—*WM*, 12/3/1895. Woodruffe also features in *PQM*, July 1894, pp. 300–1 and *WM*, 2/3/1895, 16/3/1895.
56 C. O. L. Riley to W. D. Moore, 16/10/1895, Letterbook 1866–1900, PROWA, MN 614, Acc 2467A/178, fo 172.

*4: A Slowly Expanding Front*

1 J. Y. Simpson, *WM*, 23/8/1890, pp. 6–7.
2 See p. 278.
3 St Alban's Register, PROWA, MN 614, Acc 3206A; *WM*, 31/3/1894, pp. 20–1.
4 *WM*, 11/8/1894, p. 14.
5 On the enthronement, see *WM*, 9/2/1895, p. 10.
6 C. T. Stannage, *The People of Perth*, p. 303; J. M. Medley, The Rise of Free Secular and Compulsory Education, p. 21.
7 Medley, The Rise, pp. 36–7.
8 *WM*, 26/5/1894, pp. 6, 14.
9 Dunstan's claims in *WM*, 22/3/1894, p. 3; W. A. Potts (Wesleyan) in *WM*, 23/3/1894, p. 6.
10 *WM*, 17/3/1894, pp. 22–3; *WM*, 26/5/1894, p. 14.
11 Examples in *Western Australian Parliamentary Debates, New Series*, vi, pp. 959–74; viii, pp. 1041, 1044.
12 ibid., vi, p. 789.
13 *WM*, 17/3/1894, p. 23.
14 *WM*, 26/5/1894, p. 14.
15 *WM*, 22/3/1894, p. 3.
16 *West Australian Parliamentary Debates, New Series*, vi, p. 946; see also the case of the Northampton schoolmaster referred to in p. 67, n.29, raised again as an example by G. T. Simpson as a cautionary tale, lest it be thought that the Anglican leopard might change his spots in a new society—ibid., vi, p. 949.
17 ibid., vi, pp. 795–7.
18 *WM*, 26/5/1894, p. 6.
19 *WM*, 6/10/1894, p. 4; the parliamentary debate came closest to Hackett's claim in Simpson's criticism of the amount apportioned by the Anglican church to Perth and Fremantle; this is similar to Hackett's own earlier comment that the worship of the city was characterized by 'extravagant display' and 'elaborate services'— see *Western Australian Parliamentary Debates, New Series*, vi, p. 789.
20 *WM*, 20/10/1894, p. 21.
21 ibid.
22 ibid. For comments on the wider support for the Ecclesiastical Grant, see

*Western Australian Parliamentary Debates, New Series*, viii, pp. 1125 (W. H. James), 1129 (C. Harper).
23 *Western Australian Parliamentary Debates, New Series*, vi, pp. 892-4.
24 ibid., viii, p. 897; compare viii, pp. 787-91 and v, p. 784 f.
25 J. Medley, The Rise of Free Secular and Compulsory Education, pp. 36-7.
26 J. S. Gregory, *Church and State*, especially pp. 243-55; D. Grundy, *'Secular, Compulsory and Free'*, passim.
27 *MH*, 9/1/1901, p. 2.
28 W. Walsh, *Secret History of the Oxford Movement*, pp. 80-93; the chapter following this general denunciation of confession is devoted entirely to *The Priest in Absolution*. See also Nigel Yates, 'Jesuits in Disguise', pp. 202-16.
29 D. Hilliard, 'South Australian Anglicanism', p. 53; H. J. Harrison and J. M. Truran, *St George's Goodwood 1880-1980*, pp. 29, 87.
30 Cathedral Service Registers, 1888-1908, PROWA, MN 614, Acc 2778A/32-5: Good Friday, 1889, 8.30 pm; 1890, 8.15 pm; 1892, 8.15 pm; 1895, 8.15 pm; 1896, 8.15 pm; 1899, 8.45 pm; 1900, 8.45 pm; 1901, 8.45 pm; 1903, 9.00 pm. Christmas Eve: 1899, 8.15. See also Saturday, 4/11/1893, 8.00 and 2/12/1893, 8.00.
31 G. E. Frewer, Journal, iv; and cathedral notices, quoted in *WACN*, February 1897, p. 7.
32 Leaflet inserted in St Alban's service register, 1895-1902, PROWA, MN 614, Acc 3206A/145.
33 C. O. L. Riley, Diary, 25/11/1898, PROWA, MN 369, Acc 1921A/9: 'At Claremont delivered myself on the subject of confession. I wish I had been reported'.
34 James Cowan in *MH*, 18/1/1901, p. 7, reproduced a form of confession, one of several extracts from *Before the Altar*. Concerning the circulation of that work, see *WA*, 21/10/1899, p. 10, and 'Onlooker', *WA*, 22/11/1899, p. 3.
35 *MH*, 13/12/1900, p. 2.
36 ibid.
37 *MH*, 18/3/1900, p. 3.
38 C. O. L. Riley's statement in *MH*, 14/12/1900, p. 7; also *WACN*, December 1900, p. 226.
39 Goldsmith's sermon reported in *MH*, 17/12/1900, p. 3, and in *WA*, 17/12/1900, p. 6.
40 *MH*, 18/12/1900, p. 3.
41 Both references in *WM*, 15/5/1896, p. 10.
42 *WACN*, February 1900, p. 25.
43 *WM*, 18/11/1898, p. 37, and St George's Cathedral Annual Report, Perth, 1899, p. 7, Cathedral Archives, refer to an anonymous gift of a set of frontals, and a dossal. These appear to have been the work of the Frewer family in Brede.
44 Description in *WACN*, January 1899, p. 9.
45 C. O. L. Riley, Diary, 10/1/1899, PROWA, MN 614, Acc 1921A/10.
46 *MH*, 18/12/1900, p. 3.
47 *MH*, 9/1/1901, p. 2.
48 Compare Hilliard, 'South Australian Anglicanism', p. 47. St George's Goodwood was the first Australian church to have the Reserved Sacrament, beginning in 1908.
49 *MH*, 18/12/1900, p. 3.
50 *WACN*, December 1899, p. 193.

51 *MH*, 13/2/1900, p. 2: 'At Highgate Hill . . . they also burn candles on the altar . . .'; for Victoria Park, see *WACN,* July 1897, p. 5, and for South Perth, ibid., February 1899, p. 6.
52 *WACN,* December 1897, p. 3.
53 *WACN,* October 1901, p. 170.
54 H. Braddock, in *Victorian Churchman,* 25/10/1901, p. 251.
55 *WACN,* August 1898, p. 91.
56 See p. 216.
57 H. H. Montgomery to Randall Davidson, 12/4/1901, R. Davidson, Correspondence, Official and Foreign.
58 *WM,* 17/9/1892, p. 20.
59 *MH,* 13/12/1900, p. 2.
60 *MH,* 18/12/1900, p. 3.
61 Brotherhood Diary, 29/12/1916, PROWA, MN 614, Acc 3528A/2.
62 C. O. L. Riley, Diary, 26/2/1899, PROWA, MN 369, Acc 1921A/10A.
63 *PQM,* July 1894, p. 298.
64 *WM,* 12/5/1894, p. 21.
65 *WM,* 20/10/1894, p. 21.
66 C. O. L. Riley, Diary, 30/7/1899, PROWA, MN 369, Acc 1921A/10.
67 R. H. Moore, A Short History of the Catholic Revival in Western Australia, PROWA, MN 129, Acc 1210A/12/4.
68 Church Association, *The Ritualistic Clergy List*, 3rd edn, p. 43.
69 English Church Union, *Tourists' Guide,* 1898, p. 476.
70 Photograph in possession of the family of the Reverend E. Doncaster, Renmark, S.A; his wife is the granddaughter of F. Barton-Parkes.
71 R. H. Moore, 'The Diocese of Perth, W. A., or The Story of 100 Years', PROWA, MN 129, Acc 1210A/12/5.
72 *Defender*, April 1925.
73 Hilliard, 'South Australian Anglicanism', p. 44.
74 D. J. Garland, 3/7/1896, USPG CLR vol. 209, fo. 255.
75 Hilliard, 'South Australian Anglicanism', p. 50, says that Kintore's ADC, Captain Miller, presented 'a beautiful and costly vestment' made by the All Saints Sisters, a community linked with All Saints, Margaret Street, London; but the *Defender*, April 1925, commented that it was not used regularly for almost a decade.
76 See 'The Coming of Bishop Riley', recollections of F. J. Price in *WA*, 23/10/1937, p. 5. The correspondence appears as a supplement to *WA*, 17/8/1895.
77 C. O. L. Riley, Diary, 10/1/1899, PROWA, MN 369, Acc 1921A/10.
78 *WA*, 7/12/1896, p. 6, 22/12/1900, p. 3, *WM*, 18/11/1893, p. 2, 31/3/1894, p. 20.
79 Cathedral Service Registers, 1891–99, PROWA, MN 614, Acc 2778A/33–4.
80 Cathedral Service Registers 1896–1908, PROWA, MN 614, Acc 2778A/34 and 35.
81 Description of opening in *WACN,* February 1900, p. 25.
82 H. Pitts, 25/3/1901, USPG E 1901 Australia, fo 827.
83 *WACN,* February 1900, p. 26.
84 *WACN,* December 1897, p. 3.
85 St Matthew's Guildford, *WACN*, December 1899, p. 193; South Perth, ibid., February 1899, p. 6; Bunbury, ibid., August 1898, p. 91.
86 *MH,* 13/12/1900, p. 2; on the features of mission services, see John Kent,

*Holding the Fort*, chapter 7.
[87] *MH*, 18/12/1900, p. 3.
[88] *Southern Times*, 31/10/1895, np.
[89] 'Before he had been a month in Bunbury he invited him to his house and spoke to him (Mr Marshall) concerning the matter (of the conduct of the services) . . . He would like to know where this crossing wh. Mr. Marshall indulged in was enjoined in the Prayerbook, as also the bowing to the altar . . .', ibid.
[90] St Alban's Service Register 1895–1902, PROWA, MN 614, Acc 3206A/145.
[91] Cathedral Service Registers, entries for Good Friday for 1897 and subsequent years, PROWA, MN 614, Acc 2778A/34 and 35.
[92] Hilliard, 'South Australian Anglicanism', p. 50.
[93] S. Judd and K. Cable, *Sydney Anglicans*, p. 134.
[94] H. H. Montgomery to Randall Davidson, 24/5/1900, Randall Davidson, Correspondence Official and Foreign, vol. 519, fo 249.
[95] See *WACN*, July 1898 and July 1899.
[96] 'Onlooker', *WA*, 22/11/1899, p. 3; 'Charity', *WA*, 25/11/1897, p. 7.
[97] Report in *WA*, 21/10/1899, p. 10; see also *Perth Diocesan Yearbook*, 1899, pp. 31–2.


## 5: The Critics and their Position

[1] F. M. Robinson, entry for A. E. Stone, *ADB*, xii, p. 98.
[2] *WM*, 27/10/1894, p. 23.
[3] Parker's first outburst in the press appears to be a letter in *WAT*, 22/5/1874, p. 3. He wrote later to the *Southern Times*, 19/10/1895 and 1/12/1896.
[4] On Anglicanism as the colony's religious leader 'in numbers, wealth, and quality of life of its members and clergy', see Hackett's editorial in *WA*, 5/2/1895.
[5] P. Nicholls, The Ritualist Issue and the 1900 Election in England, pp. 19–20; G. I. T. Machin, *Politics and the Churches, 1867–1921*, p. 245.
[6] See G. Bolton, entry for Alexander Forrest in *ADB*, viii, p. 542; also G. Bolton, *Alexander Forrest*, pp. 142–5; C. T. Stannage, *The People of Perth*, p. 325.
[7] Sir John Forrest, quoted by P. Boyce in 'The First Archbishop', p. 78.
[8] *WA*, 22/12/1900, p. 3 .
[9] *WA*, 25/8/1898, p. 2; the correspondence continued until 30/9/1898, p. 7, but reopened in the *WA*, 30/11/1898, p. 7.
[10] ibid.
[11] G. I. T. Machin, 'The Last Anti-Ritualist Campaign', p. 292.
[12] Examples in *WA*, 28/6/1898, Mandell Creighton issuing limits on ceremonial; *WA*, 11/7/1898, 'lawlessness in the Church'—the quashing of a sentence against John Kensit; *WA*, 23/8/1898, p. 5, headed 'Lawlessness in the church: Disgraceful scenes', describing a Lancashire Anglo-Catholic being spat on by an 'incensed [!] crowd'; *WA*, 2/2/1899, p. 2; and others in *WA*, 8/2/1899, p. 5; 10/2/1899, p. 5; 11/2/1899, p. 5; 3/3/1899, p. 6; 8/4/1899, p. 5; 11/5/1899, p. 5; 12/5/1899, p. 5; 16/5/1899, p. 5.
[13] *WACN*, October 1899, p. 51.
[14] *WA*, 20/9/1898, p. 3, 18/12/1900, p. 7.
[15] A. Hillman, *Diary*, 20/10/1878, p. 164.

16 ibid., 10/10/1880, p. 419; 27/6/1879, p. 256; 9/5/1880, pp. 363–4; 27/3/1881, p. 489; 14/8/1881, p. 549; 9/3/1884, p. 1032.
17 WACN, November 1897, p. 4.
18 T. Hayward, Southern Times, 7/5/1897; for Hayward's early place among Bunbury's settlers, see T. Barker and M. Laurie, Excellent Connections, pp. 106, 113.
19 WACN, December 1900, p. 226.
20 Perth Diocesan Yearbook, 1889, pp. 14–15; see also WM, 12/10/1899, p. 11.
21 Perth Diocesan Yearbook, 1882, Appendix G, p. xlviii; ibid., 1889, p. 64.
22 A. Hillman, Diary, 25/12/1881, p. 615.
23 ibid., 3/2/1878, p. 22; 10/2/1878, p. 28, 15/8/1878, p. 151; on his sense of being old-fashioned, see 17/2/1878, p. 38; 8/10/1881, p. 738; 8/4/1883, p. 857.
24 Southern Times, 19/12/1895, 1/12/1896.
25 WA, 29/5/1893, p. 6; WM, 3/6/1893, p. 2.
26 Joseph Withers in Southern Times, 31/10/1895; T. Hayward, Southern Times, 19/5/1896, p. 3; this may be compared with 'Looking On', Southern Times, 12/11/1895, who referred to 'some of the oldest and truest churchmen in Bunbury', appealing to Marshall to 'give up some of the ritualistic practices complained of'.
27 WM, 9/2/1895, p. 2.
28 Southern Times, 12/11/1895.
29 MH, 25/1/1901, p. 6.
30 D. Hilliard, 'South Australian Anglicanism', p. 52.
31 WA, 30/9/1898, p. 7.
32 C. O. L. Riley, Diary, 1899, PROWA, MN 369, Acc 1921A/10:
  Interviews. . .
  Called
  Mr Padbury. Left Church on a/c of Choral Celebration
  Says Faulkner went to Indepent.
33 WA, 30/5/1893, p. 6.
34 Southern Times, 9/11/1895, p. 3.
35 O. Chadwick, The Victorian Church, i, pp. 295–6.
36 D. Hilliard, '"Un-English and Unmanly": Homosexuality and Anglo-Catholicism', pp. 181–210; Machin, Politics and the Churches in Great Britain, pp. 83, 109, 236; Nicholls, The Ritualist Issue and the 1900 Election in England, pp. 7–16.
37 WAT, 22/5/1874; compare this with C. H. Worthington, quoted by Nicholls, The Ritualist Issue, p. 10: 'South Italy with its Romanism, lying, thieving and dirt ought to cure anyone of leanings towards the Papacy'.
38 WA, 22/12/1900, p. 3.
39 MH, 13/12/1900, p. 2.
40 WA, 19/9/1898, p. 7.
41 WA, 30/9/1898, p. 7.
42 Examples of Goldsmith's and Garland's use in the following chapter; see also 'An English Catholic', Bunbury, WA, 6/9/1898, p. 6, and 'Catholicus Anglicanus', Fremantle, WA, 12/9/1898, p. 7.
43 WM, 23/3/1889, p. 12.
44 WA, 21/9/1898, p. 2; 20/9/1898, p. 3: 'in England we use the word every day

with a full knowledge of its meaning'.
45 *MH*, 23/1/1901, p. 7.
46 *WM*, 16/12/1893, p. 18.
47 *WA*, 23/8/1890, p. 4.
48 *WM*, 16/12/1893, p. 18.
49 Quoted in G. Rowell, *The Vision Glorious*, p. 129.
50 *WA*, 19/9/1898, p. 7, 30/9/1898, p. 7.
51 *WAT*, 5/1/1895, pp. 4–5.
52 *WA*, 3/9/1898, p. 6.
53 *MH*, 18/12/1900, p. 3.
54 J. Scarfe, 'The Diocese of Adelaide (and the West)', p. 94.
55 *WM*, 4/10/1894, p. 4.
56 *WA*, 29/8/1898, p. 5; compare this with *WA*, 30/9/1898, p. 7.
57 *MH*, 17/12/1900, p. 3.
58 *Victorian Churchman*, 23/2/1900, p. 79.
59 See M. Maison, 'The Wicked Jesuit and Company', in *Search Your Soul, Eustace*, pp. 169–82.
60 *WA*, 8/9/1898, p. 3.
61 *WA*, 19/9/1898, p. 7, 20/9/1898, p. 3.
62 Nicholls, The Ritualist Issue, pp. 1–2; Chadwick, *The Victorian Church*, ii, pp. 355–7; and entry on Kensit in the *Oxford Dictionary of the Christian Church*, 2nd edn.
63 *MH*, 13/12/1900, p. 2.
64 *WA*, 30/9/1898, p. 7.
65 Quoted in Rowell, *The Vision Glorious*, p. 136.
66 *WA*, 5/12/1898, p. 3.
67 R. Lloyd, *The Church of England in the Twentieth Century*, p. 123.
68 Machin, *Politics and the Churches, 1869–1921*, p. 83.
69 Details in M. Wellings, 'Anglo-Catholicism', pp. 239–58.
70 *WACN*, November 1899, p. 177; *WA*, 17/10/1899, p. 7; compare 'Onlooker, *WA*, 22/11/1899, p. 3.
71 *WA*, 28/11/1899, p. 3.
72 Minutes of the Diocesan Board of Education, PROWA, MN 614, Acc 2467A/148, pp. 17, 19–20, 25–6.
73 *MH*, 18/1/1901, p. 7.
74 'Onlooker', *WA*, 22/11/1899, p. 3; compare 'Suum Quique', *WA*, 25/11/1899, p. 7.
75 *MH*, 13/12/1900, p. 2, 23/1/1901, p. 7.
76 *WM*, 31/5/1890, p. 4.
77 H. H. Montgomery to Randall Davidson, 28/5/1899, Randall Davidson, Correspondence Official and Foreign, vol. 519, fo 248.
78 *MH*, 17/12/1900, p. 3.
79 *WA*, 22/11/1898, p. 2, 7/12/1898, p. 6; for Kench's letter in the Marshall dispute, see *Southern Times*, 29/10/1895, p. 3.
80 *WA*, 22/12/1900, p. 3.
81 *MH*, 9/1/1901, p. 2, 12/1/1901, p. 6.

## 6: From the Tolerant to the Favourable

[1] A. A. Robertson, Mitres, Gaiters and Hoods, PROWA, MN 614, Acc 3568A/43/7, pp. 1–2.

[2] *WACN*, January 1924, p. 23, May 1928, p. 9.

[3] *Our Work*, July/August 1908, p. 241.

[4] R. H. Moore, 'A Short History of the Catholic Revival in Western Australia', PROWA, MN 129, Acc 1210A/12/4.

[5] *WA*, 12/3/1903, p. 3, 13/3/1903, p. 3, 14/3/1903, pp. 2–3, 16/3/1903, p. 7, 17/3/1903,

p. 5, 18/3/1903, p. 5.

[6] *Perth Diocesan Yearbook*, 1898, p. 21.

[7] *WA*, 17/10/1899, p. 7; *Perth Diocesan Yearbook*, 1900, pp. 17–18.

[8] P. Boyce, 'The First Archbishop', p. 78.

[9] C. O. L. Riley to H. H. Montgomery, 22/8/1904, USPG CLR, vol. 209, fo 340; on attacks on Kyte, see H. H. Montgomery to Randall Davidson, 24/5/1900, Randall Davidson, Correspondence, Official and Foreign, vol. 519, fos 248–9.

[10] Compare his synod charge, *Perth Diocesan Yearbook*, 1898, pp. 21–2, and C. O. L. Riley to W. W. Firth, 6/12/1895: 'The Dean is popular with some and unpopular with others—he wants to keep the whole town as one parish—I want to divide it out so that there may be churches of different complexions in the place—instead of all one colour and that high. There is the Dean and three clergy'. —C. O. L. Riley, Letterbook, 1866–1900, PROWA, MN 614, Acc 2467A/178, fo 202.

[11] Annual General Meeting reported in *WM*, 22/4/1893, p. 20.

[12] F. W. Goldsmith, 'Church Organization', in *Papers Read at the Church Congress, Sydney, 1889* (hereafter *Church Congress Papers,* Sydney 1889), pp. 179–80.

[13] C. O. L. Riley, Letterbook, 1866–1900, PROWA, MN 614, Acc 2467A/178: to the Bishop of Ballarat, 7/1/1895; to the Bishop of Manchester, 6/12/1895, fo 199; to the Primate, 6/12/1895, fo 200; to another bishop (title illegible), 6/1/1896, fo 243.

[14] Boyce, 'The First Archibishop', p. 59. Riley's comment in writing to Goldsmith that the whole situation could have been dealt with by amending the parochial statute (Letterbook, 1866–1900, PROWA, MN 614, Acc 2467A/178, fo 184) would have made no sense in this context, had the cathedral been governed by a chapter. The reminiscences of F. J. Price, the curate at the time, are the most significant source on this aspect of the clash:

> Soon after Bishop Riley came the Dean left for a holiday in England an appointed me his locum tenens, in wh. position I found myself in great difficulty on one important point. Bp. Riley had never made any secret of his disappointment at finding that what Bp. Moorhouse, of Manchester, had told him was hardly correct as to the cathedral. The Dean as rector of the parish, with the parish vestry, practically dominated the position, and although the cathedral Statute provided for a 'Cathedral vestry' no such vestry had ever been appointed. The Bishop met the parish vestry and told them he desired to have the Cathedral Statute put into practice. Several objected strongly to this 'in the Dean's absence', and, though in my heart sympathizing with the Bishop, as chairman, I felt in duty bound to support the objection. After the Dean's return and the matter was fully dealt with the Bishop said to me, "You have been

placed in an awkward position, Price, but you behaved well and did quite right in being loyal to the Dean".—*WA*, 23/10/1937, p. 5.

15 C. O. L. Riley, Diary, 2/1/1897, PROWA, MN 369, Acc 1921A/8.

16 C. O. L. Riley, Diary, 10/2/1897, PROWA, MN 369, Acc 1921A/8; 21/12/1898, PROWA, MN 369, Acc 1921A/9; 4/3/1899, PROWA, MN 369, Acc 1921A/10.

17 *WM*, 20/11/1896, p. 4.

18 Boyce, 'The First Archibishop', pp. 57, 59.

19 ibid., p. 59.

20 C. O. L. Riley, Diary, 1897, PROWA, MN 369, Acc 1921A/8.

21 C. O. L. Riley to the Bishop of Goulburn, 24/4/1896, Letterbook, 1866–1900, PROWA, MN 614, Acc 2467A/178; compare the comment of the anti-ritualist, Langham Burdett, that one of the strongest assets of the leading Anglo-Catholic clergy was their courtesy and level of education, *MH*, 23/1/1901, p. 7.

22 Boyce, 'The First Archbishop', p. 58.

23 For examples of such criticism, see G. I. T. Machin, *Politics and the Churches, 1869–1921*, pp. 237–8, 242–3, 244–5.

24 See O. Chadwick, *The Victorian Church*, ii, 351–8.

25 Machin, *Politics and the Churches, 1869–1921*, p. 235; see also G. Rowell, *The Vision Glorious*, pp. 153–6; J. Bentley, *Ritualism and Politics*, pp. 116–20.

26 *MH*, 13/12/1900, p. 2.

27 *MH*, 18/12/1900, p. 3.

28 *WA*, 15/12/1900, p. 5.

29 *MH*, 13/2/1900, p. 2.

30 *MH*, 9/1/1901, p. 2.

31 N. Yates, *Buildings, Faith and Worship*, pp. 146–7.

32 See pp. 173–4.

33 C. O. L. Riley to S. Smith, 22/3/1904: 'An appeal to Canon Law is very convenient, but is of little value—many Ritualists make such appeals when they do not want to obey their Bishops'. Primate's Correspondence, re the Establishement of the Diocese of Bunbury, 1903–07.

34 The different points at which the judgements on ritual conflicted with one another are neatly tabulated in P. Anson, *Fashions in Church Furnishings*, pp. 213–14.

35 *Perth Diocesan Yearbook*, 1898, p. 21, *WACN*, December 1900, p. 226.

36 Much of the correspondence over this issue expresses a dissatisfaction with the solutions offered within the church. See *WA*, 21/10/1899, p. 10, 22/11/1899, p. 3, 25/11/1899, p. 7 (three letters), 27/11/1899, p. 7 (two letters), 28/11/1899, p. 3, 30/11/1899, p. 3, 2/12/1899, p. 10 (two letters), 5/12/1899, p. 3, 11/12/1899, p. 7, *MH*, 13/12/1900, p. 2, 14/12/1900, p. 7, 17/12/1900, p. 3, 18/12/1900, p. 3, 28/12/1900, p. 3, 3/1/1901, p. 7, 10/1/1901, p. 3, 12/1/1901, p. 6, 9/1/1901, p. 2, 18/1/1901, p. 7, 21/1/1901, p. 7, 23/1/1901, p. 7 (two letters), 25/1/1901, p. 6, and *WA*, 15/12/1900, p. 5, 17/12/1900, p. 6, 18/12/1900, p. 7 (two letters), 22/12/1900, p. 3, 25/12/1900, p. 7.

37 See figures in R. T. Appleyard, 'Economic and Demographic Growth', pp. 219–21.

38 O. Chadwick, *The Victorian Church*, ii, pp. 396–400.

39 See *WA*, 20/9/1898, p. 3; *WM*, 23/3/1895, p. 23; *WA*, 14/6/1895, p. 17, 29/6/1895, p. 5; *Annual Report of St George's Cathedral*, 1907, p. 9.

⁴⁰ C. Holden, 'Awful Happenings on the Hill', pp. 35–52. A useful treatment of this area of Anglo-Catholic history in England is J. Shelton Reed, 'Ritualism Rampant, pp. 375–403; also D. B. McIlhiney, *A Gentleman in Every Slum*, pp. 24–46.
⁴¹ See the portrait of Lowder on the front page of *WACN*, July 1898.
⁴² *WACN*, September 1899, p. 130; Garland visited Hughes at St Peter's on his way to General Synod—see *Cross Keys* (St Peter's parish paper), October 1896, p. 8, *WACN*, February 1897, p. 2.
⁴³ *WA*, 5/12/1898, p. 3, 27/9/1898, p. 3.
⁴⁴ *WA*, 6/12/1898, p. 2, 30/8/1898, p. 6.
⁴⁵ *WACN*, October 1899, p. 151,*WA*, 15/9/1898, p. 2. Sermon reported in *WA*, 22/12/1900, pp. 36–7.
⁴⁶ Chadwick, *The Victorian Church*, i, p. 214 ff; ii, p. 315.
⁴⁷ See p. 240, n. 32: L. Burdett in *WA*, 22/12/1900, p. 3; compare 'Tocsin', *WA*, 30/9/1898, p. 7.
⁴⁸ *WA*, 15/9/1898, p. 2.
⁴⁹ 1909 Synod Charge, *BOP*, March 1910; *Bunbury Herald*, 3/12/1912.
⁵⁰ *WM*, 10/11/1888, p. 16, 31/12/1892, p. 18, 9/2/1895, p. 10.
⁵¹ *WA*, 29/5/1893, p. 6.
⁵² *WM*, 30/12/1893, p. 6,*WA*, 30/12/1893, p. 21.
⁵³ ibid.
⁵⁴ *Southern Times*, 9/11/1895, p. 3.
⁵⁵ Lambeth Conference 1908, Lambeth Conference Papers, vol. lxvi, fos. 215–19.
⁵⁶ Chadwick, *The Victorian Church*, ii, 308–15.
⁵⁷ It was inscribed *Hunc baculum pastoralis officii sacri regiminis signum reverendissimo patri Carolo Owen Lever et successoribus ejus, dedit Australiae Occidentalis ecclesia. VII. ID. Deo MDCCCXVIII. 'Pasce oves.'* It is now at St George's Cathedral, Perth.
⁵⁸ *WM*, 10/9/1891, p. 25; compare Chadwick, *The Victorian Church*, ii, pp. 310–11.
⁵⁹ Goldsmith is named as a freemason in conjunction with St George's Lodge, *WM*, 26/4/1894; see also *WM*, 26/5/1894, p. 5, 15/9/1896, p. 10.
⁶⁰ H. Braddock, in *Victorian Churchman,* 25/10/1901, p. 251. For the masonic ceremony at St Peter's Brunswick, see *BOP*, December 1907, and for freemasonry at Broome and Roebourne, *BOP*, September 1906.
⁶¹ *WM*, 13/3/1896, p. 4.
⁶² *Cross Keys*, October 1896, p. 7.
⁶³ *Cross Keys*, March 1897, p. 3, refers to the West having 'devoured' most of their choirmen.
⁶⁴ H. Pitts, 24/6/1901, USPG E 1901 Australia, fo 831, report for quarter ended 25/12/1901, USPG E 1901 Australia, fo 840.
⁶⁵ *Cross Keys*, November 1896, p. 7.
⁶⁶ *St George's Cathedral Parish Annual General Report,* 1898, p. 4.

## 7: Nationalism, Autonomy and Churchmanship

¹ For Dodd's comment, see p. 166; for Crossley's recommendation, see 'The Proper Designation of Local Churches', in *Church Congress Proceedings*, Perth, 1909, p. 148.

2 *WACN*, November 1899, p. 166.

3 On Stephen's churchmanship, see the entry on his eldest son, Alfred Hamilton Hewlett Stephen, by Ken Cable in *ADB*, vi, pp. 187–8. For A. E. Selwyn, a cousin of Bishop G. A. Selwyn, another prominent Tractarian bishop, and a loyal supporter of Bishop Tyrrell of Newcastle, see the entry by R. Davis, *ADB*, vi, pp. 103–4. The text of Selwyn's motion is given in *General Synod 1886 Official Report*, p. 43.

4 *General Synod 1900 Official Report*, p. 36, par. 99; and amendment, ibid., p. 42.

5 *WACN*, November 1899, p. 164.

6 *Church of England Messenger*, 10/9/1900, p. 138.

7 K. Rayner, The History of the Church of England in Queensland, pp. 322–3.

8 *WACN*, November 1899, p. 170.

9 *WM*, 8/9/1900, p. 38.

10 *Church Times*, 12/10/1900, p. 403. The figures given in the *Church of England Messenger*, 10/9/1900, p. 138, are: Ayes: Clergy 21, laity 21, total 42; noes: clergy 23, laity 16, total 39.

11 J. Davis, Continuity and Change, p. 61.

12 Rayner, History of the Church of England, p. 378.

13 Davis, Continuity and Change, p. 71.

14 *Age*, 4/9/1900, p. 4.

15 *WACN*, November 1899, p. 164.

16 *Perth Diocesan Yearbook*, 1888, Appendix J, p. xxxiii ff.

17 *WACN*, November 1899, p. 163.

18 See notice of a lecture on the history of early English Christianity before St Augustine of Canterbury, accompanied by magic lantern slides, in *WM*, 15/6/1899, p. 16; and a review of a series of lectures on 'The Olden Days in Britain', *WM*, 26/5/1899, p. 37.

19 *WACN*, November 1899, p. 166.

20 ibid., pp.163, 165–6, *Adelaide Church News*, quoted in *WACN*, December 1899, p. 1.

21 *WACN*, November 1899, pp. 163–4; surprisingly, only one cleric, G. Wilson, suggested that national might represent the opposite of Catholic, as something particular and divisive, ibid., p. 168.

22 ibid., pp. 164, 163.

23 ibid., p. 164.

24 See G. Rowell, *The Vision Glorious*, p. 155, and *Church Times*, 2/11/1900.

25 *WACN*, November 1899, pp. 167–8.

26 ibid., p. 165.

27 *Church of England Messenger*, October 1898, p. 161.

28 *WACN*, November 1899, p. 169.

29 ibid., p. 165.

30 Case referred to by Archdeacon Whitington in *General Synod 1910, Official Report*, Appendix XIII, pp. xxvii–xxviii.

31 *General Synod 1910 Official Report*, p. 9.

32 *WACN*, November 1899, p. 171.

33 See p. 101.

34 ibid., p. 167.

35 ibid., p. 163.

36 *MH*, 13/12/1900, p. 2; and for Riley's response, see *WM*, 22/12/1900, p. 37: 'the change of name will in no way alter our present position with regard to the Church at Home'.
37 *Mitre* and *London Church Review*, quoted in *WACN*, January 1900, p. 11.
38 *WACN*, July 1900, p. 130, refers to discussions in the *Australian Herald* (Unitarian), *Southern Cross* (Presbyterian), *Mitre*, *London Church Review* and the *Irish Ecclesiastical Gazette*.
39 *WACN*, July 1900, p. 130, except for Harmer on p. 141.
40 *Church Times*, 17/8/1900, pp. 161–2.
41 ibid.
42 ibid.
43 *Church Times*, 12/10/1900, p. 403, *WACN*, September 1900, p. 155, quoting *Adelaide Church News*.
44 H. H. Montgomery to Randall Davidson, 5/10/1891, Randall Davidson, Correspondence, Official and Foreign, vol. 33, fo 3.
45 H. H. Montgomery to Randall Davidson, 7/2/1897, ibid., vol. 50, fo 220–1; 14/5/1900, ibid., vol. 519, fo 255; 20/10/1900, ibid., vol. 519, fo 264.
46 The reports of cheering and loud applause are found in *Sydney Morning Herald*, 29/8/1900, p. 5. The text of his address is printed in *General Synod 1900 Official Report*, pp. 4–17. However, unless otherwise stated, material relating to the debate itself is taken from *Church of England Messenger*, 10/9/1900, pp. 136–8. The General Synod Minute Book 1881–1910, pp. 53–4 does not offer any material beyond that found in published sources.
47 *General Synod 1900 Official Report*, p. 15.
48 *Church of England Messenger*, 10/9/1900, p. 136.
49 ibid., p. 137.
50 ibid.
51 *Argus*, 31/8/1900, p. 4.
52 *Church of England Messenger*, 10/9/1900, p. 138; *Argus*, 31/8/1900, p. 4.
53 *Church Times*, 12/10/1900, p. 403.
54 M. Creighton to Canon McCormick, 6/8/1898, quoted in Louise Creighton, *Life and Letters of Mandell Creighton*, ii, p. 302.
55 Quoted in Dom A. Hughes, *The Rivers of the Flood*, p. 36.
56 *WAT*, 17/9/1878, p. 2.
57 *Church of England Messenger*, October 1897, p. 140.
58 *WA*, 16/2/1895, p. 6, for a nonconformist protest by S. Bryant.
59 *WACN*, April 1897, p. 9.
60 H. H. Parry, Synod Charge, in *WM*, 17/11/1888, p.9.
61 *Perth Diocesan Yearbook*, 1888, Appendix J, p. xxxiii f.
62 2/6/1900, USPG, CLR col. 209, fo 303. Although Fisher opened the letter by referring to the Perth synod motion of 1899, and did not refer specifically to Goldsmith's proposed motion at General Synod, the date of the letter and the reference to opposition to the dean's proposal as a thing of the present, make it likely that Fisher's concern continued to be fuelled by the impending General Synod motion.
63 *WACN*, November 1899, p. 166.
64 ibid.
64 ibid., p. 167.

66 *Church of England Messenger*, 10/9/1900, p. 138.
67 *WACN*, November 1899, p. 167.
68 H. H. Montgomery to Randall Davidson, 24/5/1900, Randall Davidson, Correspondence, Official and Foreign, vol. 519, fos 255, 252.
69 *Church of England Messenger*, 10/9/1900, p. 138.
70 *Church Times*, 2/11/1900.
71 See S. Smith on the nexus in *General Synod 1905 Official Report*, p. 11: 'There are bonds of a less rigid sort . . . which knit together the Mother Church in the old land with her growing daughters beyond the seas, bonds which should prevent too hasty a desire for separation . . .'
72 St Clair Donaldson to Randall Davidson, 17/10/1905, Randall Davidson, Correspondence Official and Foreign, vol. 236, fo 14.
73 *WACN*, November 1899, pp. 169–70.
74 Rayner, The History of the Church of England in Queensland, p. 285.
75 *MH*, 13/12/1900, p. 2.
76 *General Synod 1881, Official Report*, pp. 13, 36; see also the Bishop of Tasmania's motion for a code of canon law for the church in Australia in *General Synod 1886, Official Report*, p. 34, and also *General Synod 1900, Official Report*, p. 29; *General Synod 1905, Official Report*, p. 76, *General Synod 1910, Official Report*, Appendix XIII.
77 *WM*, 21/10/1899, p. 8. Riley's comments here are headed 'The Position of the Diocese', the presence of a subheading being an indication in itself that the issue was regarded as significant.
78 J. Davis, Continuity and Change, pp. 70, 77.
79 *General Synod 1910, Official Report*, p. 38.
80 *South-West Herald*, 15/2/1913.
81 *Church of England Messenger*, 12/9/1913, p. 520, *Church of England Messenger, Synod Supplement*, 11/10/1912, pp. 4–5.
82 St Clair Donaldson to Randall Davidson, 17/10/1905, Randall Davidson, Correspondence Official and Foreign, vol. 236, fo 14, J. C. Wright to Randall Davidson, 12/9/1911, quoted in Davis, Continuity and Change, p. 64.
83 Rayner, History of the Church of England in Queensland, pp. 379–80.
84 Davis, Continuity and Change, pp. 71–2.
85 Contemporary quotes in Rayner, History of the Church of England, pp. 317–18.
86 H. H. Montgomery to Randall Davidson, 14/7/1892, Randall Davidson, Correspondence Official and Foreign, vol. 36, fo 283: 'A leader in Sydney Diocese confessed that they were going to make a last fight for the Church Association and its principles. They felt they were being beaten elsewhere. But here was to be their last rally. And this is our chair of St Augustine!'
87 *Church Times*, 30/10/1908, p. 580.


*8: An Episcopal Mendicant*

1 *WM*, 23/7/1904, pp. 13–14.
2 *Church of England Messenger*, p. 63, quoting *WA* and *MH*, and p. 69, quoting *WACN*.
3 *WM*, 23/7/1904, pp. 13–14.
4 ibid., p. 14.

5 ibid., p. 12.
6 ibid., p. 14.
7 Henn Notes, F32.
8 See C. Holden, 'Rural Ritualism and Frederick Goldsmith: Anglo–Catholicism in Western Australia Before the First World War', pp. 75–95.
9 H. Braddock, in *Victorian Churchman*, 25/10/1901, p. 251.
10 C. T. Stannage, *The People of Perth*, pp. 182–90; see also J. Gregory (ed.), *Western Australia Between the Wars 1919–1939*, pp. 9–10. For Forrest's speech, see *Bunbury Herald*, 27/1/1905.
11 Concerning his ambition, see also P. Boyce, 'The First Archbishop', pp. 76–8.
12 R. A. Giles, *The Constitutional History of the Australian Church*, p. 128.
13 *WM*, 21/10/1899, p. 8.
14 C. O. L. Riley, correspondence in Primate's Correspondence re the Establishment of the Province of Western Australia.
15 C. O. L. Riley to H. H. Montgomery, 22/8/1904, USPG CLR vol. 209, fos 340–1.
16 S. Marshall, The Development of the Church of England and the Formation of the Bunbury Diocese, pp. 19–21.
17 R. Hesketh Jones, 2/11/1891, USPG CLR vol. 209, fos 226–8.
18 H. H. Parry, Diary, 13/3/1889 and 19/3/1889, PROWA, MN 134, Acc 1223A/7.
19 H. H. Parry, 11/12/1891, USPG CLR vol. 209, fos 229–31; compare his synod charge, *WM*, 10/9/1892, p. 8, where he referred to the possibility of setting up the northern districts (Gasgoyne, Roebourne, Derby/Wyndham) as an archdeaconry.
20 *WM*, 24/2/1894, p. 2. See also *Perth Diocesan Yearbook*, 1897, p. xxvii.
21 C. O. L. Riley to E. S. Clairs, 1/8/1896, in C. O. L. Riley, Letterbook 1866–1900, PROWA, MN 614, Acc 2467A/178. For Riley's public criticism of the Aboriginals' plight, see Boyce, 'The First Archbishop', pp. 67–8.
22 C. O. L. Riley, 15/10/1904, USPG CLR vol. 209, fos 348–9: 'my chief concern, however, is on behalf of the natives . . . a people to whom we owe some reparation for taking away their country . . .' Gribble, speaking at the 50th anniversary of the ABM, referred to the high aboriginal population of the state, *Church Times*, 12/10/1900, p. 402.
23 Boyce, 'The First Archbishop', p. 67; records are contained in the Minute Book of the Assistant Bishopric Committee, 1900–03, PROWA, MN 614, Acc 2467A/156.
24 J. G. Deed, 28/12/1903, USPG CLR vol. 209, fos 326–8, quoting a telegram from Riley. Concerning the inability of the Missionary Societies to help if an assistant bishop were appointed, see Tucker to Riley, 5/1/1900, USPG CLS vol. 140, fo 196, and Riley's response, stating that a suffragan was not his ultimate aim but only a stage in the process, 3/2/1900, USPG CLR vol. 209, fo 296.
25 C. O. L. Riley to H. H. Montgomery, 1/2/1904, USPG CLR vol. 209, fo 228. On Riley's desire to be rid of the goldfields, see C. O. L. Riley to Saumarez Smith, 28/11/1903, Primate's Correspondence re the Establishment of the Diocese of Bunbury, 1903–07, General Synod Archives. On Riley and his desire to establish a goldfields see, see *WACN*, April 1897, p. 6; C. O. L. Riley to H. Vere White, 17/12/1897, USPG CLR 209, fos 263–6; and for F. Barton-Parkes as archdeacon in preparation for a goldfields see *WM*, 7/5/1897, p. 9, and F. Barton-Parkes, 9/3/1898, USPG CLR vol. 209, fo 272. On the unexpected change in focus, see *Bunbury Herald*, 20/5/1904; C. O. L. Riley to H. H. Montgomery, 30/11/1903, USPG CLR vol. 209, fo 324.

26 C. O. L. Riley to H. H. Montgomery, 3/2/1900, USPG CLR vol. 209, fo 296; also his comment just after Goldsmith's consecration, 22/8/1904, ibid., fo 341—'we are anxious about the future now that a labour ministry is in power'.
27 C. O. L. Riley to Randall Davidson, 30/4/1904, Randall Davidson, Correspondence, Official and Foreign, vol. 90, fo 319 and 20/2/1905, ibid., vol. 100, fo 366; Randall Davidson to C. O. L. Riley, 1/6/1904, ibid., vol. 90, fo 323 and 20/2/1905, ibid., vol. 100, fo 367. *Crockford's Clerical Directory* and issues of *BOP* after 1905 describe him as DD, and *Bunbury Herald*, 26/5/1905, refers to the conferring of the degree; however, some sources quite incorrectly give 1904 and even 1909 as the date of conferring.
28 *WACN*, January 1917, p. 6, refers to him 'in his capacity as dean since 1904'.
29 *WM*, 11/6/1904, p. 42; see also *WM*, 30/6/1904, p. 42, and 2/7/1904, p. 42; F. W. Goldsmith to Newton Moore, *Bunbury Herald*, 27/6/1904.
30 See R. T. Appleyard, 'Western Australia: Economic and Demographic Growth, 1850–1914', pp. 222–4; claims concerning the dimensions of Bunbury trade were made in church journals such as the *Mission Field*, October 1911, p. 309.
31 The only detailed study of Bunbury is A. J. Barker and M. Laurie, *Excellent Connections*. For population statistics at the beginning of the century, see pp. 152, 163; on port development, pp. 142–3; the port and other industries as employers, pp. 155, 170–1, 188–9.
32 F. K. Crowley, *Forrest 1847–1918,* i, p. 22. On Anglican attendances, see Barker and Laurie, *Excellent Connections*, p. 89; *Perth Diocesan Yearbook,* 1889, p. 64, states that 3 eucharists per month were then offered in Bunbury. There were 150 communicants in the town altogether, but 10–13 communicated on average on each occasion.
33 Figures from Marshall, The Development of the Church of England, p. 21.
34 See F. Barton-Parkes to Saumarez Smith, 22/2/1904, and subsequent correspondence between C. O. L. Riley and Saumarez Smith in Primate's Correspondence re the Establishment of the Diocese of Bunbury, 1903–07.
35 *BOP*, December 1904.
36 ibid.
37 F. W. Goldsmith to Randall Davidson, 2/5/1905, Randall Davidson, Correspondence Official and Foreign, vol. 326, fos 1–4.
38 F. W. Goldsmith to H. H. Montgomery, 28/1/1907, USPG CLR vol. 209, fo 401A; also F. W. Goldsmith to H. H. Montgomery, 27/5/1905, ibid., fo 363: 'the work is calling for immediate effort, and if we do not respond, the nonconformists will do what we should be doing'; F. W. Goldsmith to H. H. Montgomery, 6/6/1905, ibid., fo 367, and F. W. Goldsmith to H. H. Montgomery, 28/6/1905, ibid., fo 368.
39 H. Pitts praised Roman Catholic work at Broome—24/9/1900, USPG E, 1900, fo 221; C. O. L. Riley, 15/10/1904, USPG CLR vol. 209, fos 348–9, praised Roman Catholic mission work at Beagle Bay. The same assessment had reached England, and was repeated in the *Church Times*, 28/4/1905, p. 563, and elsewhere.
40 G. Trower to H. H. Montgomery, 20/12/1911, USPG CLR vol. 209, fo 463.
41 *BOP*, December 1904, letter dated 1/10/1904.
42 F. W. Goldsmith to H. H. Montgomery, 23/12/1904, USPG CLR vol. 209, fo 350; see also SPG Standing Committee Minutes, January 1905–February 1906, entry for 2/3/1905: 'read letter fr. B. of By, 23 December 1904, applying for £150 p.a. for "Mission to the Natives in the NW of Aust." '

43 *WACN*, December 1900, p. 220; D. J. Garland, 8/1/1897, USPG CLR vol. 209, fo 261A; the best source of Collick anecdotes in print, collected from Archdeacon L. Bothamley, sometime assistant of Collick's at Fremantle, is found in A. Williams, *West Anglican Way*, pp. 271-91.
44 See G. C. Bolton, 'Black and White after 1897', pp. 129-31.
45 *The Times*, 10/4/1905, p. 9, 9/5/1905, *Parliamentary Debates . . . of the United Kingdoms of Great Britain and Ireland*, vol. CXLV, col. 1299. The whole discussion covers 20 columns.
46 ibid., col. 1307. My italics. C. H.
47 ibid., col. 1319.
48 *Church Times*, 26/5/1905, p. 696, 20/4/1905, p. 517, 28/4/1905, p. 563.
49 *Parliamentary Debates . . . 1905*, col. 1302.
50 W. Sharp, 8/8/1905, USPG E, 1905, Asia and Australia, fo 42.
51 F. W. Goldsmith to H. H. Montgomery, 27/5/1905, USPG CLR vol. 209, fo 363.
52 ibid.
53 *Church Times*, 28/4/1905, p. 563.
54 Randall Davidson to F. W. Goldsmith, 10/6/1905, Randall Davidson, Correspondence Official and Foreign, vol. 236, fo 5.
55 H. H. Montgomery to Saumarez Smith, 12/7/1905, Randall Davidson, Correspondence Official and Foreign, vol. 236, fos 6-8, H. H. Montgomery to F. W. Goldsmith, 7/7/1905, USPG CLS col. 145, fo 30.
56 Montgomery's impressions on his visit are given in *WM*, 32/6/1900, p. 37, C. O. L. Riley to H. H. Montgomery, 6/11/1905, USPG CLR vol. 209, fo 371.
57 *Perth Diocesan Yearbook*, 1905, pp. 26-7.
58 F. W. Goldsmith to H. H. Montgomery, 30/3/1906, CLR vol. 209, fo 387.
59 F. W. Goldsmith to H. H. Montgomery, 10/1/1906, CLR vol. 209, fo 378; 30/3/1906, ibid., fo 387; 14/4/1906, ibid., fo 389; 28/9/1906, ibid., fo 391; 28/1/1907, ibid., fo 402 (pearling mission lugger); 16/8/1907, ibid., fo 410.
60 On Hadley, see M. Durack, *The Rock and the Sand*, pp. 130-1.
61 *BOP*, October 1906.
62 F. W. Goldsmith to H. H. Montgomery, 28/1/1907, USPG CLR vol. 209, fo 402.
63 *BOP*, March 1910.
64 F. W. Goldsmith, 'The Anglican Communion, Australia', p. 251.
65 *BOP*, June 1906.
66 *BOP*, December 1907; concerning the see fund, in F. W. Goldsmith to H. H. Montgomery, 12/10/1907, USPG CLR vol. 209, 411A, he told Montgomery that £2,000 had already been collected, and £3,000 was expected from the Padbury bequest, leaving the need for another £2,000. (The other £3,000 of the £10,000 would be contributed by English societies).
67 H. H. Montgomery to F. W. Goldsmith, 29/10/1907, USPG, CLS vol. 145, fo 51A. See also F. W. Goldsmith to H. H. Montgomery, CLR vol. 209, fo 411A.
68 *Church Times*, 2/10/1908, pp. 404-5; 9/10/1908, p. 466.
69 *BOP*, May 1907.
70 *BOP*, October 1906.
71 J. W. S. Tomlin, *Halford's Challenge*, p. 25; on the cathedral, see J. Morris, *Pax Britannica*, pp. 502-3.
72 W. Piercy to H. H. Montgomery, 19/6/1911, USPG CLR vol. 209, fo 458.
73 H. Pitts, 24/6/1901, USPG E 1901, fo 834 on the British community; H. Pitts,

29/9/1900, USPG E 1900, fo 221 and 25/12/1900 (same folio) on the Asian community.
74 *Church Congress Proceedings,* Perth 1909, pp. 86–8.
75 G. Trower to H. H. Montgomery, 3/5/1910, USPG CLR vol. 209, fo 443, G. Trower to H. H. Montgomery, 20/12/1911, ibid., fo 463.
76 *BOP*, April 1908.
77 *BOP*, March 1910.
78 *Bunbury Diocesan Yearbook,* 1905, p. 39. The foundation was laid on 25/1/1905 and the bishop and his wife moved in to the house on 30/8/1905.
79 *BOP*, August 1905.
80 *Bunbury Diocesan Yearbook,* 1905, p. 3.
81 *BOP*, March 1906.
82 *BOP*, June 1906.
83 ibid.
84 *Bunbury Herald*, 24/9/1906, p. 3.
85 Appleyard, 'Western Australia: Economic and Demographic Growth, 1850–1914', pp. 220–1, 227.
86 *BOP*, May 1907.
87 F. W. Goldsmith to H. H. Montgomery, 28/1/1907, USPG CLR vol. 209, fo 401A; 2/3/1907, ibid., fo 406; 16/8/1907, ibid., fo 410.
88 F. W. Goldsmith to H. H. Montgomery, 2/3/1907, USPG CLR vol. 209, fo 406; 13/4/1907, ibid., fo 408; 18/7/1907, ibid., fo 409; and 16/8/1907, ibid., fo 410.
89 All preceding material is found in *BOP*, December 1907.
90 *BOP*, September 1907.
91 *BOP*, December 1907, from an unidentified *WA* country paper.
92 *BOP*, April 1908.
93 *BOP*, November 1908.
94 F. W. Goldsmith to H. H. Montgomery, 22/3/1909, USPG CLR vol. 209, fo 430.
95 *BOP*, November 1908, May 1909.
96 *BOP*, September 1909. Concerning the early history of the state school, see Barker and Laurie, *Excellent Connections*, pp. 132, 155.
97 *BOP*, March 1910.
98 T. M. Robinson, 'The Revival of Community Life', in *Church Congress Proceedings,* Perth 1909, pp. 61–6; *BOP*, May 1909.
99 *Church Congress Proceedings,* Perth, 1909, pp. 86–8.
100 *BOP*, September 1909.
101 *Victorian Churchman*, 8/4/1909, 10/9/1909.
102 *BOP*, June 1914, March 1910, February 1912.

## 9: From 'A Nation in the Mill'

1 *BOP*, March 1910.
2 W. S. Hales to Archdeacon Louch, with cover note from F. W. Goldsmith, 22/3/1912, USPG CLR vol. 209, fo 467.
3 *BOP*, June 1910.
4 *BOP,* December 1910; F. W. Goldsmith to H. H. Montgomery, 6/6/1910, USPG CLR vol. 209, fo 446; 26/5/1908, ibid., fo 422; undated letter of 1910, ibid., fo 440.
5 *BOP,* December 1910.

⁶ *BOP*, November 1911; he had confirmed 66 males and 108 females.

⁷
|  | 1905 | 1910 |
| --- | --- | --- |
| Clergy | 13 | 24 |
| Local giving to stipends | £2166 | £3472 |
| Home mission giving | £25 | £275 |
| Churches | 21 | 35 |
| Halls | 5 | 10 |
| Parsonages | 10 | 17 |

*BOP*, December 1910

⁸ See comments on Adams and the changing atmosphere of the pro-cathedral in *BOP*, March 1911.

⁹ *BOP*, March, June 1911.

¹⁰ *Southern Times*, 20/7/1911; *BOP*, February 1912.

¹¹ *BOP*, November 1911.

¹² *BOP*, June 1911. An account of the strike is given in A. J. Barker and M. Laurie, *Excellent Connections*, p. 189.

¹³ *BOP*, June 1911.

¹⁴ *BOP*, June 1911, November 1911; F. W. Goldsmith to H. H. Montgomery, letter attached to Annual Grants application, 25/3/1911, USPG CLR vol. 209, fo 455A, points out that 'the migrant intake in Australia exceeds that of Canada and the USA. The settlers have no resources'. Compare F. W. Goldsmith to H. H. Montgomery, 23/7/1910, ibid., fo 447.

¹⁵ BOP, November 1911, March 1913. A photograph of the schoolchildren from the Harcourt period is reproduced in Barker and Laurie, *Excellent Connections*, p. 209.

¹⁶ *BOP*, March 1911.

¹⁷ *BOP*, June 1911. Concerning the Bunbury lumpers, see Barker and Laurie, *Excellent Connections*, pp. 171–3.

¹⁸ *BOP*, March 1911.

¹⁹ *BOP*, February, November 1912.

²⁰ *BOP*, February 1913, reprint from *South Western Herald*, 30/11/1912. The figures are my own, based on appointments in his itinerary, *BOP*, November 1912—but in his synod charge of 1913, printed in *BOP*, January 1914, he referred to visiting 160 parishes.

²¹ *BOP*, November 1912 states six, but January 1913 reprinted an interview with Goldsmith from the *Southern Times*, 28/11/1912, giving seven, and naming them.

²² *Southern Times*, 28/11/1912, quoted in *BOP*, January 1913.

²³ *South Western Herald*, 30/11/1912, quoted in *BOP*, January 1913.

²⁴ J. Gabbedy, *Group Settlement*, i, pp. 24–5; for Moore as mayor of Bunbury during Goldsmith's episcopate, see Barker and Laurie, *Excellent Connections*, pp. 163, 176–8.

²⁵
|  | 1910 | 1912 |
| --- | --- | --- |
| Baptisms | 518 | 776 |
| Confirmations | 186 | 226 |
| Communions | 8694 | 11525 |
| Average attendance at Holy Communion on Sunday throughout the diocese | 737 | 1112 |

*Church Standard,* 17/1/1913 and *BOP*, March 1913.

26 *BOP*, January 1914.
27 *BOP*, January 1914; lengthy article in *BOP*, June 1914.
28 1913 synod charge in *BOP*, January 1914; appeal for the Grammar School in *BOP*, June 1914.
29 F. W. Goldsmith to H. H. Montgomery with March report, USPG CLR vol. 209, fo 477, *BOP*, November 1913.
30 *BOP*, October 1914.
31 ibid.
32 *BOP*, October 1914, F. W. Goldsmith to H. H. Montgomery, 10/3/1915, USPG CLR 211, WA Letters Received, vol. 1.
33 See Primate's Correspondence re the Establishment of the Province of Western Australia, 1914, Riley to Atkins, 17/3/1914, 30/6/1914, 11/7/1914, telegram 23/7/1914.
34 *Bunbury Diocesan Yearbook*, 1915, p. 12.
35 *BOP*, February 1915.
36 Death Certificate of F. W. Goldsmith; H. S. Goldsmith, entry in *Who's Who*, 1920.
37 *BOP*, September 1915. The inadequacy of the pro-cathedral had become apparent before this. Figures in PROWA, MN 614, Acc 3527A/22 for 1909 and 1910 give attendance figures above 160 for some services, including synod Sunday 1910, and when H. S. Woollcombe spoke, 500 gathered in the Bedford Hall.
38 *Bunbury Diocesan Yearbook*, 1915, p. 15.
39 On the mission, see *Bunbury Herald*, 17/4/1915, p. 8, 20/4/1915, p. 1; *Southern Times*, 27/3/1915, 17/4/1915, and especially on the Catholic atmosphere, *Southern Times*, 8/5/1915; see also *BOP*, June 1915.
40 *BOP*, June 1916.
41 F. W. Goldsmith to H H. Montgomery, 16/6/1916, USPG CLR vol. 211, WA Letters, fo 21a.
42 See S. Welborn, *Lords of Death*, pp. 53, 58.
43 *Bunbury Diocesan Yearbook*, 1916, p. 11.
44 Henn Notes, F38.
45 Henn Notes, F39.
46 Cathedral Council Meeting, 27/5/1915, PROWA, MN 614, acc 3527A/25, p. 157; *Southern Times*, 27/3/1915.
47 See PROWA, MN 614, Acc 3527A/18, George E Farrar (architect), Report to Cathedral Building Fund Executive Committee; and site diagrams, PROWA, MN 614, Acc 3527A/7-17, from which the figures quoted are drawn.
48 Interview with Mrs Jenour, née Clarke, daughter of George Clarke. For W. Balston, see PROWA, MN 614, Acc 3527A/25, where the opening pages of Annual Reports of the Council of St Paul's Cathedral, listing office bearers, gives him as warden elected by synod 1911-15.
49 For Hands, see Barker and Laurie, *Excellent Connections*, pp. 240-1, 252-4.
50 Etta Morris was the widow of a former Diocesan Secretary, whom Henn consulted in his researches—Henn Notes, F37; see also H. Adams to E. Rose, PROWA, MN 614, Acc 3527A/17.
51 Interview with Mrs Jenour; for details concerning her father, see Barker, *Excellent Connections*, pp. 177, 196, 198-9, 209, 212, 227-8, 231-2, 254-7. C. L. M. Hawtrey, *The Availing Struggle*, pp. 134-42, describes Goldsmith's failure to build as 'a great disappointment'; she seems to have drawn on the living memories of his intimates.

52 Mrs E. Morris, Henn Notes, F38–9.
53 *Bunbury Cathedral Gazette,* January 1917; *BOP*, February 1917.
54 Henn Notes, F36; *WACN*, August 1932, p. 11.
55 F. W. Goldsmith, 'The Anglican Communion, Australia', p. 260.
56 F. W. Goldsmith to H. H. Montgomery, 16/6/1916, USPG CLR vol. 211, WA Letters Received, 1, fo 26.
57 *Hampstead Parish Church Magazine,* December 1916.
58 Brotherhood of St Boniface, Diary, 29/12/1916–2/1/1917, PROWA, MN 614, Acc 3528A/2 and 3.
59 ibid., 5–6/2/1917, 8–9/2/1917.
60 *WACN,* March 1917, pp. 4–6, August 1932, p. 11.
61 *Bunbury Cathedral Gazette,* Lent 1917.
62 Brotherhood of St Boniface Diary, 9/5/1917, PROWA, MN 614, Acc 3528A/3.
63 Hawtrey, *The Availing Struggle,* p. 135.
64 *Southern Times,* 31/10/1895, p. 3; 9/11/1895, p. 3; 11/4/1896, p. 3; 6/5/1897, p. 3.
65 On the apparent alienation of Bunbury Anglicans, see correspondence in *Southern Times,* 12/11/1895; the good will of parishioners in the outcentres is clear from a description of Marshall's farewell at Ferguson, ibid., 24/7/1897, p. 3; on the offertories, see ibid., 11/4/1896, p. 3, 21/4/1896, p. 3, 5/5/1896, p. 3.
66 Barker and Laurie, *Excellent Connections,* p. 113, describe Hayward as belonging to the generation who were 'adult pioneers in the 1840s and 1850s'. Timperley had been a policeman in Bunbury in the 1860s—ibid., p. 99.
67 See pp. 107–11.
68 'A Churchman', *Southern Times,* 16/5/1896, p. 3, and Hayward's correspondence in *Southern Times,* 19/5/1896, p. 3.
69 At Darling's institution the altar was dressed with cross and lights—*WACN,* August 1898, p. 91. Since Adams restored them, Darling had obviously removed them in the meantime.
70 *WA,* 6/9/1898, p. 6.
71 *Bunbury Diocesan Yearbook,* 1910, p. 13.
72 *Bunbury Diocesan Yearbook,* 1907, p. 33. Goldsmith's terminology in this area seems to have influenced the usages of the Bunbury press in a short space of time: *Bunbury Herald,* 20/7/1904 using perfectly correct Prayer Book terminology, referred to Riley as standing at 'the Holy Table' at Goldsmith's consecration, but by 25/5/1906 used the interesting compromise of 'altar table'.
73 F. C. Mather, 'Georgian Churchmanship Reconsidered', pp. 258–9.
74 Church Association, *Ritualistic Clergy List.*
75 *BOP,* March 1910.
76 *BOP,* March 1911: 'All the authorities without exception are agreed that when a bishop possess a cope he must use it . . .'
77 Notice of the reintroduction of lights in the pro-cathedral is found in *BOP,* March 1913, reproducing *Church Standard,* 17/1/1913; for the daily eucharist at both the pro-cathedral and the House of Grace, see *BOP,* January 1914.
78 *Bunbury Herald,* 14/12/1912, p. 2.
79 *BOP,* June 1914. Merbecke was in use in the cathedral on diocesan occasions at least as early as 1909—see *BOP,* March 1910, which refers to the diocesan clergy forming a choir, accompanied on the 'organ' (harmonium) by the bishop.

⁸⁰ F. W. Goldsmith to H. H. Montgomery, 16/6/1916, USPG CLR 211, WA Letters Received vol. 1, fo 22.
⁸¹ Minutes of St Paul's pro-cathedral Council, 27/5/1915, PROWA, MN 614, Acc 3527A/25, p. 160; descriptions of the processions in *Bunbury Herald*, 17/4/1915, p. 8; 20/4/1915, p. 1; *Southern Times*, 17/4/1915,8/5/1915, but all subsequent details concerning the mission are from *BOP,* September 1915.
⁸² *Church Standard,* quoted in *BOP*, September 1915.
⁸³ W. Sharp, Report for quarter ending 25/1/1900, dated 2/5/1900, USPG E, 1900, fo 222.
⁸⁴ W. Sharp, Report for quarter ending 24/6/1901, USPG E, 1900, fo 854.
⁸⁵ Frewer Journals, ix, correspondence dated 10/10/1916. See other examples in N. Yates, *Buildings, Faith and Worship*, p. 148. See H. Davies, *Worship and Theology in England, The Ecumenical Century 1900–1965*, pp. 319–23.
⁸⁶ Henn Notes, F30, cites as sources for this, issues of the *BOP* for 1916 and 1917, copies of which I have as yet been unable to locate.
⁸⁷ See *WACN*, December 1897, p. 3.
⁸⁸ In 1922 he conducted a mission at Holy Trinity Launceston, and *Ecclesia*, the parish magazine of St Peter's Eastern Hill, commented that 'Protestant opposition to the teaching and practice of Confession and Absolution—the most vital part of a Mission—was so virulent that at times the old riots at St George's, in the city of London, seem to have come to light again'. The Reverend Anthony Bolt, who was living in Albany during White's incumbency there, remembers being shown vestments which White had been wearing when he was pelted with vegetables by irate protesters.
⁸⁹ *BOP*, February 1915.
⁹⁰ ibid.
⁹¹ Unsourced cutting in 'Volume of Newspaper Cuttings and Photographs Concerning the Bush Brotherhood, Collected by Bishop Frewer's Father in England', PROWA, MN 614, Acc 3528A/14. The occasion was Bishop Wilson's first visit to the House of Grace, and according to the cutting, there were 65 visitors present.
⁹² *Hampstead Parish Church Magazine*, December 1916; *WACN*, 1/2/1917, p. 3.
⁹³ For the expression 'returned empties', see an obituary on Goldsmith by 'J. O. S.' in G. E. Frewer, Journal, xi; also D. Hilliard, *God's Gentlemen*, pp. 125–6, on the reception of English clergy after missionary service.
⁹⁴ Obituary by 'J. O. S.', G. E. Frewer, Journal, xi.
⁹⁵ *Hampstead Parish Church Magazine*, September 1917, February 1918, February 1919.
⁹⁶ ibid., October 1917, November 1918, November 1919.
⁹⁷ *The Cultus of Our Lady, by an Old Priest*, St Thomas' Church Tracts, St Thomas, Hove, copy pasted into G. E. Frewer, Journal, x.
⁹⁸ *Hampstead Parish Church Magazine*, October 1917, July, August 1920.
⁹⁹ ibid., January 1920.
¹⁰⁰ *WACN*, January 1925, p. 21, October 1926, p. 16.
¹⁰¹ ibid., September 1932, p. 9.
¹⁰² *Hampstead Parish Church Magazine*, May 1921.
¹⁰³ Bishop Perrin, letter of 12/7/1932 in G. E. Frewer, Journal, xi. A statement to the same effect by Perrin was also quoted by P. Maryon-Wilson.

104 *Hampstead Parish Church Magazine*, October 1918.
105 *St John's Monthly Review*, April 1926.
106 M. Blatch, *A Guide to London's Churches*, p. 209.
107 *BOP*, June 1914.
108 *English Church Union Directory*, 1928, gives his address as 59 Kempshott Road, Streatham Common, SW16; the Maida Vale move and its purpose is given by E. W. Crane, *WACN*, September 1932, p. 9; *WACN*, April 1930, p. 5, gives their address as 27 Elgin Mansions, Elgin Ave, London, W9.
109 *WACN*, September 1932, p. 9.
110 F. W. Goldsmith, 'The Anglican Communion, Australia', p. 260.
111 *Magazine of the Province of North West Australia*, October 1932, cutting in G. E. Frewer, Journal, xi.
112 *WACN*, July 1926, p. 17.
113 Copy of leaflet for February–June 1927, author's collection.
114 P. Maryon-Wilson, obituary from St Mary's Somerstown parish magazine, undated cutting in G. E. Frewer, Journal, xi; on Percy Maryon-Wilson's professional career after Goldsmith's death, see B. Funnell, *Christ Church St Leonard's-on-Sea*, pp. 26–33.
115 E. W. Crane, in *WACN*, September 1932, p. 9.
116 P. Maryon-Wilson, obituary, in G. E. Frewer, Journal, xi.
117 *Diocese of North West Australia Magazine*, July 1932, in G. E. Frewer, Journal, xi, gives 24 Hyde Gardens, Eastbourne, as his address; see also Brede Parish Magazine, August 1932, also in G. E. Frewer, Journal, xi.
118 E. W. Crane, *WACN*, September 1932, p. 9.
119 P. Maryon-Wilson, obituary, in G. E. Frewer, Journal, xi.
120 J. Morris, *Pax Britannica*, p. 244; *Farewell the Trumpets,* pp. 308–11.
121 F. W. Goldsmith, 'The Anglican Communion, Australia', p. 251.

*10: Doctrine and Devotion*

1 *BOP*, June 1914.
2 Readers interested in a detailed treatment of this aspect should consult chapter 10 Neither Men nor Money in C. Holden, Ritualist on a Tricycle, pp. 367–410.
3 *WA*, 8/6/1893, p. 3.
4 *WA*, 7/6/1893, p. 4.
5 ibid.
6 See p. 217.
7 *Bunbury Diocesan Yearbook,* 1907, p. 33.
8 *BOP*, January 1914.
9 *BOP*, June 1914.
10 Foreword to G. E. Frewer, *Weekday Walking Sticks*.
11 *BOP*, November 1912.
12 Synod Charge, 1913, *BOP*, January 1914.
13 See James Bentley, *Ritualism and Politics in Victorian Britain*, pp. 124–5.
14 *Bunbury Diocesan Yearbook*, 1907, p. 25.
15 *Bunbury Diocesan Yearbook,* 1906, p. 21; *BOP,* December 1910, November 1911; *Bunbury Diocesan Yearbook,* 1907, pp. 15–16.
16 *BOP*, December 1911.

[17] *Bunbury Herald*, 3/12/1912.
[18] *Oxford Magazine*, November 1883, March 1884, quoted in K. S. Inglis, *The Church and the Working Classes*, p. 148.
[19] C. Holden, 'Awful Happenings on the Hill', pp. 42–3.
[20] G. E. Frewer, Journal, vi, copy of *Brede Parish Magazine*, May 1904; on Hopkins and his community, see P. Anson, *The Call of the Cloister*, pp. 106–22.
[21] On Weston, see G. Rowell, *The Vision Glorious*, pp. 180–7.
[22] F. W. Goldsmith, sermon, Perth synod, 1888, *Perth Diocesan Yearbook*, 1888, Appendix J, p. xxxvii.
[23] *General Synod 1910, Official Report*, p. 38.
[24] Synod Charge, 1910, *BOP*, December 1910.
[25] Synod Charge, 1911, *BOP*, November 1911.
[26] 'The Church and the Churches', *Church Times*, 17/8/1900, pp. 161–2.
[27] D. Micklem, *Principles of Church Organization*, pp. 127, 141–2.
[28] See *Bunbury Diocesan Yearbook*, 1914, pp. 42–3.
[29] *WM*, 23/7/1904, pp. 12–13.
[30] *Bunbury Herald*, 15/12/1905, 20/12/1905, 3/1/1906, 19/1/1906, 22/1/1906.
[31] See 'Tocsin', *WA*, 30/9/1899, p. 7, who claimed that the Church of England laid no claim to having Apostolic Succession, and that consequently the discussion of the doctrine was a waste of time; Langham Burdett, *WA*, 22/12/1900, p. 3, described the doctrine as 'unscriptural'.
[32] F. W. Goldsmith, sermon, Perth synod, 1888, *Perth Diocesan Yearbook*, 1888, Appendix J, p. xxxviii.
[33] *Bunbury Diocesan Yearbook*, 1906, p. 17.
[34] F. W. Goldsmith, sermon, Perth synod, 1888, *Perth Diocesan Yearbook*, 1888, Appendix J, p. xxxviii.
[35] ibid., p. xxxv.
[36] *Bunbury Diocesan Yearbook*, 1906, p. 17.
[37] ibid., pp. 17–18.
[38] *Bunbury Diocesan Yearbook*, 1915, pp. 17–18.
[39] F. W. Goldsmith, 'The Anglican Communion, Australia', p. 251.
[40] *Defender*, April 1925, p. 11ff.
[41] F. W. Goldsmith, sermon, Perth synod, 1888, *Perth Diocesan Yearbook*, 1888, Appendix J, p. xxxvii.
[42] G. J. Cuming, *A History of Anglican Liturgy*, pp. 166–7.
[43] *WM*, 17/11/1888, p. 8.
[44] *BOP*, February 1915.
[45] *Bunbury Diocesan Yearbook*, 1911, p. 12.
[46] Randall Davidson, Correspondonce, Official and Foreign, vol. 236, fo 180, and P. Boyce, 'The First Archbishop', p. 94.
[47] Cuming, *A History of the Anglican Liturgy*, pp. 135, 148, 154–6, 160.
[48] See Presidential Address, General Synod 1905, Official Report, pp. 10–11, also p. 46 ff.
[49] *Bulletin*, 19/10/1905, pp. 16–17, 16/11/1905, p. 16.
[50] St Clair Donaldson to Randall Davidson, 17/10/1905, Randall Davidson, Correspondence, Official and Foreign, vol. 236, fo 14.
[51] Smith intended in 1904 to confer with Davidson concerning the Athanasian Creed early in 1905 when he was in England: see S. Smith to Randall Davidson,

10/11/1904, Randall Davidson, Correspondence Official and Foreign, vol. 121, fos 251-2; on the possible legal ramifications, see vol. 236, fo 35.
52 Lambeth Conference Papers, vol. 66, fos 178 and 207 for the speeches of Chester and Bombay respectively. ibid., fo 202, Edinburgh, and fo 225, Ely.
53 ibid., fos 178, 220.
54 ibid., fos 215-19.
55 ibid., fo 219.
56 ibid., fos 228-32.
57 Minutebook of Committee 8, Prayerbook Adaptation and Enrichment, Subcommittee no 3 on the *Quicunque Vult*, p. 8.
58 Minutebook of Subcommittee, p. 10, and Lambeth Conference Papers C 61: Debate 31/7/1908 Proceedings of the Fifth Lambeth Conference, 1908, Report of Subcommittee—discussion in fos 76-144.
59 C. O. L. Riley, *Church Congress Proceedings*, Perth, 1909, pp. 9-10. See also his Perth Synod Charge, *Perth Diocesan Yearbook*, 1905, pp. 21-3.
60 W. S. F. Pickering, 'Anglo-Catholicism: Some Sociological Observations', p. 159.
61 *BOP*, January 1914.
62 *WA*, 11/3/1893, p. 4.
63 *WA*, 13/3/1893, p. 3.
64 On comments from the churches on proposals in New South Wales see S. Judd and K. Cable, *Sydney Anglicans*, p. 147.
65 *WA*, 26/5/1890, p. 4.
66 *WA*, 17/10/1890, p. 2.
67 ibid.
68 *WA*, 20/10/1890, p. 4.
69 *BOP*, December 1910.
70 *Bunbury Herald*, 3/12/1912.
71 See chapter 10, Neither Men nor Money, in C. Holden, Ritualist on a Tricycle, pp. 367-410.
72 H. Pitts, 24/6/1901, USPG E, 1901, fo 831.
73 R. H. Moore to H. H. Montgomery, 13/5/1905, USPG CLR vol. 209, fo 360.
74 F. W. Goldsmith to Randall Davidson, 2/6/1905, Randall Davidson, Correspondence, Official and Foreign, vol. 236, fo 2.
75 *BOP*, October 1906.
76 F. W. Goldsmith, 'The Anglican Communion, Australia', pp. 256, 260.
77 *BOP*, December 1910.
78 C. O. L. Riley to H. H. Montgomery, 25/1/1908, USPG CLR vol. 209, fo 417.
79 C. O. L. Riley to H. H. Montgomery, 1/2/1904, USPG CLR vol. 209, fo 228.
80 C. O. L. Riley to H. H. Montgomery, 1/9/1913, USPG CLR vol. 209, fo 484.
81 See C. O. L. Riley to R. Atkins, 30/6/1914, arguing that he was not obliged to have a constitution before creating a province; C. O. L. Riley to R. Atkins, same date, refusing to tolerate any further delays in the absence in England of the bishops of Kalgoorlie and the North-West; C. O. L. Riley to R. Atkins, 11/7/1914, fearing delay as the Primate goes to England—all correspondence in Primate's Correspondence *re* the Establishment of the Province of Western Australia, 1914.
82 Boyce, 'The First Archbishop', pp. 77, 85.
83 *Bunbury Diocesan Yearbook*, 1906, p. 17.
84 *Church Times*, 30/10/1908, p. 580.

85 Compare the comment by J. Davis, Continuity and Change, p. 30, that of all the churches in Australia last century, the Anglican church was the least successful in 'evolving an organization and outlook appropriate to the realities of her situation'.

## 11: Bunbury Diocese as an Anglo-Catholic Cause

1 See *Church Standard*, 30/5/1913, p. 13, 6/6/1913, p. 16, 5/12/1913, p. 5.
2 *Victorian Churchman*, 27/9/1907, p. 399.
3 *PQM*, July 1894, pp. 298, 303.
4 *Southern Times*, 6/7/1907, reprinted in *BOP*, September 1907. The description of All Saints Donnybrook, is taken from *Southern Times*, 6/7/1907.
5 *BOP*, September 1907, March 1913.
6 *BOP*, November 1912.
7 *BOP*, March 1910.
8 *BOP*, January 1913.
9 *BOP*, June 1915.
10 *BOP*, March 1913.
11 After World War I he ceased to treat All Saints Margaret Street, as the centre of his diocese's English support group as a result of the introduction of Benediction: James Norman, *John Oliver North Queensland*, p. 87.
12 *BOP*, June 1913.
13 *BOP*, January 1914, February 1915.
14 *BOP*, June 1914.
15 ibid.
16 ibid.
17 *BOP*, February 1915.
18 See especially *BOP*, June 1913.
19 *BOP*, June 1915.
20 See A. Wilkinson, *The Church of England and the First World War*, pp. 177-8.
21 See pp. 141-51.
22 *BOP*, October 1914.
23 See *WACN*, August 1922, p. 9, April 1923, p. 25; compare *Church Standard*, 17/6/1921, p. 3.
24 See articles on the Sisters of St Elizabeth of Hungary in *WACN*, July 1928, p. 14, December 1928, p. 16.
25 See for examples C. O. L. Riley, Diary, 26/2/1899, PROWA, MN 369, Acc 1921A/10; C. O. L. Riley to Saumarez Smith, 22/3/1904, Primate's Correspondence re the Establishment of the Diocese of Bunbury 1903-07, General Synod Archives; C. O. L. Riley to H. Darling, quoted in P. Boyce, 'The First Archbishop', p. 58.
26 Cutting in 'Volume of Newspaper Cuttings and Photographs Concerning the Bush Brotherhood, Collected by Bishop Frewer's Father in England', PROWA, MN 614, Acc 3258A/14.
27 Photograph of the consecration of All Saints Collie, 3/11/1915, in 'Volume of Cuttings and Photographs . . .'; circumstances described in interview with the Revd E. Doncaster, Bishop Frewer's executor.
28 Association of Prayer for the Church in Australia, Pamphlet, February–June 1927, copy in the author's collection.

29 Specimen in G. E. Frewer, Journal, iii: the dean of Perth 'desires opportunities of pleading the cause of the Diocese of Perth in England parishes, by Preaching, Lecturing, or Addressing Meetings in School Rooms, Gardens or Drawing Rooms. The Revd. G. E. Frewer, Brede Rectory, Sussex, Will be glad to hear from Clergy or laity in the Diocese of Chichester, who may be willing to receive the Dean, and assist his work as suggested above. February 1891.'
30 G. E. Frewer's preachments in these centres are scattered throughout his Journals, i–vi.
31 Obituary of Mrs Low in G. E. Frewer, Journals, viii.
32 St Jude's Bradford Parish Magazine, September 1912.
33 On the churchmanship of the Leeds churches, see particularly N. Yates, *Leeds and the Oxford Movement.*
34 See particularly Nigel Yates, 'Bells and Smells: London, Brighton and South-Coast Religion Reconsidered', pp. 122–53.
35 P. Anson, *The Call of the Cloister,* pp. 318–19.
36 *BOP,* March 1911.
37 On W. H. Mathew, see P. Anson, *Bishops at Large,* pp. 156–215, and R. P. Brandreth, *Episcopi Vagantes and the Anglican Communion,* pp. 16–20.
38 Brandreth, ibid., p. xi.
39 ibid., p. 27.
40 Anson, *Bishops at Large,* pp. 89, 214, n. 2.
41 See G. I. T. Machin, *Politics and the Churches in Great Britain 1869–1921,* pp. 242–8.
42 *Parish Magazine,* July 1908.
43 Church Association, <u>*The Ritualistic Clergy List.*</u>
44 Unsourced cutting, author's collection, by courtesy of Canon R. T. Warburton, Mansfield Vicarage, Notts.
45 *BOP,* June 1914.
46 Association of Prayer for the Church in Australia, Pamphlet, February–June 1927.
47 F. W. Goldsmith to Mother Emily, 8/5/1890, Archives, Community of the Sisters of the Church, Ham Common.
48 G. E. Frewer, Journal, viii.
49 Cutting, undated, from *Church Union Gazette,* in G. E. Frewer, Journal, viii.
50 *BOP,* June 1914.
51 F. W. Goldsmith, letter dated 28/12/1912, in *BOP,* November 1912.
52 Compare Synod Charge extracts in *BOP,* January 1914, with *BOP,* March 1913.
53 Newpaper cutting, unsourced and undated, describing the consecration of All Saints, in 'Volume of Newspaper Cuttings and Photographs . . .' PROWA, MN 614, Acc 3528A/14.
54 On returning from England, Goldsmith spoke of the donor having 'heard' of the need, which might suggest that she was part of a congregation to which he preached (*South Western Herald,* 30/11/1912, quoted in *BOP,* January 1913); but elsewhere he referred to the offer only in terms of a correspondence, and nowhere does he suggest that a direct meeting ever occurred (*BOP,* November 1912).
55 *BOP,* January 1914.
56 J. Norman, *John Oliver North Queensland,* p. 91; but Norman is quite incorrect when he states on p. 86 that Herbert Wills was a nonconformist.

57 *BOP*, October 1914.
58 Dom Placid Lawson, 'Benedictines at Brunswick', p. 46.
59 *BOP*, September 1915.
60 Percy Dearmer, *The Parson's Handbook*, pp. 87–92, 216–21.
61 *BOP*, February 1915.


## 12: Bringing Monasticism to the Bush

1 *Church Times*, 6/11/1908, p. 615: Dawes recalled meetings at which the brotherhood idea was proposed: 'Canon Body had explained that the attempt was of a tentative kind, but ventured to say that if it succeeded it would be reproduced in every colonial diocese. Thank God it has succeeded, and many another diocese followed their example'.

2 USPG Committee Minutes, 1905, p. 112, refers to the Tokyo Brotherhood, whose members did not make permanent vows, but undertook to work for a five-year period under discipline; for the Cawnpore Brotherhood, see USPG Committee Minutes, p. 730, and for the Trichinopoly Brotherhood, p. 122.

3 F. W. Goldsmith, 'Church Organization', in *Church Congress Papers*, Sydney, 1889, pp. 181, 182.

4 *WM*, 21/10/1893, p. 10.

5 See *Perth Diocesan Yearbook*, 1884, pp. 8–9, 1889, p. 12.

6 C. O. L. Riley to H. Vere White, 17/12/1897, USPG CLR vol. 209, fos 263–4; C. O. L. Riley to Canon Tucker, 4/2/1898, USPG CLS 140, fo 178; H. Vere White to Canon Tucker, 10/6/1898, USPG CLR vol. 209, fos 278–9; see also *WACN*, April 1899, p. 49, which refers to five Irish clergy coming to the West, and to H. Vere White.

7 K. Rayner, The History of the Church of England in Queensland, pp. 213–14.

8 *Church Commonwealth*, 30/12/1911, p. 12.

9 On the Brotherhood of St Aidan, see R. A. F. Webb, *Brothers in the Sun*, pp. 91–2, and for the Brotherhood of St Stephen, pp. 125–33.

10 G. Trower to H. H. Montgomery, 12/9/1911, USPG CLR vol. 209, fo 461; C. O. L. Riley to Randall Davidson, 1/9/1922, Randall Davidson, Correspondence Official and Foreign, vol. 236, fo 216; *WACN*, February 1923; C. L. M. Hawtrey, *The Availing Struggle*, p. 187.

11 Webb, *Brothers in the Sun*, p. 14.

12 K. S. Inglis, *The Churches and the Working Classes . . . ,*' pp. 156–7.

13 Dawes, addressing the English Rockhampton Auxiliary, quoted in Webb, *Brothers in the Sun*, p. 45.

14 C. Matthews, quoted in Webb, *Brothers in the Sun*, p. 74.

15 Webb, ibid., p. 73.

16 ibid., pp. 41, 77.

17 Bishop Frodsham, quoted in ibid., p. 75.

18 T. S. Groser, *The Lure of the Golden West*, p. 198.

19 'The Bush Brotherhood of St Boniface: Inauguration at Williams', *BOP*, November 1911.

20 *Southern Times*, 15/7/1911.

21 E. W. Elsey, BSB, 'The Brotherhood of St Boniface—its Work, Methods and

Needs', in 'Volume of Newspaper Cuttings and Photographs . . .' (referred to hereafter as Brotherhood Scrapbook), PROWA, MN 614, Acc 3528A/14.

[22] *WM*, 24/3/1895, pp. 24–5.

[23] *WM*, 23/3/1895, p. 23.

[24] W. Burbidge, 'The Church in the South West', p. 123.

[25] F. W. Goldsmith to H. H. Montgomery, 28/1/1907, USPG CLR vol. 209, fo 402.

[26] *BOP*, May 1909.

[27] T. M. Robinson, 'The Revival of Community Life', *Church Congress Proceedings*, Perth, 1909, pp. 61–6.

[28] F. W. Goldsmith, Synod Charge, 1911, in *BOP*, November 1911.

[29] 'The Bush Brotherhood of St Boniface—Inauguration at Williams', *BOP*, November 1911; Henry J. Adams, 'A New Bush Brotherhood', in *The Mission Field*, October 1911, p. 310; H. G. Cowin, *The Williams*, p. 123.

[30] F. W. Goldsmith, Synod Charge, 1913, in *BOP*, January 1914.

[31] *Church Standard*, 28/11/1913, p. 14.

[32] *Constitution and Rule of the Brotherhood*, Perth, 1913, in Brotherhood Scrapbook; T. Groser, *The Lure of the Golden West*, pp. 68–9.

[33] *Church Standard*, 28/11/1913, p. 14.

[34] Quoted in Webb, *Brothers in the Sun*, p. 81.

[35] ibid.

[36] *BOP*, June 1914.

[37] 'The Benediction of the House of Grace', *BOP*, January 1914.

[38] *BOP*, March 1913.

[39] Diary of the Brotherhood of Saint Boniface, Williams, 1916–17, PROWA, MN 614, Acc 3528A/2–3 (hereafter referred to as Brotherhood Diary).

[40] Mazzini Tron, one of the founding members, was the first to leave for the war, but eventually he was followed by White, Thompson and Harper. *BOP*, June 1915, refers to Tron as a chaplain to troops who left for Egypt at the end of March; White's last apparent entry as a resident occurs in the Brotherhood Diary, 11/5/1916; Harper left in 1916 to take charge of St David's South Bunbury, and subsequently served as a chaplain; Thompson enlisted in 1917.

[41] E. W. Elsey, BSB, 'The Brotherhood of St Boniface—Its Work, Methods and Needs', in Brotherhood Scrapbook.

[42] Brotherhood Diary, 7/9/1916 and 8–9/2/1917, 1/5/1916, 31/7/1916; 4/11/1916.

[43] T. Groser, *The Lure of the Golden West*, pp. 109–10.

[44] Brotherhood Diary, 29 and 31/8/1916.

[45] Brotherhood Diary, 4/6/1916, 23/7/1916; 24/9/1916 refers to Leach serving.

[46] Brotherhood Diary, 6/4/1917.

[47] The obligation to say four offices is the second item in the *Constitution and Rule of the Brotherhood*, p. 3, in Brotherhood Scrapbook.

[48] See 'The Benediction of the House of Grace', in *BOP*, January 1914, which refers to the ringing of the Angelus at noon before sext, and after Evensong, and 'A Nocturne' in *BOP*, June 1914 for the compline bell.

[49] 'Commemoration Festival at the Brotherhood House of St Boniface', cutting from unidentified source dated 1916, in Brotherhood Scrapbook.

[50] See F. W. Goldsmith, Synod Charge, 1909, in *BOP*, March 1910; see also *BOP*, September 1909. Compare the comment of T. M. Robinson that communities were

'training candidates for Holy Orders, at practically no cost to themselves', T. M. Robinson, 'The Revival of Community Life', in *Church Congress Proceedings*, Perth, 1909, p. 63.

51 *Monthly Report of the SPCK*, April 1911.
52 *BOP*, June 1914.
53 *BOP*, June 1911, January 1914, September 1915.
54 Individual volumes are held in the Bunbury Diocesan Library.
55 All in *BOP*, September 1915.
56 F. W. Goldsmith, Synod Charge 1909, in *BOP*, March 1910; for local histories of two centres in quite different parts of the Brotherhood territory, see A. Shorer, *History of the Upper Blackwood*, for details of Boyupbrook, pp. 37, 67–8, and for Chowerup, pp. 76–9, 82; and J. Parnell, *Country Cavalcade: A History of the Shire of Tambellup*, pp. 69, 73, 89, 104, 111–15.
57 Letter in *BOP*, June 1911.
58 'An endeavour has recently been made to meet this increased settlement by the establishment of a Bush brotherhood, with its headquarters at Williams', *Southern Times*, 20/7/1911.
59 *BOP*, June 1914; Groser, *The Lure of the Golden West*, p. 279.
60 Webb, *Brothers in the Sun*, p. 151.
61 *WACN*, February 1927, p. 17.
62 P. Anson, *The Call of the Cloister*, pp. 77–82, 295–6.
63 W. Walsh, *The Secret History of the Oxford Movement*, p. 163.
64 The parishes and communities were as follows: St Jude's Bradford, Society of All Saints (Sisters of the Poor); Broadstairs, Sisters of the Church; St Nicholas' Chiswick, Community of Sts Mary and John (which merged with the Community of St Margaret in 1910), and the Community of St Denys; St Mark's Hamilton Terrace, Sisters of the Church; St Saviour's Hoxton, Community of St Peter; St John the Baptist Hulme, Manchester, an unnamed sisterhood; St Stephen's Lewisham, the nursing sisters of St John the Divine; St Matthias' Malvern Link, Mission Sisters of the Holy Name; St Silas' Pentonville, Sisters of Bethany; Ramsgate, Sisters of Bethany; Pimlico and Streatham, Community of the Holy Cross.
65 Anson, *The Call of the Cloister*, p. 390.
66 *WM*, 13/11/1896, p. 11.
67 Anson, *The Call of the Cloister*, pp. 441, 587, 588.
68 ibid., p. 59; cutting ('Our London Letter') from *Church Chronicle*, 17/10/1889, in George Frewer, Journal, i.
69 Anson, *Bishops at Large*, p. 86; *The Call of the Cloister*, pp. 90–106.
70 For the foundations, see Webb, *Brothers in the Sun*, pp. 16 ff., 24 ff., 28 ff., and 33 ff. respectively for the eastern states brotherhoods.
71 Anson, T*he Call of the Cloister*, pp. 122 ff., 139 ff, 80.
72 ibid., pp. 127, 132, 142–3.
73 See photographs of brothers in *BOP*, June 1914; *Bush Brother*, lxvii, no. 2, April 1972, p. 17, has a photograph of John Frewer, and refers to the girdle as a purple one.
74 'The Brothers will live in a voluntary state of poverty, and will only receive £25 a year each, in addition to their keep. They will live under the guidance of the Warden, the Rev. A. D. Webb, and their engagement may be terminated after due notice on either side', *Southern Times*, 15/7/1911.

75 C. O. L. Riley, Synod Charge, 1896, in *WM*, 13/11/1896, p. 10.
76 For the episcopal involvement in the brotherhoods of St Andrew, St Paul, St Barnabas and the Good Shepherd, see Webb, *Brothers in the Sun*, pp. 15, 25, 29–30 and 33, respectively.
77 R. Gardiner to Randall Davidson, 17/5/1907 and Randall Davidson to R. Gardiner, 18/5/1907, Randall Davidson, Correspondence, Official and Foreign, vol. 123, fos 223–5.
78 Constitution and Rule of the Brotherhood, pp. 5–6, in Brotherhood Scrapbook.
79 G. E. Frewer, Journal, x, unsourced cutting (*Church Times*?).
80 G. E. Frewer, Journal, x, unsourced cutting.
81 F. W. Goldsmith, Synod Charge, 1909, in *BOP*, March 1910.
82 'We were led to hope four years ago that five hundred pounds of the Pan-Anglican Thank-Offering would be given to us to enable us to build—but the hope was disappointed, and we struggled on . . .', F. W. Goldsmith, letter of 28/10/1912, in *BOP*, November 1912.
83 *BOP*, September 1909, March 1910.
84 *BOP*, May and September 1909, March 1910; Synod Charge, 1910, in *BOP*, December 1910; Synod Charge, 1911 in *BOP*, November 1911 refers to the likelihood of a second house at Kojonup.
85 *BOP*, June 1913.
86 Groser, *The Lure of the Golden West*, p. 61; compare this with p. 64: 'But if the Brothers were happy in their lot, the Bishop himself was blissfully so. He loved, more than anything else, to share in their common life and rule—if only for a few snatched days'.
87 F. W. Goldsmith, speech reported in *South Western Herald*, 30/11/1912, quoted in *BOP*, January 1913.
88 'A Nocturne', *BOP*, June 1914.
89 Brotherhood Scrapbook, unsourced cutting dated 1/5/1918: 'The Rev. Thos. Groser and the Rev. A. E. White, Chaplain in the A. I. F., and both members of the Brotherhood, arrived'. 'Both members' appears to refer to Frewer and Elsey.
90 *BOP*, November 1911.
91 Webb, *Brothers in the Sun*, p. 146.
92 *Church Standard*, 17/6/1921; and an undated cutting from the *Defender* in Brotherhood Scrapbook, appealing for 'young Catholic priests in Australia' to join the Brotherhood.
93 Note that Cowin, *The Williams*, p. 123, is in error in describing him as being ordained at a later date; he does not appear in Crockford's, in diocesan ordination records, nor in clergy lists in BOP. Groser only stated that he 'relinquished the work' before going on to comment on the initial absence of any kind of vow, Groser, *The Lure of the Golden West*, pp. 68–9.
94 Webb, *Brothers in the Sun*, p. 151. Webb gives no source for this figure. An examination of the educational records of members of the Brotherhood 1911–29 shows that apart from Spargo, there were no other Australian members.
95 'The Cry of the Church', *WACN*, April 1927, p. 30.
96 Many aspects of the English ethos of the brotherhood movement are dealt with by Ruth Frappell, 'The Australian Bush Brotherhoods and their English Origins,' pp. 82–97. This concentrated treatment of the movement in Eastern Australia appeared two years after the present chapter had been written. Though neither

writer had referred to the other's work in this area, their independent researches are complementary in several areas.

97 *WACN*, August 1922, p. 9.
98 *The Mission Field*, October 1911, p. 310.
99 See pp. 327–8.
100 *Church Times*, 6/11/1908, p. 615.
101 F. W. Goldsmith to H. H. Montgomery, 1/3/1912, USPG CLR vol. 209, fo 466.
102 Groser, *The Lure of the Golden West*, p. 287.
103 *Church Times*, 2/10/1908, p. 7.
104 Quoted in Webb, *Brothers in the Sun*, p. 46.
105 *Church Standard*, 17/6/1921, p. 3.
106 ibid., 28/11/1913, p. 14.
107 *BOP*, November 1912.

## 13: Resonances

1 Athol Haesler to F. E. Maynard, undated, but among 1932 correspondence, Archives, St Peter's Eastern Hill, Melbourne.
2 *Church Standard*, 9/11/1934.
3 I disagree with Gavin Simpson's description (*West Australian*, 14/1/1995, 'Big Weekend', p. 7, which reads to me as a description of something more 'middling' than is the case.
4 C. O. L. Riley to H. H. Montgomery, 22/8/1904, USPG CLR vol. 209, fo 340.
5 See Cathedral Statute, 1904, text in *Perth Diocesan Yearbook*, 1904, pp. 40–2.
6 C. O. L. Riley, 1926 Synod Charge, *Perth Diocesan Yearbook*, 1926, pp. 17–19.
7 R. H. Moore to cathedral chapter secretary, 1/5/1918, PROWA, MN 614, Acc 3568A/25. Other comments by Moore appear in R. H. Moore, A Short History of the Catholic Revival in WA, PROWA, MN 129 Acc 1210A/12/4. On Moore and the statute, see J. H. N. Honniball, 'Archbishop and Primate', pp. 164–5.
8 See *Perth Diocesan Yearbook*, 1929, pp. 10–19.
9 D. Robarts, 'A 'Tolerable Pluralism?', pp. 50–9.
10 F. Crowley, *Australia's Western Third*, pp. 326–7; and review by J. A. La Nauze in *Historical Studies*, ix, no. 35, November 1960, p. 327; G. Bolton, *A Fine Country to Starve In*, pp. 267–9; G. Bolton, 'A Local Identity: Paul Hasluck and Western Australian Self Concept', p. 73.
11 *WM*, 11/8/1888, p. 20.
12 *WAT*, 28/9/1875.
13 See A. Burton, *Church Beginnings in the West*, pp. 115–16.
14 P. Carnley, Synod Charge, 1987, p. 63.
15 ibid.
16 P. Carnley, Synod Charge, 1989, p. 55.
17 P. Carnley, Synod Charge, 1988, p. 63.
18 I am hardly original in drawing such a parallel. It had already been made in a systematic way in R. Sharwood, Scandrett v Dowling and the Gorham Judgement, in 1992.
19 On the attempts to create further legislation to restrict Anglo-Catholics, see G. I. T. Machin, *Politics and the Churches in Great Britain*, 1869–1921, pp. 242–5.

[20] J. Davis, *Australian Anglicans and their Constitution*, pp. 102–30; see also R. Teale, 'The Red Book Case', pp. 74–89.
[21] See *WACN*, July 1923, p. 22, March 1924, p. 27.
[22] *Defender*, April 1925.
[23] K. Rayner, History, pp. 313, 315. Compare this with Bishop Dawes of Rockhampton, who had neither lights nor vestments, A. A. Fellows, *Full Time*, p. 133; K. Rayner, History, p. 252.
[24] J. Norman, *John Oliver North Queensland*, p. 49.
[25] K. Rayner, History, p. 314.
[26] ibid., pp. 283–5, and C. Holden, Ritualist on a Tricycle, pp. 401–10.
[27] Recollections of the Reverend W. Burbidge.
[28] Various anecdotes in T. S. Groser, T*he Lure of the Golden West*; incidents recalled in interview with John Elsey, son of the Rt Reverend Edward Elsey.
[29] *Mirror*, 15/10/1927, quoted in Dom Placid Lawson, 'Benedictines at Brunswick', p. 44.
[30] *Victorian Churchman*, 27/9/1907, p. 399.
[31] G. Bolton, *A Thousand Miles Away*, p. 291.
[32] K. Rayner, History, p. 360, using correspondence of Frodsham to Montgomery in 1908.
[33] T. S. Groser, *The Lure of the Golden West*, p. 287.
[34] The Reverend Nigel Pounde, incumbent of St Chad's Wolverhampton, to the author, 19/7/1989.
[35] See for example *West Australian*, 24/4/1991, p. 11.
[36] Professor K. S. Inglis to the author, 19/12/1992; Rabbi R. Brasch to Dr M. Stell, 26/11/1992.
[37] John A. Moses, 'Canon David John Garland and the ANZAC Tradition', pp. 12–21.
[38] *Church Times*, 27/11/1908.
[39] Quoted in D. Hilliard, 'The Transformation of South Australian Anglicanism', p. 52.
[40] C. S. Hardy to F. E. Maynard, 10/11/1935, F. E. Maynard correspondence, Archives, St Peter's Eastern Hill, Melbourne.
[41] Dom Placid Lawson, 'Benedictines at Brunswick', pp. 43–4; interviews with Mrs Biddy Heatley, née Ganfield, daughter of a St David's vestryman, and Mrs Molly Shaw, a daughter of a family of parishioners during this period.
[42] *BOP*, November 1911.
[43] *BOP* September 1915.
[44] Interviews: Mrs Flora Connett, née Richardson, 3/5/1991, who grew up on Corrie-Lynne, a property about eleven miles from Broome Hill, frequently visited by the brothers; Mrs Minna Terry, daughter of Joseph Craven, one of the brothers, and subsequently Rector of Manjimup.
[45] Interviews with those mentioned.
[46] See O. Chadwick, *The Victorian Church*, ii, pp. 308–14, and C. Holden, 'Awful Happenings on the Hill', pp. 24–6.
[47] J. Gabbedy, *Group Settlement*, vol. ii, pp. 191–3 comments on the English and working-class origins of group settlers of the 1920s.
[48] P. Boyce, 'The First Archbishop', p. 86; J. H. M. Honniball, 'Archbishop and Primate', p. 168.

⁴⁹ W. S. F. Pickering, 'Anglo-Catholicism: Some Sociological Observations', p. 153.
⁵⁰ Cecil Wilson in *WACN*, December 1927, p. 17.
⁵¹ I would have regarded the following statement of Foley-Whaling concerning the same synod with some caution, were it not for Wilson's own estimate quoted above: 'Another thing noticed was the strong "Anglo-Catholic phalanx"; over two-thirds of the clergy in the Bunbury diocese are Anglo-Catholic and they do stick together. We should all remember that unity is strength',*WACN*, December 1927, p. 17.
⁵² See A. Offer, *Property and Politics 1870–1914,* pp. 91–3, on the effect on the clergy of the economic 'slippery-slide'.
⁵³ Correspondence of Mrs Qona Clifton, daughter of Bishop Wilson, 3/3/1991.
⁵⁴ St Paul's Little Bardfield provided the training of 26 priests who came to Australia before 1952. Though some of the buildings remain, no records appear to have survived—Professor Ken Cable to the author, 15/1/1991.
⁵⁵ Interview with Mrs E. M. Jenour, née Clarke, daughter of George Clarke, Mayor of Bunbury.
⁵⁶ Interview with Mrs Rees, née Bussell.
⁵⁷ *WACN*, February 1929, p. 23, July 1928, p. 14, April 1928.
⁵⁸ G. Trower to H. H. Montgomery, 4/7/1911, USPG CLR vol. 209, fo 460.
⁵⁹ Quoted by Boyce in 'The First Archbishop', p. 90.
⁶⁰ On Isabell Hughes as a benefactor, see C. Holden, *From Tories at Prayer to Socialists at Mass*, pp. 96–8, 133, 134, 147, 154–5, and on Priscilla Bickford, see D. Hilliard, *Godliness and Good Order*, p. 87.
⁶¹ F. W. Goldsmith to H. H. Montgomery, 18/7/1907, USPG CLR vol. 209, fo 409.
⁶² *BOP*, May 1909, November 1908.
⁶³ *Southern Times*, 6/7/1907.
⁶⁴ *BOP*, June 1911, and obituary in *BOP*, November 1912.
⁶⁵ *Bunbury Herald*, 19/5/1906.
⁶⁶ ibid.
⁶⁷ On P. Goatcher, the mural artist, see D. Hough, 'Remembrance of Scenes Past', *Bulletin*, 15/10/1991.
⁶⁸ R. Withycombe, 'The Anglican Episcopate in England and Australia in the Early Twentieth Century', pp. 161, 168.

# Bibliography

## Unpublished Sources

### Parish and Community Records

**Brotherhood of St Boniface**

Diary, 1916–17, PROWA, MN 614, Acc 3528A/2–3, Battye Library, Perth.

Volume of Newspaper Cuttings and Photographs Concerning the Bush Brotherhood Collected by Bishop Frewer's Father in England, PROWA, MN 614, Acc 3528A/1, Battye Library, Perth.

**Bunbury**

St Paul's Pro-Cathedral Vestry Minute Books, 1899–1916, PROWA, MN 614, Acc 3527A/24–5.

Documents Relating to Purchase of New Cathedral Site, 1915–17, PROWA, MN 614, Acc 3527A/17–18.

**Cheam**

St Philip's Baptism Registers, 1881–88, Parish Archives, St Philip's, Worcester Park.

**Halling**

St John the Baptist's, Service Registers, 1886–88, Parish Archives, St John's, Halling.

**St John the Divine, Community (of Nursing Sisters) of**

Reports and Chapter Minutes, 1888–92, Archives, Community of St John the Divine, Alum Rock Road, Birmingham.

**Perth**

St Alban's Highgate:
   Service Registers, 1894–1902, PROWA, MN 614, Acc 3206A/145, Battye Library, Perth.
St Bartholomew's East Perth:
   Service Registers, 1893–1901, PROWA, MN 614, Acc 2467A/323–4, Battye Library, Perth.
St George's Cathedral:
   Minutebooks, St George's Cathedral Vestry, 1888– , PROWA, MN 614, Acc 2778/1 and 2, Battye Library, Perth.
   Service Registers, 1888–1904, PROWA, MN 614, Acc 2778A/33–35, Battye Library, Perth.
St John's Melbourne Road:
   Service Registers, 1882–1910, PROWA, MN 614, Acc 2467A/211–12, Battye Library, Perth.

*Other Unpublished Sources*

Allen, James, Notebook on Ecclesiastical Matters, PROWA, *1249A, Battye Library, Perth.
Assistant Bishopric Committee Minutebook, 1900–03, PROWA, MN 614, Acc 2467A/156, Battye Library, Perth.
Davidson, Randall, Correspondence, Official and Foreign, vols 32, 36, 39, 56, 100, 103, 121, 123 and 236, Lambeth Palace Library.
Fell, C. Y., Reminiscences of St John's College, Oxford, Ms 343, St John's College Library, Oxford.
Frewer, G. E., Journals, vols i–xii, 1888–1932, Bishopsgarth, Brede near Rye, East Sussex.
General Synod, Executive Committee Minute Book, 1881–1910, General Synod Archives, St Andrew's House, Sydney.
Goldsmith, F. W., senior, death certificate, author's collection.
Goldsmith, F. W., baptism certificate, Kent Archives Office, DRb/A1, 1876.
   Ordination Papers, Kent Archives Office, DRb/A1, 1876.
   Correspondence with Mother Emily, CSC, 8/5/1890, Archives, Community of the Sisters of the Church, Ham Common, Surrey.
Henn, W. E., Notes towards a biography of F. W. Goldsmith, author's collection.
Lambeth Conference Papers, 1888–1908, vols 21, 66 and 78, Lambeth Palace Library.
   Minute Book of Committee 8, Prayerbook Adaptation and Enrichment, Subcommittee no. 3, Ms. LC 91, Lambeth Palace Library.

Maynard, F. E., Correspondence, Archives, St Peter's Eastern Hill, Melbourne.

Moore, R. H., A Short History of the Catholic Revival in WA, PROWA, MN 129 Acc 1210A/12/4.

Parry, H. H., Diaries, 1886, 1888–93, MN 134, ACC 1223A/5, 7–8.

Primate's Correspondence re the Establishment of the Diocese of Bunbury, 1903–07, General Synod Archives, St Andrew's House, Sydney.

Primate's Correspondence re the Establishment of the Province of Western Australia, 1914, General Synod Archives, St Andrew's House, Sydney.

Riley, C. O. L., Diaries, 1895–99, PROWA, Acc 369, MN 1291A/7–10.

Letterbooks, 1866–1900, PROWA, MN 614, Acc 2467A/178.

Robertson, A. A., Mitres, Gaiters and Hoods, PROWA, MN 614, Acc 3568A/43/7, Battye Library, Perth.

Tait, A. C., Correspondence Official and Foreign, vol. 226, Lambeth Palace Library.

United Society for the Propagation of the Gospel, Correspondence:

Colonial Letters Received (CLR), 1888–1920, vols 209–11, USPG Archives, Rhodes House Library, Oxford.

Colonial Letters Sent (CLS), 1900–17, vols 140–5, USPG Archives, Rhodes House Library, Oxford.

Correspondence, Series E, 1901–06, USPG Archives, Rhodes House Library, Oxford.

Standing Committee Minutes, 1905–06, USPG Archives, Rhodes House Library, Oxford.

*Unpublished Essays and Theses*

Davis, J., Continuity and Change, Australian Anglicanism and a Constitution, 1920–1987, DD, Melbourne College of Divinity, 1987.

Holden, C., Ritualist on a Tricycle, PhD, University of Melbourne, 1994.

Medley, J. M., The Rise of Free Secular and Compulsory Education in Western Australia, BA honours, UWA.

Morgan, P., 'Jonkers under Bellamy', typescript of a paper read to the Essay Society of St John's College, St John's College Library, Oxford.

Nicholls, P., 'The Ritualist Issue and the 1900 Election in England', paper delivered to the Australasian British History Association, July 1991.

Rayner, K., The History of the Church of England in Queensland, PhD, University of Queensland, 1962.

Sharwood, R. L., Scandrett v Dowling and The Gorham Judgment, The Oxford Movement Anniversary Lecture, Adelaide, 1992.

Thompson, S., The Development of the Church of England and the Formation of the Bunbury Diocese, Graylands Teachers College, Western Australia, 1970.

## Published Sources

### Contemporary

Goldsmith, F. W., 'Australia: the Anglican Communion', in *Episcopacy Ancient and Modern*, ed. C. Jenkins and K. D. Mackenzie, London, 1930.

'Church Organization', in *Papers read at the Church Congress Held at Sydney, on the 30th April, 1st, 2nd and 3rd May, 1889*, Sydney, 1889, pp. 178–83.

'The Principles of the Church in Education', in *Official Proceedings of the Church Congress Held at Perth, Western Australia, 25th to 30th October 1909*, Perth, 1910, pp. 152–8.

### Official Publications

*Bunbury Diocesan Yearbooks* and *Synod Reports*, 1905–17, Battye Library, Perth.

Church Congress Papers: *Papers read at the Church Congress Held at Sydney, on the 30th April, 1st, 2nd and 3rd May, 1889*, Sydney, 1889.

*Official Proceedings of the Church Congress Held at Perth, Western Australia, 25th to 30th October 1909*, Perth, 1910.

*Crockford's Clerical Directory*, London, 1880–1963.

*General Synod Official Reports*, 1900–16.

*Historical Register of the University of Oxford, being a Supplement to the Oxford University Calendar with an Alphabetical Record of University Honours and Distinctions Completed to the end of Trinity Term 1900*, Oxford, 1900.

Merchant Taylors' School Register, entry, Frederick William Goldsmith,

*Parliamentary Debates*, London, 1905.

*Parliamentary Debates,* Western Australia, Perth, 1893–95.

*Perth Diocesan Yearbooks* and *Synod Reports*, 1882–1904, Battye Library, Perth.

Society for the Promotion of Christian Knowledge, *Monthly Reports*, 1911–13, SPCK Archives, Marylebone Road, London.

*Statistical Register of the Colony of Western Australia . . . compiled in the Registrar General's Office, Perth, from Official Returns*, 1896–1904.

*Who's Who*, London, 1920.

### Newspapers and Periodicals

*Argus*, State Library of Victoria.
*Bulletin*, State Library of Victoria.
*Bunbury Herald*, Battye Library, Perth.
*Bunbury Occasional Papers*, 1904–17, Battye Library, Perth.
*Church Commonwealth*, Mollison Library, Trinity College, Melbourne.
*Church of England Messenger*, Mollison Library, Trinity College, Melbourne.
*Church Standard*, Mitchell Library, Sydney.

*Church Times*, Pusey House, Oxford.
*Defender*, Parish Archives, St Peter's Eastern Hill, Melbourne.
*Kentish Independent*, Woodlands, Mycenae Road, Blackheath.
*Kentish Mercury*, Woodlands, Mycenae Road, Blackheath.
*The Mission Field*, author's collection.
*Morning Herald*, Battye Library, Perth.
*Our Work,* Archives, St Michael's House, Community of the Sisters of the Church, Ham Common, Surrey.
*Perth Gazette*, Battye Library, Perth.
*Perth Quarterly Magazine,* Battye Library, Perth.
*Southern Times*, Battye Library, Perth.
*Victorian Churchman*, Mollison Library, Trinity College, Melbourne.
*West Australian*, Battye Library, Perth.
*West Australian Catholic Record*, Battye Library, Perth.
*West Australian Church News*, Battye Library, Perth.
*West Australian Times*, Battye Library, Perth.

**Parish Magazines and Ecclesiastical Records**

*Bunbury Cathedral Gazette*, 1917, Battye Library, Perth.
Hampstead, St John's, *Parish Magazine,* 1916–26, Parish Archives, St John's, Hampstead.
Melbourne, St Peter's Eastern Hill, *Cross Keys*, 1896–98, Parish Archives, St Peter's Eastern Hill, Melbourne.
Perth, St George's Cathedral, Annual General Meeting printed reports (1889–93), copies pasted into Minute Books of St George's Vestry i and ii, Battye MN 614 ACC 2778A/1 and 2.
  Printed reports, 1897–1904, Cathedral Archives, Cathedral Office, St George's Terrace, Perth.

**Pamphlets and Tracts**

*An Alphabetical List of the Signatures to a Remonstrance Addressed to the Archbishops and Bishops of the Church of England on occasion of the Report of the Judicial Committee of the Privy Council in re Herbert vs. Purchas*, London, 1871, Pamphlet Collection, Pusey House, Oxford.
Association of Prayer for the Church in Australia, Quarterly Leaflet, June 1927, author's collection.
Bright, W., *Evening Communions Contrary to the Church's Mind and Why, being Three Articles reprinted from the Literary Churchman, with a letter to the Editor*, London, 1870, Pamphlet Collection, Pusey House, Oxford.
Church Association, *The Ritualistic Clergy List, A Guide for Patrons and Others to*

*Certain of the Clergy of the Church of England: being a list of some 9600 Clergymen who are helping the Romeward Movement in the National Church*, 3rd edn, London, 1903, Lambeth Palace Library.

English Church Union *Directories*, London, 1888–1904, 1927–32, English Church Union Archives, Faith House, Tufton Street, Westminster.

*Tourists Guide*, London, 1898, Lambeth Palace Library.

Miller, J. C., *'Subjection: No, Not for an Hour': A Warning to Protestant Christians, in Behalf of the 'Truth of the Gospel', as now imperilled by the Romish Doctrines and Practices of the Tractarian Heresy*, London, 1850, Pamphlet Collection, Pusey House, Oxford.

*The Ritualistic Conspiracy*, n.d., Pamphlet Collection, Pusey House, Oxford.

Willoughby, F. S., *A Plea for the Children's Eucharist*, London, 1898, Bunbury Diocesan Library.

## Other Books and Articles

Anson, P., *Bishops at Large*, London, 1964.
   *The Call of the Cloister*, 2nd edn, London, 1964.
   *Fashions in Church Furnishings, 1840–1940*, London, 1960.

Appleyard, R. T., 'Western Australia, Economic and Demographic Growth, 1850–1914', in C. T. Stannage (ed.), *A New History of Western Australia*, Perth, 1981, pp. 211–36.

Archbishops' Commission on Christian Doctrine, *Report, Prayer and the Departed*, London, 1971.

Barker, T., and Laurie, M., *Excellent Connections*, Bunbury, 1991.

Bentley, J., *Ritualism and Politics in Victorian Britain: The Attempt to Legislate for Belief*, Oxford, 1979.

Bignell, Merle, *Little Grey Sparrows of the Anglican Diocese of Bunbury, Western Australia*, University of Western Australia Press, 1992.

Blake, L. J., entry for Sir Samuel Wilson, *ADB*, vi, ed. G. Serle and R. Ward, Melbourne, 1976, pp. 418–19.

Blatch, M., *A Guide to London's Churches*, London, 1978.

Bolton, G. C., *Alexander Forrest*, Melbourne, 1958.
   entry for Alexander Forrest, *ADB*, viii, ed. B. Nairn and G. Serle, Melbourne, 1981, pp. 540–3.
   *A Fine Country to Starve In*, Perth, 1972.
   'A Local Identity: Paul Hasluck and Western Australian Self Concept', in *Westerly*, no. 4, December 1977.
   *A Thousand Miles Away*, Brisbane, 1963.

Bouyer, L., *The Eucharist: Theology and Spirituality of the Eucharistic Prayer*, London and Notre Dame, 1968.

Boyce, P., 'The First Archbishop', in *Four Bishops and their See, 1857-1957*, ed. F. Alexander, Perth, 1957, pp. 47-111.

Brockelbank, L., *Canon Hughes, Priest of God, Friend of Man*, Melbourne, 1944.

Burbidge, W., 'The Church in the South West', in *Four Bishops and their See, 1857-1957*, ed. F. Alexander, Perth, 1957, pp. 122-33.

Burton, A., *Church Beginnings in the West*, Perth, 1941.

Cable, K., entry for A. H. H. Stephen in *ADB*, vi, ed. G. Serle and R. Ward, Melbourne, 1976, pp. 187-8.

Carpenter, S. C., *Winnington-Ingram*, London, 1949.

Chadwick, O., *The Victorian Church*, 2 vols, London, 1966-70.

Chandos, J., *Boys Together: English Public Schools 1800-1864*, London, 1984.

Church, R. W., *The Oxford Movement*, London, 1891, reprint, Chicago, 1970.

Clark, G. K., *The Gothic Revival*, London, 1962.

'The Romantic Element, 1830-1850', in *Studies in Social History*, ed. J. H. Plumb, London, 1955, pp. 211-39.

Clunn, H. P., *The Face of London*, London, 1980.

Coombs, J., *Judgement on Hatcham: the History of a Religious Struggle, 1877-1886*, London, 1969.

Cowin, H. G., *The Williams*, Perth, n.d.

Creighton, L., *The Life and Letters of Mandell Creighton*, 2 vols, London, 1905.

Crowley, F. K., *Australia's Western Third*, London, 1960.

'Church and State in Western Australia', in *Four Bishops and Their See, Perth, Western Australia, 1857-1957*, ed. F. Alexander, pp. 225-36.

*Forrest 1847-1918: I, 1847-1891, Apprenticeship to Premiership*, Brisbane, 1971.

Cuming, G. J., *A History of Anglican Liturgy*, 2nd edn, London, 1982.

Davies, H., *Worship and Theology in England from Watts and Wesley to Maurice, 1690-1850*, Oxford and Princeton, 1961.

*Worship and Theology in England from Newman to Martineau, 1850-1900*, Oxford and Princeton, 1962.

*Worship and Theology in England, The Ecumenical Century 1900-1965*, Oxford and Princeton, 1965.

Davis, J., *Australian Anglicans and their Constitution*, Canberra, 1993.

Dearmer, P., *The Parson's Handbook*, London, 1898.

Delhine, C., *The Face of the Past: The Preservation of the Medieval Inheritance in Victorian England*, Cambridge, 1982.

Draper, F. W. M., *Four Centuries of Merchant Taylors' School, 1561-1961*, London, 1962.

Durack, Mary, *The Rock and the Sand*, Constable, London, 1969.

Eastlake, C. L., *A History of the Gothic Revival*, 1872, reprint, ed. J. M. Crook, Leicester, 1978.

Ellsworth, L. E., *Charles Lowder and the Ritualist Movement*, London, 1982.

Faber, G., *Oxford Apostles*, 2nd edn, London, 1954.

Fellows, A. A., *Full Time: the Story of How I became a Priest and of the Rockhampton Diocese, Rockhampton,* private printing, 1967.

Frappell, R. M., 'The Australian Bush Brotherhoods and their English Origins', *Journal of Ecclesiastical History*, vol. 47 no. 1, January 1996, pp. 82–97.

Frewer, G. E., *Weekday Walking Sticks: Thoughts for Daily Meditation through the Church's Year*, 1930, reprint, Perth, 1966.

Funnell, B., *Christ Church St Leonard's-on-Sea, 1859–1975*, St Leonard's-on-Sea, 1975.

Gabbedy, J., *Group Settlement*, 2 vols, Perth, 1988.

Giles, R. A., *The Constitutional History of the Australian Church*, London, 1928.

Green, V. H. H., *Religion in Oxford and Cambridge*, London, 1964.

Gregory, J. (ed.), *Western Australia Between the Wars 1919–1939*, Perth, 1990.

Gregory, J. S., *Church and State: Changing Government Policies towards Religion in Australia, with particular reference to Victoria since Separation,* Melbourne, 1973.

Groser, T. S., *The Lure of the Golden West*, London, 1927.

Grundy, D., *'Secular, Compulsory and Free': The Education Act of 1872*, Melbourne, 1972.

Harrison, H. J., and Truran, J. M., *St George's Goodwood, 1880–1980*, Adelaide, 1980.

Hawtrey, C. L. M., *The Availing Struggle: A Record of the Planting and Development of the Church of England in Western Australia, 1829–1947*, Perth, 1949.

Henn, W. E., *A Life so Rich*, Perth, 1982.

entry for F. W. Goldsmith in *ADB,* ix, ed. B. Nairn and G. Serle, Melbourne, 1983, pp. 42–3.

Hibbert, C, (ed.), *The Encyclopaedia of Oxford*, Oxford, 1988.

Hilliard, D., *Godliness and Good Order: A History of the Anglican Church in South Australia,* Adelaide, 1986.

*God's Gentlemen: A History of the Melanesian Mission, 1849–1942*, Brisbane, 1978.

'The Transformation of South Australian Anglicanism c 1880–1930', *Journal of Religious History*, xiv, 1986, pp. 38–56.

'"Un-English and Unmanly": Homosexuality and Anglo-Catholicism', *Victorian Studies*, xxv, 1982, pp. 181–210.

Hillman, A., *The Hillman Diaries, 1877–1884*, ed. B. Hillman, Perth, 1990.

Holden, C., *'Awful Happenings on the Hill': E. S. Hughes and Melbourne Anglo-Catholicism before the War*, Melbourne, 1992.

*From Tories at Prayer to Socialists at Mass, A History of St Peter's Eastern Hill, 1846–1990*, Melbourne, 1996.

Rural Ritualism and Frederick Goldsmith: Anglo-Catholicism in Western Australia before the First World War', *Journal of Religious History*, xviii, 1994, pp. 75–95.

Honniball, J. H. M., 'Archbishop and Primate: Henry Frewen Le Fanu', in *Four Bishops and their See, 1857–1957*, ed. F. Alexander, Perth, 1957, pp. 157–214.

Howell, P., and Sutton, I. (eds), *The Faber Guide to Victorian Churches*, London, 1989.

Hughes, Dom A., *The Rivers of the Flood: A Personal Account of the Catholic Revival in England in the Twentieth Century*, 2nd edn, London, 1963.

Hunt, L., entry for J. W. Hackett, *ADB*, ix, ed. B. Nairn and G. Serle, Melbourne, 1983, pp. 150–3.

Inglis, K. S., *The Church and the Working Classes in Victorian England*, London, 1963.

Judd, S., and Cable, K., *Sydney Anglicans*, Sydney, 1988.

Kent, J., *Holding the Fort: Studies in Victorian Revivalism*, London, 1978.

La Nauze, G., review of F. Crowley, *Australia's Western Third, Historical Studies*, ix, 1960.

Lawson, Dom P., 'Benedictines at Brunswick? Fr John Foley-Whaling and his Proposed Foundation in Western Australia', *Tjuringa*, no. 36, May 1989, pp. 42–57.

Littledale, R. F., and de Vaux, J. E., *The Priest's Prayer Book, containing Private Prayers and Intercessions; Occasional, School and Parochial Offices; Offices for the Visitation of the Sick, with Notes, Readings, Collects, Hymns, Litanies, etc., etc., with a brief Pontifical*, London, 1864.

Lloyd, R., *The Church of England in the Twentieth Century*, London, 1946.

Machin, G. I. T., 'The Last Victorian Anti-Ritualist Campaign', *Victorian Studies*, xxv, no. 3, pp. 277–302.

*Politics and the Churches in Great Britain, 1869–1921*, Oxford, 1987.

McIlhiney, D. B., *A Gentleman in Every Slum: Church of England Missions in East London, 1837–1914*, Allison Park (Pennsylvania), 1988.

McLeod, H., *Class and Religion in the Late Victorian City*, London, 1974.

Maison, M., *Search Your Soul, Eustace: A Survey of the Religious Novel in the Victorian Age*, London, 1961.

Mather, F. C., 'Georgian Churchmanship Reconsidered: Some Variations in Anglican Public Worship 1714–1830', *Journal of Ecclesiastical History*, April 1985, pp. 255–83.

Merchant Taylors' School Archaeological Society, *Merchant Taylors' School: Its Origin, History and Present Surroundings*, Oxford, 1929.

Micklem, D., *Principles of Church Organization*, London, 1921.

Morgan, P., 'Bellamy and His Fellows', *Oxford Magazine*, December 1961.

Morris, J., *Pax Britannica,* London, 1979.
  *Farewell the Trumpets*, London, 1979.
Moses, J. A., 'Canon David John Garland and the ANZAC Tradition', *St Mark's Review*, Winter, 1993, 12–21.
Munson, J. E. B., 'The Oxford Movement by the End of the 19th Century: the Anglo-Catholic Clergy', *Church History*, xliv, 1975, pp. 382–95.
Offer, A., *Property and Politics 1870–1914: Land Ownership, Law, Ideology and Urban Development in England*, Cambridge, 1981.
Ollard, S. L., *A Short History of the Oxford Movement*, 2nd edn, 1932, reprint, London, 1963.
Olsen, D. J., *The Growth of Victorian London*, London, 1976.
Parnell, J., *Country Cavalcade: A History of the Shire of Tambellup*, Perth, 1982.
Penhale, F., (ed.), *The Anglican Church Today: Catholics in Crisis*, London and Oxford, 1986.
Pevsner, N., *The Buildings of England: London, Except the Cities of London and Westminster,* London, 1952.
Pickering, W. S. F., *Anglo-Catholicism: A Study in Religious Ambiguity*, London, 1989.
  'Anglo-Catholicism: Some Sociological Observations', in *Tradition Renewed: The Oxford Movement Conference Papers*, ed. G. Rowell, London, 1986, pp. 153–72.
A Pioneer Sister, *Perth College, Record of the Work of the Sisters of the Church in Western Australia,* University of Western Australia Press, Perth, 1958.
Reed, J. S., Glorious Battle: the Cultural Politics of Victorian Anglo-Catholicism, Nashville, Tennessee, 1996.
  'Ritualism Rampant, Anglo-Catholicism and the Urban Poor', *Victorian Studies*, vol. 31, no. 3, 1988, pp. 375–403.
Robarts, D., 'A 'Tolerable Pluralism?", in *Women Priests in Australia: The Anglican Crisis*, ed. D. Wetherell, Melbourne, 1987, pp. 50–9.
Robin, A. de Q., *Mathew Blagden Hale: The Life of an Australian Pioneer Bishop*, Melbourne, 1976.
Robinson, F. M., entry for A. E. Stone, *ADB*, xii, ed. J. Ritchie, Melbourne, 1990.
Rodd, L. C., *John Hope of Christ Church St Laurence: A Sydney Church Era*, Sydney, 1972.
Rowell, G., *The Vision Glorious: Themes and Personalities of the Oxford Movement*, Oxford, 1983.
  (ed.), *Tradition Renewed: The Oxford Movement Conference Papers*, London, 1986.
Russell, G. W. E., *Arthur Stanton: A Memoir*, London, 1917.
  *Edmund King, 60th Bishop of Lincoln: A Memoir*, London, 1913.

'A St Peterite': see Brockelbank, L.
Scarfe, J., 'The Diocese of Adelaide (and the West)', in *Colonial Tractarians*, ed. Brian Porter, Melbourne, 1989, pp. 75–104.
Sherwood, W. E., *Oxford Yesterday: Memoirs of Oxford Seventy Years Ago*, Oxford, 1927.
Shorer, A., *A History of the Upper Blackwood*, Perth, 1968.
Simpkinson, C. H., *The Life and Work of Bishop Thorold*, London, 1894.
Smith, J. G., *Charlton: A Compilation of the Parish and its People*, 2 vols, London, 1975.
Stannage, C. T., *The People of Perth*, Perth, 1979.
(ed.), *A New History of Western Australia*, Perth, 1981.
Teale, R., 'The Red Book Case', *Journal of Religious History*, xii, no. 1, 1982, pp. 74–89.
Thompson, F. M. L., *Hampstead, Building a Borough 1659–1964*, London, 1964.
Tomlin, J. W. S., *Halford's Challenge*, Canterbury, 1952.
Twopeny, R., *Town Life in Australia*, London, 1883, reprint, 1976.
Walsh, W., *The Secret History of the Oxford Movement*, London, 1898.
Webb, R. A. F., *Brothers in the Sun*, Adelaide, 1978.
Weil, L., 'The Oxford Movement: A Retrospective Consideration of its Sacramental and Liturgical Teaching on the 150th Anniversary', *Studia Liturgica*, xv, no. 2, 1981, pp. 118–23.
'The Tractarian Liturgical Inheritance Reassessed', in *Tradition Renewed: The Oxford Movement Conference Papers*, ed. G. Rowell, London, 1986, p. 110 ff.
Welborn, S., *Lords of Death*, Fremantle, 1982.
Wellings, M., 'Anglo-Catholicism, 'The Crisis in the Church' and the Cavalier Case of 1899', *Journal of Ecclesiastical History*, xlii, 1991, pp. 239–58.
Wilkinson, A., *The Church of England and the First World War*, London, 1978.
Williams, A., *West Anglican Way*, Perth, 1989.
Withycombe, R., 'The Anglican Episcopate in England and Australia in the Early Twentieth Century: Towards a Comparative Study', *Journal of Religious History*, xvi, no. 2, 1990, pp. 154–72.
Wollaston, J. R., *Albany Journal*, ed. A. Burton, Perth, 1948.
*Journals*, vol. 2, ed. G. Bolton, H. Vose and A. Watson, with S. Lewis, University of Western Australia Press, 1992.
Yates, N., 'Bells and Smells: London, Brighton and South Coast Religion Reconsidered', *Southern History*, v, 1983.
*Buildings, Faith and Worship: The Liturgical Arrangement of Anglican Churches 1600–1900*, Oxford, 1991.
'Jesuits in Disguise, Ritualist Confessors and their Critics in the 1870s', *Journal of Ecclesiastical History*, xxix, 1988, pp. 202–16.

# Index

Page numbers in italics refer to illustrations.

Aborigines 8, 184, 194, 196, 201, 341
  evangelization 196
  population 184, 194, 254
  prisoners, at Roebourne 189, *190*
  treatment in north-west 184, 189–92
Adams, Henry 310
Adams, 'Porky' 1, 206, 207, 310
Albany 186, 222, 223
alcohol 25, 26, 45
All Saints
  Collie 213, 265, *281*, *282*, 341, *342*
  Donnybrook 260
  Margaret Street 31, 270, 279
All Souls' Day 50, 96, 225, 234
Allen, James 40, 59, 75
altars 6, 87, 88, 89, 90, 111, 134, 217, 227, 260, 278, 284, 341
  crosses 98, 99, 111
  lights 10, 16, 50, 90, 91, 98, 100, 110, 146, 163, 206, 216, 217, 223, 262, 314, 323, 324, 336
  stone 53, 87
Amended Education Act 65, 66, 67, 69, 70, 72, 79, 81
Anglican
  churches 57–60
    attendances 271
    holy tables in 87
    missionary organizations, 39
    social activities 42–4
    with two altars 89
  churchmanship 4, 63, 64, 65, 234, 239, 277
  clergy, criticism of 62–3
  Establishment 249, 271
  history 7, 253
  identity 3
  piety 107
  population 20, 23, 187, 188
  rites 89
  schools 64–5, 66, 69, 70, 79, 80
Anglican Church in Australia
  influence of Oxford Movement 241
  name change proposal 135, 153–77, 237, 331, 345
  self-supporting 193
Anglicanism 13, 16, 17, 40, 47, 73, 114, 142, 169, 237, 241, 276, 277, 319, 334
  accounts 9–11
  attacks on 81, 115
  Bunbury diocese 3, 221, 326, 335
  Catholic identity 188, 253
  Catholic tradition within 9, 114, 278
  central role 140, 242
  changes 40
  concerns 79–80, 82
  of the future 278
  future in colony 105, 168
  nineteenth-century 116, 134
  and the Oxford Movement 5, 9, 10
  polarization 111
  Protestant strength in 146
  rural 198, 343
  Western Australian 4, 12–13, 67, 125, 134, 168, 179
Anglicans
  attending nonconformist churches 111, 112
  changing allegiances 14
Anglo-Catholic
  centres 8, 34, 36, 261, 268, 270, 276, 313, 322, 323
  ceremonial 344
  churches 7, 10, 11, 36, 58, 116, 120, 149, 338, 341
  churchmanship 324, 329
  clergy 11, 15, 119, 228, 243, 261, 332, 334, 335
  control over appointments 130, 131
  dishonesty and lawlessness allegations 118, 119, 120, 147
  success 138
  devotion 224, 231–57
  influence in rural Western Australia 4, 5
  innovations 103
  lawlessness alleged 120, 128, 129
  mission 220, 276, 279
  movement 9, 47, 269, 274, 277, 296, 335
  piety 235, 262, 263, 307, 308, 309, 312, 332
  slum priests 57, 141, 142, 190
  teaching 80, 124
  terminology 15–17, 261, 275
  theology 237, 249
  vision 340–1
  vocabulary 260
Anglo-Catholicism 4–5, 6–9, 10, 11, 12, 13, 14, 47, 69, 91, 257, 325
  Anglicanism of the future 278
  concerns 31, 82, 106
  conspiracy theories 124–5
  controversy 75, 76, 82–3, 128, 137, 172
  critics 103–25, 127, 140, 141, 144, 146, 148, 321, 322
  debate 107, 114, 118, 149, 239, 318–45
  emergence 100, 277
  English opponents 113, 114, 117, 134
  lawfulness and authority 143, 144
  legislation to control 106, 134–6, 159, 172, 322
  opponents, 30, 83, 92, 97, 113, 115, 117, 118, 121, 124, 137, 142, 145, 149–50, 218, 264, 319
  in other states 322, 323, 324
  rural identity 323, 324, 325
  St Alban's Holborn 57

405

statement by Thorold 31
supporters 141, 142, 143, 146
triumph 228
unrest over 242–3
use of lights 91
Anglo-Catholics 16, 33, 324
Anglo-Papalists 16
Anstey, H. G. 74
anti-ritualist
  complaints 134, 270
  issues 103, 104, 139, 147, 150, 151, 217, 218
  press 105, 106, 107, 111, 119
  writers 121, 301
anti-ritualists 30, 261
Anzac Day dawn services 330
'Apocalypse' (writer) 83, 87, 88, 89, 90, 117, 125, 135
Apostolic faith 240
archdeacon, first 5
Assisted Schools Act 65, 69
Assisted Schools Grant 64, 65
assisted schools system 64–7, 70
Association of Prayer for the Church of Australia 266
Athanasian Creed 243–4, 245, 246, 247, 248
Australian church 153, 237
  and brotherhood movement 304, 307, 326–7
  critics 305
  legal status 172, 174, 237, 243
  religious community in 292
Australian Church Union 314, 343
authority 16, 47, 48, 131, 143, 144, 249
  bishop 253, 316–18
  church 250, 251
  episcopal 252, 253
  over Cathedral 316–18
autonomous movement 154–77, 237, 238, 243, 255, 256, 257, 331

baptism 35
Barlee, Lady 87
Barton-Parkes, Frederick 93, *94*, 160, 165, 185, 188, 287
Bignell, Merle 9
bishoprics 184, 185
  goldfields 185, 238
  independent 188
  north-west 192, 193, 196, 254, 255
bishops
  appointments 253, 343
  assessment of 242
  authority and power 316–18
  Bunbury 344
  conference 241, 242
  control of brotherhoods 304
  criticisms 134, 135, 218
  Perth 12
  qualifications 72
  rural 344
Bishopscourt 3, 180, 182, 197, 201, 207, 211, 214

Booth, D. L. 226
boxing 45, 46, 235
Boyce, Peter 11, 12, 130, 185
Brede parish church 2, 51, 57, 277, 279
Brooks, Archdeacon 195, 196, 201
Broome, Frederick Napier 54
Brotherhood
  movement 304, 307, 326–7
  of St Andrew 269, 287, 290, 291, 308
  of St Boniface 206, 208, 210, 211, 213, 215, 223, 226, 256, 259, 269, 280, 285–312, 326, 329, 333, 344
    Australian member 342
    Barroworn home 306
    Catholic priests 262, 265, 309
    House of Grace *see* House of Grace
    members 5
  of St Laurence 9
  of St Margaret 300, 336, 337
brotherhoods 202, 203, 208, 226, 261, 264, 285–312, 324
  bush 201, 210, 285–312, 345
  criticism 304–5
  English membership 305, 308, 309, 310, 311
  goldfields 289
  numbers 291
  recruits 305, 308, 309, 310, 311, 343
Broughton, William Grant 239
Brown, James 75
Brownlow Byron, Harriet 271
building programmes 279–84, 337, 338–41
Bull, John 117
Bunbury 4, 5, 186, *187*, *209*
  Anglicans 3, 221, 326, 335
  Anglo-Catholicism 4, 343, 344
  clergy 202, 207, 208, 211, 299
  conflict 216–17
  diocese 181, 187–8, 216, 226, 230, 259–84, 333
    inauguration 188
    journal articles 259–65
  election of Bishop Parry's successor 47, 73–6
  episcopate 179–203, 205–16
  Grammar School 201, 207, *208*, 210, 211, 212
  historic pageant 202
  lack of cathedral 203, 206, 212, 213, 214, 231
  mission 220
  new cathedral 222
  population 18, 186, 206
  press 219
  pro-cathedral 203, 206, 208, 212, 213, 214, 215, 218, 219, 220, 221, 223, 336
    daily eucharists 232
    funding 193
    rector 310

Bunbury Guild of Aid 197, 200
*Bunbury Herald* 185
*Bunbury Occasional Papers* 259, 260, 263, 264, 265, 277, 280, 281, 282, 284, 289, 290, 297, 326, 331, 332
Burbidge, Archdeacon W. 228, 269
Burdett, Langham 95, 113, 114, 115, 123, 125
Burt, Septimus 72, 75, 129, 148
Burton, Alfred 9–10
bush brotherhoods 5, 201, 210, 259, 269, 285–312, 324, 331, 344, 345
  *see also* brotherhoods

canon law 136, 147, 173
Carnley, Peter 316, 317, 318, 320
Carter, Canon 31
Cathedral Building Committee 206, 210, 212
cathedrals
  absence of crucifixes 99–100
  churchmanship 313
  new, site 213, 214
  St Boniface 5
  use of vestments 94–5
  *see also* St George's Cathedral
Catholic
  church 48, 237, 238, 241, 253
    Anglican branch 262
  doctrine 15, 16, 17, 114
  faith 240, 248, 276, 288, 334, 345
  full privileges 16, 323
  identity of Anglicanism 3, 188
  piety 262
  practices, revival of 85
  priests 91, 262, 265, 309
  religion 233
  teaching 77, 323
  terminology 115, 261
  tradition 9, 269
  worship 4, 10, 331
Catholicism 114
Catholicity 271, 278
Caton, W. C. C. 198, 290
Cavalier case 122
ceremonial 32, 265, 275, 323, 325
  advanced 274, 309
  Anglo-Catholic 344
  in churches 117, 142, 146–7, 179, 222, 262, 268, 269
  criticism 219
  English judgements 173
  eucharistic 15
  full Anglo-Catholic 274
  of high mass 222, 341
  Holborn 40
  impressions 125
  restrained 8, 36, 111, 145, 146, 314
  Riley's distaste for 134, 179, 182
  and spirituality 233
  support 148
  usages 50, 110, 218, 242, 328
Chadwick, Owen 144, 146
Chapel of the Good Shepherd *54*, 89

# INDEX

Charlton parish 32, 33, 34
Cheam 34, 35, 37
Cheek, Raymond 332
Christian Church 231
Christian Social Union 8
Christian Socialism 8, 236, 237
Christianity 23, 115, 240
  muscular 329
Christmas
  liturgy 58
  midnight mass, first in colony 59
church
  authority 250, 251
    broad 17, 324
  brotherhood 287
  history 9–14
  in 1907, definitions 235
  terminology 240-1
Church Association 124, 218, 275
Church Book Depot 101, 143, 149
Church, Dean 246
Church of England 36, 40, 169, 170, 191, 230, 237
  'English' church 168
  establishment 249, 271
  self-government 159, 160, 172, 175
  Temperance Society 45
  Wales, disestablishment 249, 250
Church of England in Australia and Tasmania, name change proposal 135, 153–77, 237
Church of England Men's Society 198, 212
Church of South Africa 159, 160
*Church Standard* 259, 292, 311, 312, 314
*Church Times* 58, 91, 269, 330
churches
  altars *see* altars
  Anglican 57–60, 255
  Anglo-Catholic 36, 58, 338
  architecture 6, 32, 33, 52, 53, 200, 227, 284
  attendances 23, 62, 63, 71, 107, 108, 109, 111, 112, 137, 138, 139, 140, 146, 187, 203, 220, 323
  Broome Hill 340
  building programmes 279–84, 338–41
  buildings 6, 231, 256
  'establishment' 249, 250
  Goldsmith preached in 266, 268
  government 182, 239
  illegal practices 111, 136
  inter-church relations 239–40
  journal descriptions 260
  legal status 172, 174, 175, 237
  lights 90, 91
  national 162, 163, 168, 169, 170, 174, 238, 253
  nonconformist 23, 62, 111, 112
  reunion 240, 241
  services 145, 146, 148
  south-west 199, 200, 201, 207, 215
  state aid 47, 61, 62, 63, 64, 78–82, 212
  teaching of doctrines 70
  Victorian 146
churchmanship 29, 36, 37, 40, 51, 59, 166, 284, 329, 332
  advanced 30, 36, 56, 90, 101, 107, 176, 222, 257
  Anglican 4, 63, 64, 65, 127, 234, 239, 277
  of Anglican clergy 80, 93
  Anglo-Catholic 324
  broad 105, 172, 260, 309, 310, 324
  Bunbury diocese 12, 74, 78, 259
  critics 40, 103–25
  debates 10, 11, 12, 78, 146, 313
  differences 76, 176
  different 2, 7, 8, 38, 93, 136, 150
  disputes 108, 111, 128, 139, 268, 318–19
  divisions 4, 60, 154, 265, 337
  extreme 63, 65, 80, 91, 165
  of goldfields clergy 86
  high 15, 25, 33, 57, 71, 77, 120, 260, 323, 337
  issues 6–14, 47, 51, 61, 71, 99, 103, 104, 141, 216, 217, 222, 223
  low *see* low
  Marshall's 112, 217
  moderate 8, 142
  negative responses to 61–4, 73, 74, 111
  particular 58, 81, 111, 145, 146, 173, 220, 260
  and the press 103, 104, 105
  Purnell 40
  single 130
  uniform 57, 60, 122
  *see also* under Goldsmith
churchmen
  attending nonconformist churches 111
  conference 222
Clairs, E. S. 184, 239, 290
Claughton, Thomas Legh 29, 30, 31
clergy
  Anglo-Catholic 15
  appointment of 57, 343
  of Australian birth 155
  colonial 225, 226
  English 8, 110, 111, 285, 324, 325, 335, 336, 337
  high church 15
  and laity 154
  organizations 36
  ritualist 114
  vote on autonomous church 155, 174, 175, 176
  *see also* under Anglo-Catholic
Colenso case 159, 160, 165, 166
Collick, Edward Mallan 8, 9, 141, 146, 190
Colonial Bishoprics Council 184
Colonial Clergy Act 165, 225

'coloureds' 196, 202
communicants
  guild 48, 49
  nonconformists 241
  numbers 37, 38, 137, 138, 139, 140, 141, 187, 188, 212, 215, 219, 220, 277, 294, 295, 296
communion 48, 90, 107, 108, 110, 159, 240
  Anglican 168, 170, 174, 175
  figures 59, 89, 108, 109, 138, 139
  of saints 55, 234, 260
  table 54, 87, 217
confessions 15, 16, 37, 53, 86, 87, 95, 143, 144, 220, 227, 271
  advertising 84, 85, 220, 225
  auricular 83, 86
  controversy 118, 121, 122, 123, 124, 135, 151
  debate 144, 146
  orphanage girls 85, 86, 121, 123, 136
  promotion 48, 223
  revival of 83, 84, 121, 122
  sacramental 120
  teaching 40
confirmations 35, 37, 198, 206, 225
  candidates 35, 56, 199, 206
  female candidates 56, 145
Confraternity of the Blessed Sacrament 36
Congregationalists 14, 64, 67, 69, 72, 80, 81, 95, 125, 149
conservatism 14, 24, 25, 26, 28, 42, 47, 50, 75, 95, 104, 140, 236, 242, 249
  of the laity 75, 99, 175
  theological and liturgical 243–4
Coolgardie 185
cope and mitre 218, *219*, 261, 265, 274, *281*, 337, 345
Cornish, Vernon 315
Courthope, K. E. 74
Cowan, James 101, 122, 123, 135, 148
Cox, James Bell 30, 31
Crane, E. W. 226, 227, 229
Crane, Stephen 2
Craven, Joseph 226
crosses 98–9, 100, 111
  veneration of 99
crucifixes 40, 55, 98, 99, 100, 284, 341

Darling, Harry 91, 134, 206, 217
Davidson, Randall 171, 176, 186, 189, 192, 193, 243, 245, 247, 251, 304
Davies, Douglas 332
Dawes, Bishop 124, 184, 285, 286, 287, 288
dawn services 330
*Defender* 265, 309, 343
Delamark, George 230

denominations
  in colony 64
  Protestant, 189
devotion 57, 97, 220, 221, 231–57, 340
  eucharistic 16
  Marian 226
  sacramental 264
devotional
  attitudes promoted 36
  books, sale of 101
  practices 264
  preferences 276
dioceses 182
  Bunbury and North West (1904–1910) 179–203
  country 210, 232
  Kalgoorlie 210
  new 184, 185, 188, 253
  northern missionary 184
  Perth, division of 185, 188
  Rochester 28, 29
  south-west 255
  southern 184
divorce 43, 250
Dodd, R. P. 166, 170
Dolling, Robert 141
domestic violence 45
donations 53, 279, 280, 281, 324, 337, 338, 339
Dunstan, E. T. 67, 69, 80, 231, 232

ecclesiastical
  disputes 134, 135, 136, 137
  law 135, 143
  statements 240–1
Ecclesiastical Grant 62, 63, 64, 71–2, 80, 81
  abolition of 79, 81, 104
education 22, 104
  Anglican, in south-west 201
  for clergy 343
  debate 61, 66–7, 69–70, 72
  dual system 65, 66, 70, 79, 80, 81
Education Act 66, 69
Ellis, J. 93
Elsey, Edward 211, 220, 223, 224, 226, 262, 269, 277, 285, 288, 289, 294, 307, 308, 327, 343, 344
English
  bishops 176, 267
  Catholic term 115
  church 168, 169
    and Anglicanism 114, 167, 168
  clergy 285, 324, 325
  law 135, 136, 143, 173, 174
  population 149
  response to Anglo-Catholicism 113, 114
English Church Union 16, 36, 40, 100, 124, 125, 268, 269
episcopacy 237, 238, 239, 241, 252, 253
  rural 344

episcopates 10, 11, 219, 238, 253, 337
  in Australia 227, 228
  Bishop Parry 318
  Bunbury and north-west 179–203
  Claughton 29
  election 73–6
  rural 323
  south-west 205–15
eucharist 221, 223, 232
  Holy Sacrifice 261
  theology 52
eucharistic
  ceremonial 15
  devotions 15, 16, 261
  doctrines 36
  ministers 264
  sacrifice 101
  vestments 15, 16, 34, 40, 57, 77, 91–5, 260, 313
  worship 231
eucharists 15, 16, 36, 40, 49, 50, 59, 87, 138, 143, 148, 187, 206, 220, 221, 222, 328
  All Souls' Day 225
  celebrations 5, 34, 35, 49, 58, 73, 93, 97, 109, 182, 215, 228, 294
  centrality 49, 222, 232, 235
  for children 35–6
  choral 37, 38, 57, 111
  daily 219, 224, 232, 271, 295, 336
  description 232, 233
  doctrine 88
  and matins services 34, 35, 49, 221, 222, 272
  prayers for the departed 95–7
  priority 232, 272
  sung 51, 52, 60, 78, 99, 140, 141, 146, 221, 272
evangelicals 31, 91, 98, 110, 128, 242, 263, 309, 313

Fairbridge, Kingsley 210
Firth, W. W. 129
Fisher, James 169
Foley-Whaling, John 5, 128, 222, 265, 281, 327, 331, 336, 337
Forrest, Alexander 62, 63, 71, 105, 148
Forrest, Sir John 41, 71, 81, 105, 129, 141, 148, 180, 182, 187, 341
Foster, Ernest 316, 317, 318
Frewer, Cyril Charsley 229, 230, 267, 277, 306, 308
Frewer, Edith Emma 2, 33, 197, 267
Frewer, George 260, 263, 266, 268, 277, 278, 285, 302
Frewer, George Ernest 33, 35, 36, 37, 49, 51, 56, 221, 222, 236, 266, 267
Frewer, George Herbert 33, 36, 267

Frewer, John 2, 5, 88, 207, 228, 229, 295, 300, 306, 307, *325*, 343, 344
Frewer family 33, 35, 36, 197, 237, *267*, 277
Frodsham, Bishop 289, 292, 311, 324, 328
Fryer, Arnold 211, 219, 220, 262, 297, 326, 336
fund-raising 41, 197, 200, 201, 207, 210, 211, 212, 228, 256, 266, 279, 340
funding 64, 324, 337, 338, 339
  *see also* state aid

gambling 42, 44, 46, 104
Garland, D. J. 69, 74, 86, 92, 94, 101, 120, 129, 131, 136, 142, 143, 155, 160, 172, 184, 318, 330
Gegg, Joseph 20, 38
gifts 279, 280
Gillett, F. C. 40, 75, 108
goldfields 8, 254
  new diocese 8, 19, 185, 238
Golding-Bird, Cyril 211
Goldsmith, Edith Emma (Frewer) 19, 33, 44, *267*
Goldsmith, Frederick 219, *267*, *281*
  Anglo-Catholicism 124, 136, 325
  appointment at Halling 35–7
  attacks by Hackett 65–6, 67, 73, 74, 79–80, 81, 104, 105
  baptism 22
  birth and childhood 21–3
  churchmanship 6, 11, 36–7, 39, 47, 48, 59, 60, 65, 72, 79, 89, 123, 217, 332
    criticism of 61, 63–4, 66, 73, 74, 80, 104, 105, 111, 141
    rejected by Dunstan 69
  conflict with Riley 78, 129–31, 254
  consecration 179, 186
  conservative values 9
  curate at Charlton 28, 30, 32–4
  curate at Cheam 34–5
  deaconing at Rochester 29
  death 229, 230
  education 24–8
  election of Bishop Parry's successor 73–6
  enthronement 105, 179, 186
  episcopate 179–203, 205–15
  father 21, 22, 211
  first Bishop of Bunbury 5, 129, 151, 179, 180, 182, 32
    resignation 214, 215
  health 207, 226, 227, 229
  management of orphanage 186
  marriage 33
  motions on church name change 135, 154, 165, 174, 175, 177, 331, 345
  new dean of Perth 19–21, 28, 37, 41–2

ordination 28
piety 306
public attitudes towards 180, 182
relatives 207
retirement 226, 227, 230, 277
social issues 42–7
theology 50
vicar of Hampstead 224–7
visit to England 193, 197, 200, 208, 216
visit to north-west 194–5
visit to south-west 198, 199
Goldsmith, Herbert Symonds 211
Goldsworthy, Stanley 344
government 44, 79
 aid *see* state aid
 relation to the church 251
Great Depression 8
Greatorex, Theophilus 200
Green, Arthur Vincent 74
Gregorian chant 39, 40
Grimshaw, Arthur 314
Grogan, J. D. 212
Groser, Charles 40, 66, 69, 75, 285, 292, 295, 306, 307, 308, 310, 318
Grundy, D. 82
Guildford Grammar chapel 338, 340

Hackett, John Winthrop 6, 19, 20, 44, 47, 48, *68*, 69, 71, 72, 81, 104, 106, 131, 150
 attacks on dual system of education 6, 65–7, 70, 79, 80
 attacks on Goldsmith 6, 65, 66, 67, 73, 74, 104, 105, 146
 description of disestablishment 249
 distaste for Anglo-Catholicism 265
 editorials 111, 112, 115, 117, 179
 vote on successor to Bishop Parry 75
Hadley, Montague Sydney 194
Hale, Mathew 6, 10, 12, 39, 40, 71, 319
Halifax, Viscount 100, 125
Hampstead parish 22–3, 224–7
Harcourt, Bertha 207
Harcourt, Sir William 106
Hare, Annie 58
Harmer, J. R. 183
Harper, Charles 75, 104, 285, 297
Harper, H. H. 293, 294, 297, 306, 307
Harvey, George 332
Hawkins, Ralph 337, 344
Hawthorn, Sydney 91, 94
Hawtrey, C. L. M. 10, 12, 288
Hay, Allen 272, 273
Hayward, T. 108, 110, 216, 217
Hazelwood, John 315, 316
Henn, Wilfrid 11, 180
high
 celebration 58

church 27, 60, 129, 161, 257, 309
 centres 129, 130
 clergy 124, 142, 165, 236
 doctrines 111, 112
 fooleries 109
 terminology 14, 17
churchmanship 15, 25, 33, 51, 57, 71, 77, 120, 159, 171, 260, 323, 337
churchmen 28, 29, 39, 67, 75, 99, 112, 129, 154, 160, 166, 171, 172, 265
mass 15
Hillman, Alfred 56, 61, 62, 107, 108, 109, 110, 111, 112, 145
Hoare, Georgina 270
Holdsworth, Gordon 5
Holy Communion 96, 217
Holy Eucharist 221, 223, 261
Holy Trinity 231, 244
Holy Week 31, 32, 55, 56–7, 109, 276
Hopkins, Charles Plomer 136
Hornsby, Harold Grist 311
House of Grace, Williams 90, 92, 210, 211, 212, 215, 219, 223, 234, 265, 285, 286, 298, 325, 341, 343
 celebrations 224
 Chapel *283*, 284
 daily eucharists 232
 descriptions 261–2, 294
 life 286, 294, 295, 307, 308
 statue of St Boniface 5
Hughes, E. S. 94, 141, 142, 161

Illingworth, F. T. 81
immigrants 47, 209, 235, 236, *333*
incense 15, 40, 57, 90, 100, 117, 163, 222, 223, 268, 270, 272, 274, 275, 314
Irish 105, 150

James, W. H. 81
Jamieson, Hamish 344
Johnson, William Wardell 6

Kalgoorlie 210, 228, 344
 Bishop of 211, 226
 Bishop's Chapel *339*
 diocese 4, 183, 254
Keble, John 15
Kelly, Herbert 292
Kench, W. T. 95, 125
Kidson, George 149
Kilburn, E. E. 273
King, Bishop 98, 246, 247
 trial 50, 51, 134
Knight, Bishop 214, 344
Kyte, Joseph Bertram 95, 123

laity 36, 37, 75, 99, 223, 246, 255, 272, 290
 and clergy 119, 134, 154
 support for ceremonial 147, 148

vote on autonomous church 155, 174, 175, 176
Lambeth Conferences 245, 247, 248, 328
Latham, H. G. D. 186
Laurence, Herbert 39, 40
lawful authority 143, 144
Le Fanu, Archbishop 7, 8, 9, 11
Lefroy, Anthony O'Grady 19, 20, 89, 122
Lefroy, C. E. C. 158, 159, 160, 170, 172
Lefroy family 55, 148
legislation 134, 135, 137, 143, 159, 160, 172, 173, 174, 175, 250, 322
 Bunbury diocese 188
 divorce 250
 formation of province 211
 to control ritualism 16
lights *see under* altars
Lincoln Judgement 16, 50, 90, 98, 100, 110, 159
liturgical
 aims 232
 conservatism 243–4
 innovations 99
 life 295
 matters 36, 49, 50, 222
 observances 231
 practices 16, 17, 36, 77, 89, 96, 116, 172, 173, 222, 224
 revision 248
 scholarship 14
 singing 141, 221
liturgy 15, 27, 52, 57, 83, 90, 110, 219, 228, 249, 274, 284
 advanced 226
 Anglican 90
 Anglo-Catholic 117, 120, 340
 for children 3
 Christmas Day 58
 Commission report, 99
 Pinjarra 261
 Report of the Commission on 99
Loton, T. 71
Louch, Thomas 40, 69, 75, 98, 220
Lovekin, Arthur *105*
low
 church 17, 271, 313
 churchmanship 176, 260, 268, 324, 340
 churchmen 159, 160, 161, 166, 171, 175, 176, 262, 263, 277, 309
Lowder, Charles 100, 141

McClemens, T. 160, 170
McDonald, John 332
Mackonochie, A. H. 141
Manolas, Graeme 332
Marian doctrine and devotion 15, 16, 226, 314
marriage 44, 121, 123
Marshall, S. 183, 185
Marshall, W. F. 75, 81, 98, 99, 108, 110, 111, 112, 117, 125, 137, 145, 216, 217

Maryon-Wilson, George 33
Maryon-Wilson, Percy 228, 229
Maryon-Wilson, Sir Spencer 215
Maryon-Wilson family 20, 28, 29, 32, 33, 225
masonic community 147
mass 15, 90, 117, 222, 229
  Christmas midnight 59
Mathew, W. H. 272, 273
matins 34, 35, 49, 50, 78, 221, 224, 272
Matthews, B. C. 67, 70
Matthews, Charles 288, 290
Maynard, F. E. 84
media 100–1
  see also press
meditation 233, 234
Medley, J. M. 82
men
  addresses for 36, 44
  and boxing 45, 46
  communities 301–2, 303
  dealing with 47, 202
  masculinity 327–8, 329
  population 41
  in World War I, 212, 213
  young 43
Mercer, H .F. 317
Merriman, Bishop 128
*Merriman v Williams* 160
Methodism 14, 45
migrants 198, 209, 310, 311, *333*, 334, 336, 337
missionary
  dioceses 184, 195
  life 310, 311
  societies 184, 189, 193
mitre 5, *219*, *281*
Montgomery, H. H. 171, 176, 183, 192, 193, 194, 195, 199, 200, 211, 212, 310, 311, 316
Moore, J. J. 226, 336
Moore, Newton 209, 299
Moore, Robert Henry 8, 9, 91, 93, 128, 160, 252, 314, 317, 318, 337
Moore, W. D. 75
*Morning Herald* 83, 85, 90, 91, 103, 105, 107, 124, 160
Murphy, W. A. 157, 169, 170
Murray, David 332
Muschamp, Cecil 5
music 51, 127, 141, 146, 232, 262, 296
  see also singing
Myerson, E. H. 107, 141, 290


nationalism 114, 153–77, 324, 325, 329, 330, 331, 337
Neale, John Mason 6
Newman, John Henry 3, 66, 77, 87, 125
Newton, Sir Adam 32
Nicholas, Father 189, 191
Nicolay, C. J. 75
non-eucharistic services, 107, 138

nonconformists 3, 67, 69, 79, 80, 82, 121, 124, 125, 149, 239, 241, 319
  churches 23, 62, 111, 112
  clergy 149
north-west 179–203
  archdeaconry proposal 255
  bishopric 192, 193, 196, 254, 255
  diocese 189, 194, 201
  independent see 251, 252
  see, funding 193, 195, 196, 205
Noyes, Mrs 265, 280
Nugee, George 32


Ornaments Rubric 136, 218
Oxford Movement 5, 6, 7, 8, 9–13, 15, 16, 28, 40, 42, 48, 62, 63, 72, 83, 95, 107, 108, 144, 147, 179, 188
  acceptance of 78, 151
  and the arts 5
  critics 66, 110, 115, 137, 239
  doctrines 231
  emphasis on episcopacy 237, 241
  in England 340
  future in colony 77
  impact in Western Australia 9
  influences 24, 40, 127, 129, 139, 146, 148, 149, 160, 182, 221, 242, 268, 313, 314, 323, 324
    on Anglican community 5
  supporters 180, 252
  see also Tractarianism


Padbury, Walter 111, 112
parishes 130
  Charlton 32, 33, 34
  collections for Bunbury 279
  English 222
  Goldsmith preached in 266, 268, 269, 270, 271, 273, 274, 276, 301
  independent 138, 139, 140
  rural 324
  self-supporting 343
Parker, E. H. 104, 110, 113, 115, 148, 319
Parry, Henry Hutton 6, 12, 19, 38, 39, 50, 57, 60, 72, 90, 91, 109, 168, 184, 250, 286
  attitude to Anglo-Catholicism 39–40
  death 47, 60, 61, 73, 78, 96, 287
  election of successor 47, 73–6, 103
  proposal to create diaconate 289, 290
Payne, James 314, 315
Perry, Bishop 51, 56, 242
Perth English Committee 38
*Perth Gazette* 113
piety 107, 108, 198, 233, 235, 255, 256, 260, 262, 263, 264, 284, 306, 307, 308, 309, 312, 332

Pitts, Howard 91, 97, 148, 149, 189, 196, 252
population 109, 127, 148, 149, 151, 183, 197, 198, 199, 251
  Aboriginal 184, 194
  Anglican 20, 23, 188
  Bunbury 18, 186, 206, 209
  Hampstead 22, 23
  heathen 201
  immigrants 209
  native 254
  Perth 20, 21, 41, 44, 141
  south-west 186, 206, 299, 332, 333
Pownall, George 6, 273
Prayer Book 16, 28, 51, 56, 99, 228, 232, 242, 244, 245, 261, 273, 276, 302, 303, 333
  revision 242, 243, 244, 248
  rubrics 32
  services 114
prayers
  defined 48
  for the departed 95–7, 138, 220, 234, 262
  for the war dead 220, 225
preaching
  complaints 61–2, 81, 111, 117
  engagements 31, 208, 266, 268, 269, 270, 271, 273, 274, 276, 301
  standards 62, 71, 112, 117
press 55, 62, 73, 74, 78, 82, 83, 85, 87, 88, 96, 103, 137, 224
  on Anglo-Catholicism 106, 136, 140, 143, 151, 239
  Bunbury 111
  church name change coverage 155, 156, 161
  on churchmanship 6, 12, 103, 107, 139, 264
  criticism of Goldsmith 6, 12, 46
  Goldsmith's election 179–80
  hostility to ritualism 105, 111, 137
Price, F. J. 62, 74, 75, 78, 85, 86, 94, 95, 106, 118, 120, 122, 125, 129, 138, 143, 159, 165, 318, 330
priest-confessors 83
'Prominent Churchman' (writer) 85, 86, 91, 98, 107, 108, 114, 118, 120, 121, 123, 135, 160
Protestant Anglican community 216
Protestantism 113, 114, 115, 116, 125, 150, 278
Protestants 110, 113, 143, 145, 189
province of Western Australia proposal 183, 210, 211, 238, 253, 254
Public Worship Regulation Act 29, 30, 31, 128, 134, 159, 172, 173, 218, 273, 321, 322
Purchase judgement 33, 34
purgatory, doctrine 95, 96
Purnell, R. H. 40, 98

INDEX

race and culture issues 201
radicalism 9
Randall, George 72, 80, 81
'Red Book case' 322
Redding, Donald 337, 344
religious instruction in schools 66, 67, 69, 70, 251
requiems 95, 96, 97, 220, 229
   choral, for Parry 73
reservation of the consecrated elements 90
Rice, Charles Hobbes 34, 37
Richardson, B. G. 88, 97, 287
Ridge, A. J. 208
Riley, C. O. L. 7, 8, 9, 10, 11, 12, 20, 25, 45, 57, 71, 86, 87, 89, 92, 93, 96, 98, 117, *132*, 160, 195, 196, *281*, 323, 343
   ambition to be first archbishop 253, 254, 255
   ambition to be first Archdeacon of Perth 131, 182
   churchmanship 259, 265
   conflict with Goldsmith 130-1, 133, 254
   critical of treatment of Aborigines 184, 192, 254
   criticisms 135
   diary entries 101, 112, 127, 133, 136, 144
   distaste for ceremonial 94, 134, 147, 179, 182, 265
   election 47, 76
   election of Goldsmith 179, 180, 182, 183
   enthronement 78, 115, 145, 168
   hope for goldfields brotherhood 289
   insecurity 131, 132, 133
   intolerance of Anglo-Catholicism 127, 128, 129, 130
   letter from Sir John Forrest 105
   Lincoln Judgement 90, 110
   ritualism 136
   scheme for a province 210, 254
   sermon on confession 85
   SPG 287
   supporter of autonomy movement 166, 172, 173, 174
   views on authority 316, 317
   visit to war front 213
Riley, Elizabeth 128, 160
ritualism 11, 29, 30, 31, 38, 39, 49, 55, 56, 69, 89, 116, 129, 141, 150, 175
   churches 53, 114
   clerical movement 120
   critics 71, 117, 124, 125, 146, 268
   debate 75, 77, 85
   doctrines 95
   hostility to 106, 137, 218
   legislation to control 15
   Marshall's 111, 216
   opponents 12, 54, 86, 88, 91, 93, 95, 98, 99, 103, 113, 114, 139, 150
   practices 98, 99, 135
   Riley's views 136
   St Alban's Holborn 39
   *see also* anti-ritualist
*Ritualistic Clergy List* 93, 124, 218, 275
ritualists 49, 50, 55, 101, 127, 135, 136, 265
Robarts, David 315, 316, 317, 318, 320
Robertson, A. A. 128
Robinson, T. M. 201, 290
Roebourne 189, 190, 196, 252
Roman Catholic
   churches 86
   community 81
   doctrine 88
   mission work 189
   schools, funding 82
Roman Catholicism 3, 14, 80, 91, 98, 113, 114, 116, 118, 144, 150, 241
Roman rites 57, 89, 90, 91, 99, 117, 220, 228, 273
Rose, Edwin 213, 214
Roth report 191, 192, 197
Rowe, G. E. 125
Rowley, William 60, 160
Royal Commission on Ecclesiastical Discipline 242, 243, 244

sacramental
   confession 120-3
   reservation 248
   theology 14, 264
sacraments 36, 48
St Alban's
   Highgate 58, 59, 75, 86, 90, 94, 99, 106, 137
      attendances 138, 139, 140
   Holborn 39, 57, 116, 141, 142
   Marradong 108
St Augustine, Order 32
St Bartholomew's 59, 60
St Boniface 263
   cathedral 5
St Cyprian's Clarence Gate 226, 227
St David's
   cathedral, Hobart 149
   South Bunbury 221, 222, 331
St George's
   Brede 277, *279*
   Carnarvon 92, 94, 195, 260
St George's Cathedral *54*, 91, 115, 116, 117, 313-16
   altar 87-9
   Anglo-Catholic centre 313, 314, 315
   archbishop and dean roles 316, 317
   attendances 112, 137, 139, 140, 145
   churchmanship 139, 313

411

   communicants 109, 138, 139
   cross 98
   daughter churches 58-60
   deans 314, 315, 316-18
   lights request 10, 50
   music 141
   new building 41, 52-6, 146, 341
   parish organizations 42-3
   parishes issue 130, 138
   sermons 61-2, 232
   services 48-52, 57, 60, 109, 110, 145, 146, 232
   surplices 56
St Giles South Mymms 271, 272, 273, 278
St John's
   Fremantle 58
   Hampstead 215, 224, 226
   Melbourne Road 138, 139
   school 64
   West Perth 59, 60
St Mary's West Perth 139, 315
St Matthew's Guildford 58, 90
St Nicholas' Australind *88*
St Paul's
   Bunbury 8, 187, 203, 206, 212, 222
   Carr Street 7, 8, 10, 11, 112, 157, 315
   Palmerston Street 93
   Preston 128
St Paul's Cathedral 39, 144
St Peter's, Eastern Hill 149
St Saviour's Hoxton 273, 274
salaries 311, 337
Sambell, Geoffrey 9, 316
Saunders, E. 91
Scarfe, Janet 10
schools
   Bunbury 201
   church day 22
   government funding 64, 65, 66, 67, 69, 70, 82
   *see also* state aid
   religious instruction 66, 67, 69, 70, 251
   teaching of Anglo-Catholic doctrine 80
   *see also* Anglican schools
science, and religion 249
Scott, Walter 220, 228, 291, 324
Scrambler, T. H. 239
sermons
   in Bunbury 197
   complaints 61-3, 78, 117
   on confession 85
   in England 200, 208
   high church 78
Sharp, W. 92, 93, 94, 192, 221, 318
Shepherd, Peter 317
Simpson, G. T. 81
singing
   the liturgy 221
   practices 50, 51, 60, 109, 111, 141, 148, 212, 220, 262
Sisters of the Church 8, 141

'six points' 16, 33, 49, 50, 53, 56, 100, 223, 268
Smith, Saumarez 163, 164, 165, 166, 183, 193, 210, 245, 248
social issues 8, 9, 42–7, 235–7
Social Services Committee 235
social work 8, 44
Society for the Propagation of the Gospel (SPG) 183, 184, 185, 189, 190, 192, 193, 195, 198, 205, 210, 254, 287, 294, 297, 333
South Mymms parish 271, 272, 273, 278
south-west 181, 185, 197
  churches 199, 200, 201, 207, 210, 212, 215
  clergy 226
  diocese 186, 197
  initiatives 197–9
  population 206, 332, 333
*Southern Times* 110, 264, 303
Spargo, Frederick William 206, 285, 309
spirituality 52, 116, 233, 285
sporting controls 46, 47
Stannage, Tom 182
Stansfield, J. E. 268, 269
Stanton, A. H. 141, 183
state aid 64, 67, 69, 70, 71, 72
  abolition of 62, 65, 70, 72, 78–82, 124, 149
  debate 74, 82, 105
  for religious bodies 47, 61, 63, 64–5, 77, 81
state control of the church 159, 160, 172, 249, 250, 251
Steere, Ernest Lee 338, 340
Stone, Justice Edward 21, 74, 75, 80, 89, 95, 103–4, 148, 234
Street, G. E. 271, 272
Stretch, Bishop 239
Stubbs, G. S. 201, 206, 285
*Sunday Times* 129
Sunday trading 45
surpliced choir 36, 56, 57, 148, 268
surplices 15, 109
Sweeting, Canon 74
Symons, Herbert 230

Tarr, Albert 149
temperance 42, 104
  movement 25, 44, 45
Temperance Society 45
Temple, Frederick 121, 167, 240, 247
theological conservatism 243–4

theology 27, 50, 231, 235, 254, 255, 256
  Anglo-Catholic 141, 237
  of the eucharist 52
  incarnational 235
  liturgical 232
  sacramental 14, 264
  social 236
  Tractarian 237
Thompson, Alan 219, 262, 295
Thorold, Anthony Wilson 31, 32, 35, 38, 39, 40, 270
Timperley, W. H. 98, 217
*Tocsin* 114, 115, 117, 118, 119, 120
Tooth case 29–30, 172
Tractarian
  centres 31
  churches 52
  influences 226
  movement 5, 10, 27, 53, 104, 119
  opponents 121
  terminology 15, 17
  theologians 241
  theology 237
Tractarianism 9, 11, 19, 55, 56, 66, 76, 77, 83, 107, 110, 115, 118, 120, 144, 238, 242, 248, 251, 257
  identified with Roman Catholicism 113
Tractarians 29, 34, 35, 59, 246, 260, 271, 274
Tron, Mazzini 206, 211, 212, 285, 297, 329
Trower, Gerard 189, 196, 205, 265, 288, 337, 344

vestments 15, 27, 34, 40, 57, 77, 91–5, 117, 136, 222, 260, 268, 269, 313, 314, 324
*Victorian Churchman* 259, 275, 328, 331

Walsh, Walter 118, 124, 301
Watkins, D. G. 74, 131, 168
Webb, A. D. 206, 285, 306, 310, 312
Webb, L. E. 314
Webb, R. A. F. 300, 309
*West Australian* 6, 12, 19, 34, 44, 62, 71, 72, 85, 95, 103, 105, 116, 124, 140, 264
  anonymous correspondence 106, 107
  clerical work account 309
  Goldsmith's election 179

*West Australian Church News* 91, 97, 100, 101, 105, 106, 108, 142, 143, 160, 161, 179, 182, 264, 309
*West Australian Times* 113, 117
*Western Mail* 103, 155
Wheatley, Mr 124, 125, 142, 143
White, A .E. 220, 223, 234, 285, 297, 307, 308, 311, 329, 330
Whitington, F. T. 94, 171, 173, 196
Wilberforce, Samuel 29
Wilberforce, Wilbur 120
Williams, A. E. 10, 47, 246, 329
Wills, Monica 208, 234, 280
Wilson, Cecil 11, 211, 214, 222, 226, 262, 264, 336, 337, 344
Wilson, Sir Samuel 20
Wimborne, Lady 117, 120
Wise, Percy 84
Withers, Joseph 98, 99, 110, 112, 217
Wollaston, John 5
women 117
  in Anglican communities 301
  confirmation candidates 56
  home for prostitutes 44
  migrant workers 43, 44, 47, 198, 235
  ordination of 13, 14, 17, 319, 320, 321, 322
  religious communities 31, 34
working classes 38, 44, 45, 46, 142, 150, 222, 331, 333
Working Men's Association 36, 37, 38, 40
World War I 17, 31, 210, 211, 212, 213, 220, 225, 226, 234, 243, 264, 282, 284, 294, 324, 334
World War II 332, 334, 337
worship 222, 227
  buildings for 231
  Catholic 4, 331
  Cheam 34
  effects of war 234
  eucharistic 231
  exotic 32
  high church 260
  of Holy Trinity 231
  non-eucharisic 107
  patterns 109, 110, 296
  statistics 23, 187, 203, 212
  styles 109, 110, 141, 145, 146, 220
  symbol and ceremony within 147
Wright, J. C. 210

Young, James 148
Young Men's Society 43